Also by Thomas E. Ricks

First Principles

Churchill and Orwell

The Generals

The Gamble

Fiasco

A Soldier's Duty

Making the Corps

WAGING A
GOOD WAR

WAGING A GOOD WAR

A MILITARY HISTORY OF THE

CIVIL RIGHTS MOVEMENT,

1954–1968

THOMAS E. RICKS

FARRAR, STRAUS AND GIROUX   NEW YORK

Farrar, Straus and Giroux
120 Broadway, New York 10271

Library of Congress Cataloging-in-Publication Data
Names: Ricks, Thomas E., 1955– author.
Title: Waging a good war : a military history of the civil rights movement, 1954–1968 /
    Thomas E. Ricks.
Other titles: Military history of the civil rights movement, 1954–1968
Description: First edition. | New York : Farrar, Straus and Giroux, [2022] |
    Includes bibliographical references and index.
Identifiers: LCCN 2022023645 | ISBN 9780374605162 (hardcover)
Subjects: LCSH: African Americans—Civil rights—History—20th century. |
    Civil rights movements—United States—History—20th century. |
    Nonviolence—United States—History—20th century. | Military art and
    science—United States—Miscellanea. | Tactics. | Strategy.
Classification: LCC E185.61 .R515 2022 | DDC 323.1196/073—dc23/eng/20220601
LC record available at https://lccn.loc.gov/2022023645

Designed by Gretchen Achilles

Our books may be purchased in bulk for promotional,
educational, or business use. Please contact your local bookseller or the Macmillan
Corporate and Premium Sales Department at 1-800-221-7945, extension 5442,
or by email at MacmillanSpecialMarkets@macmillan.com.

www.fsgbooks.com
www.twitter.com/fsgbooks • www.facebook.com/fsgbooks

1   3   5   7   9   10   8   6   4   2

For those who marched, including my wife

They were loyal rebels: loyal in their sorrow, determined in their rebellion.

—ERIK ERIKSON,
Gandhi's Truth: On the Origins of Militant Nonviolence

CONTENTS

N

ILLINOIS

INDIANA

Columbus ★

Oxford

OHIO

Ohio River

WEST
VIRGINIA

Washington, D.C. ★

PENNSYLVANIA

MARYLAND

D

MISSOURI

Ohio River

KENTUCKY

VIRGINIA

ARKANSAS

Nashville ★

TENNESSEE

Greensboro

NORTH
CAROLINA

Raleigh ★

Memphis

Oxford

MISSISSIPPI

Greenwood

Birmingham

Anniston

ALABAMA

Philadelphia

Jackson ★

Selma

Meridian

Montgomery ★

McComb

Atlanta ★

GEORGIA

Albany

Rock Hill

Columbia ★

SOUTH
CAROLINA

Atlantic Ocean

★ Tallahassee

St. Augustine

FLORIDA

LOUISIANA

Gulf of Mexico

© 2022 Jeffrey L. Ward

0 Miles   100   200

0 Kilometers   200

PREFACE

A Different Angle on the Civil
Rights Movement

I n the 1960s the United States became a genuine democracy for the
first time in its history, as laws and practices that prevented many
Black Americans from voting were challenged by the civil rights
movement. By the end of the decade, almost all adult citizens finally
were able to vote. This may sound mundane, but the vote is the fundamental building block of our nation. It is our primary means of
bringing about political change nonviolently. It determines policy and
actions—where money is spent, which roads are paved, how schools
are run, and whether police act as antagonists or protectors. Now, six
decades later, a significant part of the American political establishment
has succeeded in repealing many of the voting gains of the 1960s.

This national arc led me to go back and read hundreds of books
on the civil rights movement. The more I delved into that history, the
more I found myself calling on my own experiences as a war correspon-
dent to interpret what I was reading. I saw the overall strategic thinking
that went into the Movement, and the field tactics that flowed from
that strategy. Problems I was familiar with from covering military operations in Somalia, Bosnia, Afghanistan, and Iraq, and from writing

books about World War II and the conflicts in Korea and Vietnam, were all addressed in careful, systematic ways by those in the civil rights movement—recruiting, training, planning, logistics, communications, and more. I began to see the Movement as a kind of war—that is, a series of campaigns on carefully chosen ground that eventually led to victory. The Siege of Montgomery. The Battle of Birmingham. The March on Washington. The frontal assault at Selma.

There were other echoes. The same antidemocratic faction of American life that opposed the Movement in the 1960s has been resurgent lately, not only seeking to restrict access to the vote but actually storming the Capitol building on January 6, 2021, as a presidential election was awaiting certification. The question facing us is whether those antidemocratic forces will once again defeat the forces of democracy as they have before. When laws are passed inhibiting the ability of people to vote, accompanied by laws limiting the ability of teachers to teach history, these are signs that we are once again threatened by the ancient and powerful forces of caste and oligarchy.

If America is to have what most Americans want—a multiracial, multiethnic democracy—we will need to renew the promise of the peaceful voting rights crusade that is the subject of this book. But to do so we need to have a clear view of that Movement. We should resist wrapping it in a gauzy sentimentality to be gingerly handled and admired every Martin Luther King Day, reducing it to a simple and misleading "public fable," to borrow the phrase of the historian Jeanne Theoharis.

There is a second, related reason now to look back at the civil rights movement. As we move toward the middle period of the twenty-first century, a diminishing number of Americans possess memories of the Movement. That era is now receding into the unexperienced past, taking its place alongside the Civil War, another series of events that fundamentally reshaped the nation.

For more than a century, the Civil War was swathed in historical sentimentalism. Only after that did it begin to come into clearer focus. It now may be time to gain a longer, more strategic perspective on the civil rights movement. The number of eyewitnesses who walk and breathe among us is diminishing daily. There are few additional interviews to be done. Certain documents remain unavailable to us, some of which might be unearthed, but all in all, the historical record is fairly complete. The question now becomes how to better understand it. Key to my motivation for writing this book is that much of that material—tens of thousands of pages of speeches, sermons, diaries, memoirs, letters, oral histories, court proceedings, and transcripts of the internal deliberations of the Southern Christian Leadership Conference (SCLC) and the Student Nonviolent Coordinating Committee (SNCC)—has not been read with an eye to discerning strategic decision-making.

I offer here a different way to look at the civil rights movement, one that I think is essential to understanding its success. The Movement brought about a major change in the United States in only ten or so years, an accomplishment that can be better understood if it is viewed in military terms, especially those of strategy and tactics. Recently, a new generation of scholars has offered new assessments of the Movement, in particular emphasizing the roles that women played, the importance of grassroots efforts, and the significance of protest actions before the Montgomery boycott. Studies published in the past few years have explored multiple subsidiary subjects. There are even studies of the connection between civil rights and major league sports, and of the role of food in the civil rights movement. At the same time, scholars such as Erica Chenoweth and Deva Woodly have brought new rigor and insight to the subject of how and why nonviolent social change occurs.

But to my surprise no studies have looked at the Movement through the prism of its similarity to military operations. A search of the American Historical Association's database of doctoral dissertations in recent decades found more than 250 that studied the American civil rights movement, but none that looked at the Movement in this way.

Given that the civil rights movement relied heavily on nonviolent approaches, it may seem surprising or even jarring to think of it in military terms. Yet participants in the Movement often invoked the analogy. James Lawson, a key figure in developing the Movement's phi-losophy and tactics and in training a cadre of influential leaders, once commented, "Protracted struggle is a moral struggle that is like warfare, moral warfare." Another activist, Charles Sherrod of the Student Non-violent Coordinating Committee, in looking back, said, "It was a war. Though it was a non-violent war, but it was indeed a war." Cleveland Sellers said of the 1964 Freedom Summer campaign in Mississippi, "It was almost like a shorter version of probably the Vietnam War." And remember that the central tactic of the Movement—the march—is also the most basic of military operations. Indeed, even in war, marching sometimes is more decisive than violence. For example, Napoleon ob-served that his great victory at Ulm in 1805 was achieved not by arms but by legs, as his foot soldiers outmaneuvered his Austrian foe.

As the comments by Movement veterans indicate, the perspective of military history is helpful, even perhaps imperative, if we are to discern how to apply its lessons to our predicament today. No, the civil rights movement was not a traditional army with weapons and a single com-mand structure. Yet from 1955 to 1968 a disciplined mass of people waged a concerted, organized struggle in dedication to a cause greater than themselves. Many died; many more shed blood; thousands were put behind bars. In conducting their campaigns, activists made life-changing decisions with inadequate information while operating un-der wrenching stress and often facing violent attacks—circumstances that are similar to the nature of leadership in war, making the military lens a useful one in understanding what happened and why. There is a good argument to be made, says the historian Peter Onuf, that the civil rights movement was really America's "good war," and that the people in it were truly our "greatest generation." The sacrifices of Movement leaders and rank-and-file members led to a realized, if imperfect, de-mocracy. If we are to hold on to their gains and reinforce them, we must recognize the nature of their effort so that we can properly prepare ourselves to safeguard and sustain our democracy. From the Movement, we may be able to abstract principles and approaches that we need in order to apply them to our situation now. Some followed nonviolence as a way of life. Many more pragmatically adopted it as an effective tactic, especially in the face of the overwhelming power of state forces. And a few prominent voices utterly rejected nonviolence, most notably Robert F. Williams and, later, Malcolm X.

This book will show how the civil rights movement took the form of a series of campaigns, most of which were carefully planned. Viewed in military terms, the Freedom Rides of 1961 are a classic example of a long-range raid behind enemy lines. Similarly, the problems that plagued the desegregation campaign in Albany, Georgia, the following year are instantly recognizable to any military historian who has studied how a clever, adaptive enemy can stymie an offensive. And Mississippi's Freedom Summer is treated here not as a somewhat starry-eyed white liberal program to advance integration, but instead as a calculated campaign to expose privileged white northerners to the same risks of violence that Black southerners daily endured, and through that hard process to help Black Mississippians gain a voice in politics. War also offers a vocabulary that peace does not: The Montgomery bus boycott was primarily defensive, in that it was a withdrawal of patronage, while the Nashville sit-ins were offensive, in that they were demands for service. And we can understand the arc of the Movement better if we track and measure the nature and scale of the violence used against it, and see how the forces of segregation counterattacked in 1961, 1963, and again in 1964.

Framing the Movement in terms of strategy and tactics highlights some of its thinkers who should be better known to the American public, such as James Lawson and the strategists Diane Nash and Bayard Rustin. The more I examined another key Movement thinker, James Bevel, the more he struck me as the Movement's equivalent of William Tecumseh Sherman. That Civil War general was volatile, even a little insane at times, but in understanding the nature of the war he stood far ahead of his peers. Just as Sherman would invent a new way to fight in the Civil War, crossing Georgia without logistical support or even a line of communications, Bevel would devise a risky new approach to civil rights marches that shocked some yet proved essential to the Movement's single biggest victory, the Birmingham campaign of 1963.

Again and again, from Montgomery in 1955 to Selma in 1965, viewing the Movement's campaigns in this unfamiliar way underscores the audacity of its tactics, a quality that constantly kept segregationist foes off-balance. It even sheds new light on well-known figures such as Martin Luther King, Jr., underscoring that a significant aspect of his greatness was his ability to formulate strategy and then—equally important—to explain it to his followers and to the world at large. Strategy is a deceptive problem, seemingly simple when it works, but devilishly complex when it doesn't. King looms over this book, but he is hardly presented here as the sole substantial Movement leader. He figures prominently in eight of the chapters that follow, but not much in another five.

Overall, the civil rights movement was better organized and its participants far more methodical and careful than tends to be recognized now. It is a point that movement veterans make again and again in discussing their approach to bringing about social change, and is worth heeding today. Charles E. Cobb, Jr., a veteran of the Movement who served for years in Mississippi, summarized it as "struggle—disciplined, thoughtful, creative struggle." That is a summary worth exploring. Discipline in military operations is most often thought of as following one's training and obeying legal orders, and both of those are indeed crucial. But the foundation of it all is self-discipline, most often in simply being persistent, of putting one foot in front of the other, day after day, of keeping control of one's own emotions and fears in order to serve a greater good. In the civil rights movement, an additional form of discipline was maintaining the message that is being sent out to the world. Again and again, members of the civil rights movement emphasized and exhibited self-control in their public actions. As King once put it, "Those of us who love peace must organize as effectively as the war hawks."

The views of Mohandas K. Gandhi on tactics and strategy are quite relevant here. Civil rights leaders did not study military history and were not affected directly by military principles, but several—especially King and Bevel—were deeply influenced by Gandhi, who often invoked military analogies. The great activist for Indian independence taught, "There is no civil disobedience possible, until the crowds behave like disciplined soldiers." Gandhi's impact on King and the Movement, both directly through his writings and indirectly through American followers such as the Black educators Mordecai Johnson and Howard Thurman, probably has been underestimated, even now. The major reason for that misapprehension by historians, I suspect, is that the influence of Gandhi generally is more evident in King's actions than in his words—as will be seen in the discussions of the campaigns in Birmingham, Selma, and Chicago.

Looking at the civil rights revolution as military history additionally can teach us a few things about the significant but elusive subject of strategy—which also is important to the future of our country. Strategy is a misunderstood concept, often confused with tactics, which deal with the subject of how one actually fights. Strategy, by contrast, involves the larger subject of understanding who you are, and next identifying one's goals, and only then developing an overarching plan for using tactics to achieve those goals. One of the Movement's great strengths was that its leaders formulated a strategy, then developed tactics that fit their approach, and finally gave to the people who were assigned to execute those tactics the training they needed to do so. Each of these three levels fit together, with each action carrying a message—the flesh carrying the word, as it were. That meshing is harder than it looks. The contemporary American military, by contrast, often tends to be good tactically while lacking an overarching strategy. That's a major problem, because tactical excellence without a strategic understanding resembles a Ferrari without a steering wheel—the vehicle may be powerful and look good, but it won't get you where you need to go.

I realize that, as a military historian, I am an outsider to the subject of American civil rights. But I think that my decades of experience in witnessing, analyzing, and writing about American military operations enable me to write about the Movement in a new way that can deepen our understanding of it. Indeed, I don't think the workings of the Movement, or its victories, can be fully understood without using a military perspective.

WAGING A
GOOD WAR

INTRODUCTION

Stirrings, 1865–1954

There is a direct relationship between wars and struggles for civil rights. If "war made the state," as Charles Tilly famously observed, it also stimulated some of the social movements that went on to change the state.

The lesson holds well for the United States. After the Civil War, and the emancipation it enabled, formerly enslaved Blacks in many parts of the South were elected to office, opened schools, and served as sheriffs and police chiefs. White supremacists retaliated with a prolonged campaign of terrorism, killing Black law enforcement officers, lynching teachers, and beating or shooting almost anyone who fought back or sought to better the condition of the newly freed. Sometimes Blacks simply were killed for owning land. Political violence was especially aimed at young Black men who challenged the dominant caste. In the part of Louisiana around Shreveport, for example, about 10 percent of Black males between the ages of eighteen and forty-five were killed during the eleven years after the Civil War ended. The North was weary of fighting and looked the other way as the states of the old Confederacy passed Jim Crow laws enforcing racial segregation. By the end of the 1870s, Blacks in the South had been reduced to second-class citizens at best, serfs at worst. They were excluded from the official and political worlds that made the decisions that affected their lives. Only a small percentage could vote; none held major elective office. All this was enforced by systemic terror.

Then came World War I, in which more than 370,000 Black men served in the U.S. Army. In its aftermath, Black veterans challenged Jim Crow and were suppressed violently. Whites rioted against Blacks in Chicago, Washington, D.C., and Omaha. In a related action, at least 100 and perhaps 240 Blacks were killed in 1919 after Black sharecroppers tried to unionize in rural Elaine, Arkansas. In 1921, armed Black vets in Tulsa, Oklahoma, led a group to the courthouse to try to prevent a lynching. The ferocious white response killed between 150 and 300 Black people and burned down the city's Black business section. Thereafter, segregation in the South remained rock-solid for decades.

World War II brought another, even further-reaching change. The novelist and essayist James Baldwin called it "a turning point" in the relationship between white and Black America. After that war, one million returning Black veterans, many of them from the South, mounted a new challenge to the white supremacist structure. They conveyed the sense, said Bayard Rustin, that "we are not going to put up with this anymore." Having fought racist Nazis abroad, they were now prepared to challenge racist Americans at home. Charles Dryden, a Black fighter pilot during World War II, wrote that when he and his comrades finished fighting in Europe, they prepared "to help defeat domestic enemies back home: Jim Crow attitudes and practices in government, schools, jobs, churches— everywhere!" Even so, Dryden was stunned by what happened when he returned to the United States before the war ended on an assignment to train newer pilots. Stationed at Walterboro Army Airfield, in rural South Carolina, he was amazed to see that German prisoners of war, readily identifiable by the big "PW" painted on the back of their fatigue shirts, were allowed to use the "white" part of the base cafeteria, but that he and his fellow Black U.S. Army officers were not.

"I think it was World War II that provided the essential foundation for the kind of struggle that unfolded across the South during the

1940s, '50s and '60s," concluded Charles E. Cobb, Jr., the SNCC veteran of Mississippi. Across the South, returning Black World War II vets such as Mississippi's Amzie Moore, Aaron Henry, and Medgar Evers; Alabama's Ralph Abernathy; and North Carolina's Robert F. Williams, to name a few, stepped into leadership roles in their communities.

As a young Black man in rural Mississippi in the 1920s and '30s, Amzie Moore had assumed that God somehow loved white people more. "We had a terrible idea that it was sinful to be black, that God only loved white people," he recalled. "I had assumed, reluctantly so, that it had to be something wrong with me." His travels during World War II, and in particular his service in the Burma theater, opened his eyes. "I lost my fear of whites when I was in the armed forces," he said. "I found out I was wrong. People are just people, some good, some bad, some rich, some poor."

When Moore returned home to Mississippi after the war, he went to work in the post office—a federal job that would give him a bit of protection against local retaliation—and also used his savings to open a gas station. At that station, on Highway 61, then the main artery between Memphis and New Orleans, he refused to put up "White" and "Colored" signs to racially segregate the restrooms. To defend this act, Moore sat in his living room with rifles and pistols in anticipation of attacks. Moore would go on to be what one civil rights activist called "the father of the Movement" in Mississippi, the man who sheltered activists like Bob Moses in the early 1960s and introduced them to a low-profile network of supporters across the state. The quiet but persistent way Moore operated in Mississippi has the feel of a successful regional chief of the French Resistance in World War II.

Segregationists were wary of the returning Black veterans, and confrontations came quickly. In the first six weeks of 1946, police in Birmingham, Alabama, killed several Black vets, perhaps five in total (though the number is not certain due to careless official record-keeping). In the same year, local whites around Monroe, Georgia, murdered George Dorsey, a newly returned vet, along with his wife and two other Blacks. It was a slaughter. The victims were shot a total of sixty-six times. Clinton

Adams, a ten-year-old white farm boy, covertly witnessed the killings on Moore's Ford Bridge. He was shocked because he knew Dorsey, a neighbor he had found friendly and helpful. One of the alleged killers, Loy Harrison, a cotton grower, years later told Adams, "Up until George went in the army, he was a good nigger. But when he came out, they thought they were as good as any white people." And that was sufficient to justify a multiple murder, Harrison thought.

The first big postwar fight erupted in Columbia, Tennessee, in February 1946. It had its origin in a dispute between Gladys Stephenson, a Black woman, and a white clerk at the Castner-Knott department store. Stephenson had left a radio there to be repaired, only to be told later that the radio had been sold. She argued with the clerk, William Fleming. As she and her son, James, a Navy veteran, were leaving, Fleming ran out and hit James Stephenson in the back of the head. It was a bad move. James had boxed in the service as a welterweight. He wheeled and punched Fleming, who went through the store's plate-glass window. An arriving policeman clubbed James Stephenson. Gladys Stephenson protested and was hit in the face. The mother and son then were arrested.

Crowds gathered in Columbia, which had a history of lynchings and racial friction. Black veterans took up lookout positions with weapons in the town's Black business section. When police attacked the neighborhood, four of them were wounded. Before dawn the next morning, the Tennessee Highway Patrol raided the section, shooting into houses, ransacking businesses, and confiscating weapons. Eventually, some twenty-five Black men were charged with attempted murder of the white policemen. The prosecution presented a bungled case—there was no proof that some of those charged even had been in the area—and the jury acquitted all but two of the men. The state then dropped the charges against those two, knowing they would almost certainly win on appeal.

As the details of the Columbia fight emerged, news also emerged of a vicious attack on another Black veteran. Sergeant Isaac Woodard, traveling home on the day he was discharged from the Army and while still in uniform, was beaten and blinded by the police chief in Batesburg, South Carolina, a small town about midway between Columbia, South Carolina, and Augusta, Georgia. The police chief drove the stock of his long-handled blackjack into each of Woodard's eye sockets. President Harry Truman was shocked by the incident and would cite it in a letter explaining his 1948 executive order mandating desegregation of the armed forces. "I can't approve of such goings on," he wrote to an old friend and former Army comrade. "I am going to try to remedy it."

New lines of struggle were forming. Blacks wanted change, but whites held almost all the power and the money, controlling local and state governments, the police forces, the economy, and, most important, access to the ballot box. Schools were both rigidly segregated and vastly unequal. Yet the "dominant caste," to borrow an illuminating phrase used by Isabel Wilkerson and others, had one great vulnerability: it had nothing to offer Blacks but more of the same treatment. The major tools that segregationists held were oppressive: Blacks challenging the system were often kicked off the land they worked; fired from their jobs; and, if they persisted in their protests, beaten or murdered.

"I remember 1949 as a very bad year," said Rosa Parks, who then was an official with the local chapter of the National Association for the Advancement of Colored People (NAACP) in Montgomery, Alabama. She recalled that the racist system was so overwhelming and oppressive that many crimes against Blacks, even murders, went unreported. In the summer of 1955, Emmett Till, a fourteen-year-old Chicagoan, while visiting relatives in the Mississippi Delta, was lynched for whistling at a white woman, and his corpse was thrown into the Little Tallahatchie River. When asked in an interview about the murder of Till, Parks offered an unexpected response: Instead of discussing Till, she spoke about a young Black minister in Montgomery who at about the same time was killed in a similar incident—which, she said, never came to public light. The man had a singing group and played a request for a white woman. "This is supposed to have led to him being in church with this [white] person," Parks said. In response, white vigilantes took the minister to a bridge over the Alabama River and forced him to jump from it. "They told his mother she had better keep quiet about it, which she did,"

Parks recalled. Incidents like that were widespread, she implied. In her work as secretary of the Montgomery branch of the NAACP, Parks had learned that many abused people were too intimidated to sign an affidavit or even give a statement of fact. They knew the score.

One startling fact about the extent of Black disenfranchisement is that in 1950 in Sunflower County, Mississippi, Blacks made up 68 percent of the population, yet they made up less than 0.5 percent of the county's voters. In some parts of Mississippi, Black men who registered to vote, such as the Reverend George Lee and Lamar Smith, were murdered in retaliation.

By this point, the pieces of a civil rights movement were in place. They had been developed by scores of pioneers in earlier decades. Among those pioneers were Ida B. Wells, who deftly used newspapers to publicize lynchings; W. E. B. Du Bois, who organized intellectuals in the Black middle class; A. Philip Randolph, who similarly galvanized part of the Black working class; Lillie Carroll Jackson, who explored the use of focused boycotts to protest stores that did not employ Black clerks; and Homer Plessy, who in 1896 went to the Supreme Court to test separate-but-equal segregation laws. There even had been sit-ins and bus rides for liberation. In the mid-1950s all these elements came together, in part because for the first time, the southern Black church joined the struggle. Participation by ministers would make the difference in Montgomery, Alabama, in 1955 and 1956, as the city's Black religious leaders broke with tradition and stepped forward.

The Supreme Court acts

In 1954, the Supreme Court rejected the notion of "separate but equal" public schools, calling the approach "inherently unequal." The court's unanimous decision in *Brown v. Board of Education* was a key point in our national history because it cracked the bedrock beliefs of the Jim Crow South and would lead, eventually, to huge changes in American society. The ruling, the culmination of decades of work by the NAACP, altered the strategic context in the South by shifting the weight of federal law from supporting white supremacism to, in some forms, opposing it. At first impression, it seemed to address the issue of segregation completely. "That was almost like getting religion again," recalled the Reverend Fred Shuttlesworth, a leading Black activist and minister in Birmingham. "I felt like now we have arrived. Now, you know, we're going to get somewhere."

But with time it became evident that the Supreme Court ruling did not solve the problem as much as it raised a series of questions: How much had the law changed? The decision applied to public schools, but what about public accommodations and commerce? And how would the federal ruling by a faraway court change the actual situation on the ground? What kind of actions were needed, and what kinds of organizations would have to come into existence to launch those actions? What role would the federal government, and especially the executive branch, play in dealing with recalcitrant states? How would any of this be enforced?

These questions could only be answered by prolonged direct testing of both the system and the culture of the South, in schools, buses, restaurants, and other locations. Shuttlesworth said a few years later, "It takes massive organization to overcome massive resistance." Indeed, it would take more than a decade to produce the first set of answers, while some of the other questions still hang in the American air nearly seventy years later.

1.
MONTGOMERY, 1955–1956
Besieging a City

The siege of Montgomery, otherwise known as the Montgomery bus boycott, marks the first major effort of the modern civil rights movement. The leaders and most of the participants certainly knew history was against them. But by the mid-1950s they were better prepared than earlier generations. Here the pieces came together for the first time—the awakening southern Black church; the returning Black soldiers, indignant at being denied access to the democratic rights for which they had fought; and a population weary of subjugation and ready to act.

The basis for action was organization. As in the military, even before discipline, the all-important beginning point was how people were organized and trained. These are subjects that deserve far more attention in studies of the civil rights movement.

What do you want to do? What are you going to do?

Long before the day in December 1955 when she sat down on a city bus in Montgomery, Alabama, Rosa Parks had begun training for that moment. The previous summer, Parks, then an official with the Montgomery affiliate of the NAACP, had attended a session at the Highlander Folk School, a leftist, pro-labor, racially integrated outpost in the hills of eastern Tennessee. Founded in 1932, Highlander at first focused mainly on training union organizers for the hard task of operating in the South. In 1953, its leaders decided to turn more toward working for civil rights. Soon the head of its workshops was Septima Poinsette Clark, a brilliant, remarkable woman who had a powerful effect on a generation of civil rights activists. Born in South Carolina in 1898, the daughter of a formerly enslaved person, Clark had worked for decades to bring literacy to Blacks in the South, seeing the ability to read as enabling people not just to lead more productive lives—and perhaps eventually to register to vote—but also to elevate their sense of themselves. She had lost her job as a schoolteacher for belonging to the NAACP.

Along the way, Clark had developed a strategic way of thinking. She once commented, "I have a great belief in the fact that whenever there is chaos, it creates wonderful thinking. I consider chaos a gift."

Each Highlander training session of one or two weeks began with a strategic question: "What do you *want* to do?" It ended with a tactical discussion of how to reach that outcome: "What are you *going* to do?" Significantly, the session Rosa Parks attended at Highlander was titled "Racial Desegregation: Implementing the Supreme Court Decision." That decision was the ruling the previous year by the high court in *Brown v. Board of Education* that racial segregation in schools was illegal. Highlander's teachers found Parks shy at first, especially around white people, but they drew her out by asking her to describe her civil rights work in Alabama. She found the experience liberating.

Clark wrote to friends, "Had you seen Rosa Parks (the Montgomery sparkplug) when she [first] came to Highlander, you would understand just how much guts she got while being here." Parks took page upon page of notes during the sessions. She was struck by the idea that the goal of protest was not to influence attitudes, but to force change. "Desegregation prove[s] itself by being put in action," she wrote in her notes. "Not changing attitudes, attitudes will change." In other words, don't try to begin by changing the way people think. Rather, change the way they actually live, and their thinking will follow.

Parks reveled in the novel experience of living alongside white people on a basis of equality. She emerged from her two-week session a changed person. "At Highlander, I found out for the first time in my adult life that this could be a unified society," she later said, "that there was such a thing as people of different races and backgrounds meeting together in workshops, and living together in peace and harmony." She had found herself laughing when she "hadn't been able to laugh in a long time." She added, "It was a place I was very reluctant to leave." But depart she did, returning to Montgomery by summer's end.

Rosa Parks sits

Parks and other civil rights leaders in Montgomery had been mulling the bus situation for years, and lately had been contemplating a boycott. There had been multiple cases of driver violence against Black passengers who talked back or moved too slowly for the taste of the dominant caste. Parks was close to Claudette Colvin, a scrappy teenager who in March 1955 refused to give up her seat on a bus, tussled with the police who came to move her, and was arrested. But other activists thought Colvin, who was unmarried and had become pregnant a few months after her arrest, was not the right person on whom to base a boycott campaign. By contrast, Parks—a quiet, steel-willed woman of forty-two—was perfect. She literally was a Sunday school teacher, at the St. Paul African Methodist Episcopal Church.

On the cool, wet afternoon of December 1, 1955, Parks finished her work as a department-store seamstress and did some shopping. "I was quite tired after spending a full day working," she recounted the following year. It was just another gray Thursday when she boarded a crowded bus at Court Square and sat down in the fifth row. On that bus, there soon was a white man standing in the aisle. The bus driver,

Jimmy Blake, then told the Blacks nearer the front of the vehicle to give up their seats so the white person could have the row, as was the custom. At first, none of the four moved.

"You all make it light on yourselves and let me have those seats," Blake emphasized.

At this, one Black man and two Black women followed his instructions. Parks stayed in her seat. The driver left the bus and returned a few minutes later with two policemen. Blake pointed at Parks. One of the police officers approached her. "Why don't you stand up?" he asked.

"I don't think I should have to stand up," she said. Then she added a human inquiry: "Why do you push us around?"

"I don't know," he said, "but the law is the law and you're under arrest."

Parks noticed with dismay that as she was taken from the bus, no other Blacks spoke in her defense or otherwise came to her aid.

So began the modern American civil rights movement, which would transform the nation over the following ten years. The story of Parks is a familiar story now, a modern American parable taught in elementary schools, some of them named after her. Parks had been readying herself for that moment for years. She had seen Blacks abused repeatedly—humiliated, raped, and even lynched—only to have police turn a blind eye. She felt the Black community had given up hope and was mired in despair.

Moreover, she had prepared in Highlander's training program, which was rooted in the philosophy of well-disciplined nonviolent direct action—that is, of confronting problems and calling attention to them. Her quiet and dignified defiance on the bus may have been her answer to the parting question that ended each session at Highlander: What are you going to do? The movement's great strength would be its determined adherence to nonviolence, even under the extraordinary stresses of church bombings, home burnings, jailhouse torture, and far more, as well as an endless stream of notes and telephone calls threatening all those things.

In the person of Parks, the city's civil rights activists felt they now had the right person at the right time. When E. D. Nixon, Parks' long-time colleague at the Montgomery chapter of the NAACP, heard she was being held in the jail because of her action on the Cleveland Avenue bus, he drove downtown to bail her out. Then he went home to his wife and said, according to his account, "Baby, we've got a case that we're goin' boycott the Montgomery city [bus] line." Jo Ann Robinson, the president of a group of Black Montgomery women, surreptitiously mimeographed thirty-five thousand copies of a call for a one-day boycott to be held on the following Monday, December 5, 1955.

Early that Monday morning, Martin Luther King, Jr., a young minister new to town, watched with his wife out their front window as a bus from the South Jackson line passed. It was empty. So, too, was the second bus. The third one carried two white passengers. King, who at this point was simply an interested observer of the boycott, had hoped for a 60 percent success rate in the one-day boycott, but it turned out to be closer to the high 90s. Montgomery's Black population clearly was responsive to the call, and certainly was tired of being abused during bus rides. Bus drivers complained that day that Black children mocked them and stuck out their tongues as the empty buses rolled by.

The ministers of the town followed up with a mass rally that Monday night at Holt Street Baptist, the biggest church in town. Thousands responded. "We had never seen a crowd like that before," recalled the Reverend Ralph Abernathy, a friend of King's who was far more established in Montgomery. There were too many attendees to fit into the church, so loudspeakers were set up to convey the proceedings to the crowds outside.

In a preliminary meeting that afternoon, King had been asked to speak that night at Holt. He had only a short time to prepare. His friend Elliott Finley drove him to the church, but because of the throng gathering outside it, they had to park blocks short of it and then make their way on foot. Struck by the surprising size of the crowd, which totaled about five thousand, King observed to his friend, "You know something, Finley, this could turn into something big."

King speaks

King's debut speech in the civil rights movement is remarkable for how well grounded it is in strategy and American history. As his first major public address, it would be worth dwelling on in any event. But even more, it requires attention because in it he outlined the stance that the Southern Christian Leadership Conference (SCLC) and indeed much of the Movement would take. It is intensely American, strongly nonviolent, and rooted in Christian faith, especially a vigorous belief in love and forgiveness. In it, King signaled that the Montgomery bus boycott and later the entire Movement would be a campaign not just to free Black people but also "to redeem the soul of America," as he would put it years later to an ally in the Movement.

He began, as he often would, by establishing the context. "We are here this evening for serious business," he said. "We are here in a general sense because first and foremost we are American citizens." With that, he established the central claim of the Movement, the demand to be treated as equal members of American society. It frankly is amazing that he expressed the strategic goal so clearly in his first speech. That he did so goes a long way toward explaining his swift rise to leadership.

Next he reviewed the facts of the arrest of Parks on the previous Thursday.

Then he struck his second theme, a very human one: that Black Americans simply were tired of being abused. He did not say they were bitter or angry. Rather, he said, "We are here this evening because we're tired now. And I want to say that we are not here advocating violence. We have never done that. . . . The only weapon we have in our hands is the weapon of protest." Jesus was providing the spirit, King later said, while Gandhi was furnishing the method.

The question of King's commitment to nonviolence at this point is complex. Bayard Rustin, who later advised him on the subject, would assert that King initially did not know much about nonviolence. For example, Rustin said, King employed armed guards at his house after it was attacked.

But the historical record indicates that there was a lot Rustin may not have known about King, such as that when King was a student at Pennsylvania's Crozer Theological Seminary, he had heard a talk by Howard University's Mordecai Johnson on Gandhi and got "fired up" and "began to read all the books on Gandhi he could lay his hands on." Also, at his next school, as a graduate student in theology at Boston University, King became friends with Howard Thurman, a dean and a key figure in twentieth-century Black American theology. Thurman, who had been raised by a grandmother who was born enslaved, developed a philosophy of Black American nonviolence, depicting Jesus, writes one historian, as "a persecuted religious minority, a nonviolent political insurgent who courageously and strategically defied the demands of an empire and permanently altered the course of human history." Thurman memorably wrote in 1925, "Jesus is still unknown in this land that is covered with churches erected in his honor." Thurman also asserted that "implicit in the Christian message is a profoundly revolutionary ethic." Subscribing to this view was not difficult, he added, but figuring out how to implement it was.

And in 1936, Thurman had traveled to India and met with Gandhi. The Indian leader asked him why American slaves had not become Muslims. Their interview ended memorably with Gandhi's farewell comment that "it may be through the [American] Negroes that the unadulterated message of non-violence will be delivered to the world." Speaking with another American in the 1940s, Gandhi asked about the treatment of its Black people and then said, "A civilization is to be judged by its treatment of minorities."

King also was familiar with Thurman's classic study, *Jesus and the Disinherited*, which portrays Christianity as a "survival kit" for "people who stand with their backs against the wall." So King may not have been showing all his nonviolent cards to Rustin and other out-of-town experts. And if he consciously put a Christian face on Gandhi's philosophy, as he appears to have done, following Thurman's lead, that was an act of strategic genius.

In his speech that night at the packed Holt Street Baptist Church, King next linked the Montgomery action to Black Americans' status as citizens. "The great glory of American democracy," he said, "is the right to protest for right." He then soared for the first time:

> We are not wrong in what we are doing. If we are wrong, the Supreme Court of this nation is wrong. If we are wrong, the Constitution of the United States is wrong. If we are wrong, God Almighty is wrong. . . . If we are wrong, justice is a lie. . . . We are determined here in Montgomery to work and fight until justice runs down like water and righteousness like a mighty stream.

He came back down to earth with a tactical admonition: "Not only are we using the tools of persuasion, but we've come to see that we've got to use the tools of coercion." He was saying that they would shun the buses of this city until they were desegregated. The tactical business at hand was to continue the boycott beyond the one-day wild-cat action. That interesting word "coercion" left hanging a question of just who was being coerced. Was it simply the bus company? Or was it also reluctant Blacks of the sort who had not aided Rosa Parks but who would now be seen as breaking with the community if they rode a bus?

King finished with a second leap, this time into history itself: "When the history books are written in the future, somebody will have to say, There lived a race of people . . . who had the moral courage to stand up for their rights, and thereby they injected a new meaning into the veins of history and civilization."

It was an amazing presentation. King, just twenty-six years old, the son of the pastor of one of Atlanta's major churches, and holder of a doctorate from Boston University, had grasped the root of the matter, never an easy task in the middle of swirling events. He had laid out the way forward for the Movement, planting the flag of nonviolent action.

And he had taken a long historical perspective in which he foresaw ultimate victory. He did it all in just sixteen minutes.

It helped King that the one-day boycott had been an enormous success. The Montgomery campaign, recalled Fred Shuttlesworth, the Black minister and activist watching from Birmingham, would be "the first actual massive uprising." A major reason for that, he said, was King and his message: "Doctor King spoke with a new voice. Not only was it a new movement, but it was a new voice, that you must love, you must not hate. The . . . best thing to make out of your enemy is a friend. So, this had a very profound effect upon not only Blacks, but whites at this time." Something different was happening in Montgomery, and it would eventually win the attention of the world.

That night the crowd voted, by standing, to extend the boycott indefinitely, under the auspices of a new organization which that night was dubbed the Montgomery Improvement Association. It tends to be forgotten that the boycotters' initial demand was not for full integration; rather, they presented three requests that fell short of that—first, that sitting Blacks would no longer have to turn seats over to whites; second, that drivers act with courtesy; and third, that some Black drivers be hired. This modest approach would be dropped when it became clear that white officials were not interested even in such a gradualist compromise.

King would go on to lead an insurgency, not just in the city of Montgomery but across the entire region as well. To assert that King's role was central is not, I think, to fall into the "great man" trap of relating history. Rather, it is to pose the beginning of a series of questions: What did he do, and what did others do? How and why did they do it? Why did they fail sometimes, but why did they succeed more often? All that is the subject of this book.

The strategy and tactics of nonviolence

The point of departure in answering those questions must be the strategy and tactics of nonviolence. As King's first speech showed, nonviolence would be at the heart of the nascent civil rights movement, from how it attracted people and prepared them for action to how it later deployed them on the streets. It would inform the recruiting of volunteers, with trainers constantly asking people if they were capable of practicing nonviolence while under duress, while being taunted or beaten or having ketchup poured over their head while others spat on them at a segregated lunch counter. It was at the core of how these volunteers were trained. In the field, the dignity of marchers, declining to counterattack the hoodlums sometimes set upon them, would catch the attention of the media and thereby of the nation.

The goal of the Movement, the purpose of its strategy, was to end the treatment of Blacks as second-class citizens and so to reorder the nation's public culture. It wanted to desegregate public accommodations—buses, restaurants, parks, and such—and to win for Blacks the right to vote, consistently denied to them in the South. The mode of challenge was to mobilize the Black population of the South to show white southerners that Black people were not content with their lot and very much desired to receive equal justice before the law. Beginning in Montgomery, the central tactic of the Movement was nonviolent protest. It was an inspired choice.

The Movement had the tremendous advantage of facing a stubborn adversary wedded to brutal methods that had worked for a century. The dominant caste had used violence or the threat of it to rigorously enforce the second-class status of Black southerners. But the Movement's nonviolent actions would baffle the southern power structure. "If there had been any violence at all, they [white southern officials] were prepared to deal with that," said Rustin, one of the key strategists of the Movement. "But they could not deal with people who were not being violent."

Yet make no mistake: the Movement was militant from the start. Its approach could be quite aggressive, almost the opposite of "passive resistance," a confusing and misleading term. As Gandhi put it, nonviolent resistance "does not mean meek submission to the will of the evildoer, but it means the pitting of one's whole soul against the will of the tyrant." One seeks conflict with the adversary, ideally making him show the system's true face—not the one it would like to show to the world (and perhaps believes in), but rather the true face of oppression, which fundamentally rests on violence. Just before launching his famous Salt March to the sea in 1930, Gandhi wrote to the British viceroy of India to explain his intentions. "Many think that non-violence is not an active force," he explained. "My experience . . . shows that non-violence can be an intensely active force."

One key difference between military violence and militant nonviolence is that the latter flummoxes the foe. Police and vigilante groups in the South were well versed in the use of force, but not in this new approach. Ultimately, this righteous insight would be key to the success of the Movement. It was a smart approach not just strategically but tactically. As Richard Gregg, an American disciple of Gandhi, wrote in the 1930s, "Your violent opponent wants you to fight in the way to which he is accustomed. If you utterly decline, and adopt a method wholly new to him, you have thus gained an immediate tactical advantage." When the civil rights movement was able to keep a nonviolent stance, it generally prevailed.

Militant nonviolence possessed multiple approaches well beyond just being beaten by policemen without retaliating. The nonviolent arsenal includes the march, the fast, the picket, and the one-day general strike, general noncooperation with authorities such as nonpayment of taxes, overwhelming the jails with prisoners, and even, in the extreme, setting up a parallel government to police the people, teach in Movement schools, and collect Movement taxes. The greater the variety of tactics, the less certain the foe will be on how to prepare to respond. Unpredictability can make operations more effective. As observed by the Harvard political scientist Erica Chenoweth, a specialist in nonviolent social change, the diversity in approaches gives members of a social movement "the capability of maneuver when the state begins to ramp up violence against them."

Indeed, a nonviolent campaign could even take the form of a large portion of a city's population simply but resolutely declining to use that city's public transport system.

The nuts and bolts of a bus boycott

So began the Montgomery bus boycott. It would last 381 days, far longer than anyone expected, ultimately continuing through almost all of 1956, ending only after another Supreme Court ruling. Effectively, Montgomery's Black population besieged the city for more than a year. The key to its success was the ability of the Black community to sustain its protest, showing an amazing capability for endurance and patience.

How did they manage to persist? More than anything else, they were well organized.

The first issue facing the boycott leaders was developing secure lines of communication in order to inform the Black citizenry about the boycott and encourage those already active to remain so. From the very start, the boycott was plugged into a key infrastructure: the Black churches of the city. The importance of those churches cannot be emphasized enough. They provided meeting places, and, more important, their ministers used their pulpits to transmit information and instructions, an essential role given that Blacks had no political representatives. The endorsement of ministers gave institutional backing to King's call for Black resistance to be rigorously nonviolent. And the churches provided a kind of shield against outsiders. When strange voices telephoned requesting information about the boycott, they were instructed to call their own church. The Montgomery Improvement Association promoted a slogan, "Don't ride the bus 'til you hear from us."

The second issue for the boycott movement was figuring out how to provide rides for some of the 17,500 Black citizens of Montgomery who normally used the bus system to commute to and from work. King called his friend T. J. Jemison, a minister who in 1953 had run a semi-successful eight-day-long bus boycott in Baton Rouge, Louisiana, to ask about organizing carpools. Some people could walk, he learned, but others would need car rides, and so a transportation committee was formed. Soon more than three hundred people volunteered at a mass meeting to drive their cars in the pool. By mid-December, a system had been worked out with the drivers following regular routes past designated collection points. It helped that as the boycott got under way, college students at home on Christmas break were willing to drive their parents' cars, which provided a short-term stopgap as longer-term arrangements were developed.

Soon it was clear that a small staff would be needed to field service complaints, answer queries, and acknowledge and record contributions. The transportation committee also hired about eight dispatchers who directed carpool traffic and also were assigned to track gasoline use in order to prevent "spongers" from taking more fuel than they were using in the carpools and stop gas stations from submitting "phony invoices." The entire boycott operation required about $5,000 a month (the equivalent of more than $50,000 today). Cautious of the reach of the antagonistic Alabama state government, the association was careful to deposit most of its funds in out-of-state banks, most of them Black-owned.

Two Black-owned properties in downtown Montgomery would become key to the success of the boycott. One was a parking lot, the other a drugstore. Both had enough space for carpool drivers to drop off and pick up passengers, and so became the downtown exchange points for the system. By contrast, one of the biggest problems in organizing the system was finding spots in white neighborhoods where Blacks could gather to wait for their rides without people calling the police on them.

There were setbacks. At the beginning of many wars, one of the usual difficulties is figuring out which potential allies actually will rally to the cause. Distinguishing friend from foe from neutral entities is a major aspect of the early phases. There are always surprises and disappointments, as Winston Churchill and Franklin Roosevelt learned with the Vichy French during World War II. King went into the Montgomery boycott expecting that many white Christian clergy in the South would support him. He was chagrined to find out the contrary. Indeed, the organization of white ministers in Montgomery declined even to meet with its Black counterpart. "The most pervasive mistake I have made," he later said, "was in believing that because our cause was just, we could be sure that the white ministers of the South, once their Christian consciences were challenged, would rise to our aid. . . . I ended up, of course, chastened and disillusioned." Some white ministers even became adversaries, King observed. Eight years later, his enduring disappointment in the southern white religious establishment would energize his single most memorable piece of writing, the "Letter from Birmingham Jail."

To maintain momentum, retain support, and reinforce the philosophy of nonviolent resistance, King and the Montgomery Improvement Association began holding mass meetings twice a week, which he later cut back to one. His message again and again was dignity and discipline. Not all speakers toed this ideological line. One night a minister rambled on about white people as "dirty crackers," for which he later received a quiet rebuke. To maintain what now is called "message discipline," the association decided that only King would be allowed to speak to the media on its behalf.

There also was some initial ambivalence or confusion about the practice of nonviolence. Some participants wanted to follow a system of nonviolence under which they would not initiate violence but would defend themselves if attacked. A few even suggested that it might be a good idea to kill some white people to show that the boycotters were serious, King recalled. Regular meetings helped tamp down such dangerous thinking. "At the beginning of the protest these twice-a-week get-togethers were indispensable channels of communication, since Montgomery had neither a Negro-owned radio station nor a widely read Negro newspaper," King noted. These sessions, he added, also built organizational cohesion as Black professionals sat side by side with working men and women.

"The mass meetings were so stimulating that it just engulfed everybody," recalled one frequent attendee. There were hymns, prayers, and speeches. "You couldn't resist the influence of the mass meetings. Mainly because of the dynamic personality of Reverend King. No person could inspire the people like him."

Montgomery officials counterattack

King and other boycott leaders underestimated the intensity of white opposition to altering bus segregation even in small ways. For the city's white leaders, the issue was not legal but cultural and political. "If we granted the Negroes these demands," the bus company's lawyer remarked at a meeting at which King was present, "they would go about boasting of a victory that they had won over the white people, and this we will not stand for." As might be expected, the meeting concluded without progress being made. Stances on both sides hardened.

White officialdom proceeded to commit a series of unforced errors. This was a pattern of behavior that would help the boycott and appear again in subsequent civil rights operations. On December 8, three days into the boycott, the bus company halted service on eight lines in predominantly Black neighborhoods. This effectively reinforced the boycott, as vacillators now had no choice but to rely on the boycotters' alternative means of getting to and from work.

One of the more bizarre errors by the white establishment occurred on Saturday, January 21, 1956, when the city of Montgomery announced that it had reached a boycott settlement with three "prominent Negro ministers." The announcement did not identify these ministers by name. As it happened, a few clergymen had met with city officials, but none of them were involved in the boycott. The city's statement seems to have been an attempt to confuse the rank and file of boycotters into riding the buses on the following Monday, or perhaps to discourage contributions.

King and the other boycott leaders responded with alacrity. They drove around the city that night to put out the word in clubs and bars that the announcement was incorrect, and the next morning the message was passed from the pulpits of Black churches across the city. The result of the city's clumsy effort was to stiffen Black resistance and erode any credibility that white officials might still have had with Montgomery's Black citizens. "Did they think we were fools?" wondered the activist Johnnie Carr.

Soon after that misstep, W. A. Gayle, the mayor of Montgomery, stated that it was time to get tough. The city's officials, he said, were "tired of pussyfooting around with the leaders of the boycott." He also expressed concern that "the Negroes are laughing at the white people behind their backs." He was ready to retaliate. Clyde Sellers, the commissioner of police, singled out King for criticism.

The crackdown came quickly. That same day that the mayor announced his new hard-line approach, King was arrested for allegedly driving his Pontiac at 30 miles per hour in a zone with a speed limit of 25. Unusually, instead of simply being issued a ticket, he was arrested, fingerprinted, and briefly jailed, for the first time in his life. The next night, back home, a telephone caller told him, "Nigger, we are tired of you and your mess now. And if you aren't out of town in three days, we're going to blow your brains out and blow up your house." Most death threats are just efforts to frighten someone, but this one may not have been. On January 30, just a few days later, a small bomb rolled onto the front porch of King's house and exploded, filling the front room with smoke and broken glass. A crowd of Blacks soon gathered in front of the house, displaying their unhappiness to the mayor and the police chief, who arrived to try to show that they had the situation in hand.

King hurried home from the church where he was speaking and, after checking on his family, stood on his front porch and calmed the gathering while the odor of dynamite still lingered in the air. "Don't get panicky," he ordered. "Don't get your weapons. . . . We are not advocating violence." Go home, he said, "and know that all of us are in the hands of God." It was a magisterial performance that underscored the difference between the boycotters and their segregationist opposition.

A college student asked King two years later about his greatest moment of fear. He said it had come in January 1956, when the death threats mounted to "thirty and forty" a day. He hadn't expected that, he confessed, because he hadn't seen Montgomery as a violent city. "So I started out with an illusion," he said. Then, he added, "I had certain religious experiences that gave me something within to confront all of these threats."

The bombing incident also cemented King's role as a leader in his community. He clearly already had the eloquence needed. He was learning to deal with violence, and also how to oversee a large organization while operating under pressure. He was growing in credibility with both his Black supporters and his white opponents. Erna Dungee Allen, the Montgomery Improvement Association's financial director, watched him learn: "He listened a lot and thought a lot. He got by himself a lot."

Meanwhile, no ploy seemed too petty for white officials to try. Fred Gray, the young attorney for the Montgomery Improvement Association, was informed that his draft classification had been changed from 4-D, a deferment given because he was a practicing minister as well as a lawyer, to 1-A, a status making him eligible for immediate conscription.

The city issued indictments on February 21 and the following day began arresting people it suspected of leading the boycott, which was technically illegal under state law. In all, about a hundred people were charged, including Rosa Parks and some twenty ministers, but eventually only King was tried. He was convicted on March 22 and fined $500. Failing to pay that, he would have to serve 386 days at hard labor. He appealed.

The indictments were a major misstep by white officials. Arresting a score of ministers was so unusual that it made national news, which in turn spurred a flood of contributions. Before King's arrest, the Montgomery Improvement Association was receiving about $10,000 a month. In the month after it, the association was given about $60,000. With money pouring in from around the country, the association was able to purchase fifteen new station wagons, making them the property of participating churches, with the name of each church emblazoned on the sides and fronts of the wagons. People called them rolling churches. Whites were infuriated by the sight, thought Ralph Abernathy, King's closest friend in Montgomery. "They were used to seeing Blacks driving around in ten-year-old Buicks," he explained, "not in brand-new Ford wagons." The new fleet of automobiles was a physical manifestation of the Black challenge to the existing social hierarchy.

James Lawson, a major theorist of nonviolence, would recall that these manifold pressures forced King to dig deep spiritually. "The threats on his life that began almost immediately in Montgomery made him very aware of how fragile his life was," Lawson said, "but it also made him profoundly aware of how dangerous the struggle was and also how he had to have the spiritual and moral fortitude to work through it and live through it."

By the spring of 1956, the boycott began to gain attention even overseas. One day in a town almost exactly in the middle of India, a young Black American picked up the local newspaper, the *Nagpur Times*, and saw a news story about the Montgomery boycott. He was so elated he began shouting. This American was none other than James Lawson. He had moved to India to study Gandhi's philosophy of non-violent resistance, but now he began thinking it was time to head back to the United States. A few years later he would become an adviser to King, a key figure in shaping the civil rights movement's direction, and a major point of transmission of Gandhi's teachings to the American civil rights movement.

King's take on nonviolence

Lawson thought people generally did not understand the term "nonvi-olence." He said in one interview, "The definition that most Americans have of nonviolence is that if you get hit in the face then you take it, you don't do anything. . . . That, you know, it's laying down." He preferred the Sanskrit word *satyagraha*, which can be loosely translated as "the te-nacious power of the soul" or more understandably, as "clinging to the truth." In practical terms, Lawson continued, nonviolence was much more confrontational than passive resistance: "It meant trying to find superior skills in resisting." One of Gandhi's veteran followers, Krishnalal Shridharani, went even further, flatly asserting that satyagraha is "an instrument of aggression" that in fact has "more in common with war than with Western pacifism."

Well into the boycott, King reported to Bayard Rustin, who was becoming a frequent adviser to him, that he saw "a growing commitment to the philosophy of non-violence" in Montgomery's Black community. "Even those who were willing to get their guns in the beginning," he added, "are gradually coming to see the futility of such an approach."

King didn't list himself in that letter to Rustin as among those who were changing their minds, but he well might have. In his memoir, King reported that his understanding of nonviolence changed over the course of the boycott. Theory was one thing; practicing the philosophy was another. "The experience in Montgomery did more to clarify my thinking on the question of nonviolence than all of the books that I had read," he later wrote. "As the days unfolded I became more and more convinced of the power of nonviolence. . . . Many issues I had not cleared up intellectually were now solved in the sphere of practical action." Drawing this distinction between theory and practice also may have been King's way of achieving some distance from seasoned activists such as Rustin who wanted to guide the younger man. He was not going to act merely as a vehicle for the views of others.

Reading King's correspondence for the year 1956 makes one wonder if there were days when he felt like he was being sent letters of advice by every American liberal who ever had made a pilgrimage to India. Indeed, a rivalry developed between two old hands in nonviolence, Glenn Smiley and Rustin, about who would be King's guru, and King was aware of the wrestling between the two.

But King had good instincts here. Advice from elders was fine, but in the civil rights movement, as in war and many other endeavors, it was almost always best to have the leader on the ground make the big decisions. During the course of the crucial year of 1956, through the experience of seeing thousands of Black citizens express their grievances daily without violence, King became more dedicated to nonviolence, not just as a tactic but as a way of life. As Rustin summarized it, "The glorious thing is that he came to a profoundly deep understanding of nonviolence through the struggle itself." That assessment may be both romantic and condescending. As noted earlier, King may not have let on to outsiders how deeply he had studied Gandhi and nonviolence. Rustin could be high-handed, noted Harris Wofford, a sympathetic white adviser to King and later an aide to President Kennedy, and he sometimes "acted as if King were a precious puppet whose symbolic actions were to be planned by a Gandhian high command."

The best way to summarize King's relationship with Gandhi's philosophy is that the Indian thinker was a major influence on King, but not a direct model. There are many differences between the two. Gandhi created a movement, while a movement found King. Having spent two decades of his adult life in South Africa, Gandhi was a bit of an outsider in India, whereas King never was a stranger in the American South. As the political scientist Gene Sharp observes, "it is usually forgotten how un-Indian Gandhi was in many ways." Gandhi worked constantly at self-denial; King often indulged in food, alcohol, and the pleasures of the flesh. Gandhi immersed himself in rural India as King rarely did in the rural American South. Gandhi was not tied to weekly sermons at a church inherited from his father. And Gandhi thrived when confined to jail, while King languished when imprisoned.

Yet there are impressive similarities. Both led transformative campaigns. Both also had tendencies to announce wildly ambitious goals and then leave them behind. This propensity suggests that they did not always necessarily think they would reach those goals but sometimes talked about them perhaps in the hope of expanding the imaginations of their followers and even of their adversaries. They were offering different views of the world and asking people, or even forcing them, to consider those views. Both were notably adept at using the media to advance their causes. Both saw nonviolence not just as a political tactic but as a life-encompassing philosophy. And the lives of both ended with assassination. Some of King's most impressive victories involved taking plays from Gandhi's book. This would be especially true when the Movement strategist James Bevel, who also was deeply influenced by Gandhi, became involved.

A stunning moment in court

On the morning of November 13, 1956, King was back in court, dealing with a city injunction that sought to shut down the boycotters' make-shift transportation system of carpools. It was a low point for him. He expected the judge to rule in favor of the city, and he didn't know how to encourage boycott participants, except to say that things would work out somehow. "They had backed us up, and we had let them down," he recalled. "It was a desolate moment." Yet that low mood was soon to be lifted.

While King sat in a courtroom near despair, a reporter came over and told him that the Supreme Court had just declared that bus seg-regation in Montgomery was illegal. In a word, the Movement had won. There would be a waiting period while the city appealed, but the end was in sight. By mid-December, the city had exhausted its legal challenges to the high court ruling. On December 20, the bus boy-cott, more than a year old, was over. The emerging civil rights move-ment had won a major victory in its first campaign, which had been waged primarily in the streets, not in the courts. It had done more than change how the local government treated local Blacks; it had changed how local Blacks thought about themselves as they stood up visibly to protest Jim Crow.

That month, King paused to record some of the lessons of the boy-cott. The first was that Montgomery's Black population could come together and maintain a unified position. "We have discovered," he declared, "that we can stick together for a common cause." Another was that white aggression could be handled, especially if there was high morale and unity in the Movement. "Threats and violence do not necessarily intimidate those who are sufficiently aroused and non-violent," he explained. And as a result of the boycott, Blacks' self-image had improved: "We have gained a new sense of dignity and destiny."

In a similar document also written that month, Bayard Rustin reflected on two other aspects that helped the boycott succeed. First, it was built upon the existing infrastructure of Black churches, which kept the entire community involved. Rustin wrote in a letter to King, "It thus had the strength of unity which the school integration efforts have lacked, thereby leaving the fight to heroic but isolated individuals." Rustin did not say so, but there was a Gandhian connection here: The southern Black church was essentially conservative in its values, respectful of established ways. So, too, was Gandhi, who sought to compel his opponents to live up to their belief in their own humanity. Second, the nature of the boycott required daily participation by everyone, and this was visible to the entire community.

The southern Black church was effectively a citadel for the Movement. It was not just a reliable refuge in a hostile world but also what the sociologist E. Franklin Frazier called "a nation within a nation." But its presence on the front lines represented a shift. Historically, the Black church had been seen by activists such as the great historian W. E. B. Du Bois as an impediment. As the historian Richard Kluger notes, Du Bois thought Black ministers were "consumed by trivialities and their own personal influence among their congregants; their sermons were out of date and provided no leadership." Now they were stepping up and leading the people. In military terms, the churches had become the command posts of the Movement, secure locations where plans could be made, training sessions held, and orders issued.

There was one other relevant aspect to the presence of the Black church. King's friend the Reverend Ralph Abernathy knew the ministers of Montgomery better than did King, a relative newcomer to the city, and so was able to run interference for King. As Andrew Young put it, "Adept at the internal politics among Black Baptist preachers, Ralph was able to protect and promote Martin among the other preachers, freeing Martin to lead." It is easy to overlook the importance of such arrangements that free up the top leader of an organization to do what he or she does best. The motto of the senior commander should be "Do only what only you can do." Everything else should be left to subordinates. During World War II, for example, Dwight Eisenhower tried to focus on the absolutely essential, while delegating to others the merely important.

Endings

All campaigns, like all wars, must end at some point. The conclusion is too often neglected in war, often with devastating consequences, as in the American failure to plan for an occupation in Iraq in 2003. But the civil rights movement, to its great credit, was remarkably attentive to the question of endings. Nonviolent philosophy emphasizes that the final step in an action should always be reconciliation. Thus deep consideration of the ending was built into Movement campaigns from the very start.

King had the foresight to see that a victory in Montgomery would need to be consolidated. Since October 1956, he and others had been preparing the boycotters for a successful outcome, emphasizing that they should resume riding the buses with dignity and courtesy. Any boycotter who could not behave on the buses with restraint, they instructed, should "walk for another week or two." And when integrated rides began, the Montgomery Improvement Association assigned two ministers to ride on each line at the morning and evening rush hours to monitor passenger behavior.

Before waiting television cameras, King boarded a bus at six o'clock on the morning of December 21, 1956, and paid his fare.

The driver—white, of course, as the company did not hire Blacks for those jobs—greeted him with a smile and said, "I believe you are Reverend King, aren't you?"

"Yes, I am," King replied.

"We are glad to have you this morning," the driver said.

It all seemed so simple and polite.

In war, the outcome of major events sometimes turns on mundane forms of transport. And so in memories of war, those means can become mythologized, because they tend to capture the desperation of the moment—the fleet of Paris taxis that took the French army to the battle of the Marne in 1919, or the small boats that helped rescue the British army when it was pinned by the Germans against the North Sea at Dunkirk in the spring of 1940. The iconic image of the civil rights movement would be buses, in Montgomery in 1955 and in the Freedom Rides in 1961. Those two campaigns would have an echo in 1963 when buses were the means by which most participants arrived at the March on Washington for Jobs and Freedom, the biggest civil rights march in American history. The sad opposite echo would come two decades later, when whites in the northern city of Boston reacted violently to the court-ordered desegregation of schools through what was called, in political shorthand, busing.

The end of the beginning

The Montgomery campaign was over, yet the war for civil rights for American Blacks was just getting started.

There are three basic ways to measure conflict: scope, duration, and intensity. The geographical scope of this effort would be the South. Just what its duration would be was anyone's guess—some predicted many decades. And in the weeks following the success of the boycott, it became evident that the fight would be intense. The goal was simple: for Black Americans to be treated as humans like anyone else.

A white backlash began within days. Someone fired a shotgun into King's home at 1:30 a.m. on December 23, 1956. Shots also were fired into buses rolling through the city. Two nights later, Fred Shuttlesworth was lying in his bed in Birmingham, ninety miles north of Montgomery, when sixteen sticks of dynamite exploded on the other side of the wall from him, under his bedroom window. James Roberson, a neighbor, recalled, "It felt as if the Earth had just erupted. You could feel the thrust of it and the smell of it. It was so powerful. You can think of a shotgun shell and how loud it is and multiply that by maybe two thousand." The wall of Shuttlesworth's house blew out and the roof collapsed, yet he found himself still lying in his bed, somehow alive, probably because the mattress had been wrapped around him by the blast. "At that moment, all fear was taken from me," he said later. "I never feared anything since that time."

When Shuttlesworth emerged from the smoking wreckage, a police officer—white, as there were no Black police in Birmingham at that time—gazed at him and said, "Reverend, if I were you, I'd get out of town as fast as I could."

Shuttlesworth was an unusual man—a moonshiner turned minister—and was always a fighter. He responded, "Officer, you are not me. You go back and tell your Klan brethren that if God could keep me through this, then I'm here for the duration."

Then, on January 10, 1957, a wave of bombings shook Montgomery. Ralph Abernathy's house was struck, along with four Black churches and the home of the sole white minister (a missionary from the North) who had supported the boycott. Two weeks later, a bomb was left on King's front steps but failed to detonate. Thus was a pattern established: successful civil rights efforts would be followed by quick waves of vengeful white violence.

Most strikingly, a young preacher new to Montgomery had done a remarkable job in leading and holding together the city's Black population through a trying year of terrorist attacks and official harassment—and had prevailed. It helped that King was, as his adviser Andrew Young later put it, "an extremely disciplined person."

Each campaign sets some of the conditions for the next. The success of the Montgomery boycott captured the attention of Blacks across the South. That was more meaningful than was understood at the time and is understood even now. Historians tend to measure events in the civil rights campaign by whether they resulted in changes in laws or practices, but this neglects the effect that each episode had on inspiring others to join the Movement or to support it financially. Such instances of rallying to the cause were certainly as significant as legal results in sustaining the Movement. In 1955, for example, John Lewis was a tenth-grader living in rural Alabama, fifty miles southeast of Montgomery. In the evening, he recalled, after a day of hoeing weeds or—even harder on the hands and body—picking cotton, Lewis and his family would listen to the radio news about the Montgomery boycott. "It created a sense of hope, a sense of optimism," he recalled. Lewis of course would go on to become one of the enduring leaders of the Movement.

2.
NASHVILLE, 1960

Developing a Nonviolent Cadre

The Montgomery bus boycott had been large and well organized, but it was not an offensive action. Rather, it was a withdrawal of patronage. The next big step for the civil rights movement would be a confrontational presence demanding service, in 1960. This was a major escalation in the war for equality and genuine citizenship.

Looking back now from the twenty-first century, the three years after the Montgomery bus boycott often look like a time of inaction in the Deep South, except for the skirmish over the integration of Little Rock High School in the fall of 1957, off in relatively distant Arkansas. Yet behind the scenes, this period was a time of organization, training, and preparation. Many activists were asking the same question: What exactly had happened in Montgomery, and what might the next steps be? The boycott had shown a way to conduct a long-term mass campaign. "The idea was to understand the power of nonviolent direct action as it had been proven in Montgomery," recalled the Reverend C. T. Vivian, who in the late 1950s was a seminary student in Nashville and would go on to become a stalwart of the Movement. "People said, 'Great victory in Montgomery, what does that mean for us? What can we do?'" It took some time to answer those questions.

One of the major lessons of the Montgomery boycott's success was the need for a regional organization that would plan actions, recruit and train volunteers, raise funds, and maintain discipline during campaigns. King took the first big step by inviting sixty Black ministers and community leaders to his father's church in Atlanta for a meeting on January 10, 1957, just a few weeks after the end of the boycott. There, at the suggestion of Bayard Rustin, who had prevailed in his rivalry with Glenn Smiley about advising King, they formed a group they at first called the Negro Leaders Conference on Nonviolent Integration, which soon would be renamed the Southern Christian Leadership Conference.

The SCLC got off to a shaky start. In May 1957, King delivered a well-received speech titled "Give Us the Ballot," and three months later the SCLC decided its first effort would be the Crusade for Citizenship. This campaign started the following winter with mass meetings in a score of cities across the South. The ambitious goal stated on its letterhead was "to double the number of qualified Negro voters in the South" by 1960. The impulse for the campaign was rooted in the fact that Blacks in the South often were simply denied the ability to vote, usually by refusals to register them. But this early effort was made of gossamer and went nowhere.

In mid-1957, King received an offer from Mordecai Johnson, president of Howard University, to become dean of that institution's School of Religion. He considered the invitation for several weeks, but ultimately declined, stating, "I have come to the conclusion that my work in the South is not quite complete." Then, while in New York City, he was stabbed in the chest with a letter opener by a mentally ill woman, and took several weeks to rest and recuperate. And early in 1959, he went on an extended pilgrimage to India. King still had a lot to learn about setting strategic goals and overseeing an organization. It did not help him that in another act of harassment by officials, Alabama authorities indicted him for allegedly filing false tax returns. He was eventually found not guilty, despite being tried before an all-white, all-male jury.

A loss of momentum often occurs in war, and is usually a sign of either misstated objectives or poor leadership. Both factors were at work here: King was distracted and the SCLC was adrift. By the following summer, Ella Baker, a veteran organizer who at one point was the organization's sole staffer, warned King in a memorandum that "we are losing the initiative in the Civil Rights struggle in the South." The following spring, at a meeting in Montgomery, Baker "gave him the devil for not spending more time with the SCLC." Later that year, King wrote to an AFL-CIO official reassuring him that the SCLC was not "fading away." He also sent a letter to an influential journalist in which he half conceded that the Crusade for Citizenship had fizzled, observing, "The fact remains that no organization has done an adequate job in the area of registration and voting. The job is too big for any single organization." King was enormously active—he traveled constantly and delivered more than two hundred speeches in 1958 alone—but it wasn't clear that he was leading the SCLC toward achieving its political goals.

A military maxim holds that one should never reinforce failure. Part of being a leader is being able to recognize when something is not working and then to take steps to cut losses and move in a different direction. In late 1959, King did just that. In an internal memo, he began edging away from voter registration. "While the voting drive still holds a significant place in our total program, we must not neglect other important areas," he wrote, a bit stiffly. "Therefore, I recommend that we begin thinking of some of the other areas that should gain our immediate attention." Opportunities were out there, but it wasn't clear precisely where. Another part of being a leader is biding one's time and waiting for the situation to develop.

King encounters Lawson

Meanwhile, February 1957 had brought a quiet but key moment in the history of the civil rights movement. King was speaking at Oberlin

College when he met James Lawson, a veteran practitioner of nonviolent protest who had been jailed during the Korean War for declining to cooperate with draft laws, refusing even to seek a student exemption. Asked on a conscription form about his race, Lawson had recorded that his was "human." After serving eleven months in prison, Lawson had moved to India to study Gandhi's philosophy of nonviolent resistance and consider how it might be applied to the United States. He was the young American who had read about the Montgomery bus boycott in the Nagpur newspaper. He then returned to the United States to complete his studies at Oberlin.

King and Lawson shared a meal, had a good conversation, and agreed to stay in touch. "[We] found ourselves to be very much in sync with one another as people," Lawson later said. When Lawson said he planned to work in the South after finishing his graduate studies, which would take several years, King responded, "Don't wait, come now, we need you." Lawson responded that he would arrive just as soon as he could.

Extending that invitation to Lawson to come south may have been the most historic thing King did during these years. Lawson soon would inject a new energy into the wandering movement. Heeding King's call, he moved to Nashville, Tennessee, and enrolled at the divinity school at Vanderbilt University, which had begun admitting a handful of Black students a few years earlier, and only at some of its graduate schools. Lawson began his civil rights work in Nashville not with a demonstration or some other public action, but with a low-profile yet intense program of training that lasted for months.

Training and readiness

The civil rights movement was often creative, but it was rarely spontaneous. Its members did not just take to the streets to see what would happen. Rather, weeks and even months of planning and preparation went into most of its campaigns. Lawson set the example by taking his time. Diane Nash, a Fisk University student who became one of Lawson's most effective trainees, later explained, "The first step was investigation, where we really did all the necessary research and analysis to totally understand the problem. The second phase was education, where we educated our own constituency to what we had found out in our research. The third stage was negotiation, where you really approached the opposition, let them know your position." Only then would come marches, sit-ins, or other forms of demonstration. "The purpose of demonstrations," Nash explained, "was to focus the attention of the community on the issue, and on the injustice." This would be coupled with withdrawal of cooperation from the system—boycotts, strikes, and other forms of simply not working with existing structures. If the civil actions were successful, the final stage would be reconciliation, the working out of a new, postcrisis relationship.

Putting that systematic approach into practice required a good deal of training. The preparation of soldiers is a neglected subject in most military histories, often treated as the necessary but dull preliminary to the real story. But it is of critical importance. Every military leader knows that intense training is essential to everything that follows, playing a large role in whether an organization fails or succeeds. The more rigorous and realistic the training, the better. The ancient historian Josephus wrote of the Roman army, "Their exercises lack none of the vigor of true war, but each soldier trains every day with his whole heart as if it were war indeed. . . . He would not err who described their exercises as battles without blood, and their battles as bloody exercises."

The civil rights movement paid close attention to training as well. It was in lectures, discussions, and role-playing sessions that the philosophy of nonviolence was imparted. Those sessions prepared new volunteers for the ugly violence many would endure, and also made them familiar with the overall strategy of the Movement. Indeed, a 1934 book by the Gandhi disciple Richard Gregg concluded with two full chapters on training. Gregg's work was influential in the Movement. King had read his book in 1956, recommended it to others, and contributed a prologue to an American edition published in 1959.

Gregg wrote that the ideal size for a group being trained is no more than a dozen. "When there are more than twelve, it is very difficult to have free, active and steady discussion," he observed. He had settled on an interesting number, one familiar to every soldier. In modern infantry units, squads are usually made up of eleven to thirteen people. Smaller than that, and the group becomes vulnerable when it suffers combat losses; bigger than that, and it is difficult to develop and maintain tight cohesion. Hence this small unit is the basic building block of military organization. Gregg had recognized what most civilians never see—that the "primary group" of about a dozen people is all important in predicting success in conflict. And of course, Lawson, a deeply religious man, had another example before him: twelve disciples had gathered around a leader named Jesus.

"A small group of twelve gets to know one another well and comfortably," Gregg wrote. "They can easily feel strongly as a unit, can think and plan effectively as a unit and can act swiftly, perseveringly and effectively as a unit." Gregg endorsed the analogy between nonviolent actions and combat operations because he thought that many of the same behaviors and techniques that humans had developed over thousands of years to wage war could be repurposed for nonviolence. He wrote, "The nonviolent resister will, like soldiers, need courage, self-respect, patience, endurance and the ability to sacrifice himself for a cause."

Done right, a thoughtful training program also will identify potential new leaders—the soldiers who learn fast, show persistence and self-discipline, and are able to help others. The Nashville civil rights movement is particularly striking for its development of leaders. Out of its initial small group of about forty or fifty students grew a cadre of people who would become a major force in the civil rights effort—first in sit-ins, then in the Freedom Rides, then in forming the Student Nonviolent Coordinating Committee (SNCC), then in the Birmingham marches, and finally in Selma. In addition to Diane Nash, this group included John Lewis, James Bevel, Bernard LaFayette, Jr., and Marion Barry.

Nashville was an interesting choice. It was home to a Black seminary and several Black colleges, as well as two white ones. The city prized its reputation for political moderation, which had led it to take some tentative steps toward desegregation. Lawson would soon put those steps to the test. It also had a community of engaged Black ministers who were paying close attention to the Montgomery bus boycott. Inspired by the formation of the SCLC, in January 1958 they created their own group, the Nashville Christian Leadership Conference, as an affiliate.

Conditions were ripe in Nashville, but Lawson was to be the city's "special ingredient," said one of the NCLC's leaders. Lawson believed that he could turn the city into "a laboratory for demonstrating nonviolence," and that doing so could plant the seeds for "many Montgomerys." He set to work, conducting on March 26, 1958, the first of what he called "workshops" but the American military would call intense training and indoctrination. These took place on Tuesday nights, Saturday mornings, and Sunday evenings in church basements, at first with about ten participants, none of them students. But in the fall of 1958, students began to participate, and the workshop group doubled.

The purpose of the workshops, explained Lawson, was to train people so that when conducting an action, they would coordinate their approach with an understanding of the ultimate goal. "You have to have a common discipline when you have twenty-five people on a protest," he said. "A protest cannot be spontaneous. It has to be systematic. There must be planning, strategy." What Lawson called "a common discipline" is known in the U.S. military as "doctrine."

One of the first students to attend Lawson's meetings, which focused on the nature of justice, was John Lewis, a bright but awkward son of Alabama sharecroppers who had been puzzled as a boy that he was not allowed to set foot in his town's public library. "Those Tuesday nights . . . became the focus of my life, more important even than my classes," Lewis recalled. "It was something I'd been searching for my whole life." He was a student at American Baptist Theological Seminary, which trained Black ministers. Tuition cost him $42 a semester. To help pay that bill, Lewis worked part-time as a dishwasher and then as a janitor at the college.

James Bevel, a friend of John Lewis' and of Lewis' roommate, Bernard LaFayette, Jr., had heard Lawson talk and had been distinctly unimpressed. Then one day Bevel dropped by at the end of a session to give Lewis and LaFayette a ride. Lawson was talking about a man who was spat on and asked his assailant for a handkerchief, used it, and returned it with a word of gratitude. Bevel was astonished, thinking to himself, "He thanked the man who spat on him for letting him use his damn handkerchief?" Lawson said that the act was so simple yet so profound that it disarmed the attacker. "That amazed me," Bevel recalled. "At the same time it felt like lights going on. The possibilities and the uses of nonviolence became instantly apparent." Bevel himself went overnight from skeptic to devotee. Never one for half measures, he visited the Nashville Public Library and left carrying every book it had by or about Gandhi.

Lawson sent Lewis, Bevel, and LaFayette to a session at the Highlander Folk School, the same place that had helped prepare Rosa Parks for her moment in history. For the first time in his life, Lewis saw white and Black people cooking, eating, and cleaning together. He also got some advice in workshops about not letting older people take over their embryonic movement. He was especially impressed by Septima Clark, the regal woman running the workshop. "I left Highlander on fire," he would write years later.

The students at Lawson's sessions soon outnumbered the adults, especially at the meetings held near Fisk University. Recruiting took off. Long before the U.S. Army discovered the value of an all-volunteer force, the civil rights movement lived by it. In particular, one of those recruits, James Bevel, later observed that there was a particular type of person who made a valuable addition to the nonviolent movement: "They have a sense of rightness, fair play and justice about them. They have open hearts and minds. They listen."

One such addition was Diane Nash. Determined, attractive, and stylish, Nash had grown up in Chicago. In September 1959, when she enrolled at Fisk, she was surprised to encounter rigorous legal segregation for the first time. Angry and frustrated, she heard about the workshops on nonviolent protest that Lawson was conducting. She was taken with them. She also was taken with Bevel, and eventually would marry him. As a couple, they would become a Movement powerhouse, greatly influencing the campaigns in Birmingham and Selma.

The theory and practice of nonviolence

The first step in the workshops was to explain the theory and philosophy of nonviolence. The next step was to introduce tactics—how to translate theory into practice. The third was to determine procedures—how to implement those tactics, step by step.

Lawson began with an overview of religion and philosophy, contending that all the great religions essentially sought to find justice. He would go on in later classes to review specific episodes and thinkers—Henry David Thoreau's resistance to the American government, the American abolitionists, the German resistance to Nazism, and Gandhi's campaign against British colonial rule. He threw in a bit of Chinese philosophy.

He ended with a big dose of Christian faith. He taught that segregation was wicked and that it was wrong to submit to it. But he emphasized the necessity not to inflict suffering in attacking it and instead to take suffering upon oneself. "When you don't retaliate with a personal insult, but instead offer a friendly gesture," Lawson explained, "that's what Jesus meant when he said, 'turn the other cheek.' You cause the other person to do searching." Accepting suffering changed not only the person experiencing it but also those inflicting it, and even those witnessing the interaction.

So, Lawson taught, the first principle of nonviolent resistance was this: "We will not injure you, but we will absorb your injury of us because the cycle of violence must be broken. And if we respond to your violence with violence, then all you do is escalate the violence. We want the cycle of violence in America and racism stopped. So we will take it on ourselves, we will not dish it out in kind." The essential action was to look your attacker in the eye and try to register with him as a fellow human being, and to see him the same way. Lawson said if that seemed difficult, then imagine the assailant as a baby who had not yet learned the ways of segregation and hatred.

The corollary to this practical application of nonviolent theory was that one must never be passive about absorbing violence. An attack required a response, albeit a nonviolent one. "When the enemies proceed to do violence against us," Lawson said, "we must not let their violence stop our movement." That, he added, became "a kind of a cardinal notion in the Movement all across the South." The idea was to take the release of destructive energy and recycle it into a positive action. The usage could take a variety of forms—a march, a boycott, a general strike, and so on. But it became Movement doctrine that it was essential to respond in some form. Some of the most striking moments in Movement history came when this lesson was applied.

Advanced training: Role-playing

Once the basic principles had been imparted, the volunteers would begin to practice their roles. In evening sessions, they sat at long tables, pretending they were at lunch counters, and submitted themselves to the abuse of others playing the role of harassing whites. Nonviolence meant far more than simply not responding when hit. It was an entire way of thinking about the world. Workshop participants learned, recalled one volunteer, C. T. Vivian, how to "take the blows," not just physically but mentally. "The fact that you were being spit on and still respond with some sense of dignity. . . . We actually poured coffee on people . . . kicked chairs out from under them."

A major goal of the role-playing was to teach participants to recognize the "fight or flight" reaction and learn how to control it. This was good training, akin to the military adage "Train like you fight."

Another technique, said Diane Nash, involved how to protect a fellow protester: "If one person was taking a severe beating, we would practice other people putting their bodies in between that person and the violence. So that the violence could be more distributed and hopefully no one would get seriously injured. We would practice not striking back, if someone struck us." After each role-playing session, Lawson would review how it had unfolded, offering suggestions to each participant according to how others had handled it.

These workshops were not purely tactical. Nash, who would go on to play a major role first in the Freedom Rides and later in shaping Movement strategy, also learned something deeper in Lawson's classes. "There were several principles that I learned in those workshops that I've been able to really use in the rest of my life," she said. "For example, I discovered that practical and real power of truth and love. . . . I've gained a respect for truth, not because it has anything to do with being good, or right, or anything, but it is being in touch with reality." Here Nash illuminates the basic lesson that good strategy-making must begin with a clear-eyed, honest assessment of the situation. If one's understanding is mistaken, whether by accepting false information or through self-deception, everything that follows will be corrupted by that misstep. This insight comes directly from Gandhi, who taught, "Non-violence demands the strictest honesty, cost what it may." In military terms, this means gathering the intelligence you need, even if it is not what you would like to hear.

Scouting the targets

But even after all that training, Lawson still was not ready to make a public splash. Instead, in November and December 1959, he dispatched students in threes and fours to conduct informal dry runs, just sitting down at lunch counters in downtown Nashville and seeing what happened. They would report back to the larger group on what they had sensed about the physical setup and the attitude of the waitresses and managers. These were the equivalent of military scouting parties, and indeed Lawson was thinking in those exact terms. He recalled that these early forays and subsequent discussions were "part of a focusing in, that places were going to be our targets down the road." The trips downtown made the sit-ins more real to those who would participate—they could picture the ground on which they would fight. Likewise, thoughtful military leaders always try to conduct reconnaissance missions before going into combat. Terrain can be decisive in ways that can only be imagined when one stands on it.

These three steps—training, role-playing, and scouting—made the emerging activists feel they were well prepared for the novel tasks they were about to take on. Bernard LaFayette summarized his preparation this way: "We had a nonviolent academy equivalent to West Point. We knew how to organize a community, how to negotiate. We were warriors."

Then came a welcome surprise from an adjoining southern state. C. T. Vivian was scouting a downtown lunch counter in Nashville when he heard that on February 1, 1960, four freshmen from North Carolina A&T University had conducted their own sit-in at a Woolworth's lunch counter in Greensboro. It was an electrifying experience, said one of those Greensboro protesters, Franklin McCain. "If it is possible to know what it is like to have your soul cleansed," he recalled, "I probably felt better on that day than I've ever felt in my life." Gandhi would not have been surprised by that reaction. To be ready to die for what one held to be true was a chance to live fully, he taught. Gandhi believed that the divine manifested itself not in a person but in an action, and that indeed seems to have been the experience of some early sit-in protesters.

Other students reinforced the Greensboro protesters the next day. Soon came similar actions in Winston-Salem, Durham, and Raleigh, and then in neighboring states. "I mean, it was like a flash fire," recalled Cleveland Sellers, then a student in South Carolina. "Within two or three days, the other areas were mobilizing and organizing to carry out their portion of the sit-in demonstration."

It is striking how often sit-in participants mentioned the killing of Emmett Till five years earlier, how seeing the photograph of his bloated face in *Jet* magazine had hit them in a personal and direct fashion. Had Till lived, he would have been of college age in 1960. Sellers said, "I think the first real impact on me as a student, and many of the other students of my age, was Emmett Till. . . . I think it became very clear to us that there was something incessant in American society, . . . that it had the potential for killing children." Similarly, Junius Williams, who termed himself a "grunt" in SNCC, said decades later, "The picture of Emmett Till sticks in my mind now. . . . I could just picture myself in that same situation. . . . That was one of the sparks that really lit the Civil Rights Movement in a lot of people's hearts."

As it happened, the minister working with the Greensboro students was a friend of Lawson's and called him to discuss what was occurring. The Nashville student community had been watching. Some five hundred showed up at a meeting on the evening of February 5. Another session a week later was even bigger.

Readiness and timing were constant issues in the civil rights movement. Was it time to go public? The ministers in the Nashville Christian Leadership Conference urged delay, feeling that conditions were not yet right, but the students felt primed to move. James Bevel, always edgy and ready to push harder, responded that the Movement had to take some risks: "If you asked us to wait until next week, then next week something will come up and you'd say wait until the next week, and maybe we'd never get our freedom." He would make his mark in the Movement as a risk-taker, most notably with daring tactics three years later in Birmingham.

"There was no stopping this thing now," recalled Bevel's friend John Lewis. "We were young, free and burning with belief—the perfect foot soldiers for an assault like this." Indeed, Lewis would become like a dedicated infantryman for the Movement, one who "traveled constantly and . . . traveled light," for whom "comfort was simply not a concern."

Finally, Lawson had prepared his cadre for a long effort. This would not be a matter of a few demonstrations or marches, he told them. As he would put it later, "Protracted struggle is a moral struggle that is like warfare, moral warfare. I don't like using that language, but it means that tension is in the air, disruption is in the air, that a lot of people think that their lives have been unduly interrupted." Here Lawson was touching on a fundamental fact that still is insufficiently recognized: by challenging the established order in novel and unexpected ways that confounded and baffled officials, practitioners of nonviolent tactics could be extraordinarily aggressive.

The Nashville sit-ins begin

On the snowy morning of February 13, 1960, Lawson was ready to launch his first full-scale sit-ins. He deployed 124 students to three downtown lunch counters, in the stores of Woolworth's, S. H. Kress, and McLellan's Five-and-Dime. They were the civil rights equivalent of paratroopers—an elite force of volunteers, well trained and highly motivated, stealthily dropping in on unsuspecting targets. Lawson reminded the students to follow their training, warning that failing to do would undercut the entire effort. A leader appointed for each group would speak for it, and also keep an eye on those under his or her wing. In groups that were mainly Black but usually had one or two white students, they slipped into the lunchrooms, sat down, and politely asked for service. They simply wanted to be served at the lunch counters in the stores where they shopped. But, as the saying had it, they were asking for more than a hamburger. They were asking for equal treatment as citizens— and as human beings. By getting it, they would change both how white southerners treated them and how they thought of themselves.

Lawson deployed observers with instructions for them to stay at the edge of each protest. Their primary tasks were to keep a detailed running account of what was happening, to send information back to headquarters via runners, and to call the police when mobs attacked protesters, which would deprive the authorities of the excuse that no one told them. But the presence of informed observers also may have encouraged those sitting in to follow their training. Lawson related, "We had white people who stayed in the background and out of place but kept an eye on what was going on, so if we needed to have court witnesses and information and a whole lot of other things, we had it in place." This shrewd anticipating of consequences and preparing for them was one more sign of a well-planned, tightly organized operation. They were miles ahead of their opponents.

The purpose of the sit-ins was to underscore the unfairness of stores allowing Blacks to spend their money there on goods, but not to sit down and eat. At Woolworth's, white men heckled the students, saying things such as "Niggers, go home" and "What are y'all doing here?" Receiving absolutely no response, the hecklers left, a vindication of Lawson's approach and training. At another store, Diane Nash recalled, an odd moment occurred when two of the women sitting in went to the women's room. While they were there, an older white woman opened the door, saw them, threw up her hands, and, nearly crying, exclaimed, "Oh, nigras everywhere!"

During one Nashville protest, a young white man reared back and spat in the face of Leo Lillard, a student at Tennessee State University. Remaining low-key and following the rules, Lillard responded, "Sir, do you have a handkerchief?" The man began to reach for his pocket, then caught himself and said, "Hell, no." But Lillard felt that for a moment he had reminded the man of their common humanity.

Such reactions could only deepen the students' belief that they had been thoroughly prepared for their missions, a feeling essential to maintaining the morale of those on the front lines. "When they knocked me out of the chair and spit on me and drug me, I was prepared for that because I'd been trained day in and day out," recalled one participant, Joe Goldthreate. Thorough training makes people feel they can handle whatever comes at them and are not simply being buffeted by events, including the unexpected.

The pressure of the sit-ins on Nashville quickly mounted. The surprised old woman who saw Black people everywhere was more correct than she had known. Five days later, the number of students nearly doubled, to two hundred, and they were able to include a fourth establishment, Grants. Then, on February 20, Lawson fielded more than three hundred sit-in participants. White patrons of the stores began to complain. The ministers in the Nashville Christian Leadership Conference asked the mayor of Nashville, Ben West, for a meeting, but he declined.

"Big Saturday"

Two weeks into the Nashville protests, on Friday, February 26, the city's chief of police, Douglas Hosse, met with Lawson and other leaders and warned them there would be trouble if the actions continued. The next day, Lawson had some four hundred volunteers on hand. Thirty of them were deployed to conduct a sit-in at Woolworth's. It was the weekend, which was significant, because white teenagers were out of school and many would be in the stores that were the sites of the protests.

Because the numbers were increasing, and some of the volunteers were newcomers who had not received Lawson's thorough training, the studious and serious John Lewis wrote up a list of basic demonstration rules to be followed. Because Lewis worked as a janitor in his seminary, he had the keys that enabled him to slip into an office and mimeograph them.

DO NOT:
1. Strike back nor curse if abused.
2. Laugh out.
3. Hold conversations with floor walker.
4. Leave your seat until your leader has given you permission to do so.
5. Block entrances to stores outside nor the aisles inside.

DO:
1. Show yourself friendly and courteous at all times.
2. Sit straight; always face the counter.
3. Report all serious incidents to your leader.

4. Refer information seekers to your leader in a polite manner.
5. Remember the teachings of Jesus Christ, Mahatma Gandhi and Martin Luther King. Love and nonviolence is the way.

The role of the group leader was much like that of a squad leader in a military unit—that is, to make sure the rules were followed, and to buck up group members who faltered.

Until this point, the police had maintained a presence at the protests, which deterred some attacks on the students. But, recalled Lawson, "On this Saturday, very suddenly the police disappeared." The sudden and total withdrawal left the protesters vulnerable to waiting white mobs, which were behaving just as Lawson had taught they would— spitting, jabbing, heckling. It is always reassuring when one's training is validated by real events in the field, even when those events are threatening. It gives participants faith in their leaders and their instructions.

One of those sitting in, Paul LaPrad, a white student enrolled at Fisk University, a historically Black institution, wrote that the white youths began "insulting us, blowing smoke in our faces, grinding out cigarette butts on our backs, and finally, pulling us off our stools and beating us. Those of us pulled off our stools tried to regain them as soon as possible. But none of us attempted to fight back in any way." The students sitting with him followed their instructions and did not turn around, but in the long mirror they faced, they could see the fists flying downward against LaPrad, being pummeled on the floor. After the beatings, the police moved back in to arrest those sitting in yet detained none of the whites who had attacked them.

But the students' next move flummoxed the police. When the first set of protesters had been hauled away, another wave, notified by observers and runners, moved in to take their places. Lawson here was following the nonviolent equivalent of the military's "concentration of force." That time-honored principle is based on the recognition that troops can't be strong everywhere but can focus on one spot, outnumber the enemy there, and hit repeatedly. One nineteenth-century military analyst summarized the thought as follows: "The principle should always be kept in view, that the power of most rapid concentration upon the decisive point is the guarantee to victory." Perhaps the most famous example is the German military's use at the beginning of World War II of tanks, mechanized infantry units, strike aircraft, and radio communications to carry out the fast-moving assaults that the Allies labeled "blitzkrieg," although the Germans didn't use that term.

So, rather than dispersing his students across the downtown, which would make it harder for him to monitor and easier for the citywide police force to counter, Lawson brought them together. After the second set of arrests, Lawson sent in a third wave. "No matter what they did and how many they arrested, there was still a lunch counter full of students, there," Nash recalled. "It was interesting to watch their response. . . . They didn't quite know how to act." Indeed, when the police had arrested about eighty students, they stopped, likely because the jail's intake system was full. At this point Lawson still had not committed his reserves—he had several hundred more students waiting at the nearby First Baptist Church.

Jubilation in the jail

The next step brought a powerful tactical inversion: The protesters welcomed jail.

This is worth pausing to consider, because it represented a fundamental cultural shift. White bystanders were surprised to see the students who were being put in paddy wagons singing as they shuffled along. They seemed elated. This was a decisive moment for the protesters. Lawson had taught that redemption and freedom came from directly challenging an evil system, refusing to cooperate with it any longer. Being jailed for mounting such a challenge, he taught, was a badge of courage, a visible outward sign of an inward change in mentality.

One of those arrested on Big Saturday was John Lewis. "[It] was the first time that I was arrested, and growing up in the rural South . . .

it would bring shame and disgrace on the family," he recalled. It was also dangerous: In the Deep South, it was common for police to beat arrested Blacks. Those who protested or even fought back were deemed "uppity"—that is, insufficiently submissive—and sometimes turned over to lynch mobs or simply killed by the police. As Dr. William Anderson, a civil rights activist in southwestern Georgia, would put it, "There were many Blacks who were arrested in small towns in Georgia never to be heard from again." But heading to jail, Lewis was exhilarated. He felt he had found his life's work. And he was not alone.

With those fourscore of arrests on Saturday, "The social terrain had now begun to shift dramatically," comments Barry Lee, one of the best chroniclers of the sit-in movement. Lewis and others had been taught that only bad people were locked up. Now he and others were volunteering to do so. It was, concludes Lee, a decisive generational discontinuity, signaling the beginning of the breakup of the glacier of fear that had gripped southern Blacks for decades and centuries. As James Lawson had taught, "If you dare to pray such prayers . . . then you must be prepared to go where you did not plan to go, and do what you did not plan to do. But you will be astonished at the life you discover."

The students treated the experience of jail as an opportunity. They organized their days with set periods for sermons, lectures, and quiet time. For the seminarians among them, it brought to mind the acts of the Christians of the first century. "We created our own church services," said C. T. Vivian. It became a bonding experience for those behind bars. This was a major lesson, learned in the relatively benign atmosphere of the Nashville city jail. It would help some activists the following year when they would wind up in Parchman Farm, Mississippi's far harsher state penitentiary.

When assigned to shovel snow on city sidewalks, the jailed protesters threw themselves into it enthusiastically and then requested more work. Gandhi mandated that the nonviolent prisoner should show a "cheerful acceptance of jail discipline and its attendant hardships" so that "by his exemplary conduct he reforms even the criminals surrounding him, he softens the hearts of jailors and others in authority." When they were finally released, recalled Bernard LaFayette, the warden shook their hands and congratulated them for being "the best prisoners I've ever had."

The act of going to jail had political as well as personal results. In Nashville's Black community, the moral burden shifted to those who were not locked up. Where had they been, and what were they doing to help change the situation? Such questions helped attract Black adults to the cause. Persuaded that the students were serious, and willing to take risks, Nashville's adults began to make more donations to the NCLC. Flem Otey's grocery store sent sandwiches to the jail. In military terms, this was a "rallying," a process of encouraging allies to come forward. It was at this point, concludes the historian Benjamin Houston, that the sit-ins stopped being the action of students and became a broad popular movement, with adults providing financial support and some even marching with students.

Political shifts, nationally and locally

The tactic of withdrawal by the police, allowing white youths to attack the protesters, had backfired strategically. "The city fathers . . . see their image being destroyed," recalled Vivian. For decades, white southerners had reassured concerned northerners that they possessed special knowledge on how to deal with the Blacks of their region. Yet missteps such as the police pullback indicated otherwise.

Also, because of the violence, both Blacks and whites became reluctant to shop downtown—Blacks out of solidarity with the protesters, whites for fear of the violence. Speaking about the first sit-ins, Bevel recalled, "We learned that asking for change—no matter how overdue and correct the change is—will usually create chaos in people's minds."

Further damaging Nashville's image, the footage of the beating of LaPrad, the white student from Fisk, had been broadcast on national television. "It marked one of the earliest instances where Americans were shown firsthand the kind of anger and ugliness that the peaceful movement was prompting in the South," wrote John Lewis. Lewis didn't say so in that passage, but the outcry over the image of that assault instructed movement leaders in an unhappy truth about the country: Americans responded much more vigorously to seeing white protesters being beaten than they did to seeing similar suffering among Blacks. It was a severe but realistic lesson that the Movement would apply repeatedly in the following years.

Politicians tend to be hypersensitive to increases in political power, even if they don't know quite how to respond. Two days after the mass arrests, the mayor of Nashville finally agreed to a meeting. However, he used it to denounce the students as criminals. Lawson responded that "where the law was used simply to oppress people, then it wasn't really a law," because it was neither just nor Christian.

The major result of this meeting with the mayor was unexpected: Vanderbilt's divinity school expelled Lawson as a graduate student. This was another sign that the white people running Nashville still had not fully grasped what they were up against. The expulsion of Lawson resulted in a wave of faculty protests and denunciations from universities across the country, damaging Vanderbilt's national reputation, which was valuable to Nashville's establishment. More than half the faculty of the divinity school threatened to resign. Ultimately, the university offered to reinstate Lawson while removing the dean of divinity, an outcome Lawson rejected as equally unacceptable. The mishandling of Lawson ultimately provoked the American Association of Theological Schools to place the divinity school on a year of academic probation. Thus, ironically, the school wound up in more trouble than Lawson.

The NAACP's critique

Surprisingly, there was another institution uncomfortable with the demonstrators: the NAACP. Roy Wilkins, its executive secretary, took a dim view of the student protests, and also of Martin Luther King, Jr. "It was essential to keep the sit-ins and the prospect of direct action within proportion. The students were young, committed and valiant, but they were not organized," he wrote. Those last two words were both incorrect and dismissive. Wilkins was more accurate in his assessment of the future: "They would have no staying power beyond a few short years' time. My own experiences had taught me that the struggle would still be going on long after they were out of college and immersed in other concerns. Only a strong organization like the NAACP could survive the wear that went on year after year."

The problem with the NAACP's approach of working mainly through the courts to gain access to graduate and professional education was that it was both incremental and remote from the concerns of most Blacks. The NAACP's lawyers had challenged "separate but equal" public education for nineteen years before finally succeeding, massively, in 1954. They had begun in the 1930s by chipping away at segregation in law schools in states such as Maryland and Missouri, and then went after such schools in Texas, Louisiana, and other states. Generally, write the historians August Meier and Elliott Rudwick, "direct action did not form a significant part of NAACP tactics." The NAACP's wary approach, focused on the courts and legislatures, probably was the best way, and perhaps the only way, that progress could be made against official American racism at that time. But strategically it was a problem, because the focus on professional educational opportunities for African Americans on the periphery of the South meant that its efforts were quite distant from the everyday lives and immediate concerns of most Black Americans. And, as King noted, even after the 1954 ruling, the South's power structure sought to delay integration through years of court actions. King quoted Eugene Cook, the attorney general of Georgia, as saying that it was possible that integration in the South could be forestalled by "a century of litigation."

Even Thurgood Marshall, who led the NAACP's legal crusade, found the process wearing. He once told the psychologist Kenneth Clark, his academic ally, "Sometimes I get awfully tired of trying to save the white man's soul." Not surprisingly, for the rising generation of Black Americans, the NAACP's legalistic approach simply was too damn slow. "A lot of the younger people started seeing that NAACP wasn't moving fast enough for us," said Willie Thomas, an Ohio University student who would participate in the July 1961 wave of Freedom Riders. Another Rider, even younger, would be Alphonso Petway, who said simply, "I wanted to participate in my own struggle." By staying mainly in the courts and so failing to provide adequate opportunities for people to participate, the NAACP had created an opening that other organizations would fill.

Wilkins wasn't wrong in his assessment of the extended nature of the effort. But the civil rights movement was not always a gradual and steady series of events. Rather, like a war, it sometimes was quiet for prolonged spells but sometimes moved in leaps and bounds. For most of the 1960s, Wilkins' NAACP lagged far behind the vanguard. James Baldwin, probably the most important writer of the time, captured the situation when he wrote in 1961 that the NAACP's magazine, *The Crisis*, "reveals the state of mind of the Negro bourgeoisie. *The Crisis* has the most exciting subject matter in the world at its fingertips, and yet manages to be one of the world's dullest magazines." This is not trivial, he insightfully added, "because this dullness is the result of its failure to examine what is really happening in the Negro world."

King got wind of some cracks Wilkins was making about him. Jackie Robinson, who had broken major league baseball's system of segregation in 1947, wrote to admonish King about the squabbling. King responded vehemently:

I have refused to fight back or even answer some of the unkind statements that I have been informed that NAACP officials said about me and the Southern Christian Leadership Conference. Frankly, I hear these statements every day, and I have seen efforts on the part of NAACP officials to sabotage our efforts. But I have never said anything about it publicly or to the press.

The fact of the matter was that King had reached into the lives of Black Americans in a way in which the NAACP either could not or would not do. Stanley Levison, a left-wing New York businessman who was an adviser to King, recognized the shift when he wrote to King about the sit-ins. "This is a new stage in the struggle," Levison stated. "It begins at the higher point where Montgomery left off." The students, he added, in what appears to be a direct critique of the NAACP, "by example are demonstrating the bankruptcy of the policy of relying upon courts and legislation to achieve real results."

While the NAACP's legal strategy had focused on professional schools on the periphery of the Deep South, the new civil rights movement would be based in its heartland. The Montgomery bus boycott, of course, had taken place in the first capital of the Confederacy. The Freedom Rides would cut across the South and terminate in the capital of Mississippi, the hardest state in the region. The Birmingham campaign would tackle the hardest city in Alabama, and Freedom Summer would challenge the entire obdurate state of Mississippi. What's more, these efforts had an immediacy that conveyed what one of King's interlocutors called his belief that "everyone should be involved in his own liberation."

A small, cohesive movement

The Nashville student demonstrators were in fact creating their own liberation—and in the process, many were experiencing profound personal transformations, discovering a new sense of self-confidence. "The movement had a way of reaching inside me and bringing out things that I never knew were there, like courage, and love for people," said Diane Nash. "It was a real experience, to be among a group of people who would put their bodies between you and danger. And to love people that you work with enough, that you would put yours between them and danger." Military specialists would recognize this phenomenon as "unit cohesion," strongest when tested in the crucible of combat. Cohesion is more than a helpful thing for a unit to have; it is essential to maintaining combat effectiveness. Cohesion reflects the presence of deep trust, which results in both short- and long-term benefits. Its presence tends to ease decision-making and communication, enabling a unit to operate with greater speed and impact. Remarkably, soldiers who see combat while in units with notably strong cohesion also tend to suffer less from post-traumatic stress disorders.

In this early phase, the Nashville sit-in movement was small, co-hesive, and nimble. The Nashville students met often, usually every morning at six, to enable those with eight o'clock classes to attend. They gathered again in the afternoon or early evening. Thus, by the time the city government and business leaders convened to mull events and to plan their next steps, the students already had decided on their course and were considering their follow-on actions. "The students managed to move so fast that other forces in the community couldn't keep up with us," Nash recalled. At another point she said, "We just moved so fast in terms of organizations I've been in since then."

Lawson also taught them that after each action, the participants should gather and discuss what happened: What had worked? What hadn't? Why? Would there have been better ways to handle a problem? What should we try next time? He referred to this reflection and analysis as an effort "to keep the movement as creative as possible." The U.S. Army, which has a similar process, calls this sort of session an "After-Action Review." It leads to tactical adaptation, which is essential, because if a foe is paying attention, then what works one day may not work the next. Learning from the enemy is key to any successful campaign.

In early April, several of the Nashville students were invited to a weekend retreat at the Highlander Folk School. Among other activities, they heard Guy Carawan, the school's music director, sing several Black and labor songs—"We Shall Not Be Moved," "Keep Your Eyes on the Prize," and "We Shall Overcome," the last of which Carawan and oth-ers at the school had adapted from an old church hymn. Gregg's 1934 manual on nonviolence taught that singing together was a primary way of developing unity. And, he noted, it cost nothing and required no equipment. Oddly, with the exception of words chanted while running or marching in boot camp, at the very beginning of military careers, modern armed forces seem to have lost this tradition, probably to their detriment.

The songs of the Movement had powerful positive effects on participants. Belting them out with one's fellows "made you bigger," recalled the Freedom Summer volunteer Pam Parker. "It made you large enough that the fear was there but you were no longer your fear, and you were something bigger and you were doing it with others. That sense of collectivity that we weren't doing it just as individuals, we were doing as part of this thing that we called the Movement." Songs even could educate participants in strategy, as with the admonition in "Keep Your Eyes on the Prize"—that is, focus on the strategic goal, not on the lesser issues. They also could be altered to fit the circumstance. Bernard La-Fayette recalled singing the following verse:

I don't know the song but I know the note
They're marching in Selma for the right to vote
Hold on, hold on,
Keep your eyes on the prize, hold on

Vocalizing also was a reliable way of maintaining cohesion, keeping the pace in a march, and boosting morale while in difficult situations, such as being in jail. Once, when Andrew Young went to check on a civil rights march in southeastern Georgia, he would be immediately concerned that "there were no marshals, and no one led freedom songs—a clear sign of poor training."

The bombing of Nashville—and a quick reaction

The situation grew more intense later that month. Sit-ins had spread to more than one hundred towns across the South, with some fifty thousand people estimated to have joined in. In Nashville and other cities, some major businesses—owned by whites, of course—were suffering.

Around dawn on the morning of April 19, 1960, as Diane Nash

was getting dressed in her dorm room, she "heard this big boom." In the cafeteria she learned that the sound had been made by a bomb detonating at the home of Z. Alexander Looby, a Black city council member (one of the first elected since before World War I) and lawyer who had defended the students sitting in. Born in the West Indies, Looby had been orphaned at the age of fifteen. He made his way to America by signing on as a hand on a whaling ship. The blast nearly destroyed his house and blew out 147 windows at a hospital across the street. Looby, however, was not injured.

One of the lessons the students had learned in nonviolence training was to use attacks as a catalyst, to turn negative energy into positive action. So as the students conferred about the attack, they began with the notion that something had to be done, that the bombing could not go unanswered. "We decided to respond that day and before the dust cleared from the bombing," said Bernard LaFayette. They would march.

That afternoon, more than 2,500 students from Fisk and the other historically Black colleges in Nashville walked across the city in ranks of three. They maintained silence, a sign of resolve. "Everyone was very intense, but very disciplined and very orderly," wrote John Lewis. They reached city hall. While they waited for the mayor, Highlander's Carawan played his guitar and sang "We Shall Overcome." It was the first major march of the civil rights movement, "a turning point," recalled C. T. Vivian. Whites on the street stood back and watched. "There was a fear there," Vivian said. "There was an awe there. And they did not know what to do, but they knew this was not to be stopped, this was not to be played with or to be joked with."

When Mayor West emerged, Vivian and Nash walked up the stairs of city hall to speak with him. Vivian read a statement to the mayor accusing him of failing to lead the city. West reacted angrily. Nash intervened. She thought West looked vulnerable. Trying to connect as a human being, she asked him in an almost gentle voice whether discrimination based on color is moral. Trying to be informal, but instead coming off as awkward and condescending, West addressed Nash as "little lady." No, it is not, he conceded. So, she said, should the lunch counters be desegregated? "Yes," the mayor responded. They shook hands. With that exchange, the desegregation of Nashville began. But it would take several years for all the city's restaurants, movie theaters, and hotels and motels to comply.

The birth of SNCC

The next night, Martin Luther King, Jr., came to Nashville and spoke to a packed auditorium downtown. The victor of Montgomery lauded the Nashville sit-ins as "the best organized and most disciplined in our Southland today." This was high praise, but it also was an interesting choice of words, underscoring not religious inspiration or redemptive suffering but preparation and self-control. King's phrasing would not be out of place for a general visiting a victorious subordinate unit to review and congratulate it.

The NAACP was less impressed. Thurgood Marshall, its star lawyer, would publicly call C. T. Vivian "the most dangerous man in all Nashville." Marshall did not mean it as a compliment. He was worried that sit-ins and other direct actions by Blacks would be provocative but unproductive, and also might alienate the courts, which he considered the best ally of Black Americans. Marshall may also have sensed the deeper philosophical challenge to the NAACP presented by Lawson, Vivian, and others. Nonviolent direct action amounted to a rejection of the existing approach in the civil rights struggle. As the historian Anthony Siracusa puts it, "While a series of legal shifts seemed to remove chinks from the armor of Jim Crow, Lawson suggested that the limits of legal change were real and acute." All in all, the comment made Marshall look truculent, and it reflected the condescending father-knows-best attitude that the NAACP often would tend to take with newer civil rights organizations. Another move later would underscore the NAACP's skepticism about Lawson and nonviolence: King wanted to hire Lawson to work for the SCLC, but Roy Wilkins threatened to retaliate against the SCLC if he did. King dropped the idea.

On May 10, the six downtown lunch counters were desegregated. The sit-ins also taught a financial lesson: national attention aided fundraising. By the end of that month, the balance in the Nashville Christian Leadership Conference's bank account had increased from about $87 when the sit-ins began to about $22,000. The psychological effect on Nashville's Black citizens also was notable. "A general feeling of dignity and self-respect has come into everyone's life," said Vivian.

The effects reached far beyond Nashville. *Sit In*, a compelling NBC documentary about the Nashville movement, filmed and aired in 1960, depicted how the students were organized and emphasized their respectful, restrained conduct at the lunch counters. The documentary—made by Robert M. Young, who would go on to a career as a director of feature films—conveyed the self-control of the protesters so well that it was adopted by the Movement as a training film, used to teach students across the country about how to go about protesting. Septima Clark said, "Throughout the Southland, we took that movie for them to see how a community rallied around to see suffering inflicted upon these kids, to see the way they were able to take suffering, and leadership developed from this was most marvelous."

The documentary provided one of the first major indications of how influential television news would be in the coming years for the civil rights movement. It turned into a powerful recruiting device, sending a call across the nation to like-minded young people. In New York City, Andrew Young, a youthful minister from New Orleans working for the National Council of Churches, was riveted by the documentary. "It was rare enough that Black people were featured on television, but the story of the Nashville student action against segregation was extraordinary," he later wrote. He added that, by the time the hourlong documentary ended, "I knew that it was time to return home." Young soon went to work at the Highlander Folk School, and then moved from there with Septima Clark to the SCLC. Elsewhere in New York City, Bob Moses, a Black math teacher at an elite prep school, saw news of the sit-ins and was inspired to see that "somebody was doing something." He decided he had to be part of it.

As for the Nashville students, many went on to become the core cadres of the Student Nonviolent Coordinating Committee, which was formed in April 1960, with the strong encouragement of the SCLC's Ella Baker, and soon became one of the foremost organizations in the civil rights movement. Several early SNCC leaders also would move on to roles in the SCLC. At SNCC's foundational meeting, Lawson described how the new group would be different. "This movement is not only against segregation," he stated. "It's against Uncle Tom Negroes, against the NAACP's over-reliance on the courts, and against the futile middle-class technique of sending letters to the centers of power." Rather, he said, it was dedicated to carrying out a "nonviolent revolution." The NAACP's leaders would not be pleased by this critique.

As Lawson indicated, the Movement's operations had much in common with an insurgent force. Its leaders were directly involved, staring both friend and foe in the face. They recruited people, trained them, and sent them out into the field. They were taken captive, interrogated, and beaten. They met to discuss strategy and map out future efforts. They planned and led marches. They conducted operations in which there were rarely front lines, which meant that there were few genuinely safe places where one could relax—a situation that dramatically increases stress. Visiting their offices in Alabama and Mississippi, wrote Howard Zinn, a sympathetic historian, was like visiting combat outposts.

3.
THE FREEDOM RIDES, 1961

A Raid Behind Enemy Lines

I n the war over civil rights, the two sides faced very different tasks. The enforcers of segregation were committed to maintaining the status quo everywhere. This put them at a disadvantage because they had so much territory to defend. The civil rights movement, by contrast, usually could pick the time and place of engagements. Once a campaign got under way, it also generally could set the tempo of action. Authorities could respond with harassing actions, ranging from traffic tickets to injunctions to even banning the state's chapter of the NAACP, and they often resorted to violence. But even so, the initiative remained almost always with the forces of desegregation.

One of the best examples of the variety of novel operations available to the Movement was the Freedom Rides. In them, a small band conducted the equivalent of a daring but almost suicidal foray behind enemy lines. The best military analogy may be the Doolittle Raid, the American bombing attack on Japan early in World War II. In April 1942, just five months after the Japanese attack on Pearl Harbor, sixteen American B-25 bombers, each with a crew of five, took off from an aircraft carrier in the North Pacific—a job that their pilots had never done before and for which the planes had not been built. They flew toward Japan without their usual escort of fighter planes, making them enormously vulnerable if detected. What's more, they left behind some of their defensive machine guns, in order to make the planes lighter and so extend their range. The fliers knew their mission was dangerous. Indeed, some of them would be captured by the Japanese and kept on starvation diets. Three of those taken prisoner were executed as war criminals.

The point of the American raid was not to inflict significant damage, but simply to boost the morale of the American public and damage that of the Japanese public by showing that the American military could retaliate for Pearl Harbor. The planes did in fact bomb the Japanese capital and five other cities. A less predictable consequence was the effect on the embarrassed Japanese military. As the military historian Adrian Lewis puts it, "The Doolittle Raid caused the Japanese to act rashly, which led to their defeat at Midway"—which became a major turning point in the war.

Likewise, the Freedom Riders—a small group of committed activists organized in May 1961 by James Farmer, national director of the Congress of Racial Equality (CORE)—rode buses from Washington, D.C., into the Deep South. They traveled light and penetrated deep into enemy territory, unprotected, to take their segregationist enemies by surprise both in their tactics and in their strategy. The sit-ins had taken place mainly in urban areas in the Upper South—Tennessee, North Carolina, and Virginia. The purpose of the Freedom Rides was, like a military raid, to carry the flag of the cause into previously untouched areas, even into rural areas of the Deep South. "We somehow had to cut across state lines and establish the position that we were entitled to act any place in the country, no matter where we hung our hat and called home, because it was our country," Farmer explained.

A secondary goal was to get the attention of the Kennedy administration and try to push it off the fence on the issue of civil rights. The organizers had some reason to believe that the administration was ready to move. Just as the first Freedom Ride was getting under way, Robert Kennedy was preparing a speech on civil rights. It would be his first formal address as the attorney general in his brother's fledgling administration. When he delivered it at the University of Georgia on May 6, 1961, he appeared to endorse the civil rights movement. "If one man's rights are denied, the rights of all are endangered," he stated. It was high time, he said, for the South to make some "difficult local adjustments."

But even as Kennedy spoke, he was being overtaken by events. Before the month was out, the Freedom Rides would push him to put action behind his words challenging the South to begin making difficult changes. Unfortunately, he would fail that test.

From D.C. to the Deep South

A persistent advantage of the civil rights movement was that it was innovative and so was able to keep its opponents off-balance. Tactically, the Freedom Rides were "something new," recalled Floyd Mann, then the director of the Alabama State Police, "something that the state police had not been confronted with in the past. We'd had local demonstrations by local people, but this was the first time we'd had an interstate movement on the part of people. . . . It was just totally something new to law enforcement in Alabama. . . . It caught them . . . off guard."

The situation was ripe for exploitation. The Supreme Court had ruled in December 1960, in *Boynton v. Virginia*, that state segregation laws could not be used against interstate travelers. Yet court rulings and legislation mean little if they are not implemented on the ground. In this case, the Interstate Commerce Commission had failed to enforce the high court's ruling. Waiting rooms, restaurants, and toilets across the South remained segregated.

Carrying out the Freedom Rides involved far more than simply boarding a bus. All too often, the civil rights movement is remembered only for its visible actions, such as marches, speeches, and other public events. That neglects the key fact that successful civil rights campaigns almost always were based on extensive planning and reconnaissance. It was essential to know beforehand what you were getting into, where your confrontations were likely to take place, and who your local allies might be. So before launching the Freedom Rides, CORE dispatched a young staff member, Tom Gaither, a Black South Carolinian and veteran of sit-ins, to scout the planned route. Gaither had been one of the people to conceive of the Freedom Rides, inspired in part by a biography of Gandhi he had been reading. His task was to travel the planned route, make maps of bus terminals, and find places where the Freedom Riders could safely stay overnight between their bus rides. Gaither also assessed the state of racial tension in each town. He reported back that he was most worried by two cities in Alabama—Anniston and Birmingham.

Raids and other commando operations, moving fast and light through enemy territory, require "troops with above average combat skills and high training levels," admonishes the military expert James Dunnigan. The same was true for the men and women who volunteered for the initial Freedom Ride foray, for whom the equivalent of combat skills was a deep and abiding commitment to the cause.

CORE held preparatory meetings in Washington, D.C., for its handful of recruits. Gaither told them what he had seen on his reconnaissance assignment. A lawyer briefed them on the legal issues they would face, focusing on what to do if and when arrested. The presence of Black riders in "White Only" areas of bus terminals would force local authorities to face the contradiction that their segregation laws were at odds with national law governing interstate travel. A social scientist discussed the culture of the white South. In military terms, they were being introduced to the terrain of their area of operations.

The recruits then went through three days of intense role-playing, with racial taunts and drinks being thrown. After experiencing this, one volunteer dropped out, a sign that the exercise was effective. Acting out the scenarios had the obvious function of preparing people for what they might face, but it also gave the Riders a sense of one another's personalities and characters, always helpful for a unit going into combat. On the night before they left Washington, the Riders went out for Chinese food, a taste that was new to John Lewis. "It was like the Last Supper because you didn't know what to expect going on the Freedom Ride," he remembered.

Historians differ on the number of Riders who left the capital on the first day, Thursday, May 4. It seems to have been thirteen to fifteen Riders, and three accompanying journalists—about the same as the number of aircraft in the Doolittle Raid. There is no question that, in terms of social movements, it was a small group. Yet as Gandhi had taught, "it is never the numbers that count; it is always the quality, more so when the forces of violence are uppermost." The greater the chance of a fierce reception, the more imperative it is that nonviolent activists are disciplined and cohesive. Indeed, for his famous Salt March in 1930, Gandhi restricted his column to seventy-eight people, all well trained and deeply dedicated. But as it proceeded hundreds of miles toward the sea, his small group was greeted by crowds as large as fifty thousand.

The Freedom Riders departed Washington, D.C., in two groups— one taking a Greyhound, the other a Trailways bus. The plan was for both groups to hop buses from city to city. Their route had been designed to place them each night in towns with Black communities where they could find refuge, and also where they could meet with local groups and explain their mission with the hope of sparking longer-lasting local actions. The plan was to reach New Orleans by bus on May 17. As it happened, that geographical endpoint was never reached, but in the process the Riders achieved their strategic goal by forcing the segregation power to show the world the degree of violence it was willing to use to enforce the suppression of the rights of Black people. In addition, the fact that segregationists would attack white people got the attention of Americans nationwide.

And so they rolled south, at first not attracting much attention, but braced for the violence they knew was inevitable. "I was like a soldier in a nonviolent army," recalled John Lewis. On May 6, as Attorney

General Kennedy spoke at the University of Georgia, they traveled across southern Virginia from Petersburg to Lynchburg.

The Ride passed without incident until Tuesday, May 9, when Lewis, in the lead, stepped off a bus in Rock Hill, South Carolina, and walked into the waiting room marked "White." White toughs waiting there punched him to the floor and began kicking him. Albert Bigelow, Lewis' assigned seatmate, a white grandfather from Connecticut, interposed his body, and soon he was clubbed down as well. Then a white female Rider stepped up and was knocked to the floor. Lewis was proud that they had passed the test of not being provoked to respond to violence. After this incident, Lewis had to leave the Ride for an interview in Philadelphia about getting a fellowship in Africa or India. He did that, then returned home to Nashville, planning to rejoin the Freedom Ride in Birmingham.

The situation grew even more perilous in Winnsboro, South Carolina, a mill town with a huge Confederate memorial and a reputation for hard-core racism. Henry "Hank" Thomas, a Black Rider and a Howard University student, was arrested at the bus station for trespassing by being in the white waiting room. But making a legal case was not always the purpose of detaining someone. The charge was dropped, and Thomas was released around midnight and driven by a police officer to the bus station—which was about to close, and where a group of surly whites waited outside holding sticks and baseball bats. The police officer ordered Thomas out of the car. Thomas began thinking about old movies he had seen "about blacks being taken out of southern jails in the middle of the night."

As Thomas reluctantly stepped out of the police car, a Black man rolled up in his own vehicle. It was driven by the courageous Reverend Cecil Ivory, a civil rights activist leader and pastor of a Presbyterian church in Rock Hill who had been asked by CORE to keep an eye on the Howard student while he was in jail. Ivory, who used a wheelchair as a result of childhood injuries to his spine, told Thomas to hop in. "He didn't have to tell me twice," Thomas recalled. "We hightailed it out of there." Good planning and organization pay off in ways that no one but the participants might ever notice—but that can mean the difference between life and death. For Ivory to intervene, several things had to happen: CORE had to know that Thomas was detained, had to have someone to contact with that information, and had to hope that the person contacted would prove reliable in a hazardous situation, as Ivory did.

Burned in Anniston

On May 13 the Riders stopped in Atlanta, where Martin Luther King, Jr., met them and gently warned a journalist traveling with them, "You will never make it through Alabama." Here James Farmer, the CORE official who had organized the Freedom Ride, left it because his father had died.

The town of Anniston sits about halfway between Atlanta and Birmingham. A crowd of whites led by the local Klan leader awaited the bus at the town's Greyhound terminal. On Sunday, May 14—Mother's Day—the Greyhound rolled in with seven Freedom Riders aboard, plus two accompanying journalists. The crowd smashed the windows of the bus and tried to puncture some of its tires. After twenty minutes of this, local police arrived and cleared a path for the Greyhound driver to pull out. But it did not leave alone. The bus was followed by a caravan of angry whites. Six miles outside town, one or two of the damaged tires gave way and the driver pulled over. The whites surrounded the bus, waving chains, clubs, and sections of pipe. They rocked the bus in an attempt to topple it over. After another twenty minutes, a firebomb was thrown through the smashed back window of the bus. "Across the highway, in a state patrol car, three or four of the police sat joking and laughing," recalled Albert Bigelow. The bus began to fill with oily black smoke as seats caught fire.

One Freedom Rider heard someone outside shout, "Let's burn the niggers alive." The surging crowd held the doors shut. Then a white man who had been sitting at the front of bus and had appeared to be just another civilian passenger, unrelated to the Freedom Riders, pulled a pistol and displayed a badge, revealing that he was a state law enforcement official working undercover. He ordered the belligerent whites to move back from the doors of the bus. Some passengers spilled out, choking, and fell to the ground. One of the Riders, Hank Thomas—the same man who had been rescued by Cecil Ivory in Winnsboro, South Carolina—staggered around on the grass. A white man approached and asked if he was okay. Yes, Thomas replied. The man then swung a baseball bat into his head. A white child who lived nearby brought them water, an act for which she and her family would be ostracized. When the gas tank on the bus detonated the crowd moved back, allowing ambulances to collect the Riders and take them to Anniston's hospital.

While the Riders were being treated inside the hospital, Klansmen began to gather outside it. Contacted in Birmingham, the intrepid Reverend Fred Shuttlesworth, tough and pugnacious, put together a convoy of about ten cars, with some passengers toting shotguns, to pick up the beleaguered Riders. Some of the convoyers had never signed up to the notion of nonviolence, while others argued that even while following it, they retained an inalienable right to self-defense. This ambiguity in the Movement's stance was useful, because it meant that the forces of the dominant caste never could be quite sure when they might wind up staring into the barrel of a shotgun.

On that day, the entire war for civil rights changed shape. The Anniston attack on the Greyhound bus passengers represented a radical escalation by segregationists. The white hecklers at the sit-ins had been nasty but not murderous. This was different. Segregationists, given a green light by law enforcement officials, had nearly killed a busload of people. To many white Americans, it mattered that some of the people on that bus were white. Skin color was not a protection from sadistic segregationist violence. In sum, the war for civil rights had increased in intensity and expanded in scope.

The Freedom Rides at this point captured the attention of the nation. As the historian Raymond Arsenault notes, they had hardly been noticed until now. The bus burning outside Anniston put them on the front pages of newspapers across the country. Burke Marshall, the antitrust specialist whom the Kennedy administration had inexplicably picked to run the Justice Department's civil rights division, said, "The Freedom Rides didn't really come to our attention until Anniston and, then, of course, when the bus was burned in Anniston it came to our attention in a very, very dramatic fashion. . . . It was sort of incomprehensible to us." The success of the Freedom Rides would have been far more comprehensible to John Singleton Mosby, the daring Confederate cavalry commander who led incursions behind Union lines. "The military value of a partisan's work," the raider observed in his memoirs, "is not measured by the amount of property destroyed, or the number of men killed or captured but by the number he keeps watching." Mosby meant the number of soldiers diverted to the task of monitoring rear areas for raiders, but the Freedom Riders now had much of the nation watching.

In the following days, the more the Riders were attacked, the more coverage they received, and the more people across the country decided to join them. Ultimately, some three hundred people would volunteer to become Freedom Riders.

Mother's Day in Birmingham

The other shoe dropped later that same Sunday. The second bus, from the Trailways line, left Atlanta an hour after the Greyhound, carrying among its passengers several people who had nothing to do with the civil rights movement, plus seven Riders and two journalists. At Anniston, several white men boarded and began beating the Freedom Riders, with one holding them up while others punched their faces. "They used my husband's head for a football," reported Frances Bergman, whose spouse, Walter Bergman, suffered brain damage from the attack.

The assailants then hauled their victims to the back of the bus and threw them in a pile. "Doggone, it looks like there has been a hog killing

on this bus!" remarked one of the passengers who was not a Freedom
Rider. A policeman stepped aboard the bus, surveyed the bloody scene,
and assured the Klansmen, "I ain't seen a thing." The bus departed for
Birmingham with its gory cargo aboard.

When the bus pulled into the Trailways terminal in Birmingham at
4:15 that Sunday afternoon, there were, by prearrangement, no police
officers present except for two plainclothes detectives. Rather, the Riders on the Trailways vehicle were met by thirty members of the Ku Klux
Klan. Theophilus Eugene "Bull" Connor, Birmingham's commissioner
of police, had made a deal with the Klan, according to a Federal Bureau
of Investigation memo wired to the bureau's headquarters two days earlier: the Klan would be given fifteen to twenty minutes to beat the Riders before any law enforcement officers came on the scene. "By God, if
you are going to do this thing, do it right," Connor told the Klansmen,
according to the FBI. This meant that pistols should not be used, but
clubs and bats were welcome. If the Riders sought refuge in the men's
room at the bus depot, the memo stated, "Klansmen are to beat them
in the rest room and 'make them look like a bulldog got ahold of them';
then remove the clothing of the victim and carry the clothing away."
The Klansmen had a free hand to be vicious, and they used it.

Howard K. Smith of CBS television, who was in the station waiting
for the bus to arrive, reported that "one passenger was knocked down at
my feet by twelve of the hoodlums and his face was beaten and kicked
until it was a bloody pulp." James Peck, the man who owned that pulped
face, awoke in an alleyway in a pool of his own blood. He tried to get
up, he later said, but "was too tired to care. I lay down again." There was
no pretense of law and order in Birmingham. This was permitted dominant caste terrorism, intended to draw a bright line showing that the
city would fight integration tooth and nail. That night, Birmingham
police Detective W. W. "Red" Self called the Klan to congratulate them
on their work at the Trailways terminal.

One might expect Birmingham's rights activists to reel in horror
from the day's events. But that would neglect the fact that they understood well that this kind of violence was a frequent tool of the white

power structure. The rest of the world was seeing what they lived with constantly. The Klan attack simply had displayed that vicious system to a national audience. At a meeting at Bethel Baptist Church that Sunday evening, Fred Shuttlesworth was ecstatic. Not only had the sharpened teeth of the system been shown biting, the Riders had kept on coming, even after the incident in Anniston. "This is the greatest thing that has ever happened to Alabama," Shuttlesworth exclaimed to an audience of about fifty. "And it has been good for the nation. It was a wonderful thing to see these young students—Negro and white—come, even after the mobs and the bus burning. When white and Black men are willing to be beaten up together, it is a sure sign they will soon walk as brothers. . . . Others may be beaten up, but freedom is worth anything." This may sound cold, but it echoes how military leaders tend to think of casualties—always regrettable, but sometimes necessary in order to fulfill the mission.

On Monday, May 15, newspapers across the country carried front-page photographs of the Greyhound bus burning in Anniston. But that did not mean that everyone was sympathetic to the Freedom Riders. President Kennedy snarled at his aide Harris Wofford, who before joining the administration had been among the many people advising Martin Luther King, Jr. "Can't you get your goddamned friends off those buses?" the president snapped. "Stop them."

That same morning, the bloodied Riders in Birmingham voted to continue their mission. They planned to take a Greyhound to Montgomery that afternoon. But while they sat in the terminal, the company canceled that run. After hours more of waiting, the Riders grew nervous and decided to fly out of the city to Montgomery. Shuttlesworth took them to the airport. Their flight was canceled after a bomb threat was phoned in. Feeling besieged, they instead decided to catch a Capitol Airlines flight to New Orleans. Another bomb threat got their flight canceled. Klansmen were arriving at the airport, and the Riders were afraid to go outside. John Seigenthaler, an aide to Attorney General Kennedy, flew into the airport from Washington. After assessing the situation, he went to the airport manager and told him to slip the Riders on a night flight to New Orleans without announcing the departure until the last minute, and then not to answer the phone after that. The gambit worked.

Once on the ground in New Orleans, this initial group of Riders formally disbanded. Their Freedom Ride was over. They felt they had made the point that the law forbidding segregation in interstate travel was not being enforced.

But the operation was not over. Indeed, it was about to expand in size and effect.

Nash and Bevel intervene

In Nashville, Diane Nash, James Bevel, and their compatriots watched the disbanding of the Ride with horror. They felt that Farmer and CORE had committed a strategic error by starting a high-profile civil rights action and then abandoning it. They had not just retreated; they had given up. This violated "one of the most basic tenets of nonviolent action," wrote Lewis. "That is, that there can be no surrender in the face of brute force or any form of violent opposition. Retreat is one thing; surrender is another."

The Freedom Riders had found a national spotlight. Letting segregationist violence stop them now would invite a wave of new violence, and possibly bring the civil rights movement to an abrupt end, Nash worried. "The message would have been sent," she said, "that all you have to do to stop a nonviolent campaign is inflict massive violence." It might in fact mean open season on the Movement, perhaps the killing of large numbers of activists in future protests, she thought. "That was a very dangerous thing to happen," she recalled.

On top of that, the Nashville students had been taught by James Lawson that acts of great violence should be seen as presenting an opportunity, albeit a highly hazardous one. As Nash put it, "The nonviolent strategy understands that when that type of negative image is directed at you, one of the important things to do is find ways to convert it to, to positive energy, which we were able to do as a result of continuing." Their training had prepared them to see moments of great shock and dislocation as occasions to surprise the world, to mold the moment when circumstances are hot and unpredictable. The very fluidity of the situation invited quick action. But it also demanded that there be available people who had the capability and the will to act quickly. As it happened, Lawson in Nashville had developed just such a cadre.

There also was a simple tactical reason to go, Nash recalled. The Freedom Riders had done their best. Now they needed help. And in her group in Nashville, she recalled, "We were fresh troops." What's more, they were trained and cohesive. They talked over the situation and made plans in meetings that stretched over two days. They understood that time was crucial, but they also knew that the Movement always was more effective when considered discussion preceded action.

James Bevel, a man who knew about commitment, was given the task of selecting who could go on this dangerous mission. He looked in each volunteer for spiritual conviction. He would ask, "How do you want your body buried?" After that, he'd say, "All right, now write out your eulogy." Bevel's test of each statement was whether he felt that he could look parents in the face and tell them why their child died. If so, he would give them a green light. "If I can't explain to your folks why you're dead, I'm not going to send you," he told volunteers.

And then, on May 17, they dispatched a group to Birmingham to continue the Rides. "We got ready to be burned up," Bevel recalled. Bevel here was wrestling with a problem that many military commanders face at one time or another in combat: the possibility of sending good soldiers to their deaths. At the key Civil War battle of Gettysburg, for example, General Winfield Hancock ordered the 1st Minnesota Regiment to plug a gap in the Union line, even though that unit was vastly outnumbered, in order to buy enough time for reinforcements to be brought up. The regiment's officers responded with alacrity, and within five minutes the majority of their soldiers were dead or wounded. As Elliott Ackerman, who served five tours of duty in Iraq and Afghanistan as a Marine officer, put it, "If you're in any type of leadership position, . . . you might find yourself at a moment of consequence where you have to make a decision in order to accomplish the mission, in which you are ordering your friends, these people, in my case, it was Marines who you love, to certainly get wounded, sometimes get killed. And so really, the central dilemma in war is that you have to ultimately oftentimes destroy the very thing that you love."

Reinforcements from Nashville

The Nashville Riders selected Diane Nash, who had left college to be a full-time activist, to be their coordinator for this operation. That is, she would be the trusted insider who would remain behind, not riding the bus, and so stay outside the control of authorities. Her assignment was to keep track of events and movements and to maintain communications from the Riders to Movement groups, to news organizations, and to federal officials. As the group prepared to leave, some made out their wills and others gave sealed letters to Nash. "That's how prepared they were, for death," she said.

Attorney General Robert Kennedy called his aide John Seigenthaler. "Who the hell is Diane Nash?" he wanted to know. The attorney general of the United States was being outmatched in political chess by a twenty-one-year-old college dropout who was living at a YWCA. Seigenthaler was still figuring out the answer to Kennedy's puzzled inquiry. He had told Nash that she didn't understand the situation, that "people are going to be killed." She replied that she understood that. Yet he kept repeating it. She responded that if the initial Nashville Riders were killed, others would follow them. Indeed, on her tiny budget, she had more volunteers on hand than she could afford to send. It was at about this time that the singer and actor Harry Belafonte, who was friendly with the Kennedys and also a steady financial contributor to the civil rights movement, gave a bit of advice to Robert Kennedy. "If you want to know what they're going to do next, just read Gandhi," he said.

"The whole blueprint for what the movement is doing is right there." But, Belafonte recalled, the suggestion went over Kennedy's head. The attorney general responded that political power came from the vote, not from demonstrations.

Nash herself was becoming frustrated with the Kennedy administration's inability to understand that the group was willing to die rather than put up with segregation. "We knew that we couldn't let the government lead the Movement, that was ridiculous," she said.

Seigenthaler was not accustomed to such zeal. He worried to a friend, "She is going to get those people killed." Here Nash's experience points to a larger lesson about the Movement and strategy. Seigenthaler and his boss, Robert Kennedy, were thinking tactically. Nash was speaking at a higher level, operating in a strategic context.

Carl von Clausewitz, the Prussian philosopher of war, emphasized that the first and most important task of a commander is to understand the nature of the war in which one is engaged. Nash had done that. She had addressed the most basic of questions: *Who are we, and what are we trying to do?* Her answer was, emphatically: *We are people who would rather die than tolerate subjugation.*

From that extraordinary act of strategic self-definition flowed the necessary tactics. "We were going to be rid of segregation," she later said. "One of the things that I have learned over the years is that you really can't change anyone but yourself and what we did in the South was change ourselves from people who could be segregated into people who could no longer be segregated. The attitude became 'well kill us if that's what you're going to do, but you cannot segregate us any longer' and once you change yourself the world has to fit up against the new you." Once again, this was a message that Lawson had channeled straight from Gandhi, who taught his acolytes, "Every one of you should, from this very moment, consider himself a free man or woman and even act as if you are free and no longer under the heel of imperialism. . . . What you think, you become." It was a message so powerful that one SNCC leader, Ruby Doris Smith, who died of cancer in 1967, chose it for her epitaph; the headstone on her grave reads, "IF YOU THINK FREE,

YOU ARE FREE." Nash's view was that her group intended to live like people who were free. If the people enforcing segregation didn't like that, well, that was their problem, not hers.

Making that mental leap was incredibly powerful, Bevel noted, and intimidating to opponents: "Since we agreed we could only lose our own lives, we quickly discovered something important: We could always make the last decision." That is, the Riders' determined approach, their willingness to pay the ultimate price, gave them the upper hand in confrontations.

Genuine strategizing is exceedingly difficult. There is a saying among seasoned military strategists that if you are not weeping occasionally, you're not making strategy. Indeed, Nash found the emotional toll of formulating and executing the strategy, which involved taking such a novel and uncompromising stance, to be enormous. It was, she recalled, "like being at war." She added, "I cried every night, profusely. And I needed to, as an energy release. It was so much tension."

The initial contingent of Rider reinforcements from Nashville numbered ten, aboard an early morning bus heading for Alabama. Shuttlesworth, always inclined toward confrontation, telegrammed Bull Connor to tell the police commissioner he was being given a second chance to protect the rights of Freedom Riders. Connor accepted the challenge: when their Greyhound arrived at the Birmingham city limits, the group was taken off the bus, bundled into "protective custody," and held in jail without charges. They responded by going on a hunger strike.

At 11:30 the next night, they were taken from their cells and put into a convoy of cars. John Lewis found himself in a station wagon with Connor at the wheel. They were driven back to the Tennessee border, where they were dumped in the middle of the night near the small town of Ardmore. Worrying that they were being set up to be lynched by the Klan, the Riders found a telephone and called the hotline in Nashville that Nash had set up and reserved solely for their incoming calls. Somehow, perhaps because the stakes were so high, Nash had intuited that communication can be as decisive as action—an essential lesson in military operations. American soldiers and Marines are trained to "shoot, move, and communicate." That last word means that it is essential to stay in touch, letting comrades know where you are, what you are doing, and what you are seeing and hearing. Nash and her cohort were developing a nonviolent variation on that—confront, move, and communicate.

Nash dispatched a car from Nashville. The Riders told the driver, Leo Lillard, an old comrade from the Nashville sit-ins, that no, they did not want to go to Nashville. Rather, they wanted to be taken back to Birmingham. This remarkably courageous request comported with the training they had been given, which was to find ways to wear down their opponents and keep them off-balance. It also evinced a gritty perseverance. People who had been escorted out of the state by Bull Connor usually didn't race him back to Birmingham, the city he dominated.

On top of that, Nash had located more money and was shipping a second group of Nashville activists to Birmingham to join the Ride. Quite brilliantly, she was managing to catch both Bull Connor and the Kennedy brothers on the back foot. It was a remarkable effort on her part, and also a testimony to the power of thoughtful strategy and preparation.

Welcome to Montgomery

On Friday, May 19, the Nashvillian Riders, now numbering nineteen, tried to board a Greyhound bus from Birmingham to Montgomery, only to have the company cancel several runs. Robert Shelton, a top Klan leader, wearing his black robes indicating his status, led a group of Klansmen into the waiting room in the Birmingham Greyhound terminal to harass the waiting Riders. A hostile crowd surged outside. The city disconnected the telephones in the waiting room. The surrounded Riders wound up sleeping on benches.

Early the following morning they finally were able to board a bus to Montgomery. Shuttlesworth appeared with a ticket and intended to join them, but officers arrested him to prevent him from doing so. The state police escorted the bus to the Montgomery city line, where the highway patrol took over.

Arriving at the Greyhound terminal in downtown Montgomery at 10:23, the nineteen Riders found it eerily quiet. It was deserted. There were no waiting passengers, no bystanders—and no police around. The absence of law enforcement personnel was a terrible warning sign. The Riders didn't know it, but lookouts had spotted their bus and a hostile throng was lurking nearby. Catastrophe loomed in the air. "And then, all of a sudden, just like *whoosh!*, magic, white people, sticks and bricks, 'Nigger! Kill the niggers!'" recalled one Rider, Frederick Leonard.

John Lewis said, "The moment we started down off the steps of the bus, an angry mob . . . came out of nowhere—men, women, children, with baseball bats, clubs, chains." Hundreds of them swirled around the Riders. Someone swung a wooden Coca-Cola crate against Lewis' head. He tasted his own blood. "Everything turned white for an instant, then black," he remembered Then he fell unconscious to the pavement.

Following him, James Zwerg, a white college student from Wisconsin, stepped off the bus with his head bowed and walked into the mob, closing his eyes and reciting Psalm 27: "The Lord is my light and salvation; whom shall I fear? The Lord is the strength of my life; of whom shall I be afraid? . . . And now shall my head be lifted up above mine enemies round about me." Hands grabbed him. He was soon beaten and kicked in the face.

Seigenthaler, the aide to Robert Kennedy who had failed to dissuade Diane Nash from continuing the Freedom Rides, tried to usher one of the female Riders into his car. She told him that it was not his fight and he should leave her. "You're going to get hurt," she warned. At that moment a section of pipe cracked against the back of Seigenthaler's skull, and he fell to the ground, where he was kicked under his car.

That attack represented yet another escalation in southern white violence: Not only was Seigenthaler white, but he was an official of the federal government, indeed a personal assistant to the attorney general of the United States. He would wake up in a Birmingham hospital bed with a fractured skull and several broken ribs.

By attacking him, the forces of segregation had handed the civil rights movement a victory, because President Kennedy and his brother took the attack on Seigenthaler personally. To them, it was one thing to beat activists and quite another to attack one of their personal representatives. "The president was mad," recalled Burke Marshall, the head of the civil rights division at the Justice Department. Robert Kennedy ordered a detachment of federal marshals who were assembling at Maxwell Air Force Base, on the western outskirts of Montgomery, to be ready to intervene.

Floyd Mann of the Alabama state police, seeing that the city police had deserted the area, called in a group of state troopers he had stationed nearby, though he officially lacked jurisdiction. He fired his pistol twice in the air to get the mob's attention and to end the beatings. Hearing the weapon's report, one of the new Riders from Nashville, Bernard LaFayette, who was fleeing the scene, thought that some of his comrades were being shot behind him. While Mann waited for his state policemen to arrive on the scene, he intervened to stop a man beating a Birmingham television reporter. "I just put my pistol to the head of one or two of those folks who was using baseball bats," Mann recalled, "and told them unless they stopped immediately they was going to be hurt." Years later, a federal judge would conclude that Montgomery police authorities had willfully, deliberately, and unlawfully withdrawn police protection when the bus arrived.

A civil rights confluence in a besieged church

Moments of crisis can bring together great forces or suddenly drive them apart. On Sunday, May 21, at a mass meeting at Ralph Abernathy's First Baptist Church, not far from the Montgomery bus station, the Nashville student movement joined hands with the older one. As Andrew Young noted, the Montgomery movement had been church-based, while

Nashville's was philosophical and grew out of that city's colleges and seminaries. The older ministers and the younger students now began to work with one another.

About 1,500 people, almost all of them Black, but with a few reporters and some local white liberals, gathered inside the church. Outside were at least that many shouting whites, many of them affiliated with the Ku Klux Klan. Trucks carrying loads of cinder blocks and sledgehammers pulled up, and the crowd began cracking the blocks into pieces to have objects to throw at the church windows. People in the mob also hurled firebombs at the church. "I thought they were going to burn down the church with us inside," recalled LaFayette.

Kennedy's small force of federal marshals, now deployed into the city, tried to keep the crowd at bay. But the marshals were not really prepared for the task. To be fair, they were a pickup team of U.S. Border Patrol officers, Internal Revenue Service agents, and federal prison guards. What's more, quelling a large and angry mob is no easy job, especially at night and on unfamiliar turf. It requires a good deal of training. Mann, the director of the Alabama State Police, thought the marshals appeared unready. "They began to throw tear gas and they threw it into the wind. And the gas began to affect the marshals more than . . . the people that they were trying to control." Most of the marshals did not have gas masks, he added.

The gas also wafted through the broken windows of the church and began to irritate the eyes of the crowd huddled inside. "It was a horrible night. . . . Awful," recalled Wyatt Walker, selected the previous year to replace Ella Baker at the SCLC, and effectively serving as King's chief of staff. The English author Jessica Mitford, who was in town to write an article about the South for *Esquire* magazine, had borrowed a Buick from local friends to attend the church meeting and had parked directly outside it. The crowd overturned the car and torched it. Its gas tank exploded with a bomb-like detonation, sending another wave of fear through the people inside, who then sang hymns to raise their spirits.

While they went through "Love Lifted Me," King was in an office in the church's basement, on the phone to Robert Kennedy. He told the attorney general that the situation was desperate. Kennedy asked King for a cooling-off period, which was the administration's standard response to the Movement at this point. James Farmer was also in the church, returning to the Ride that evening after his father's funeral, in part to reclaim the operation for CORE. "Farmer was determined to share the spotlight in Montgomery," writes Raymond Arsenault, the most thorough historian of the Freedom Rides.

King found Farmer to tell him about the attorney general's request. To his credit, Farmer said he would need to consult with Diane Nash, who had moved her coordination effort to Montgomery and was inside the church. She shook her head and said that the Nashville students would not stop. Farmer walked back to King and said, "Please tell the attorney general that we have been cooling off for 350 years. If we cool off any more, we'll freeze. The Freedom Ride will go on."

Robert Kennedy also was talking that night to the governor of Alabama, John Patterson. But Kennedy did not know that the governor had an eavesdropping system that enabled him to monitor Kennedy's calls to Justice Department aides waiting at Maxwell Air Force Base, on the edge of the city. When Kennedy asked those aides about whether to deploy U.S. Army troops, Governor Patterson got a step ahead of him and instead called in the Alabama National Guard to keep the mob from burning the besieged church. At 10:00 p.m., the Guard soldiers moved in and set up a protective ring around the church. The 1,500 people inside lay down and slept on the pews or on the floor. Just before dawn, National Guard trucks began transporting the people who had been trapped in the church all night to their neighborhoods.

At this point, Robert Kennedy thought that King and others were in his debt for having protected them. But from the perspective of the Movement, he simply had done his duty as the nation's top law enforcement official.

In a speech that night from the pulpit, King saluted the Freedom Riders for their moving "example of strong courageous action devoid [of] violence." He added that "honesty impels me to admit that we are in for a season of suffering." And he declared, "We will present our

physical bodies as instruments to defeat the unjust system." That last
sentence left a question hanging in the air: Was King presenting his
own physical self as a Freedom Rider? That is, would he be on a bus
from Montgomery into Mississippi?

King and jail

Great people tend to have great flaws. "Every human being has some defects, some weaknesses," Bayard Rustin once observed. "Martin Luther
King had several, and by truly understanding those defects he becomes
not less a great man, but more a great man, because it's not a matter of
putting him on a pedestal and therefore obscuring what he really is."
Heroes especially tend to have dark and even destructive sides, notes the
military veterans' therapist Jonathan Shay. Gandhi once remarked to a
journalist interviewing him, "I am very imperfect. Before you are gone
you will have discovered a hundred of my faults and if you don't, I will
help you to see them."

King's flaws were numerous. One was that, as a graduate student,
he engaged in what the editors of his papers delicately term "unacknowledged textual appropriations" and what one writer has bluntly
called "chronic plagiarism." Another was that, though married, he was
sexually promiscuous, at times recklessly so.

But in tactical terms, his greatest shortcoming may have been his
profound dislike of being behind bars. Those involved in the struggle
for civil rights knew that being jailed was an essential step, a rite of passage, a sign of commitment, and a part of the bonding process inside
the Movement. Yet being imprisoned made King miserable and carried
lasting emotional costs. "Jail is depressing because it shuts off the world,"
he once wrote while behind bars. "It is almost like being dead while one
still lives. To adjust to such a meaningless existence is not easy."

Andrew Young attributed King's "almost paralyzing fear of being
alone in jail" to an incident in 1960 in which Georgia sheriffs had arrested him on a technicality involving his driver's license. It wasn't the

first time he was jailed—that had occurred in Montgomery—but this episode was particularly chilling. The lawmen placed him in a strait-jacket, handcuffed him, and shackled his legs with irons, then drove him two hundred miles to the state prison, while not telling him what they were doing. He later recounted his experience to his wife, Coretta, who said, "He just broke down and cried and then he felt so ashamed of himself." This vulnerability would cause tension between him and other movement leaders. The contrast here to Gandhi is striking: the Indian leader described jail as "a palace" in which he could write, rest, and reflect. He once wrote from his prison cell, "I am quite at peace & none need worry about me."

On the evening of Monday, May 22, and into the early morning hours of Tuesday, May 23, several leaders of the Movement met with the Freedom Riders. King, Farmer, Abernathy, and the other older ones sat in the available folding chairs, while the Riders generally took to the floor. Farmer got on John Lewis' nerves as he asserted control of the Freedom Ride mission. "He talked loud and big, but his words seemed hollow to me," wrote Lewis. "His retreat after the attacks in Anniston and Birmingham had something to do with it, I'm sure, but he just struck me as very insincere. It was clear to everyone that he wanted to take the ride back now, when we all knew that without our having picked it up, there would have been no more Freedom Ride." Farmer was losing the support of the people carrying out the mission, a major mistake for any leader.

James Bevel told King that the way forward was clear, if open-ended: "We'll have Freedom Rides going on until all people can ride buses without being harassed. We don't care what the cost is, or what the danger is."

But there was another issue on the table, one raised by Diane Nash. In his speech at the beleaguered church on Sunday night, King had associated himself with the Freedom Riders. So, Nash boldly asked King, given that embrace, would he be on the bus with them to Mississippi? She and he both knew that being jailed there was all but certain—if they survived the Ride itself.

No, King responded, he couldn't join them, because he was on probation.

This was too much for the Riders. King could have been honest and said he was scared to go, or that he was too central to the Movement to risk his life. But his offered reason was ludicrous. "I'm on probation, too," one Rider shouted.

"We're *all* on probation," said another.

King answered, with a bit of irritation, "I think I should choose the time and place of my Golgotha," a reference to the site where Jesus was crucified. This was consistent with the teaching of nonviolent philosophy that everyone had to make their own choices and should not be coerced into agreeing with the group. But the Riders had had enough. They stood up and left the room.

King had handled his explanation badly, yet in retrospect he was correct in his decision, especially if one looks at the Movement as a sustained struggle. Everyone involved had a role. King's was as a spokesman, a fundraiser, a symbol, and a provider of the long-term vision. The Riders were like Special Operations troops going on a hazardous raid. Having him along would be like having a top general accompany such a mission, which would be an inappropriate use of a senior officer. Also, the Freedom Rides were not an SCLC operation. That said, King's disquiet over the prospect of being jailed would come back to trouble him.

At a press conference on May 23, King, flanked by Farmer, Abernathy, and Lewis, announced that the Rides would continue. "Freedom Riders must develop the quiet courage of dying for a cause," King said, his voice cracking. "We all love life, and there are no martyrs here. . . . I'm sure these students are willing to face death if necessary." One can only wonder if under King's message to the public, there also was a quiet message to the students: Welcome to the world I have been living in for the last seven years, of bombs and death threats.

That night, James Lawson, who had arrived from Nashville, gave the Freedom Riders a refresher course in nonviolence. This was a smart move, because the makeup of the group had changed somewhat, with some veterans of the Ride returning to college under threat of expulsion and some fresh faces recruited mainly by Nash. Also, Hank Thomas, having recuperated from being clubbed at the Anniston bus burning, was back. Thomas was a classic example of a good soldier for the Movement. "He was one of the most impressive young black men I'd ever met. . . . I really admired Hank," wrote the prominent organizer Stokely Carmichael, who joined a Freedom Ride from New Orleans to Jackson, Mississippi. "Whatever he said he would do, you could absolutely count on."

Lawson's intense efforts would make sure they all had some familiarity with one another, always an intelligent step to take before going into battle. According to the historian Raymond Arsenault, "Several of the Freedom Riders would look back [on this session] . . . as a life-changing experience, one that deepened their theoretical understanding of nonviolent struggle and sacrifice, preparing them as nothing else had for the difficult challenges ahead." Cohesion is an ineffable but powerful force in military operations. It is more than simply familiarity or bonding. After World War II, American scholars investigated a historical puzzle: Why had German army units held together and fought with stubborn tenacity long after they had suffered losses that would have caused units from other countries to disintegrate? In a renowned article, the sociologists Morris Janowitz and Edward Shils concluded that cohesion is a product not of political loyalty or indoctrination, but rather of faith in one's comrades, leaders, and training. When cohesion is present, everything works better. When it is absent, friction and failure often follow. Cohesion was the ineffable but essential ingredient the Nashville contingent possessed. Developing it was perhaps the greatest contribution James Lawson made to the civil rights movement.

The Rides resume

Persistence is a neglected virtue in many walks of life, but it is prized in the military world—and was in the civil rights movement as well.

The Nashville contingent demonstrated its extraordinary tenacity once more on Wednesday, May 24. Not only did the Nashville students resume the Freedom Rides, but they did so in a way that yet again kept the authorities off-balance.

State and federal officials thought they had the situation under control. At around eight in the morning, a Trailways bus carrying twelve Riders, led by Lawson, departed Montgomery for Jackson, Mississippi, under the protection of an array of law enforcement officials. Also on the bus were several other Nashville vets—C. T. Vivian, James Bevel, and Bernard LaFayette—as well as a dozen reporters and six soldiers from the Alabama National Guard, toting rifles with fixed bayonets. It was an unusual set of passengers—the Guard had made sure that no ordinary travelers were allowed to board. A military convoy escorted the bus to the state border, where it was turned over to the custody of the Mississippi National Guard.

But Diane Nash and her comrades had another tactical surprise waiting. For some reason, officials had assumed that there would be only one busload of Riders. Four hours after that first one left, another fifteen Riders appeared at the Greyhound terminal in Montgomery and purchased tickets for Jackson. This group included John Lewis and Hank Thomas. There was one odd hiccup just before this Ride began. Lewis looked out of the bus and saw James Farmer waving farewell. The Riders had assumed he would join them. Farmer reached up to shake the hand of one Rider, Doris Castle, who was just shy of turning nineteen. "My prayers are with you," Farmer said.

She whispered to him, wide-eyed, "Jim, you're coming with us, aren't you?"

Farmer was full of excuses. He replied that he was too busy with CORE to do that, with his job as director, and all the paperwork that was stacking up. Castle listened, stared at him out her bus window, and then said, "Jim. *Please.*" Farmer, by his own account, was shamed aboard. Yet in his hesitancy, Farmer had committed a third major mistake. At key moments, leaders must lead from the front. He hadn't.

To be sure, it was not easy to step up into that bus. "It was like a death kind of scene. Everybody knew that this is a suicide mission, in a sense," recalled Dave Dennis, one of the Riders. The bus was seen off by a jeering crowd of two thousand.

Both groups arrived in Jackson, Mississippi, that afternoon, where they were protected from mob violence but were arrested upon stepping into white waiting rooms even though under federal law, interstate travel could not be segregated. Unknown to them, Robert Kennedy had cut a deal with the governor of Mississippi, Ross Barnett, that was guaranteed by the state's powerful senior U.S. senator, James Eastland. Under it, the Riders were arrested, despite having the law on their side, in exchange for Barnett's promise that there would be no violence against them. The attorney general had given away their federal protection.

The next morning, the headline on the front page of Jackson's *Clarion-Ledger* read, "27 Mixers Jailed on Arrival Here." With that odd word "mixers," it is as if the newspaper lacked the vocabulary to describe what was happening—which after all is the foremost task of daily journalism. The Riders were indeed presenting a different view of the world to Mississippi's power structure. When Robert Singleton, a UCLA economics student, was arrested in Jackson, a policeman said, "You're a black son of a bitch, aren't you?" Singleton pleasantly responded, "Isn't that a beautiful color?" He recalled that the officer "just froze. He didn't know how to respond to that."

Once behind bars, the Riders were so keyed up after their harrowing day of travel that life felt surreal. "I saw one person just start beating his head against the wall," remembered Dennis. "Girls started pulling, just pulled a handful of hair out." These are combat levels of stress, in which it becomes difficult to hear clearly, let alone think or speak.

Many of them wound up in the notoriously harsh Mississippi State Penitentiary, known as Parchman Farm. Here their experience in the Nashville jail served them well. They organized and sang. "It became almost a university of nonviolence," Arsenault said in a documentary interview. The female Riders were especially active in this regard, holding political seminars, French classes, ballet lessons, and a series of lectures on Roman history and Greek culture. It was as if they were defining the world differently from their captors.

In a variety of ways, they made the point that they were not normal prisoners, and they were not being broken by Parchman. One day, Bernard LaFayette, who had acquired the nickname "Little Gandhi," spoke back to one of the bosses of the prison, known to them as Deputy Tyson, who ordered, "You shut yo' mouth, boy." LaFayette mischievously responded, "Deputy Tyson, do you mean anything derogatory when you call us 'boy'?" One Rider who had operatic training discovered that the metal punishment box called "the hole" happened to offer perfect acoustics for his baritone, and treated his fellow prisoners to a series of beautiful songs that reverberated through the entire building. One listener described it as "the most moving concert I have ever heard." The constant singing of "freedom songs" got on the nerves of the guards, who took away the prisoners' mattresses in reprisal.

Governor Barnett kept his pact with Kennedy, and the Riders generally were not beaten by the prison guards. Even so, they endured hard time, with the guards free to inflict other sorts of suffering and humiliation. They were greeted with threats, ordered to strip, left naked in a holding cell for hours, and then issued only T-shirts and underwear. One of Parchman's punishments was to hang prisoners from their cell bars by handcuffs. Some of them were set to hard labor on chain gangs.

White Mississippi was indeed prepared to fight. Ross Barnett had campaigned for governor as an ardent segregationist, telling one audience that whites needed to be prepared to battle for the cause. "We must identify the traitors in our midst," he said. "We must eliminate the coward from our front lines." But the Riders were no less willing to continue their confrontation. After Bevel and LaFayette emerged from Parchman, they escalated again by recruiting teenagers in Jackson to conduct their own sit-ins and Freedom Rides. The two were arrested and charged with contributing to the delinquency of minors. The prosecutor offered a deal under which the charges would be dropped if they agreed to leave the state. They declined.

Robert Kennedy had cut a deal with the segregation power, but despite that disreputable sellout he had not achieved his goal of ending the Freedom Rides. A call went out for more Riders. Hundreds responded, with two arriving in Jackson one day, ten the next, and so on. New Rides were launched almost every week during the rest of 1961. In one, an interracial group of fifteen Episcopal ministers, one of them the son-in-law of New York governor Nelson Rockefeller, arrived at Jackson's Trailways terminal. Eventually Parchman would hold three hundred of the activists.

Robert Kennedy confronts King

Robert Kennedy thought the Riders were embarrassing him and the nation. He called King, who was in Montgomery at the house of Ralph Abernathy. Kennedy and King had a snappish telephone conversation. Kennedy was concerned by the image of America that the situation was producing, especially as his brother was preparing for a trip to Europe that would culminate in a summit meeting in Vienna with the Soviet leader Nikita Khrushchev. He was worried about what would happen to the imprisoned Freedom Riders in the hands of Mississippi prison guards when national attention had moved on and there were no television cameras or reporters around. King told Kennedy that the Riders would reject any efforts to free them. Kennedy left the conversation unhappy. "The president is going abroad and this is all embarrassing to him," the attorney general told an aide.

King put down the telephone and walked into Abernathy's living room. "You know, they don't understand the social revolution going on in the world, and therefore they don't understand what we're doing," he said.

He was right. It was Robert Kennedy who embarrassed himself as he was outfoxed by segregationist politicians. The attorney general had begun May 1961 with a rousing speech in Georgia in which he had vowed to enforce civil rights laws across the country. He ended that month by cutting a deal with a segregationist governor that resulted in the Freedom Riders being arrested for exercising their legal rights. When challenged by the Riders to enforce the nation's laws, Kennedy instead had retreated from his stated position and sided with the forces of segregation. This was not moderate pragmatism, as some historians have argued, but rather a shoddy showing by the nation's chief legal officer, who was head of the Department of Justice, not the Department of Order. He was only partially redeemed by a petition he filed on May 29 to the Interstate Commerce Commission asking it to adopt stringent desegregation regulations. As one historian put it, "For all their talents, the Kennedy men suffered under a colossal misconception— they thought they could steer and control the Movement for full black citizenship. They thought they could do it with brains, charm, diligence, logic, and back-room negotiation. They did not know it, but they were already being swallowed up by the movement." Kennedy had shown that in a crisis he could be backed down, a terrible signal to send to southern officials.

To be fair to the attorney general, the Freedom Rides were subject to doubt even within the Movement. On July 10, delivering the keynote address at the NAACP's national convention, the Reverend Stephen Spottswood belittled the Rides, calling them "useful" but more "a signal flare" than an artillery barrage. His analogy badly underestimated the effects of the Rides. Across the South, the Riders again and again had demonstrated that local segregation laws were in conflict with national laws. The nation had seen mayors and sheriffs seeking to protect their customary but now illegal ways. The Rides had not ended the segregation power across the South, but they had given it a sharp rap that was felt even in areas they hadn't visited. Indeed, later that year, all CORE had to do to force forty-seven restaurants in Maryland and Delaware to desegregate was to announce that it planned sit-ins there. Almost an equal number of restaurants along the highways in the area failed to agree to integrate, but CORE was happy to collect the quick victory gained by a press release. With the target set for CORE cut in half merely by a deft act of public relations, the holdout restaurants were then hit by demonstrations.

A strategic assessment of the segregation power

It is worth pausing here to assess the strategic state of white supremacy. As noted, the forces of segregation appeared in 1961 to be in an advantageous position, even an overwhelming one. In the terms by which power is usually measured, they were dominant, a regional monolith that stood under the banner of "massive resistance." They held the vast preponderance of economic power, directed and peopled law enforcement, and controlled the courts and the schools. They proclaimed "Segregation forever" and pinned on buttons stating "NEVER." The veteran Georgia politician Roy Harris, a dedicated segregationist and the president of the white supremacist Citizens' Councils of America, had stated in 1959 that whites would oppose desegregation so intensely and broadly that failure was unthinkable. "There won't be any integration in Georgia," he confidently informed a reporter. Indeed, some 75 percent of southern whites surveyed said they supported segregation.

The methods by which they had subjugated Blacks were ugly, ultimately resting on violence or the threat of it, but they had been successful for centuries. Not only was violence effective, but Klansmen and others who attacked Blacks enjoyed what one historian has called "a general immunity from arrest, prosecution, and conviction." So it seemed there was no reason for segregationists to worry.

Yet in many ways the status quo was a hollow force, a clumsy dinosaur with a small brain and atrophying muscles. As Erica Chenoweth observes, "Oppressive systems tend to be much more fragile than they appear." There were several reasons for this vulnerability.

First, as noted at the outset of this chapter, the segregation power was in the position of having to defend everywhere, while the Movement could choose the times and places of its confrontations.

Second, after the Supreme Court's decision in 1954, segregation no longer had the federal law entirely on its side, a problem that led segregationists to rely on hazy, subjective nonlegal phrases about "our way of life," as when Alabama, in reaction to the Freedom Rides, enacted a law making it a crime to "outrage the sense of decency and morals or . . . violate or transgress the customs, pattern of life and habits of the people of Alabama." Similarly, Mississippi outlawed "encouraging disobedience to any law of the State of Mississippi, and nonconformance with the established traditions, customs, and usages of the State of Mississippi." This approach would not stand up to sustained legal scrutiny.

Third, the forces of segregation had little to offer in reality, so their efforts would largely be expressed in two ways. To whites, they promoted cultural myths, such as the superiority of the white race—and the cultural and social power of such fictions should not be underestimated. To subjugate Blacks, their primary tool was economic power. This had the advantage of being effective without making headlines. Blacks who tried to register to vote—and so gain a bit of political power—often were asked by the registrar who they worked for, and then sent away unregistered as the person's employer was notified with the understanding that registration would result in the loss of their job. As the lawyer for the Citizens' Council in Selma, Alabama, put it in November 1954, the organization's plan was "to make it difficult, if not impossible, for any Negro who advocates desegregation to find and hold a job, get credit or renew a mortgage." This was not an empty threat. Rather, it was a time-tested formula. In August of that year, nineteen Blacks in the Selma area had signed a petition against school segregation. By September, sixteen of them had lost their jobs. Newspapers helped by publishing the names and addresses of those who tried to register.

The fallback line of defense was tying up desegregation in the courts, fighting it in every county and school district. This approach produced much delay but few long-term victories.

The final line of defense always had been and remained white violence, threatened or real. For most of American history, this had been a reliable tool for the dominant caste. Theodore Bilbo, a Mississippi governor and senator, as well as an avowed member of the Klan, said in a speech in Jackson in the summer of 1946, "White people will be justified in going to any extreme to keep the nigger from voting. You know and I know what's the best way to keep the nigger from voting. You do it the night before an election. I don't have to tell you more than that. Red-blooded men know what I mean."

But in the 1950s, a technological reason made white aggression harder to deploy: the rapid expansion of television networks. They operated first around New York City, then in the late 1940s expanded to the Mississippi, and early in the 1950s to the West Coast. The networks broadcast images that began changing how Americans saw their nation and so what they thought about it. The first commercial stations opened in the South in 1948, in Richmond, Atlanta, Louisville, Memphis, New Orleans, and Fort Worth. The effect of television—present but slight during the Montgomery bus boycott—intensified with each passing year, amplifying the sit-ins, the Freedom Rides, the Birmingham campaign, the March on Washington, and the Selma campaign. As Bayard Rustin put it, "Now you were having brought into every American living room in America the brutality of the situation. So I think that if we had television fifty years earlier, we would have gotten rid of lynching fifty years earlier." In other words, the strategic context had changed for the essential tool of maintaining the subjugation of Black southerners, because the viciousness of the system could no longer be denied. Looking back in 1967, Dr. King said that "in the South, in the nonviolent movement, we were aided on the whole by the brutality of the opponent."

In addition, the white segregationists complicated their position through their own missteps. Everybody makes mistakes in war; the key is not repeating them. Victory often goes to the side that is able to recognize its errors and make effective fixes.

The first error the segregationist South committed, repeatedly, was not understanding the enemy. In the wake of the Montgomery bus boycott, southern officials focused on the NAACP as the foe. In 1956, a judge in Alabama effectively banned the organization after it declined to turn over its membership and financial records. States across the South followed suit, tying up their local NAACP chapters with lawsuits and injunctions. "In destroying the NAACP, the state of Alabama had pushed Negro protest into its revolutionary form: a mass struggle, based in the church and on the notion not of an organization but of a movement," comments the memoirist Diane McWhorter. That is, the absence of the gradualist, legalistic NAACP moved the action from the courts to the streets, and so created an opening for less stodgy, more radical civil rights activists. "Closing down the NAACP," McWhorter writes, "might have been the best thing the segregationists could have done for the civil rights movement." Coincidentally, in October 1956, the French government made a remarkably similar mistake during the Algerian war for independence: it captured the existing leadership of the Algerian insurgents—who, it developed, were older and more moderate than those who soon moved up to fill the French-created vacancies. Sometimes the enemies you have are more pliable than their unknown replacements waiting in the wings.

A graver mistake the segregationists made was to believe their own lies. This is a constant danger in wartime, and one of the greatest unrecognized causes of defeats. The foremost self-deception was believing that the Blacks of the South were largely content with their second-class status or sufficiently cowed by segregationist oppression, and were only being stirred up by outsiders. As the mayor of Jackson, Mississippi, put it, "It has been a policy of mine and the city council, the police department and the people to maintain what has worked for the past hundred years to bring happiness, peace and prosperity. That has been to maintain a separation of the races—not segregation, we don't call it segregation—to maintain peace and order and to keep down disturbances. . . . The policy we have adopted here has been to maintain happiness and contentment between the races and to live together in peace and quiet."

It is never wise to base a strategy on believing one's own misperceptions, but it happens surprisingly often. Few nations go to war expecting to lose. This is one reason that commanders who are both wise and self-confident create "red team" cells to attempt to discern the enemy's perspective on war plans. These small internal think tanks immerse themselves in the worldview of the adversary and then emerge to probe for the vulnerabilities in their side's approach.

Casting a cold eye on your team's plans tends to make everyone uncomfortable, which is one reason that in the American military, red cells are one of the first things to be eliminated when budget cuts are needed. One of the most notorious examples of informed opposition thinking was the simulated attack that Rear Admiral Harry Yarnell launched against the U.S. Navy base at Pearl Harbor, Hawaii, in a war game on Sunday, February 7, 1932. Yarnell, who was an innovative tactician, left behind his battleships and brought two aircraft carriers, the *Lexington* and the *Saratoga*, to the north of Hawaii. He then launched 152 planes. The defenders never caught him. A Navy panel dominated by battleship admirals rejected the exercise's results as unrealistic, arguing that in real warfare, the carriers would have been detected. Japanese military planners found the scenario's results quite plausible and copied them nine years later for their surprise attack on Pearl Harbor. The blindness shown by the battleship admirals is not a disease solely of the American defense establishment. Newspaper publishers and editors do the same thing by using financial excuses to rid themselves of nettlesome ombudsmen.

A second self-deception by the segregationists was their depiction of their enemy's actions and motivations. Words, like bombs and bullets, are tools of war. When words are misused, they are like mis-aimed weapons. All too often, the language of the segregation power rang false. Blacks who tried to exercise their rights as citizens often were characterized as committing acts of "aggression." Equally off base was the charge that the secret goal of Blacks was racial mixing. That was especially illogical in light of the long history of southern white men raping enslaved Black women. As the memoirist Diane McWhorter put it, "The slaveholders had written the book on miscegenation." Indeed, James Eastland, who for decades served as a U.S. senator from Mississippi, by one account supposedly used to tell his weekend guests arriving at his family's sprawling cotton plantation in Sunflower County to "pick out a nigger girl and a horse."

In another misstep, some segregationists also targeted Jews and Catholics. Not all did—some taking the longer view realized that was an error, because one principle of war is to have as few enemies as possible. As a result, writes the historian David Chappell, the forces of segregation "never organized concerted, consistent propaganda that might have undermined the increasing (and increasingly confident) public authority of civil rights leaders."

More accurate was the segregationist charge that the Movement was influenced by the American far left. It was indeed true that some key figures such as Bayard Rustin had been sympathetic to the Communist Party. Their pasts would give the FBI director J. Edgar Hoover an opening to intervene against the Movement. The damage Hoover's FBI did probably still has not completely been revealed, more than half a century later. Yet ultimately the charge of being communist-influenced did not resonate with the American people. As King would note, he didn't need someone in Moscow to tell him that a white man's knee was on his neck.

In addition, the white supremacists had to deal with the fact that not all whites, even in the Deep South, supported them. Here they again responded with threats. They would not consider compromise, as officials in Nashville, Charlotte, and even Atlanta had done. Yet the ground shifted. Many whites tended to support segregation as long as doing so was cost-free. But when civil rights campaigns threw an unwelcome spotlight on the violence of segregation and began scaring away investors, that cost calculation would begin to change, especially in the southern business community.

Finally, leading segregationists never offered a plausible vision of a successful outcome. In strategic terms, they had no "theory of victory" they could place before their followers and others. In attempting to come up with one, they sometimes appeared profoundly irrational, as when the Citizens' Council backed a Senate bill calling for the "voluntary repatriation in [sic] Africa of those Negroes who wish to leave the country." An Alabama legislator sought to ban a children's book about the marriage of two rabbits, one white, one black. Even more absurdly, on June 14, 1963—that is, Flag Day—Black children in Jackson, Mississippi, were arrested for carrying small American flags. This was because the town had banned all public displays by Black people. It was barely a blip in the history of the Movement, yet its very extremity captures a strategic point: a policy that forbade American children to wave the flag of their country was the fruit of a doomed point of view.

All this meant that there was never a clear path forward for white resistance. The sole hope was to wear down the enemy and prevail through attrition. A strategy of that sort is not necessarily doomed. For example, it can succeed if it is based on an overwhelming advantage in people and other resources, as the United States, Britain, and the Soviet Union enjoyed when facing Germany and Japan during World War II. But when one lacks the advantage in resources, an attritive approach is most often a recipe for a long, slow, bitter, retrograde action, like the one the overmatched Nazis waged long after it was clear that their defeat was inevitable.

The national effect of the Freedom Rides

The Freedom Rides were more than a successful regional raid. They also had a national effect of attracting new recruits to the cause. We are so accustomed nowadays to stable systems of raising a military force that we tend to forget that one goal of a battle can be to attract new soldiers and to rally people to the cause, as it indeed was for George Washington when he surprised the Hessian garrison in Trenton, New Jersey, at the end of 1776. Likewise, the Freedom Rides caught the attention of young people across the country. Hollis Watkins, a young Black refugee from rural Mississippi, was looking for work in Los Angeles when he saw the Freedom Riders on television. "I felt that I wanted to check them out and find out what they were about," he recalled, so he went back home to Mississippi, where he ran into Bob Moses. The charismatic young teacher was by then working almost alone for the NAACP on voter registration. Watkins signed on to help Moses.

After the Freedom Rides, the civil rights movement began to feel different. "It was the first time that we had put out a national call for people to come south and support and participate in the civil rights movement," recalled Diane Nash. "It moved the movement to a dimension of a national effort." A lesson here was that, like it or not, the presence of white faces being slugged got national attention. The harsh fact was that white lives mattered to the media more than Black lives did. Thus dealing with the media required great discipline on the part of the Movement: newspaper and television coverage was essential to making progress, yet the choices that journalists made often were inherently repellent, as they had a tendency to neglect violence against Blacks, considering it routine and expected, and so lacking in news value.

As it learned to deal with the media, at the end of 1961 the Movement was in an enviable strategic position: It was fighting in only one region of the country, but it was drawing on resources—people, money, and attention—from across the breadth of the United States. White supremacism, meanwhile, had only a regional base, the eleven states of the former Confederacy, and really could not even depend on support from the ones at the fringe. And though still present in the U.S. Congress, the segregationist power was steadily becoming more isolated. A study of roll call votes in Congress in 1957 found that there were essentially three political parties in America: Northern Democrats, Republicans, and the South.

The problems of success

Yet, as civil rights leaders would experience, success always brings its own problems. By going national, the small, intensively trained nonviolent force that arose in Nashville inevitably lost some of its robust self-discipline. Inviting hundreds of people less steeped in nonviolence, or perhaps not even committed to it at all, changed the feeling of the Movement. Armies learn to their sorrow that the addition of lots of new soldiers can have disruptive effects: The newcomers are not known to the old-timers. They are not trained the same way, and perhaps not trained as well. Most of all, they have not earned the trust of the more seasoned people they are joining. In military terms, this is called lack of horizontal cohesion. This adds friction, one of the reasons that war makes even easy things hard.

"I could see that discipline eroding," recalled John Lewis of the Movement at the end of 1961, "crumbling a little at the edge where the outsiders were stepping in." Consider Stokely Carmichael, a volunteer who later would attain national prominence but was then just a premed student from Howard University. He invited violence on a Nashville picket line, Lewis said, "outright daring the white hecklers to attack him." As it became a mass force, the Movement was less able to intensively train newcomers. It was a problem that would only worsen with time. The more people the Movement attracted, the less nested it was in the kind of enormously effective self-control that had been displayed by Lawson's followers in the Nashville sit-ins. Lawson looked into Carmichael's behavior at demonstrations and then, he recalled, "we booted him out of Nashville." Carmichael's own recollection, a bit hazier, was that Lawson presided over a formal review of Carmichael's behavior but that the tribunal did not reach a conclusion.

King himself seems to have been a bit confused at this time about what he was to do. At one point he seriously considered playing the role of a U.S. senator in Otto Preminger's film *Advise and Consent*. Indeed, he had sought and received the permission of the SCLC's administrative committee to do so. He dropped the idea after newspapers began mentioning it. King might have entertained the notion because it would bring money to the SCLC, but even flirting with it was a basic mistake. Had he asked himself that first defining question of strategy— Who am I, and what am I trying to do?—he would not have considered such an offer. He was not a creature of Hollywood. Yet he lacked people around him who could tell him that he should not even consider a role that would project that sort of image. Ralph Abernathy appears not to have called him on it. Wyatt Walker, the SCLC's executive director from 1960 to 1964, was an effective tactician but not a reliable strategic thinker. Bayard Rustin could think strategically with the best, but for several reasons he had grown distant from King around this time.

In this small incident there was a larger lesson. King needed the calculated insights of people like Diane Nash and James Bevel. He would have it later, in Birmingham and Selma. But he did not have it yet, and that lack would hurt him in his next campaign.

4.
THE ALBANY MOVEMENT, 1961–1962

Stymied by an Adaptive Adversary

E arly battles in war often are most valuable as learning experiences. Those first encounters sometimes explode long-held but unexamined expectations. The harsh calculus of combat also sometimes clarifies who is a real leader and who just talks a good game. But early battles also can be misleading, especially if they are more successful than expected. Thus in the fall of 1961, the situation for the civil rights movement was a bit like the beginning of the American Revolution. In 1775, the American rebels had done unexpectedly well at Lexington and Concord, and then at Bunker Hill, with the result that they went into the campaign in and around New York City the following year overconfident of their abilities. Likewise, the civil rights movement overestimated itself going into the obscure southwestern Georgia town of Albany in the fall of 1961. It was not as strong as it thought, and the goals it set there were far too ambitious.

Like many battles, the confrontation in Albany began almost accidentally. At a meeting at the Highlander Folk School, the Student Nonviolent Coordinating Committee, which was just over a year old, assigned Charles Sherrod, one of its young and untested field secretaries, to go into Terrell County, Georgia, to conduct a voter registration campaign. That assignment proved even tougher than expected. "I couldn't do anything in Terrell County," Sherrod later said. "Those people were scared to death." Sherrod retreated to nearby Albany, which he found a bit more accommodating. Also, the town's population of about fifty thousand made it easier for him to disappear among the 40 percent who were Black. Local students were intrigued by his talks about changing the racial dynamic in the town. Sherrod was joined by Cordell Reagon, SNCC's youngest staffer, who had joined the Nashville sit-ins as a high school student and in 1961 was still only eighteen years old.

On November 1, 1961, the day that the Interstate Commerce Commission was supposed to start enforcing tougher rules against segregation in interstate bus terminals, Sherrod and Reagon sent a group of students into the "whites only" section of the town's bus station. They then put together a coalition of groups called the Albany Movement with the announced purpose to desegregate the entire town. The students were then expelled from school, a punishment that provided Sherrod with an instant staff. "They had nothing else to do," he recalled, "so we used them to spread out even wider."

Like most southern towns, Albany was utterly segregated, with no Black police officers, no Black officials, and no Black clerks in downtown stores. Sherrod and his local allies tackled this entire system. As the historian Aldon Morris puts it, "The goals of the Albany movement differed drastically from those of previous movements: This movement, it was decided, would end all forms of racial domination in Albany. Demonstrations were to be held against segregated buses, libraries, bowling alleys, restaurants, swimming pools, and other facilities." The military term for setting goals that are too big is "overreach."

The Albany Movement's far-reaching ambitions were based partly on a strategic miscalculation. "Some of us really didn't think they would get arrested, because this was a federal mandate," recalled Sherrod. "Nobody is gonna mess with the federal government, we thought." To be blunt, SNCC's people were operating on some unexamined assumptions, always dangerous in warfare or other forms of disruptive conflict. An essential part of devising strategy is looking deeply at one's understanding of the situation: When we take an action what do we think will happen? Why do we think that? What evidence supports that view, and what other information challenges it? In Albany, the civil rights movement would learn hard lessons about the need to address those questions.

There was one other looming problem for Sherrod and Reagon. The Albany chief of police, Laurie Pritchett, at the age of thirty-four, was both relatively young and unusually well educated for a southern cop, with some college and also some professional training. He would prove to be tactically adaptive in dealing with SNCC.

Chief Pritchett's plan

Through November and into December, SNCC's local recruits demonstrated and the police arrested them. SNCC demonstrated again against the trials of those arrested. At those actions, the police made more arrests. The more people SNCC threw into the fight, the more arrests Chief Pritchett made, far beyond the capacity of his own jail. In most cases, this pattern of growing detentions would swamp the system and thus provide at least a momentary victory for the Movement.

But Pritchett had a plan. After learning that his town would be the target of a civil rights campaign, he sat down and studied how the Movement worked. He discerned that its two major tools were the use of nonviolence and the use of being arrested and declining bail to overwhelm a town's jail system. To counter the tactics of nonviolence, Pritchett ordered his men to handle protesters with respect and even gentleness. To prevent the city jail from being flooded, he researched all locations where people could be held within a radius of fifty to sixty miles from Albany. "So when these mass marches started, we were well prepared," he explained. When he arrested demonstrators, he would charge them not with violating segregation laws, which would invite a legal challenge to those laws, but with charges such as disturbing the peace or unlawful assembly. Together, these three steps—acting gently, relocating prisoners, and avoiding legal challenges—relieved pressure on the city government to negotiate. By contrast, SNCC, a new organization, had neither much of a plan nor sufficient resources, such as bail money on hand and lawyers standing by, both of which would come to be considered essential in subsequent operations.

And so the situation ground on, with demonstrations mounted and arrests made. One of the most accurate statements made about war is that it consists of long stretches of boredom punctuated by moments of sheer terror. Days in the trenches or on patrols pass with hardly an event worth noticing, and then in mere moments the world can become a chaotic swirl of gunfire, shouts, and movement. Keeping attentive during the long, often dull lulls requires discipline. The life of the civil rights activist was similar. John Lewis records that it consisted of "days and days of uneventful protest that took place outside . . . courtrooms and jails. People silently walked a picket line for hours on end, or simply stood in line at a [voter registration] door they knew would not be opened, hour after hour, day after day. . . . Waiting. Keeping the pressure on by simply maintaining a relentless presence." Again, to do this requires steady persistence.

By mid-December 1961, more than five hundred demonstrators were being held in the environs of Albany. At about this point, the Albany Movement ground to a halt. Bill Hansen, a SNCC worker in the town, said, "We ran out of people before he [Pritchett] ran out of jails." Among those behind bars were Sherrod and Reagon, SNCC's two local leaders. While they were out of touch, other leaders of the Albany Movement, led by William G. Anderson, a young Black doctor in the town who had become an ally, mulled the next move. "We were in a situation where we had several hundred people in jail, no bond money, people wanted to come out of jail and people had been fired off their job," explained Anderson. "We did not have money, we did not have a legal staff, we did not have any experienced civil rights workers."

Anderson had a bright idea. He called an old schoolmate named

Martin Luther King, Jr., and asked him to drive down to Albany and give a speech. King thought that it was just a visit, that he would give the speech and then head back home, but when his talk ended, Anderson announced that King would lead a march the next morning. "Martin felt like he'd been put in a trick," recalled King's aide Andrew Young. "He had not come to lead a movement, but only out of friendship for Dr. Anderson." One can only wonder if there is an element of postmortem regret in Young's account. After all, King largely had been a bystander to the sit-ins and Freedom Rides, and may have felt it was time to get back into the thick of the civil rights fight.

Chief Pritchett, an interesting figure, was intrigued by the Movement. At one point, much later, and deep into the campaign, he was meeting with King when an aide came in to hand him a telegram. The chief read it and looked bothered. King asked if everything was okay. Pritchett told him that the telegram was from his wife, reminding him that the day was their wedding anniversary. He explained that during the demonstrations he had been staying downtown and hadn't seen his wife in weeks. According to Pritchett, King responded, "You go home, take your wife out to dinner. Enjoy yourself. Nothing would happen in Albany, Georgia today or tonight. In the morning at eight o'clock, we'll take up where we leave off." It was a human moment that shows King following the Gandhian principle of attacking the system, not the person, and so trying to avoid imposing unnecessary problems on your foe. For example, in India, Gandhi's followers once had postponed a planned action when they realized it would conflict with the British occupiers' observance of Easter Sunday.

King and two hundred others marched and by December 17, 1961, were arrested and jailed for parading without a permit. A total of seven hundred activists were now behind bars. But jailing King in Albany, Georgia, meant less than it did in other campaigns. The problem in Albany, in Andrew Young's analysis, was that King's presence tended to be effective because of all the preliminary work that usually accompanied it—that is, organizing marches, holding meetings to recruit people, and then training them. The Albany leaders, he said, mistakenly had believed that "a spontaneous appearance by Martin Luther King could bring change," not grasping "that it wasn't just a spontaneous appearance by Martin Luther King, it was the planning, the organizing, the strategy that he brought with him, that brought change."

At this point the Albany story becomes murky, with several different accounts appearing in various histories. One version is that King, in an incautious moment, supposedly vowed that he would stay jailed until there was an agreement to desegregate the city. The city then offered an unwritten "truce" under which almost all protesters would be freed, all bond money would be returned, the city buses would be desegregated, and a biracial committee would be formed to study further steps. In return for this, King would agree to leave town. Nothing was put in writing, which made King suspicious. But Anderson, the local leader who was his friend, assured him that the offer was a good one. In any event, the "truce" terms soon evaporated, and nothing changed.

Another version, endorsed by Taylor Branch, an encyclopedic historian, is that King told reporters through the bars of his cell that he would not accept bond and expected to spend Christmas in jail. This was taken by one reporter as meaning that King planned to remain in jail "as long as necessary." Meanwhile, Anderson, a novice in protest and imprisonment, was suffering a mental breakdown, calling King "Jesus" and hallucinating about "extraterrestrial events." King and Abernathy decided it was essential to get Anderson out of jail, but he would not leave without them. Anderson's condition may have provided King, who as noted earlier had an understandable fear of being behind bars in southern jails, with a convenient excuse for leaving confinement.

King and the jail problem, again

In July 1962, King had to return to Albany to face the charges from the previous December. In the meantime, the protests in the town had continued without much change or progress.

Nerves were tight. Chief Pritchett appeared at the door of a church where a mass meeting was being held. When his presence was noted from the podium, he was invited to speak. He accepted the challenge. He began by thanking the church for welcoming him. "Many people misunderstand your policy of non-violence, but we respect your policy," he said, speaking from where he was standing. "I ask your cooperation in keeping Albany peaceful." Pat Watters, a reporter who witnessed this unusual event, thought that Pritchett enjoyed dealing with the Movement and found it a relief from the daily drudgery of running a police force.

To be sure, from another perspective, Pritchett was "a sophisticated segregationist," as Ralph Abernathy put it. John Lewis called him "a cunning man, as deceitful as he had to be." Yet in 1966, when Pritchett was seeking to become the chief of police in High Point, North Carolina, a suburb of Greensboro, Andrew Young "took the leap and gave him a good recommendation on race matters."

Pritchett, ever alert to points of vulnerability in his opposition, and perhaps relying on inside intelligence from moles, had noticed the squabbling between leaders of the SCLC, SNCC, and the NAACP. King was sentenced to a choice between a $178 fine or forty-five days in jail, and chose to serve the term. But just three days into it, his fine was paid by someone who has never been identified. Pritchett privately had wanted King out. "I knew that if he stayed in jail," Pritchett said, "we'd continue to have problems, so I talked to some people. I said, we've got to get him out."

According to Pritchett, King said he didn't want to leave jail, saying, "I'll lose face if I go." Pritchett told him he had to go.

King later wrote that Pritchett used "the moral means of nonviolence to maintain the immoral ends of racial injustice." King managed to get back in Pritchett's jail by the end of the month, but by then the Albany Movement began to run out of steam. After that third arrest in Albany, he agreed to stop demonstrating and to leave town.

"In the end, the Albany movement wound down inconclusively," wrote Andrew Young, "without us winning any substantial or noteworthy achievements." Some demonstrations continued, but in far smaller numbers. It was a messy situation. "Dr. King vowed to refuse bail on two occasions, December 1961 and July 1962. However, because of extraordinary circumstances, he failed to honor the pledge," states the historian Barry Everett Lee, in a judgment that may be too harsh. King may have done the best he could when facing an unexpectedly cunning adversary.

Organizational rivalries fester

Nothing provokes internal friction as much as does failure. King, Abernathy, and the SCLC felt that SNCC had bitten off more than it could chew in Albany and needed to be helped out by the more mature people from the SCLC. King, they felt, was being treated as a resource to be tapped to solve SNCC's problems. "In Albany, we were like firefighters," said Wyatt Tee Walker, the executive director of the SCLC, and effectively King's chief of staff at the time. "The fire was already burning, and I try to say this as charitably as I can: SNCC was in over its head. And they wanted the international and national attention that Martin Luther King's presence would generate, but they did not want the input of his organization."

SNCC's leaders in the town, by contrast, felt that King and his cohort came in and tried to take over the campaign. They especially disliked Walker's authoritarian style. "People who had done the fighting felt they were being given a back seat," said Marion Page, executive secretary of the Albany Movement. "We were trying to get up, then, the hugest demonstration ever, but the air went out."

Both viewpoints may have been accurate. The failure in leadership on both sides came in them not finding a way to address their differences. But to do that requires trust. King's erratic handling of being jailed probably undercut that valuable commodity in this circumstance. With confidence in leadership, armies and other organizations can perform extraordinary feats. Without it, even small tasks become difficult. King seemed to come away with a new recognition that he needed to handle campaigning better. He had been pulled into a campaign without adequate planning or preparation, or an understanding of what he was being asked to do, or of the forces arrayed against him. "When Martin left Albany, he was very depressed," Andrew Young recalled.

SNCC's Charles Sherrod, for his part, would insist for the rest of his life that the Albany Movement had not failed. "We needed to make certain mistakes, . . . to retreat and then come back again," he maintained. "It was a war. Though it was a non-violent war, but it was indeed a war." Eventually, he noted, Albany was integrated because of the passage of the Civil Rights Act in 1964. "Where's the failure?" he asked. However, in retrospect, he also conceded, "We didn't know what we were doing."

The conclusion of Anderson, the local leader of the Albany Movement, was simpler, and probably closer to the mark: "We were inexperienced as civil rights activists." Indeed, the Albany campaign bears a resemblance to the first battle of Bull Run, which took place one hundred years earlier, in 1861. In this first battle of the Civil War, Union forces, badly led and undertrained, but confident they would prevail, clashed with the Confederates in Virginia, about thirty miles southwest of Washington, D.C. It did not end well for the North. The main lesson the soldiers took away from the battle as they retreated was that the conflict would not be won in an afternoon. Some may also have realized that they had a lot to learn about making war.

Learning from Albany

Agile leaders use failures as opportunities to reexamine their strategy and tactics. After being defeated in New York City in the late summer and fall of 1776, George Washington began to reconsider his approach to fighting the British. Likewise, after Albany, King decided that the entire campaign had been too diffuse, going after the entire system of segregation, and should have had specific targets, such as integrating lunch counters or confronting stores that did not hire Black clerks.

"The mistake I made there," he later said about Albany, "was to protest against segregation generally rather than against a single and distinct facet of it."

There were some victories, he said, in that many Blacks in Albany did register to vote, and the Black population gained a new sense of dignity. Even so, the Movement learned in Albany to choose its fights more carefully. As King put it, "When we planned our strategy for Birmingham months later, we spent many hours assessing Albany and trying to learn from its errors." Septima Clark, a wise observer of the Movement as well as one of its leading trainers, once commented, "Just think of how much Martin Luther King, Jr., grew in his life. That was the greatest thing about him."

After Albany, the Movement never again would seek a confrontation with a sheriff or police chief adept enough to adapt his response to the Movement and neutralize its tactics. What the Movement needed to target was not a thoughtful official who tried neutrally and respectfully to enforce the law, but an ogre who treated the race conflict as a gang war and who saw nothing wrong about collaborating with the Ku Klux Klan. In Birmingham and Selma there waited two law enforcement officials with just that sort of dogged, brutal mindset.

King's people also would plan long and hard before going into Birmingham. Albany had taught them, noted Andrew Young, that "passion and enthusiasm were no substitute for sound, strategic planning. . . . When people operated purely on emotion, without organization and planning, it simply didn't work." This is a lesson that militaries learn again and again: dash and vigor are generally attractive assets, but they are no substitute for robust organizing, thoughtful planning, and intense training. The gods of battle are not romantics; they are unforgiving stoics.

5.
OLE MISS, 1962

A Racial Confrontation That Lacked Movement Input

On the warm afternoon of September 20, 1962, James Meredith, escorted by federal marshals, arrived at the Lyceum, the oldest building on the campus of the University of Mississippi, its construction having begun in 1846. Inside he was confronted by Mississippi governor Ross Barnett, the son of a Confederate veteran. "I want to register at the university," stated Meredith, a Black veteran of the U.S. Air Force. Barnett responded by reading aloud a proclamation asserting that, as governor, he had the right to ignore a federal judge and so was denying admission to Meredith. So began "the battle of Oxford."

The confrontation between the Kennedy administration and the Mississippi state government over the enrollment of Meredith was, in retrospect, a sideshow in the history of the civil rights movement. But for the purposes of this study, it is worth stopping to examine because it provides an unusual and instructive example of how a racial confrontation during this era unfolded when no leaders of the Movement were present or involved. In many ways, the major lesson of the Ole Miss incident lies in who was not there and, as a consequence, what did not happen.

The contrast between the Ole Miss fight and formal civil rights campaigns is instructive. Movement leaders brought a seriousness of mind to their campaigns, with advance planning, training, role-playing, and rehearsals. They mapped out the terrain and even made contact with their antagonists, to allow key issues to be discussed before emotions grew hot and to give everyone a sense of how the crisis might be resolved. What is most striking about the incident at Ole Miss is that none of that sort of careful preparation occurred. Instead, both sides improvised as they went along, with ugly consequences. Snap decisions led to a series of blunders that made both the federal government and the government of Mississippi look oafish. The theory of nonviolence was conspicuously absent, with both sides relying on brute force. The incident degenerated into what is known in American military parlance as a shitshow.

It began badly, as a grudge match between the U.S. attorney general, Robert Kennedy, and the state's governor, Ross Barnett. A year earlier, as discussed in chapter 3, Barnett had tied Kennedy in knots during the Freedom Rides. In a surprising retreat, Kennedy had wound up agreeing to the violation of the Riders' constitutional rights simply in order to stop public bloodshed. Effectively, because of Kennedy's waffling, the threat of segregationist violence had been allowed to prevail.

Now, sixteen months later, Kennedy and Barnett faced off again over a racial issue—in this case, the admission of Meredith to the University of Mississippi. To a surprising degree, the civil rights movement was uninvolved in this showdown. Its leaders saw Meredith as an irascible loner, not a member of any group, and not working in conjunction with them except to seek legal support from the NAACP. Even so, the national media portrayed the situation at Ole Miss as part and parcel of the civil rights movement.

Meredith indeed was an odd figure. He saw himself as a soldier in an army—but his was an army of one. Isolated and mistrustful, he never associated with the Movement as such. When the NAACP's Thurgood Marshall tried to determine in a telephone conversation whether Meredith had the character needed to persevere in a test case, Meredith hung up on him. Meredith in reality possessed a single-mindedness that would enable him to endure a monthslong ordeal. "I was at war," he said later, "and everything I did I considered an act of war." Truth be told, Meredith resembled the prickly dissidents who challenged the Soviet Union in the 1960s and 1970s, which was appropriate, because the state of Mississippi was as close as a part of the United States has ever come to having a totalitarian regime. Medgar Evers, the NAACP's top official in Mississippi, and himself a man of great courage, said of Meredith, "He's got more guts than any man I know, but he's the hardest-headed son-of-a-gun I ever met. The more you disagreed with him the more he became convinced that he—and he alone—was right." Indeed, in a memoir of his time in Mississippi, Meredith would make an astonishing assertion: "I have never made a mistake in my life, because I never make arbitrary or predetermined decisions." And he was determined to enroll at Ole Miss.

A charade of resistance turns real

The University of Mississippi, located in the town of Oxford, in the northern part of the state, was wrapped in the myths by which the unrepentant Old South lived. During the Civil War, almost its entire student body had enrolled in the Confederate Army, forming the A Company of the 11th Mississippi Regiment. That unit suffered a 100 percent casualty rate during Pickett's Charge, the doomed culminating action of the battle of Gettysburg on July 3, 1863. The school's nickname, which dates back to the Jim Crow period, appears to be a reference to the manner in which enslaved people sometimes addressed the wife of the owner of a plantation—the old mistress, or "ole miss." As one booster rhapsodized in 1932, Ole Miss evoked "the romance, the chivalry, the beauty, the culture, the graciousness and the finest traditions of the Southland." Not much had changed in 1961, when the student yearbook portrayed the campus as "the land of mint juleps and antebellum columns" where "you can lean back after the sun sets on the levee, cast away all those earthly cares, and listen as the darkies sing softly in the moonlight." It was a false image, a dominant-caste fairy tale. Yet people cling to their cherished myths and often are willing to spill blood to defend them. They can live without facts but apparently not without beliefs, however false.

Of the many odd facts about the University of Mississippi, the most relevant in 1962 was that enrolling there was forbidden to 43 percent of the state's citizens, because they happened to be Black. James Meredith was not the first to try to enroll in an all-white public institution in the state. Two Black Mississippians had tried before, with one being shipped to an insane asylum and the other to the state penitentiary at Parchman Farm on a seven-year sentence for allegedly stealing $25 worth of chickenfeed. Meredith had been fighting an eighteen-month-long legal battle that culminated on September 10, 1962, with a ruling from Supreme Court justice Hugo Black—himself a former member of the Ku Klux Klan in Alabama—that effectively ordered the University of Mississippi to admit Meredith.

On the night of September 20, after Barnett denied admission to Meredith, the Justice Department filed contempt-of-court charges against two university officials for not complying with Justice Black's order. A lawyer for the university, seeking guidance from Barnett, was surprised to hear the governor reply, "I'm bluffing. But you wait and see. I'll bluff the Justice Department into backing down." Put simply, Barnett had no plan; he was making it up as he went along. What he was looking for was to maintain segregation at Ole Miss, at best, and not to be blamed for it if, at worst, integration occurred. "He knew that Meredith was going to the University of Mississippi," said Burke Marshall, of the Justice Department. "He just didn't want it to be his fault."

Complicating matters, Robert Kennedy was also making it up as he went along. On September 25, Kennedy told federal officials to try a new ploy by taking Meredith to the university's office in the Mississippi capital of Jackson and registering him there. Barnett went to that office, however, and again refused admission to Meredith.

The next day, the federal marshals took Meredith back to the Ole Miss campus, where he once again was denied entry, this time by the lieutenant governor, substituting for Barnett, whose aircraft was unable to fly to Oxford because of fog.

On September 27, the federal officials again moved Meredith toward the campus. Barnett at this point proposed to the federal government that he stage a charade under which all the federal marshals would draw their weapons on him, and he then would step aside. But as negotiations continued between Barnett and the Kennedy administration, the situation on the campus was becoming more dangerous. The Oxford area was seeing an influx of Klansmen and vigilantes from across the South, some of them toting pistols and hunting rifles. The situation looked so volatile that the attorney general ordered the federal caravan of cars carrying Meredith toward Oxford to stop and head instead to Memphis, Tennessee, where Meredith was housed in a Navy installation on the outskirts of town—not just on federal land, but in another state, well beyond the reach of Mississippi law enforcement officials. The administration then began notifying the 82nd Airborne Division and some other Army units that they might be needed in the coming days.

Meantime, Barnett came up with yet another plan: Meredith could quietly register in Jackson, and Barnett would feign surprise but allow him to begin attending classes. But then, on September 30, the governor changed his mind following an emotional experience: he attended an Ole Miss football game and was cheered by tens of thousands as he exclaimed, at halftime, "I love Mississippi! I love her people! Our customs! I love and respect our heritage!" After that exuberant moment, he rescinded his decoy plan and went back to advocating the "drawn guns" plan. "I have to be confronted with your troops," he informed Robert Kennedy.

But the attorney general rejected that as too risky, a situation that easily could get out of hand with all the firearms pouring into town. Losing patience, Kennedy threatened to have the president, John F. Kennedy, tell the world on television about Barnett's sneaky plan to have Meredith registered quietly. Barnett, feeling cornered, came up with a counteroffer: he suggested that Meredith be registered that afternoon, even though it was a Sunday. The attorney general, improvising as if he were playing touch football, agreed to this last-minute proposal. He then set the U.S. Army scrambling to get in place to back up the small force of federal marshals who would escort Meredith. But Barnett did not spread the word to state officials about the quiet deal he had made.

The battle of Oxford

In the battle of Oxford, thousands of white segregationists would confront the federal forces on and around the campus. By the time the sun came up on Monday, more than a hundred of the federal representatives would be injured, and two onlookers—a foreign reporter and a local man—would lie dead.

A force of 125 U.S. deputy marshals, augmented by 300 Border Patrol officers and 97 federal prison guards, had been assembled at that small Naval station just outside Memphis, but not all of them were sent to the campus. Those deployed were hurried aboard Air Force C-130s for the short flight to the Oxford airport, where they were loaded onto seven Army trucks and driven to the campus, arriving at about four in the afternoon. A separate small group was sent to protect Meredith, with orders to shoot if he was attacked. The majority were under the direct control of U.S. deputy attorney general Nicholas Katzenbach, who was inside the Lyceum, which contained the office of the university's registrar.

But what to do with these federal newcomers? There were neither plans nor even a place set aside for them to eat and rest. This was the opposite of the meditative process the Movement was learning to use in order to form strategy and then develop a plan for direct action that would be a physical manifestation of that strategy. Katzenbach, the senior federal official on the scene, asked George Yarbrough, the president pro tem of the Mississippi state senate, who was there representing Governor Barnett, if he could put the marshals in the gym building, where their presence would not be provocative, a "red flag," as Katzenbach thought of it. Yarbrough did not agree to that request. He also told the federal officials, "You have occupied this university and now you can have it." To that end, he said, he was preparing to order the state highway patrolmen to withdraw from the campus. "As soon as the highway patrol drove out, it was almost as though that was a signal to people for the riot to begin," recalled Katzenbach.

Lacking a plan, writes the historian William Doyle, "Katzenbach decided simply to line his men up around the Lyceum." Without any preparation for what they should do once they were in place, the marshals formed a defensive semicircle around the front of the Lyceum. Standing shoulder to shoulder, they covered the front of the building and most of its two sides. It was, in military terms, a show of force.

The problem with shows of force is that they can be interpreted by the adversary as a challenge. For that reason, it is unwise to mount such a display when one is outnumbered, because doing so all but invites attack. There were more than a thousand people milling outside the administration building, many of them armed. Indeed, at one point there may have been 2,500. The crowd started "to get mean and get ugly," said John Doar, a Justice Department official who was inside the building.

Nor did the federal forces have on hand what a unit prepared to control a riot normally would possess. "We were sent in unprepared, with nowhere near the equipment we should have had," recalled one marshal. Doyle lists the missing articles: "a public-address truck, mobile telephones, bullhorns, walkie-talkies, floodlights and generators, oxygen equipment, police barriers, flak jackets, stretchers, first-aid equipment, and backup supplies of gas." Doyle does not mention it, but any serious riot control effort also would be supported by officers and detachments specializing in communications, intelligence, and co-ordinating action between units. Such an effort also would have placed snipers atop buildings, both to deny the use of rooftops to the other side and to protect exposed comrades below. This is a basic tactical step in military operations: never place soldiers in a vulnerable, visible position without having someone else watching over them. Indeed, the snipers providing overwatch also would need other soldiers to watch their own backs and the doors accessing the rooftops while the sharp-shooters focus on the action below. Experienced sergeants and officers would be put in place to coordinate these protective operations. Mean-while, farther away, staff officers would track the situation, monitoring troop locations and supply problems, and communicate with aides at the White House, which would free up the president and the attorney general to think about the larger picture. Done right, riot control work gets complicated very quickly, as it balances on the knife edge between police operations and military combat.

But the marshals and other officials standing outside the Lyceum in their prominent white helmets and orange vests had little more at hand than tear gas and some concealed pistols. Nor did any university officials appear to try to control or restrain the crowd, which as the sun went down was quickly degenerating into a mob. When darkness fell, "the scene became a nightmare," recalled Charles Moore, a freelance photographer on assignment for *Life* magazine. "There was teargas floating on the air. We could hear shots being fired. Molotov cock-tails were being thrown. Cars in the crowd were set afire." Many of the people milling around the Lyceum assumed, incorrectly, that Meredith was inside it. The mob closed in on the federal officers, throwing rocks and lighted Coca-Cola bottles filled with gasoline. Just before eight o'clock, the marshals began to respond with tear gas. Soon the federal supply of that weapon began to run low.

There really was an Army general present that night—but he was there to resist the federal government. Around nine o'clock, the recently retired Major General Edwin Walker, a complex hard-right racist, ap-peared on campus and stood at the base of the Confederate monument outside the Lyceum. "Keep it up all night," he urged the crowd. "We've got more people coming." (Seven months later, oddly enough, Lee Harvey Oswald would take a shot at Walker, just missing him. And seven months after that, of course, Oswald would shoot and kill President Kennedy.) After Walker's pep talk, the crowd surged forward.

Inside the Lyceum, behind the marshals, Katzenbach's communications system to the White House consisted of a pay phone in a hallway that he kept open with a collect call. Every time the front door was opened, shots were fired at it. The federal law enforcement officials moved in and out by crawling on their stomachs. Katzenbach had experienced combat—he had been a bomber navigator during World War II, and had been shot down and held as a prisoner of war, even participating as a helper in what became known as "the Great Escape" from Stalag Luft III. Katzenbach heard gunshots coming in. Just after ten, he told Robert Kennedy that his men could not hold by themselves, and that the Army should be brought in. But that was easier said than done. "Getting the Army from Memphis to Oxford became a comedy of errors and made a long night even longer," he wrote decades later. Some Army units driving in convoys from Memphis were confronted at the Mississippi state line by highway patrol roadblocks. With no time to negotiate, the soldiers used their trucks to push aside the police cars.

In the meantime, at around 10:30 that night, an Oxford-based unit of the Mississippi National Guard, which had been "federalized"— essentially, taken over by the president—arrived on campus. These local men were shocked to find themselves under attack by the mob. The Guard unit was commanded by Captain Murry Falkner, a nephew of the novelist William Faulkner, who spelled his name differently. Falkner and his little convoy of three jeeps and four trucks drove through and over improvised barricades of park benches while being shot at and hit by bricks. Falkner later found in his vehicle seven bricks, along with an unexploded Molotov cocktail, and a bullet hole in the radiator.

Fortunately for historians, President Kennedy had a taping system working in the White House that night, capturing both his meetings and the conversations he and Robert Kennedy had with Governor

Barnett. "I haven't had such an interesting time since the Bay of Pigs," the president sardonically remarked at one point, referring to the botched CIA-led effort in April 1961 to invade Cuba and oust Fidel Castro. Reading the transcripts of deliberations at the White House that evening, it is striking that the president and his aides had no plan and no backup troops waiting nearby. They also had neglected to establish a communications network, especially with Army units on the move. Faced with all these problems, they did what overwhelmed commanders often do, which is to regress from the strategic level, where they generally should have been—asking the hard questions about what they are trying to accomplish—and instead dwelled overmuch on tactical problems. They repeatedly discussed small-scale issues such as when the resupply of tear gas to the marshals would occur. These are pieces of the puzzle that should have been tracked continually by staffers plugged into a group of liaison officers. But the Kennedys had failed to establish such a supporting net. So, as often happens with micromanagers, they blamed the people and organizations reporting to them. "Damn Army!" Robert Kennedy exclaimed at one point. "They can't even tell if . . . the MPs have left yet"—that is, the military police unit actually trained for operations such as riot control.

Around 2:15 a.m., that much-needed company of regular military police soldiers arrived on the campus. For the first time in the incident, there was a unit actually trained and prepared for the task at hand. The mob greeted them with Molotov cocktails. The MPs watched the bombs arc toward them and then marched through the resulting flames with bayonets fixed to their rifles. Each soldier carried a loaded M-1, as well as 180 rounds to spare. Some had riot-control shotguns. The MPs also delivered another surprise: some of them were Black, which shocked members of the crowd. The MPs reinforced the besieged marshals, and then began launching small counterattacks, pushing the rioters off the campus. One later-arriving unit, settling in on the edge of the campus, shot out the streetlights along an adjacent highway and dug foxholes in the lawns of houses to protect themselves from shooting coming from cars on that road.

Over the course of the night, twenty-six marshals were hit by gun-fire, one in the throat. Many had been peppered by shotgun pellets. Well over a hundred other marshals were injured by rocks, cinder blocks, pieces of park benches, and other thrown objects. In addition, forty-eight soldiers reported injuries needing treatment. No members of the mob were ever convicted of a crime.

At dawn on Monday, October 1, the riot was essentially over. On the shocked campus, bedecked with burned cars, smashed park benches, and tear gas lingering in the air, James Meredith registered and then went to his first class. John Doar, one of the Justice Department officials, said he "had no feeling of elation about what had been accomplished. It just seemed to me that . . . it was just another step in a long, long effort to break the caste system."

But Klansmen and their allies still were converging on Oxford, so the Kennedy administration continued to pour Army units into the area. By the middle of the week, those thousands of soldiers outnumbered local citizens by a two-to-one ratio. President Kennedy had General Walker arrested on charges of seditious conspiracy and insurrection, but a federal grand jury would decline to indict him. The president also contemplated detaining Governor Barnett, but ultimately dropped that idea.

Two weeks later, the Kennedy administration lurched into the Cuban Missile Crisis, a standoff with a nuclear superpower, and the confrontation at Ole Miss was all but forgotten.

A lack of understanding

Katzenbach, the Justice Department official who had been the federal commander on the ground at Ole Miss, later recalled that Hugo Black, the Supreme Court justice whose order had set in train the Ole Miss incident, told him more than once, "Neither you nor Bobby [Kennedy] understand the South." This was one point on which all parties in the South seemed to agree. Robert Kennedy in particular "was very naïve about the South," concluded Andrew Young, who effectively served as Martin Luther King, Jr.'s emissary to the dominant caste. In the first two years of the Kennedy administration, he said, both Robert and his brother "really didn't know how to deal with the civil rights movement."

The Kennedy administration especially thought it should be in charge of events. But it was not. The Kennedy brothers were surprisingly slow to realize that they were not driving events, but instead reacting to them. The civil rights movement was in large part a battle for public opinion. The American people watched the fight on television and were pulled in by it. Public opinion began to focus on civil rights as a major issue in the country.

The Kennedy administration was hardly alone in not comprehending the civil rights movement. Justice Black notwithstanding, southern officials often were even more perplexed by it. The Movement acted more quickly than they could follow, and the way its leaders thought about the world was often beyond the ken of older white male officials accustomed to a world where their views and instructions went unquestioned by Black people. For example, James Bevel and Diane Nash married in the fall of 1961, and the following spring, Russell Moore, a judge in Mississippi, trying to act humanely, quizzed Bevel about why he would stand by while his heavily pregnant wife insisted on serving a two-year sentence in the state's primitive jails. Nash herself responded that a Black child born anywhere in Mississippi was born imprisoned.

"You know, son," Moore told Bevel, "you people are insane."

"Judge Moore, you don't understand Christianity," Bevel replied. "All the early Christians went to jail."

Significantly, the Bevel-Nash gambit worked: The judge chose to release Nash and simply ignore her prison sentence.

It was at about this time that the SCLC hired Bevel to become its field secretary for the state of Mississippi, focusing on voter registration in the Delta, to the west of Oxford. He found the going hard in the state. "We waited for the people of Mississippi to take up the fight. But nobody did," he recalled. "In Mississippi we'd come up on a people repressed. A people in silence." Amzie Moore and others had worked long and hard, but the state's Black population remained frozen under a near-totalitarian regime, with Blacks living under a constant threat of violence and no tolerance by the dominant caste for any form of dissent, Black or white.

That said, some southern officials clearly recognized that the presence of television cameras was changing the equation for them. "You are witnessing one more chapter in what has been termed the television revolution," Governor Barnett told NBC News. "Information media, including the TV networks, have publicized and dramatized the race issue far beyond its relative importance in today's world." The real issue, he argued, was not race but the growth of the power of the federal government. But then those two issues had always gone hand in hand in America. Back in 1818, North Carolina senator Nathaniel Macon had warned, "If Congress can make canals, they can with more propriety emancipate."

The missing ingredient at Ole Miss

There was one more crucial ingredient missing at Ole Miss. The Movement always tried to engage in the concluding step that civil rights leaders saw as essential: reconciliation. Without it, the fight was just sound and fury. The last step was the payoff for a campaign, the very purpose of the entire exercise. They sought to provoke a crisis that would force their foes to come to the negotiating table. There they would try to find a resolution, and after that they would take the last step of engaging in postcrisis efforts to bring the two sides together—not to love or embrace each other, but at least to find a peaceful way forward.

But the Movement approach was wholly absent in Oxford. Instead, after the battle of Ole Miss, both the government of Mississippi and the federal government simply stepped back from confrontation. In Gandhian terms, the Ole Miss incident concluded not in establishment of a new truth, but in a far lesser outcome, a cease-fire. In other words, it ended with a cessation of violence but not a creation of peace. There was no follow-up of the kind that King, Lawson, and others taught was essential, to remain in dialogue with the opponent and ensure that promises were kept.

The university's administrators, again derelict in their duty, left James Meredith to endure a year of harassment. Students yelled at him as he walked to classes. "Why doesn't somebody kill him?" one female student asked out loud as she watched him. The answer to her murderous query was that Meredith always had federal marshals or soldiers escorting him, or watching nearby. He also was protected by four marshals working undercover as students. He was generally shunned in the cafeteria. A handful of white students who one day sat down to eat at the same table as his were ostracized. At night, undergraduates would bounce basketballs in the dormitory room above his to interfere with his studies and sleep. The tires on his car were slashed and the antenna snapped off.

The result was something cruel and ugly, falling far short of genuine integration. "Most of the time, I am perhaps the most segregated Negro in the world," Meredith wrote. Underscoring the point, the editors of the college yearbook made no mention of Meredith, and printed no photographs of him. As one watching journalist put it, James Meredith was less a student than he was a "prisoner of war." Still, on August 19, 1963, he would receive his diploma from Ole Miss.

However, the absence of the civil rights movement at Ole Miss may have taught the Kennedy administration a vital and lasting lesson: the Movement might have been irritating to them, but the battle of Oxford had shown them that it was not the problem. It had not even been in the area. The Kennedys, inadvertently, had seen their consciousnesses raised. After Ole Miss, the president and his brother no longer would attempt to take a neutral stance aimed at finding a balancing point between the two sides. The executive branch of the federal government finally stood ready to become engaged. That meant in turn that Congress also would have to become involved. In the 1940s and 1950s, when the

NAACP had led the civil rights fight, it addressed mainly one branch of the federal government, the judiciary. But in 1963, all three branches would finally focus on racial justice, and that would prepare the way for the Movement's victory in winning bills on civil rights and voting rights that had some teeth in them to ensure they would be enforced.

6.

EARLY BIRMINGHAM, SPRING 1963

Putting Children on the Front Lines

A labama governor George Wallace, upon taking office in 1963, in-
famously declared, "I say, segregation now, segregation tomorrow,
segregation forever." Grandiosity in rhetoric is a sign that leaders
are detaching from reality. So James Bevel, hearing Wallace's wild talk,
assessed it, correctly, as more a wish than a promise. He recalled, "By
'63 we were pretty confident that we had developed a science that
would allow us to eradicate segregation."

Out of that confident assessment came Project C. Perhaps the organizers chose that name for its sheer obscurity, to shield their plans
from the prying eyes of the federal government, but even then there
was a poetry to it. Was it a project to "see"? Or a plan perhaps to part
the waters of the segregationist "sea"? The Birmingham minister Fred
Shuttlesworth, always inclined to the combative answer, said the "C"
stood for "confrontation." The history is a bit murky, because various
people have claimed credit for urging that Birmingham, Alabama, be
made the target of the next big civil rights campaign. Winning the
fight there would be the Movement's equivalent of the Union's victory
at Gettysburg during the Civil War, a turning point that had occurred
exactly one hundred years earlier.

Ultimately, however, whether intended or not, "C" would come to mean "children." The movement's campaign would bring all the heat of the moment to bear upon Birmingham, which King would label the most segregated city in America. "If you can break the back of segregation in Birmingham, Alabama, then you can break the back of segregation all over the nation," promised Shuttlesworth. That sounds grandiose, too—until one considers that his assessment ultimately proved correct.

In contemplating a campaign against Birmingham's white power structure the organizers knew they were tackling a tiger. At the end of a preliminary planning meeting, King warned, "Some of us are going to lose our lives in Birmingham." As dozens of histories note, the city's chronic violence had earned it the nickname "Bombingham." The city enforced segregation so rigorously that a 1930 ordinance made it illegal for Blacks and whites to play each other in checkers or dominoes.

Shuttlesworth vs. Connor

The battle of Birmingham would be typified by leaders in the city on either side: the Reverend Fred Shuttlesworth and the police overseer Theophilus Eugene "Bull" Connor.

Wiry and tough, Shuttlesworth is another civil rights leader who should be better known. There were people around King who "were far more learned than Fred Shuttlesworth," commented J. L. Chestnut, a Black lawyer in Alabama. "There weren't any there who were more courageous though." His house had first been bombed back in 1956, yet Shuttlesworth had kept on challenging the city's oppressive white power structure. As discussed in chapter 3, he also had come to the aid of the Freedom Riders after they were attacked in Anniston and Birmingham in 1961.

If King represented the nonviolent Christian approach, Shuttlesworth embodied the Black church militant. Preaching in June 1962, he proclaimed, "We believe that if we stand as Christians, if we contend for our rights as righteous soldiers in the Army of Christ, if we endure the hardness and madness of this hour . . . then in God's own time . . . He will do that which is right and give us the victory so help us God!" He then warned, "Our battle is hard but the end is not yet. There is yet much more land to be conquered." It is interesting that two leaders with such divergent viewpoints as Shuttlesworth and King were able to work together. Yes, they clashed, as will be seen later in this chapter, but they usually managed to find a way to combine their approaches effectively. It is the rare leader who is able to perceive value in such a sharply different person.

Shuttlesworth had battled the local police for years. The Birmingham police force posed a special problem, notable even in the South. It was led by Bull Connor, who had been born in Selma, Alabama, in July 1897. Connor was no Laurie Pritchett. He first made a name for himself as a radio announcer for the local minor league baseball team, the Birmingham Barons. He used the prominence that job gave him to run for public office. In 1936, he was elected public safety commissioner, a position from which he would oversee both the city's fire and police operations for most of the next twenty-seven years.

Connor was a hard-core segregationist throughout his reign, but that was hardly the only flaw of his police force. The city's police were poorly paid, receiving "less than the average railroad worker or truck driver," as one historian puts it. As a result of the low wages, turnover was high—in 1951, nearly half the force had less than two years of experience. The police were regarded by Black Birminghamians as deeply corrupt, demanding protection money from speakeasies, brothels, and gambling houses. In 1954, a burglary ring of police officers was exposed, with twenty-three accused of committing forty-one crimes. A reformist Birmingham police chief estimated around that time that 45 percent of the force was on the take, and that another 45 percent would be if they could find someone to pay them.

Most of all, the Birmingham police were notorious for their pervasive brutality toward Blacks, operating in those neighborhoods like the occupying force of a hostile power. "The Birmingham Police

Department was like an armed military," said James Roberson, a neighbor of Shuttlesworth. "They did what they wanted to do. . . . Shooting
a black was not a big thing." One policeman alone, James Albert Hale,
was involved in the killings of five Black men between 1943 and 1950.
In 1951, the city's police shot and wounded or killed twenty-eight
Black men. Washington Booker III, a Marine veteran, said the police "terrorized the community." Other Birmingham law enforcement
agencies were hardly better. In March 1960, after a handful of Black
college students staged a Prayer Vigil for Freedom, a group of white
men charged into the house of one of the protesters and beat him,
his mother, and his sister with iron pipes and blackjacks. The mother
was taken to a hospital. The next day she was visited there by a pair of
sheriff's deputies—and to her horror recognized two of them as having
been among her attackers.

Planning and training for a campaign

The preliminary plan for the Birmingham campaign was devised in
Dorchester, Georgia, a small town outside Savannah. In Dorchester
there stood an old missionary school that was closed, its main building
left vacant. Andrew Young knew through his contacts in the Congrega-
tional church that it was available. During the winter of 1962–63, the
SCLC's leaders began to meet there.

After the plan was formed came the training needed to execute it.
Shuttlesworth selected potential leaders from the major Black sections
of Birmingham. These people traveled to Dorchester to be prepared by
James Bevel, Dorothy Cotton, Septima Clark, and Andrew Young, who
all wound up on the staff of the SCLC, an extraordinary lineup of seasoned, determined, and captivating teachers. "We planned to go into
Birmingham with trained leaders in every key neighborhood," wrote
Young. "The demonstrators in Birmingham would be under tremendous pressure and we knew that a large number of well-trained folk
would be necessary to maintain discipline in the face of the violence

that was sure to come from Bull Connor and his men." To endure the brutalities of Connor's jails, the trainees were instructed to wear to demonstrations clothes that could keep them warm while behind bars, and also to put in their pockets a comb, a toothbrush, and a tube of toothpaste. They also were taught how to organize their days behind bars with education, exercise, and contemplation, to make it a meaningful experience and also to maintain cohesion.

One day Young flew on a chartered aircraft from Atlanta to Savannah and then drove to Dorchester. Arriving hungry, he began to walk to the front of the cafeteria line for food. Septima Clark, an old hand from the Highlander Folk School, where she had worked with Rosa Parks, had found Young a bit bourgeois. She held him back from cutting in line. The people getting off the bus who were arriving for classes haven't eaten yet, she told him, and you shouldn't eat until after they do. This episode resonates with anyone familiar with the long-standing practice of the American military that officers should eat only after the troops have been fed. Clark may have heard about this from World War II vets like Hosea Williams or Amzie Moore. Or she may have been aware that Gandhi had once written, "I wish to be in tune with the life of the poorest of the poor among Indians. . . . It is our duty to dress them first and then dress ourselves, to feed them first and then feed ourselves." Or she may have just sensed it herself. In any case, she enforced it—and in the process taught Young a lesson.

The significance of the SCLC's Citizen Education Program at Dorchester should be noted. Funded in large part by the Marshall Field Foundation, the education program has been called the school for the noncommissioned officers (NCOs) of the civil rights movement. In the military, promising young soldiers who are promoted to be sergeants— that is, NCOs—get special schooling to help them discharge their new responsibilities. That's meaningful because sergeants are the backbone of most modern militaries, the people who live with the soldiers, know them well, and provide hands-on guidance.

The school's leaders were also its recruiters. They focused on counties in the South that had a majority Black population yet few Black voters. When they began there were 188 such counties. They went into them and asked local Black leaders to identify men and women who showed potential—intelligence, commitment, and energy. "What we used to look for," said Young, "was the person with the Ph.D. mind in a community who had not had an opportunity to get a formal education, but who was respected by everybody as one of the wise leaders of their community." Thus chosen, these people would travel to Dorchester for a week of training in how to register voters and how to deal with hostile officials while seeking one's rights. One specific lesson was how to make a long-distance telephone call, a new experience for many of them. They also were taught how to hold a meeting. Some also saw the ocean for the first time. The core purpose of the week, said Dorothy Cotton, the director of the Citizenship Education Program, was to change how the forty or fifty students thought about themselves.

Soon after arriving at Dorchester, the students were served a big welcoming meal of southern comfort food—fried chicken, okra, lima beans, corn bread, and apple pie. Then they would have a familiarization session in which they would introduce themselves, discuss the situations they faced back home, and sing Movement songs.

Cotton would begin one class on citizenship by asking what the term "habeas corpus" meant. Usually, no one knew. This would begin a discussion Cotton called "What Is a Citizen?" People would respond with answers about being good people and obeying God's rules. At some point, a participant would mention the Constitution, at which point Cotton would distribute copies of sections of that document. She would focus them on a pressing question: Which amendments were applicable to the struggles of every person in the room? Cotton recalled that their faces would light up when they realized that the First Amendment applied to them, that they had the right to peaceably assemble to express grievances against the government. At the end of the day, Cotton would again ask what habeas corpus was. It didn't matter, she explained, because they knew their rights. They had learned they had more power than they knew.

In another exercise, students were paired off and told to take long walks in which each would explain to the other the struggle they were engaged in back home. When they reconvened, the one who had been the listener would be asked to summarize the other person's situation. This session carried multiple lessons—in empathy, in public speaking, in the common nature of their struggle, and in the possibility of there being multiple approaches to problems.

After these sessions, they went back home to towns across the South to labor in anonymity. Many of the participants were natural leaders, such as Fannie Lou Hamer, who attended a session in the spring of 1963 as part of a group led by Diane Nash. Cotton estimated that in total about seven or eight thousand people passed through the school during the 1960s.

The trainees became the seeds of future actions, in a kind of virtuous feedback loop. They would go home newly empowered, use their skills and knowledge, and "get in trouble with the local authorities," said Andrew Young. "Then we would go in to help rescue them, and that's the way most movements begin." And when another group in another city requested the help of King and the SCLC, often the first step in the response was to send in a team to meet with the group and invite some to come to Dorchester. Thus training was a continuing and dynamic part of the core process of the entire Movement.

Building King's staff

In between those field stalwarts and the celebrated leaders of the Movement was a middle level, the staff members. An often-neglected part of building an organization is choosing key staff people. As a young minister, King had almost no experience in this, and he learned the hard way.

In Montgomery, Ralph Abernathy had begun as King's senior, the more experienced, older hand, better known in the city. At first he acted as if he were King's partner, essentially a coequal. Yet it became clear over the years that his vital contribution was not as a leader but rather as King's best friend, someone with whom King could relax. Abernathy was especially notable in helping King endure his times in jail. "Abernathy was his brother," said Wyatt Walker, King's chief of staff in the early 1960s. "He was closer to Abernathy than he was to his brother, A.D."

In Albany, Georgia, Walker himself had rubbed SNCC the wrong way. Even internally, he acted in an authoritarian, hierarchical way that others disliked and that was uncommon in the civil rights movement. He eventually was eased out and replaced by Andrew Young, another Black minister, but one with a lower-key, more conciliatory approach. Externally, Young became a kind of foreign minister for King, especially in dealing with white officials and businesspeople. Internally, Young's role became that of the cautious adviser who calculated the risks, offsetting the two people who emerged as King's two idea men, James Bevel and Hosea Williams. Both were as excitable as Young was calm—and frequently vented against each other. Young played the balancing role well, but he grew weary of it. In one meeting, on a whim, he decided to go along with whatever Bevel and Williams proposed.

King, growing suspicious, pulled Young out of the meeting and asked him what he was doing. "When people get irrational and emotional like that, your job is to kind of be cool and calm things down," King admonished.

"I get tired of being the Uncle Tom," Young responded.

"That's your role," King shot back. "You have to take the discussion as far to the right as you can to give me enough leverage in between so that I can come down. . . . I don't mind risking my life, but I don't want to throw it away over some foolishness." Young said that his inherent caution created space for King "to come down in the middle."

One result of this approach was that staff meetings could be loud affairs. "You had an executive staff of fourteen highly egotistical, stubborn, arrogant people, who were strongly convicted, but willing to lay aside their strong convictions for a unity," said Randolph Blackwell, the SCLC's program director from 1964 to 1966. Such contentious sessions can be a strain, but they tend to be a sign of a healthy process of developing and assessing strategy. Groupthink is a constant danger in military planning. All assumptions need to be recognized—a process that is not easy—and then questioned. What was true yesterday may not be true tomorrow, especially when facing an adaptive adversary. Fortunately for the civil rights movement, the segregation power was particularly sluggish in adjusting in response to events.

As the SCLC prepared for Birmingham early in 1963, racial violence increased in the South, even as the national media began to pay more attention to the region. One morning in Greenwood, Mississippi, one hundred Blacks stood for hours to try to register to vote; when the registrar closed the office, they marched toward a church, only to have the police sic their dogs on them. The next day President Kennedy saw a photograph of a German shepherd biting the Reverend D. L. Tucker, and pinged the Justice Department about it. Yet the civil rights bill that Kennedy proposed in February 1963 was surprisingly modest, in large part a collection of small fixes and half measures. The bill would make it harder to use literacy tests to restrict Black voters, but it did not do away with them. It would provide temporary federal monitors on voting in locales where Blacks were alleging voting rights violations. It would require courts to expedite voting claims. The Republicans on the House Judiciary Committee issued a statement calling the proposals "belated" as well as "timid and almost reluctant."

Preparing the battlefield

Implementing a classic Gandhian nonviolent campaign involves several distinct steps. The Birmingham operation is almost a model of these. The first step, as we've seen, is educating yourself by studying the situation. Next comes formulation of demands and a private presentation of them to the opposition, so it knows what you want and is able to begin measuring whether any fight is worthwhile. While those negotiations are under way, you prepare your own followers for direct action. Then you begin holding meetings to stir people up. Fourth, you go public, issuing a statement, really an ultimatum, making it clear what your goals are and what will happen if your demands are not met. That leads to direct action, which can take several forms—boycotts, strikes, acts of civil disobedience, marches. When everything goes right, this should lead to a negotiated settlement and, finally, some form of reconciliation.

The first phase in the Birmingham campaign, the training in Dorchester, Georgia, took place far away from Alabama. Surprisingly, the next phase, the educational steps, took place even farther away, in two distant cities. SCLC staff reached out to allies in Washington and New York to bring them into the plan so that they would understand the campaign as it unfolded. Thus the northerners would be able to knowledgeably explain events to reporters who called them for comment. As Andrew Young put it, they could "function as a part of a national network without day-to-day contact because they had been briefed in advance."

Similar briefings on methods and goals were given to an advisory committee of middle-class Blacks in Birmingham. This reflected long-range thinking on the part of Movement strategists. The city's Black bourgeoisie was not likely to play a major role in demonstrations— indeed, most were wary of King and of actions in the streets—but they were expected to play a role in the closing phases of the campaign. The Movement viewed the endgame—what the U.S. military would call Phase IV post-conflict operations—as the time for reaching genuine understanding with the opposition. At that point, it would be essential to have the Black middle class engaged. These were the teachers, ministers, independent business owners, and other professionals regarded as pillars of the community. "Had they not been involved at all through the process, they wouldn't have been prepared to bring leadership in the period of reconciliation that followed," Young later explained. Treating this group as initially neutral or worse, but potential allies in the end-game, was a brilliant move.

Then came meetings with Birmingham's white economic power structure—the leading store owners and the Chamber of Commerce officials. They were told what the Movement's demands were and what would happen until those demands were met. It was helpful, Young said, to meet with them before people began to get caught up in the anger and tumult of the moment, with blood on the pavement and perhaps tear gas in the air. In war, before launching a battle, armies often use "preparatory fires," artillery barrages to make the enemy take cover and perhaps kill a few in the process. The civil rights equivalent was going to foes and telling them what was about to happen—that is, shaping the environment. "Basically, what we were doing was educating our opposition," Young said. "In Gandhian terms, it was . . . to come together from our different perspectives to seek a new truth—this situation in Birmingham was intolerable."

Young informed Birmingham's white business leaders what the Movement wanted them to do: desegregate the city's store and lunch counters, hire Blacks as clerks and cashiers, and drop charges against nonviolent demonstrators. The Movement also called for a committee to develop a way forward for school desegregation, but according to Ralph Abernathy, that demand was included simply to give white negotiators something to throw out.

The white businessmen were not much interested in any of the demands. It became clear, Young recalled, that "they were not going to change until we made them uncomfortable. It was not a test of reason or justice that we were being required to meet: it was a test of power." The whites were quite comfortable with the existing arrangements that kept Blacks subjugated.

Birmingham's white establishment responded to this initial contact by going instead to the city's leading Black businessman, A. G. Gaston, to ask for help. Gaston told them they needed instead to speak to the Reverend Fred Shuttlesworth, who had been fighting for civil rights in the city for years. The pugnacious Shuttlesworth agreed to confer with the white men, but he cut them no slack. Oh, sure, they were talkative *now*, he told them. But consider this, he added: "I been here now sufferin' for five and six or seven years. Church been bombed twice, and nobody said nothing." But *now*, he said, they wanted to talk.

Sidney Smyer, the head of the Birmingham Chamber of Commerce, pleaded with Shuttlesworth, "We just wanna know how we can help [keep] Dr. King . . . outa here." This was tantamount to a confession that the city was vulnerable to Movement pressure. It must have been music to Shuttlesworth's twice-bombed ears.

Going public

Then it was time to move. On April 2, 1963, the SCLC set up its command headquarters in Room 30 of A. G. Gaston's motel, near downtown Birmingham and a block south of the Sixteenth Street Baptist Church. The next day, under the name Alabama Christian Movement for Human Rights, the Movement issued the Birmingham Manifesto. This kickoff statement began, as King had done in Montgomery at the beginning of the boycott there, with a statement of the facts of the matter: "Birmingham is part of the United States and we are *bona fide* citizens. Yet the history of Birmingham reveals that very little of the democratic process touches the life of the Negro in Birmingham." It said that civil rights leaders in the city had tried in good faith to negotiate desegregation, but their efforts had resulted only in broken promises and hesitant steps that were reversed. The call for civil rights for Blacks had religion, morality, and the law on its side, it added. "This is Birmingham's moment of truth in which every citizen can play his part in her larger destiny," it concluded.

Wyatt Walker, King's chief of staff, had all the plans at hand. These were in the form of lists—who would work the phones, who would drive, who had said they were willing to be jailed—and maps, of their targets downtown and how to get there. Walker had measured the time it took to walk to each of them. He had studied the entries and exits. Like a commander of a bombing run, he even had picked what he called "secondary targets," in case the primary targets were blocked to marchers. He had a list of four hundred people willing to go to jail. He planned to stagger them, launching a new wave every couple of

days. The battle of Birmingham was planned to be more than just protest marches—it was a combination of negotiations, sit-ins, boycotts,
and demonstrations, with mass meetings at night. In military terms, it
was a combined arms operation, in which infantry, artillery, armored
vehicles, and perhaps aircraft all support one another. The purpose of
the store boycotts was to squeeze downtown storeowners so that they
might encourage city officials to seek a solution.

Walker's planning looked impressive, but there was a warning sign
hidden in all his details. In war, when a top leader becomes mired in
tactical minutiae, that often is a warning that strategy is being neglected. This had happened to the Kennedy brothers in handling the
Ole Miss incident, and it appears to have been a problem for Walker
in Birmingham.

Indeed, the early marches—the equivalent of infantry probing
attacks—did not go well. The Black establishment in Birmingham was
not comfortable with the coming of King. The city's Baptist ministers
voted against his leading a campaign in their city. Of the four hundred
Black churches in the city, only fourteen agreed to host meetings for
marches. Shuttlesworth, King's local ally, was less popular in the city
than the SCLC had realized. Shuttlesworth's "doggedness, his tenacity,
his courage, his craziness" had kept him going but had also alienated
other potential local allies, said Wyatt Walker. "Fred did not have a major church in Birmingham. He had angered a lot of people in the Black
community because he was very blunt in his language, talking about
the Uncle Toms. I don't blame him, because that is what they were."

The operation began badly, with underwhelming turnouts. At the
first preparatory "mass meeting," only sixty-five locals attended. At
the initial demonstration, on April 3, twenty people were arrested.
The charge that day and thereafter generally was parading without a
permit. On April 5, ten were jailed. On April 7, Palm Sunday, it was
twenty-six. On Monday, April 8, King spoke to 125 Black ministers
from the Birmingham area to ask for their support for his campaign.
They declined to give it to him.

The number of the jailed did not increase much: April 9, eight;

April 10, thirty-nine, a high for the entire month; April 11, twelve; April 13, six; April 14, thirty-two. And so on, into late April. This was a trickle, hardly the flood that might bring the city's power structure to its knees. "The demonstrations . . . reached rock bottom," recalled William Kunstler, an attorney who frequently aided civil rights activists.

To increase the count a bit, Walker began delaying the beginning of demonstrations, letting crowds collect and hoping they would be counted as among the marchers. Yet the very thing that made Birmingham an attractive target, its near-totalitarian racial system, also meant that city's Black population was nervous about being seen demonstrating. And who could blame them?

King responded by taking two steps that were crucial. He brought together his closest advisers to discuss what his next step should be. And he sent word to James Bevel, who had been working on voter registration in Mississippi but without much interest or support from the SCLC, that his advice was needed in Birmingham. King was not yet a national figure. As Taylor Branch notes, until the March on Washington, later that year, King's speeches often went unnoticed in white America. But Bevel's intervention would make all the difference.

King writes from the depths

On Friday, April 12, King conferred with his closest advisers in his room in the Gaston Motel, the only suite in the place. This was a council of war. Nobody had any good ideas. The Birmingham campaign seemed at an impasse. The marches were sputtering, and the city's Black middle class was suggesting that King call off further demonstrations. Money was needed to bail out three hundred volunteers who had marched and remained behind bars.

In conventional warfare, generals don't have to leave the battlefield to collect taxes to pay the troops—they leave that to the state structure. But insurgents are fighting the state, or part of it, and often have to pay attention to support functions such as recruiting and fundraising. In his treatise on guerrilla warfare, for example, the Argentine revolutionary Ernesto "Che" Guevara recommends that insurgent leaders collect taxes from the peasantry, either in the form of money or part of the harvest. The people can be reconciled to light levies, he notes, if their livestock is supplemented by giving them cattle, pigs, and other animals confiscated from large landowners. Another example of guerrilla taxes came during the Vietnam War, when the Viet Cong often fed themselves by collecting a portion of the rice harvest from locals. Hanoi's official history of the war notes that one of the hardest moments in the war came late in 1968 when the Americans and South Vietnamese focused a campaign on disrupting this tax system. "The enemy . . . collected and tightly controlled the people's rice crops in order to dry up local sources of supply for our armed forces," the history states. Communist fighters, hungry and dismayed, began to desert and defect in numbers that alarmed their leaders.

Thus King was pulled in two different directions. He was the Movement's most prominent protest leader, but he was also its most effective fundraiser. In 1963, he raised some $400,000 for the SCLC, mainly through speaking engagements, covering about half its budget, according to Walker, who was the executive director then.

At the April 12 meeting, some of King's lieutenants thought he should go on the road for a fundraising drive to raise bail money for those in jail. Others thought he should get himself arrested and reap the publicity of that move. This discussion wandered on for about two hours, at which point someone—King doesn't identify the person in his account of the moment—warned, "If you go to jail, we are lost. The battle of Birmingham is lost." The room fell quiet.

King finally made the decision by himself. He walked into the suite's other room and closed the door behind him. He stood in the center of that room. "I think I was standing also at the center of all that my life had brought me to be. . . . There was no more room for doubt." He took off his more formal garments and put on dungarees, a blue cotton shirt, and work shoes. Then he walked back into the meeting room. His clothes immediately told those waiting that he had decided to go to jail. It was like a top general taking off his office uniform and appearing before his staff in combat fatigues. King did not say so, but he was taking a page directly from Gandhi, who five decades earlier had sent a message to his followers by abandoning the frock coat he had worn as a London-trained barrister and appearing instead in the simple smock and sandals of the common Indian laborer. "I don't know what will happen," King told the others. "I don't know where the money will come from. But I have to make a faith act." This is the essence of leadership: looking at a situation in which there are no good options, and then making a decision.

It was a key moment not just in the campaign but in King's life, according to Andrew Young. As he put it, King, "not knowing how it was going to work out, . . . walked out of the room and went down to the church and led a demonstration and went to jail. Well, that was, I think the beginning of his true leadership, because that Sunday the [white] ministers published in the newspapers a diatribe against Martin, calling him a troublemaker, and a communist, and saying that he was there stirring up trouble to get publicity."

Even on this day, with King and Abernathy leading the column, there were only fifty marchers. It must have been an extraordinarily sobering moment for King. Going to jail had not become any easier for him. And this time, it developed, he would be held alone and incommunicado.

Sitting in solitary confinement in the Birmingham jail, not allowed even to contact a lawyer at first, he felt himself "in a nightmare of despair." When people are pushed beyond endurance, they sometimes descend into a frustrated, bewildered silence. At other times, such anguish can lead a different way, to a moment of clarity, of a new willingness to look squarely at harsh truths. This appears to be what happened to Martin Luther King, Jr., when, on April 16, he finally was allowed to meet with a lawyer, who showed him an item in the *Birmingham News* in which eight moderate white clergymen in Alabama called on him and his followers to slow down. Denied writing materials, he began scribbling in the margins of the newspaper and then on other paper an effervescent essay exploring the moment. In it, his anger bubbles just beneath the surface. The piece, at once highly emotional and brilliantly strategic, became known as "Letter from Birmingham Jail."

In the essay, King writes as a seasoned fighter, someone who has grown tired of white moderates telling him to slow down: "Frankly, I have yet to engage in a direct-action campaign that was 'well-timed' in the view of those who have not suffered unduly from the disease of segregation." He also was weary of their counsel to seek negotiation: Don't they know that the Movement tried that before it took to the streets? We asked for a dialogue, he explains, but we got a monologue.

He doesn't have his books with him, but he has his authorities in his head. His citations mount up: Socrates, St. Augustine, St. Thomas Aquinas, Martin Buber, Paul Tillich. Here they amount to a formidable firing squad, for King has lost patience. He has two confessions to make, he says:

> First, I must confess that over the past few years I have been gravely disappointed with the white moderate. I have almost reached the regrettable conclusion that the Negro's great stumbling block in his stride toward freedom is not the White Citizen's Counciler or the Ku Klux Klanner, but the white moderate, who is more devoted to "order" than to justice; who prefers a negative peace which is the absence of tension to a positive peace which is the presence of justice; who constantly says: "I agree with you in the goal you seek, but I cannot agree with your methods of direct action"; who paternalistically believes he can set the timetable for another man's freedom.

Then he rounds up a second firing squad: Jesus, Martin Luther, John Bunyan, Abraham Lincoln, and Thomas Jefferson. He reveals that his second great disappointment is with the men whose statement he has seen in the newspaper. His phrases are lashing:

> I have been so greatly disappointed with the white church and its leadership. . . . In the midst of blatant injustices inflicted upon the Negro, I have watched white churchmen stand on the sideline and mouth pious irrelevancies and sanctimonious trivialities. . . . In deep disappointment I have wept over the laxity of the church. . . . I love the church. . . . [But so] often the contemporary church is a weak, ineffectual voice with an uncertain sound.

Hence the challenge of the day, he says, is not to the civil rights movement. King states he has no fear or doubt that it will succeed in Birmingham, "even if our motives are at present misunderstood." He is confident of the goal of freedom. Rather, he says, the challenge is whether the wandering church at long last will find itself and side with justice.

Students at the U.S. military's war colleges are senior officers who are potential generals. The role of the war colleges is to move them from thinking tactically, at the level of field operations, to thinking strategically about how to run wars, or large parts of them. Typically the officers are taught that strategy consists of ways, ends, and means. So a comment that King made here would prick up ears in any war college classroom: "I have tried to make it clear that it is wrong to use immoral means to attain moral ends." Again, he is asserting that his tactics are part of a larger strategy. Then he salutes the "amazing discipline" of the nonviolent protesters and comments, with great foresight, "One day the South will recognize its real heroes."

It is a stunning document that lays out what the Movement is trying to do, how it is trying to do it, and why its moderate critics are terribly in error—not just mistaken, but standing on the wrong side of history. It is the best thing King ever wrote, and arguably one of the most noteworthy documents in American history. But its significance was not recognized at the time. King was not yet a national figure. An assignment editor at the *New York Times* Sunday magazine was interested in publishing King's essay but was overruled by superiors, who were bothered that part of it was published elsewhere. But other outlets picked it up, and with time, recognition of the essay spread.

Birmingham's order of battle

The enemy point of view is harder to explain. The civil rights movement left wonderfully detailed records. SNCC's meeting minutes often have a feel of a verbatim record. And, of course, conversations collected through wiretaps placed by the Federal Bureau of Investigation, which would conduct a yearslong campaign against King and the civil rights movement—about which more later—have become a rich if ironic source of information about the inner workings of the civil rights movement.

But the opponents of civil rights did not leave any such chronicle. Yes, there are documents from state and city officials. But by and large the segregationists did not rush to tell that story. That may be because much of what was discussed was in fact illegal and evil, such as having police withdraw in order to let Klan members assault protesters. But it also was because the people who led the fight to preserve segregation were not the kind of people who tend to write about their roles. George Wallace, Ross Barnett, Bull Connor, and Selma sheriff Jim Clark never penned memoirs.

Obviously, the enemies of the Movement held an overwhelming dominance in conventional power, in various arms of law enforcement. They had local police and various statewide agencies. In Alabama in 1963, the Highway Patrol effectively operated as Governor Wallace's private army. It consisted of eight hundred men with shotguns and helmets and was led by Al Lingo, who had flown Wallace's aircraft during the campaign for the governorship. For additional firepower or deniable violence, they also could employ the Klan as a kind of auxiliary arm.

Chuck Morgan, a Birmingham lawyer, described the KKK as "guerilla warriors for preservation of the order."

But the outcome was never going to be decided by numbers or sheer physical force. A comment said to have been made by Joseph Stalin famously illustrates the point. When an aide mentioned the importance of the pope, the Soviet dictator dismissively responded, "The pope! How many divisions does he have?" What this ignored was that there are other forms of power besides the sheer ability to hurt or kill someone. And it was this sort of political power that would be decisive in the war over civil rights.

Public opinion would be more decisive than firepower in this fight. The arrest of King caught the attention of the national media, and the country began to take note of him. Reporters and cameramen began pouring into Birmingham. In response, the Movement began scheduling its marches so that they would end by early afternoon, giving the television journalists sufficient time to get their film to the airport to be flown to New York for the evening news broadcasts. "We attempted to plan our demonstrations so that a distinct message was conveyed every day, first to the people of Birmingham, then to the nation," remembered Andrew Young.

But the media needed something more to see. Despite the attention given to King's arrest, the Movement's Birmingham campaign continued to falter. On Monday, April 22, only ten people volunteered to march and be jailed. "We needed more troops," said Wyatt Walker. "We had scraped the bottom of the barrel of adults" willing to go behind bars.

On April 29, King said an emergency meeting, "We've got to get something going. The press is leaving, we've got to get going."

Something new, something different, clearly was needed. But what?

Enter Bevel

James Bevel had a notion of what to do, and when he was like that, he was a hard man to stop. While King had been in jail writing, Bevel had been busy organizing. King had summoned him to the city to work on the faltering campaign and perhaps devise a new approach. Bevel, wearing his distinctive outfit of overalls, a shirt and tie, his shaved head topped by a colorful woven yarmulke-like skullcap, did just that. Under his determined and charismatic guidance, the campaign came roaring back. Bevel's particular brilliance was finding new ways to challenge the existing order.

Historians often depict Bevel as a tactician. That assessment undersells him. He was a good strategist and, as such, understood that strategy should shape tactics—that is, first you decide who you are, then you focus on what you want to achieve, and then you decide what actions to take to bring about that goal. In Birmingham, James Bevel would introduce an audacious new tactic. If there is an American military figure analogous to him, it probably is William Tecumseh Sherman. The Civil War general was volatile, even a little insane, but strategically he was far ahead of his peers. Just as Sherman would invent a new way to fight in the Civil War, crossing Georgia without any logistical support or even basic rearward communications, Bevel would develop a new approach to civil rights marches. Interestingly, Bevel was married to someone who was his equal as a strategist: Diane Nash.

Always a risk-taker, James Bevel was a "human hurricane" who "loved nothing more than stirring the pot," wrote John Lewis, who met him when both were students at the American Baptist Theological Seminary in Nashville. He was the thirteenth of seventeen children of a farmer in the tiny Mississippi Delta town of Itta Bena. But, perhaps more meaningfully, he was, he noted, "the seventh son"—a birth slot sometimes associated with mystical powers of healing or prophecy. Eventually, like too many other veterans of the Movement, Bevel would unravel—indeed, as Sherman did early in the Civil War, hovering near suicide for a time. But at this point in the struggle, in the key phase of the Birmingham campaign, Bevel had his eye on the ball, both strategically and tactically.

It isn't easy to develop strategy. Figuring out what to do is only the first phase. The next is to communicate it to followers in simple, clear terms that they can use to shape their actions. Bevel, for all his eccentricities, was extremely good at this. Addressing a Black crowd in Georgia one day in 1963, he began with a trope from southern Black folklore about how the white people back where he came from were really mean. "You think these white folks over here know how to beat up Negroes?" he asked. Nah, he said, these whites weren't half as bad as the ones back in Mississippi and Alabama. Don't be like them, he admonished. "We didn't come here to hurt the mayor, or the city," he continued. "We didn't come here to destroy anybody's business. . . . So I don't want you to be beating up white folks and throwing at them—and you become worse than they are."

Bevel also could be provocatively tart, even from the pulpit. At another time in Georgia, he was preaching in a rural church when the local sheriff and his deputies walked in. Bevel gazed at the sheriff, who was rudely smoking a cigar at the back of the church. "You know, whenever God's people go to church," Bevel mocked, "Satan will always show up. In fact he'll come in smoking on a cigar so you'll know who he is." People began laughing, and the sheriff and his men left. Early the next morning, Bevel discovered that someone had burned down the church. He and others would argue that such a violent response was part of the process of bringing to the surface and into the daylight the savagery that was inherent in the system of segregation.

Bevel was also one of those unusual people who like the process of arriving at decisions. "One should get joy out of making decisions," he said once. "Power is the ability to make decisions for yourself and get with other intelligent people and make decisions for a group of people to solve a problem." In late April 1963, he was ready to go to work in Birmingham.

The children's crusade

If the adults wouldn't march in Birmingham, Bevel calculated, the city's children might. Putting children on the front lines of the Movement was risky and irregular. It also would be a form of radical escalation. It would pose the question to Birmingham's power structure: Are you willing to jail and even beat children to preserve white supremacy? The answer would be yes. And the nation would see it on television. The idea of child soldiers may have been disconcerting, but Bevel likely would have noted that he was not arming his recruits or telling them to use force. "The act of nonviolent protest doesn't seem to have that parallel" to warfare, comments Peter W. Singer, a strategist at the New America Foundation and an expert on the subject of child soldiers. Indeed, Singer adds, nonviolent marching "is arguably the opposite of war in that it is enshrined in law/rights."

Recruiting is hardly treated as a major subject in military affairs, but even there, Bevel operated innovatively. His approach to the task was strategic. Instead of buttonholing likely volunteers one-by-one on the street, as most people might think was the way to go, he began by seeking out two disc jockeys popular with Black youth in Birmingham: Shelley "The Playboy" Stewart and Paul "Tall Paul" White. He asked them to announce on their shows the offer of a free hot lunch at the Gaston Motel's restaurant. Bevel specifically wanted the invitation extended to quarterbacks, cheerleaders, class presidents, beauty queens, track stars, church youth group leaders, and other prominent high school students. Over that meal, Bevel discussed his new strategy with them, and many of them in turn went out to become his recruiters among the city's teenagers. He, Andrew Young, and others then began intensive training of the students at evening sessions.

These new volunteers were required to sign a card reading "I PLEDGE MYSELF—MY PERSON AND MY BODY—TO THE NONVIOLENT MOVEMENT." This vow was followed by ten promises, including "I WILL . . . REMEMBER always that the nonviolent movement in Birmingham seeks justice and reconciliation—not victory. . . . REFRAIN from the violence of fist, tongue, or heart. . . . FOLLOW the directions of the Movement and of the captain on a demonstration." One volunteer, Freeman Hrabowski III, just twelve years old but already in high school, was struck by how well the leaders prepared him and his fellow recruits. "They trained us to understand strategy and discipline," he recalled.

Bevel was an assiduous student of Gandhi, who also had required volunteers to sign formal pledges to follow the rules of nonviolence. Those who were deemed unlikely to be able to follow these inviolable rules were diverted into other useful activities, such as running errands, answering phones, and distributing leaflets. Every child who marched had been trained, King later said.

At the time, however, King hesitated about allowing children to join the Movement—and how could he not? Bevel responded by playing his ace, telling King, "If we don't do this, we might wind up just like we did in Albany." It was a strategic risk—would the Movement be seen as recklessly using children, or would its segregationist foes be seen as heartlessly attacking them? It could go either way. But taking risks is almost essential to success in warfare. Avoiding them is a recipe for stalemate, at best.

Bevel designated May 2 as D Day. The "D" stood for "desegregation," but the echo of World War II would also have been caught, especially because *The Longest Day*—a Hollywood blockbuster about the D-Day landings of June 1944, featuring John Wayne, Henry Fonda, Richard Burton, and other movie stars—had been a hit the previous year. Bevel told the students to report on May 2 to the Sixteenth Street Baptist Church, on the edge of downtown Birmingham. Parents getting wind of their children's plans could forbid them from going downtown or marching, but it was harder to order them not to go to church.

Shelley the Playboy and Tall Paul, the two deejays, broadcast messages telling their listeners to come to "a party at the park" and, significantly, to bring their toothbrushes with them. Those who had been trained caught the meaning of the latter message: you might be going to jail.

"They just poured in," recalled one participant, Jimmie Hooks. Inside the church, the growing crowd sang, "Ain't Gonna Let Nobody Turn Me 'Round." Then Bevel held one of his distinctive mass meetings. King arrived. "He still had his doubts about allowing them to participate," Bevel recalled. King asked the thousand or so students in the church how many planned to demonstrate. "He expected about 15 or 20 to respond," Bevel wrote. Instead, "everyone in the church held up their hand. It almost caused him to faint. . . . He had to ask the question again. '*All* of you are going?' . . . 'Yeahhhh!' He'd never seen anything like it." Deciding on a different direction while on the battlefield usually is not easy, but King saw that Bevel had found a way out of the tactical stalemate, and he consented to the new approach. He might be seen as following the military principle of "flexibility of maneuver," but all that phrase really means is that when a situation changes, a commander must be prepared to change his or her mind. It is worth noting that King was able to do so.

The church rocked with energy. "You always left with a euphoric feeling, like you could do anything, go anywhere, and beat any odds when you went," recalled Shirley Miller, then an eighth grader, who had been trained by Bevel. It was as if Bevel's training enabled them to redefine themselves and leave behind the humiliation inflicted by a racist system.

When Bevel opened the doors of the church that day, teenagers began marching out in ranks of two. A first group was arrested. A second group emerged, and then a third, and so on. The precision of Bevel's preparation was striking, especially when compared to the slapdash federal intervention in Oxford seven months earlier, when federal marshals were thrown into a fight without the training, equipment, or supporting units they needed. "We were never just sent out," remembered Gwendolyn Gamble, who participated in about twenty of Birmingham's protests. "We were always briefed: what to say, what not to say, where we were going, what information to give, and what information not to give. . . . We were timed to the minute—'You have five minutes, eight seconds, to get to your destination.'"

Ultimately, more than one thousand children were arrested on May 2, an extraordinary number, quite different from the trickle of arrests the previous month. Indeed, by the end of the day, the city jail, with a capacity of nine hundred, was full.

Bevel also had made an insightful economic calculation. When children were jailed, they didn't have jobs to lose or paychecks to miss, so sending them marching didn't threaten the precarious finances of Black families who were struggling to pay bills and put food on the table. Yet the financial impact on the city of jailing children was the same as with adults, with the need for guards, food, and utilities. At a mass meeting that night, two thousand people crowded into a church. Dr. King's relief was evident when he said, "I have been inspired and moved today. I have never seen anything like it."

Police dogs and fire hoses

In most wars, the purpose of combat is not primarily to kill people. That is just a consequence. The true goal is usually to reduce the options or choices available to the opponents, so they wind up having to do what you want them to do—retreat, surrender, or move to a spot that makes them vulnerable. Bevel was doing something like that, taking away options from his opponent.

On May 3, Bevel sent another 2,500 people into the streets, most of them youngsters. With the city jail close to overflowing, Bull Connor had tried to obtain the use of Legion Field, a big local football stadium, but was told it was already booked for a track meet. So the policeman decided that rather than make more arrests, he would chase the children away. This was a major and memorable miscalculation on his part.

Connor played straight into Bevel's hands. This time the marching children were met with fire hoses and police dogs. One system of hoses, which combined two flows, was powerful enough to strip the bark off a tree or knock bricks out of walls. Trained on the children, it knocked them down, ripped their clothing, and sent some skittering across the asphalt. "We were taught to sit down, and if we balled up into balls, hugging together, then the water would not hurt so much," recalled Annetta Gary. "The water just washed us down the street. Forceful. It was like pins maybe, sticking you in your arms and legs." Another child marcher recalled that the force from a hose tore off some of her hair: "It was very painful."

Shirley Miller, who had emerged from the church euphoric, found the dogs terrifying. "When they brought the dogs in, we ran," she said.

The counter-escalation through dogs and hoses was exactly the wrong response for the city of Birmingham to take, because it alarmed both local citizens and people around the world. "News photographs of the violence seized millions of distant eyes, shattering inner defenses," writes Taylor Branch. Locally, Black adults were so angry at seeing the children attacked that they began to throw rocks and bottles at the police. Seeing this, Bevel borrowed a bullhorn from a policeman and ordered everyone to go home. "We're not going to have violence," he stated. His thinking, he explained later, was that if a riot broke out, it would take several days of work to reestablish the principle of nonviolent direct action.

Connor and the local forces of white supremacy had, to use a twenty-first-century phrase, lost control of the narrative. Bevel and the Movement had seized it. Determining the narrative is the nonviolent equivalent of holding the initiative in war. Once it is lost, it is almost impossible to regain it.

Was it cynical to use children? Perhaps. But it was nonetheless realistic. The parents were afraid to come out, which might have been expected in the most oppressive big city in the South. White America had made it clear that it wouldn't blink when southern whites beat and killed southern Black adults. The answer had to be to confound the enemy with some other sort of troops. In Birmingham, the answer was children. A year later, in Mississippi's Freedom Summer, the answer would be white college students from the North. Both times, the proof would be in the violent local white reaction that provoked national outrage.

Robert Kennedy was critical of the tactic of using children. "An injured, maimed or dead child is a price that none of us can afford to pay," he said. It is a haunting comment, given what happened five months later to four young girls in the Sixteenth Street Baptist Church. What Kennedy did not mention, but what many Black people knew, was that Black children already were under attack in the South. The murder of Emmett Till, who had just turned fourteen when he was lynched for a possible violation of racial etiquette in 1955, was still a recent memory.

But Bevel's new approach was having an effect on the Kennedys, more proof that it was working. The same day that the attorney general's comments appeared in the newspapers, the Kennedy administration sent a Justice Department official, Burke Marshall, to Birmingham to spur both sides toward a settlement. The national media seized on the images of Black children being knocked over and rolled down paved streets with powerful fire hoses, and of dogs being set upon them.

Young Freeman Hrabowski III led a group of students up the steps of city hall, only to encounter Bull Connor. "What do you want, little Nigra?" Connor asked.

"Suh, we want to kneel and pray," Hrabowski responded.

Connor spat in the boy's face. It is a memorable image, like seeing a hinge in time—the aging, ignorant racist showing mean-spirited contempt for a courageous Black boy who would grow up to become a notably innovative college president.

Connor had "served our purposes well," said Wyatt Walker. The police commissioner's ham-fisted brutality in response to Bevel's new tactic finally brought Birmingham's Black adults onto the streets. Andrew Marrisett, a Black Birminghamian, had not been involved in the demonstrations. He was driving a bus for his church when he saw a police dog attacking a little Black girl. "I went and stood in front of the girl and grabbed her," he recalled, "and the dog jumped on me and I was arrested." That was the spark, he said, that made him a civil rights activist. That night he attended a mass meeting.

On Sunday, May 5, Bevel led perhaps two thousand people out of a church and toward a line of firetrucks. He did not know that the chief of the fire department, John Swindle, had tired of seeing his men used as assault troops by Connor and had told the firefighters to obey only those orders that came from him. As the marchers neared, the firemen stepped back and watched them. When Connor ordered the hoses turned on, Swindle did not pass along that instruction, so they were not. This moment was more significant than it might at first appear. In discussing the characteristics of successful civil resistance movements, Erica Chenoweth writes that "security force defections dramatically increase the chances for nonviolent resistance to succeed." She notes that these need not be complete transfers of allegiance, but rather can be simply declining to carry out orders, as was the case here. Such quiet refusals of orders can be enormously destabilizing, especially if the security forces are having morale problems.

By Monday, May 6, there were three thousand demonstrators in jail, many of them stashed in improvised confinement facilities on the state fairgrounds. Audrey Faye Hendricks, an eight-year-old marcher held there, was repeatedly interrogated by law enforcement officials. She remembered, "They would ask silly questions about our mass meeting. They wanted to know whether we talked about any communist plots, or did we plan to overthrow the government, or something silly like that. I told them we talked about nonviolence and discrimination in our meetings, not communism." A small child being able to checkmate detectives was another proof that Bevel's approach was working. The importance of preparation is worth noting again here. Hendricks had been trained well, and remembered what she had been taught.

At this point in the campaign, there were more people marching than were being detained. Bevel now introduced another tactical variation, sending demonstrators not just a few blocks, but all the way into the city's business district. "That was pretty frightening to some of the businessmen," recalled David Vann, a moderate figure involved in negotiations between business leaders and the Movement. Just as in Nashville three years earlier, when demonstrators flooded the downtown, shoppers disappeared—Blacks mainly to honor the boycott, whites more out of fear. The boycott began to bite deeply into downtown revenues. There also was a growing concern among the storeowners that shoppers who left might never come back, because by coincidence, Birmingham's first suburban shopping center, the Eastwood Mall, had just opened to the east of the city. The future was knocking on Birmingham's door in more ways than one.

One basic rule of combat is never to do today quite what you did yesterday. Alter patterns. Be unpredictable. Do sudden reverses. Switch it up. Not only does this create openings, but it wears out the enemy, who has to be ready for a variety of actions and to stay on alert for the unexpected. On Tuesday, May 7, seeking to keep Connor off-balance, Bevel launched Operation Confusion. He began the day's demonstration not at one o'clock, the usual time, but at noon, when many policemen were accustomed to taking their lunch breaks. Also, instead of sending out successive waves, Bevel simultaneously dispatched fifteen separate groups of about forty each, taking different routes but all arriving in the downtown business district at the same time. Suddenly, the downtown was flooded with young protesters. In response, the fire hoses came back on. Connor apparently had regained control of that apparatus.

As the day's march was ending, Fred Shuttlesworth was trying to herd the young demonstrators back into the Sixteenth Street Baptist Church. He heard a white voice say, "Let's put some water on the reverend." He turned around and a high-pressure stream hit him on the side of his chest. The force of it knocked the breath out of him and pushed him backward down a stairwell and against a wall, inflicting chest injuries sufficient to have him be hospitalized. "We thought they had killed him," said one eyewitness, Joe Dickson, a marcher. Connor, told by a reporter that Shuttlesworth had been taken off in an ambulance, responded, "I wish they'd carried him away in a hearse."

Settlement talks

The city's business community, feeling the pinch and sensing national disdain, wanted the entire situation to end, to just go away. While Shuttlesworth lay in his hospital bed, King began negotiating with the Kennedy administration to stop the demonstrations. Getting word of that, and furious that King would entertain the idea of settlement without first talking to him, a shaky Shuttlesworth checked himself out of the hospital and went to confront King. The Birmingham minister accused the one from Atlanta of repeating the mistakes of Albany, but now with national attention. "You've been Mister Big, Martin, but you'll be Mister Shit if you pull out now," he said.

At a second meeting, Andrew Young intervened, bodily, against Shuttlesworth. "We had a little confrontation where I had to physically restrain him," Andrew Young, ever diplomatic, recalled. Fortunately, Young recalled, the attorney general called to urge Shuttlesworth to consider the settlement. "Fred took the call," Young wrote, "and thankfully it satisfied his principles, soothed his wounded ego, and saved me from punching him out."

Dramatic arguments like the one between Shuttlesworth and King may seem unhelpful, but in practice they are an essential part of the process. In war, it is always dangerous to submerge differences and instead to relentlessly seek consensus. The genius of President Franklin Delano Roosevelt during World War II, for example, was to stir the pot and probe contrasting points of view. Sometimes FDR even would appoint two people to research the same question and then see which result he preferred. This caused short-term friction but also produced strategic clarity, and helped the president separate the essential from the merely important. By contrast, President George W. Bush, leading the nation into a war in Iraq in 2003, did not delve into differences of opinion among his military advisers, such as the view of the Army chief of staff, General Eric Shinseki, that the American occupation force would have to be far larger than planned. This failure to explore disagreements and to use varying perspectives to sort through major problems was a leading reason why the United States flailed in Iraq for years. Such discussions can be enervating, but they are essential to making life-and-death decisions.

The leaders and strategists of the civil rights movement were not afraid to confront one another. They saw argument and the advocacy of alternative courses of action as part of the process. Casey Hayden, one of the more reflective members of SNCC, once wrote, "All basic disagreements needed to be ironed out before we took action, so we could act in unity." There was a sound reason to make sure everyone was heard: "You couldn't ask someone to risk his or her life without agreeing on what they would risk it for."

Demonstrations were designed to bring racial tensions in a city to the surface. Likewise, examining internal tensions was seen as part of making strategy. "I think conflict can be very healthy," said Diane Nash. "In fact, lack of conflict is unhealthy." She recalled that James Bevel and Wyatt Walker "would have these sort of shouting matches."

By this point, the Movement's campaign in Birmingham had backed Bull Connor into a corner. The police commissioner asked Governor Wallace for help. The governor sent in around eight hundred state troopers. But they never got a chance to wade into the fray.

On May 8, President Kennedy held a press conference, the first one in which the major focus was American race relations. He asserted that "the ugly situation" in Birmingham was damaging the image of both that city and the entire nation. This was a message that Birmingham's business leaders could not ignore, no matter what Connor and the governor thought. This led to division within the city's white power structure. And through that crack shone the light of a Movement victory.

Soon afterward, on May 10, a settlement was reached between the city's white business leaders and the SCLC, under which the Movement appeared to win on all its demands: the desegregation of lunch counters and bathrooms in downtown stores, the hiring of some Black salesclerks, and the formation of a biracial committee on school desegregation. These would not be immediate, but would be phased in. That slight compromise follows a rule of warfare of allowing your enemy an avenue for retreat. Sun Tzu, the legendary Chinese military strategist, supposedly counseled, "Build your enemy a golden bridge to retreat across." But it also is in keeping with the Gandhian precept that one should be inflexible in means—that is, nonviolence—but open to change in ends. Compromise is entirely acceptable as long as it does not touch principle. For example, Gandhi had signed the Delhi Pact with the British government in 1931 even though it fell far short of his goals. He suspected, correctly, that the partial gain of the provisional treaty would set India on the path toward eventual independence.

As it happened in Birmingham, the compromise split the city's power structure. The business community now favored change; those who held political power did not. Desegregation would be a long and difficult process in the city. Bull Connor's sulking comment on the settlement was, "You know what's the trouble with this country? Communism, Socialism, and journalism."

Shuttlesworth had wanted a clear-cut victory. King was willing to settle for a partial one. "I don't think Fred saw the larger picture as Martin did," said C. T. Vivian. Shuttlesworth was the tougher tactician, the hotheaded General Patton of the Movement. But King was more of a General Eisenhower, the cooler head and a better strategist. Shuttlesworth was impatient with the subject of strategy. "They were doing a lot of talking," he said once of the SCLC. "They had so much to talk about. Strategy. Points about points which weren't points about anything. I told them, I said, 'We don't do this in Birmingham. We don't spend our breath arguing among ourselves. We hit the road in Birmingham.'" What Shuttlesworth, for all his valor, did not see but King did was that the Birmingham campaign was about more than just that city. The Movement's campaign there had changed the national agenda. In May 1963, for the first time, the Gallup poll reported that Americans considered civil rights "the most important problem facing the country."

King's assessment prevailed. In this case, the very appearance of victory was, in the eyes of the nation, an impressive win for the Movement. And, as Gandhi had taught, one engaged in nonviolent struggle "whilst he is ever ready for fight must be equally eager for peace. He must welcome any honorable opportunity for peace." King correctly grabbed that opening.

Bombing Birmingham

King left town. But there still was some fight left in his foe.

Laurie Pritchett, the police chief in Albany, Georgia, had been invited—it is not clear by whom—to travel to Birmingham to give Bull

Connor some advice on how to quell demonstrations. Pritchett and Connor immediately rubbed each other the wrong way. Pritchett noted that King was staying in a motel that was vulnerable to Klan attacks and suggested the police put out a guard. Pritchett later recalled Connor's response: "I'm not going to guard him, if they want to kill him, that's up to them." Of Connor, Pritchett concluded, "I didn't like his methods—frankly, I didn't like the man."

Indeed, Pritchett's advice seemed to further provoke the emotional Connor. "That was just like putting gas on the fire," said Mel Bailey, the county sheriff, who had his own problems with Connor. "You couldn't necessarily communicate with Bull. . . . Chief Pritchett tried and was run out of town."

The segregationists rarely accepted defeat gracefully. This was, perhaps, one of the unintended consequences of the 1870s. After the Civil War, the white supremacist South learned that if it continued to resist Black freedom, eventually the North would tire of intervening and let white supremacists have their way. In the wake of the Birmingham compromise, violence escalated in the city. On May 11, 1963, the Gaston Motel was dynamited, with the epicenter of the blast at Room 30, King's suite, which was destroyed. Four people were slightly injured in the attack. As if to drive home the point about who was being targeted, the Birmingham home of King's brother, the Reverend A. D. King, also was bombed.

Art Hanes, the mayor of Birmingham, maintained that the bombs were self-inflicted. "We know they were done," he alleged, "feel reasonably sure, were done by King and his crowd, and the Communists, to stir up trouble."

King returned to Birmingham. "Dogs can't stop us and bombs can't stop us," he asserted. "For we are on the way . . . to the land of freedom. . . . We shall overcome because the Bible is right, 'You shall reap what you sow.'"

The president ordered three thousand Army troops to move to near Birmingham. That indication of a willingness to use federal force seemed to discourage further bombings. On the evening of June 11,

Kennedy gave a nationally televised talk endorsing civil rights legislation. It was time, he said, to respond to "the cries for equality." He
finally had moved off the fence.

But there were always reactions, usually violent. A few hours after
the president's talk, at 12:20 a.m. on June 12, Medgar Evers, the most
prominent NAACP official in Mississippi, was assassinated; he was shot
in the back and through the heart as he arrived home. "We heard the
motor of the car coming in and pulling into the driveway," his widow,
Myrlie Evers, recalled. "We heard him get out of the car and the car
door slam, and in that same instance, we heard the loud gunfire. The
children fell to the floor, as he had taught them to do. I made a run
for the front door, turned on the light, and there he was." The bullet,
from the rifle of a white supremacist, had passed through him, through
a window and then a wall inside the house, and then glanced off the
Everses' refrigerator.

The next morning, President Kennedy expressed surprise in a telephone conversation with Carl Albert, the House majority leader, about
how the civil rights movement suddenly was dominating the domestic
agenda: "Just events are making our problems. . . . Christ, you know,
it's like they shoot this guy in Mississippi. . . . I mean, it's just in everything. I mean, this has become everything."

A few days later, Kennedy proposed a new civil rights bill—it was almost the opposite of the weak one he had envisioned just a few months
earlier. This new bill would increase the Black vote by doing away with
literacy tests for anyone with a basic elementary school education. It
would enable to the Justice Department to file suits to compel school
desegregation. It restricted federal funding for programs that discrimi-
nated on the basis of race. Most important, it outlawed segregation in
public places—stores, restaurants, hotels, and parks.

The Kennedy administration's new civil rights bill caught the public
mood. In the summer of 1963, the push for civil rights, heretofore
regional, grew into a mass national movement. More than 700 demonstrations took place in 186 cities and towns across the country, and
nearly 15,000 arrests. Corporate America threw its weight behind the

Movement, with executives pledging to donate $1 million to five major civil rights groups—the NAACP, the SCLC, SNCC, CORE, and the Urban League. The membership rolls of several of those groups also increased.

Post-victory steps

The civil rights movement was skilled at consolidating victories, even partial ones. Indeed, it generally handled that task better than the U.S. military has in recent years. As noted, this was in part because seeking reconciliation was always listed as the final goal in nonviolent campaigns. When downtown Birmingham began to desegregate, local Movement leaders used their calmest, best-trained activists to implement the agreement. In an interesting variation on sit-in tactics, these actions were purposefully low-key and nonconfrontational. "We started with one lunch counter a day; we would call in advance and avoid the busiest times," wrote Young. "We wanted the community to gradually get used to seeing African-Americans sitting down, eating lunch." This approach eased the way for the vast majority of Blacks who were not in the Movement. Seeing events proceeding peacefully, they could come in and sit down themselves. Young doesn't say it, but this step could be seen as training the white population to live with the post-segregation world. Subtly guiding the opposition population is a particularly innovative form of training, something that military planners should consider.

That spring, James Bevel told Diane Nash that "he had been thinking and decided we should have a march on Washington." Nash told him that it sounded like a good idea.

It would be "just like the 1930 march in India, when everyone arose and walked to the sea to make salt," Bevel thought.

It may be that people were thinking alike. As it happened, A. Philip Randolph and Bayard Rustin had been mulling such a march on Washington for months. Randolph, a veteran Black labor leader and the grand old man of civil rights at age seventy-four, had threatened just such a march during World War II, causing President Roosevelt to open defense industry jobs to Blacks. Later he had helped spur President Truman to integrate the American military, putting Blacks and whites in the same units. In January 1963, he had asked his old friend and longtime associate Rustin to write a short plan for how such a march could be put on.

One of King's strengths was his ability to understand the moment and to sense what the next step should be. Perhaps prodded by Rustin's planning, he was lifting his eyes to the horizon. "We are on the threshold of a significant breakthrough and the greatest weapon is the mass demonstration," he told an adviser at the end of May 1963, as he recovered from the Birmingham fight. "We are at the point where we can mobilize all this righteous indignation into a powerful mass movement." Just announcing a "March on Washington," he added, "may so frighten the president that he would have to do something."

The next day, in a conversation that the FBI wiretapped, King sounded even more confident and determined, declaring, "We are ready to go on a national level with our protests." King had assessed the size of the mobilization needed and the time it would take to generate the required numbers. He and his advisers, notes the historian Taylor Branch, "agreed that it would take a crowd of a hundred thousand to generate enough political force, and that it would take at least until August to mobilize." King was even thinking about conducting sit-ins in the offices of Congress.

7.
THE MARCH ON WASHINGTON, MID-1963

Taking the National Stage

Logistics is often the unacknowledged key to military success. It also was the decisive aspect of the 1963 March on Washington for Jobs and Freedom.

But what does that mean? Inside the military, everyone knows logistics is vital. As an old saying puts it, "Amateurs talk tactics, professionals talk logistics." But there is rarely any drama to logistics. The better it goes, the less outside attention it receives. There are few, if any, heroic films made about logistics. In a nutshell, logistics means the planned military movement of people and goods—primarily food, fuel, water, medicine, and ammunition—in such a fashion as to have everything in the right place at the time when it is needed to carry out a mission. In war, logistics is, like training, one of the preliminaries to combat, the necessary prerequisite to everything that follows. It is what makes the heroics possible. Still, the subject gets little respect. During World War I, for example, frontline German soldiers disparaged the units that supplied them as *Etappenschweine*—that is, "lines of communication pigs" or "supply swine."

In the March on Washington, too, logistical planning and execution were the unseen ingredients that made the day go smoothly, preventing the crowds from getting out of hand, keeping most police at arm's length, and ultimately making the event a triumph. What could be more fitting for a social and political force calling itself "the Movement" than to transport hundreds of thousands of supporters into the nation's capital for a day and move them back out by sundown? If the plan worked, it would look like magic.

But there was no guarantee that this massive endeavor would work. To the contrary, some members of Congress foresaw a day of mayhem. Representative James Haley, a Florida Democrat, predicted that the march could "be the spark which would touch off an ugly, bloodletting riot, accompanied perhaps by killings."

The Kennedy brothers by now were somewhat begrudging allies of the Movement, but they still worried that Black Americans were getting too pushy. One day in May 1963, the president and the attorney general assessed the state of the civil rights movement.

"They're all getting tough," Robert warned.

"Negroes?" asked the president.

Yes, Robert responded. "They're awful tough to deal with now." He went on to explain that "they're competing with one another. Roy Wilkins hates Martin Luther King."

President Kennedy then added another concern: "The trouble is the Negroes are going to push this thing too far."

Robert Kennedy was correct about the tension between King and Wilkins. And he and his brother were attuned to the political risk that came with being seen as overly supportive of rights for Black Americans. About 75 percent of white southerners and 50 percent of white northerners thought the Kennedys were themselves pushing integration too hard. But the president and his brother still had a lot to learn about the abilities, determination, and discipline of those in the Movement.

In mid-May 1963, plans for the March on Washington were unveiled, notably without listing Roy Wilkins' NAACP as a sponsor. President Kennedy responded by inviting civil rights leaders to the

White House. He told them he didn't think the march was a good idea. Holding it while legislators were only beginning to consider the administration's civil rights bill, he counseled them, "seemed to me a great mistake" that could backfire with Congress. As the meeting ended, Roy Wilkins leaned over to Arthur Schlesinger, a historian and presidential adviser, who recorded that Wilkins "whispered to me his sympathy for the President in view of the pressures playing on him, the choices he had to make, the demands on his time and energy." At a session with reporters after the presidential meeting, Wilkins disavowed participating in the march. "I am not involved at the present moment," he said.

Winston Churchill once remarked, "There is only one thing worse than fighting with allies, and that is fighting without them." The organizers of the March on Washington would have appreciated that grim observation. Like Charles de Gaulle during World War II, Roy Wilkins could be an ally, but a surprisingly bitter and suspicious one.

Fighting with allies

The difficulty with allies is that some of their interests will be similar to one's own, but they will never be precisely identical. The NAACP never much liked Martin Luther King, Jr., or his crowd. To the old hands of the NAACP, King and his fellow Baptist ministers were newcomers who were elbowing aside the veterans and capturing the loyalty of the working-class Blacks of the South. NAACP staffers felt that sometimes they would initiate an action in the South, and then King and his crowd would come in and claim the credit—and reap the subsequent reward of money from donors across the country. The NAACP, more northern and more middle class, wanted to stick mainly to its policy of seeking integration through the courts. It had the monumental decision of *Brown v. Board of Education* to point to. What did King and his ilk have to show, some in the NAACP asked, aside from getting arrested a lot?

One of the NAACP's leading field workers had been Medgar Evers, head of its operations in Mississippi. Evers, an activist anomaly in the NAACP, felt that the organization was being overly bureaucratic and so was being left behind. He asked Wilkins to reconsider its shunning of demonstrations. When Evers was elected to a senior position in the SCLC, Wilkins told him to resign from that post. Evers complied with that instruction but continued to cooperate with King and the SCLC behind the scenes. The NAACP's very pace of life was different from those of the newer civil rights organization. Andrew Young once noted that the SCLC's ideal campaign lasted about ninety days, while the NAACP could pursue a legal action for nine years.

In June 1963, after the assassination of Evers, the NAACP official Gloster Current had dismissed a suggestion from James Meredith about how to respond. "We couldn't comment on any idea a student has," he said. "We're in a titanic struggle here, and it's not a struggle in which an amateur had to give advice to those who know what it's all about." This was an odd comment to make at a time when students had repeatedly led the way in the lunch counter sit-ins, the Freedom Rides, and the Birmingham marches. But it captured the awkward position of the NAACP. Wilkins himself protested that the NAACP was the only organization capable of maintaining a sustained fight. That may have been correct—the organization is still around nowadays, after all—but it hardly meant that the NAACP was leading the way in the early 1960s or that its leaders should enjoy automatic deference from others.

When Wilkins finally did agree a month later to become involved in the March on Washington, his price was that someone other than Bayard Rustin be its director. With his communist past and homosexual present, Rustin simply carried too much baggage, Wilkins indicated. At a meeting in New York City, Randolph, seeking unity, agreed to the change: he himself, he announced, would be the march director. It looked like Wilkins had prevailed. But, Randolph continued, as the designated director, he had the right to name his deputy.

"Oh God," Wilkins said, his victory barely won.

"You've got it, Roy," Randolph replied. "That means I want Bayard to be my deputy."

John Lewis, also at the meeting, had his first chance to assess Wilkins. "I can't say I liked what I saw. . . . He came across to me as some sort of New Yorker who thought he was smarter than the rest of the group." In dealing with Rustin, Lewis thought, Wilkins was "particularly nasty."

Yet once Wilkins was on board, he threw the weight of the NAACP's unmatched national infrastructure into the effort. Wilkins canceled or curtailed the summer vacations of many staffers and told his local chapters that he wanted them to go "all out" and send "no less than 100,000 of us" to the march. This was crucial because the SCLC's financial contribution, by contrast, was what one historian terms "threadbare."

Building a national stage for the Movement

Done well, a demonstration is just the tip of a huge iceberg, the physical manifestation of months of hard work of planning, training, and organizing. The March on Washington was executed so well that it would become a model for other organizations seeking national attention for their issues, whether against the Vietnam War or for women's rights or gay rights.

The purpose of the march was to introduce the civil rights movement to the nation. This was a chance for its leaders to get beyond the sound bites shown on nightly news broadcasts and explain themselves on their own terms. "Martin and the regular civil rights leaders were presenting to America our best face, our nonviolent face, our desire to be included into American society," said the actor Ossie Davis, who helped recruit entertainers for the day. To that end, it had to be impressively large, smoothly run, and peacefully conducted.

Rustin labored for months. He set up local committees in major cities. By the end of July, the committees had chartered two thousand buses, twenty-one special trains, and ten aircraft. Each bus had a designated captain to keep track of the passengers and to maintain discipline while traveling and then while in Washington. Each captain was required to know the rules of the march and to brief the passengers about them while en route. In addition, on the ground at the event would be 1,500 marshals. A manual for them was produced listing their duties, among which was to "create, by example, an atmosphere of passive, peaceful, nonviolent behavior." Marshals were to wear white shirts, blue pants, and carry no weapons. The manual even contained an appendix with the names and ranks of D.C. police officers who would be in the area, with their planned locations.

Security for the march also was essential—it had to be provided, but it couldn't be allowed to mar the day. Rustin handled it in a novel way, approaching it from his perspective of nonviolence. "My theory of maintaining order," he later said, "is not to have somebody who is strong to take care of a situation which becomes confrontation. My theory was, you deal with avoiding confrontation." He did not want the Washington, D.C., police, who then had a poor reputation for handling race issues, to be present in large numbers anywhere near the march. Rather, he asked them and other police departments in the area to look outward and focus on preventing interference by the Ku Klux Klan. For the march itself, Rustin invited the Guardians Association, a group of Black police officers in New York City, to take the lead. Its leaders in turn reached out to other similar groups, and the march eventually would be patrolled by two thousand Black law enforcement officers. They carried no weapons—they were operating outside their jurisdictions, at any rate—but they did bring handcuffs. Rustin brought in three experts to train these volunteers in dealing with marches, one of them a Black policeman from Britain.

Delicate compromises were also being negotiated. To bring in religious groups and others suspicious of militancy, Rustin announced in early August that there would be no sit-ins or other acts of civil disobedience associated with the march. Another adjustment was the result of so many big-name performers, from Josephine Baker to Harry Belafonte to Bob Dylan, having signed up: Rustin decided to divide the day into two parts, with a concert in the morning and speeches in the afternoon.

Rustin also produced a military-style "Operating Manual" for the march that first laid out its sponsors and its goals, and then instructed prospective attendees on how to prepare to attend: publicize the march, organize transportation, get unemployed people involved, and ask government and other employers to give workers the day off. Marchers were instructed not to bring their own placards; only signs provided by march organizers were allowed. Participants were advised to wear flat shoes and bring hats and sunglasses, and they were "strongly advised" not to bring children.

Rustin also set up a hotline to handle medical emergencies, staffed around the clock for the three days before the march to the day after. He even instructed people on what to pack for lunch: no sandwiches with mayonnaise, which might spoil, but peanut butter and jelly would be good, as would apples and raisins; lots of water; no alcohol. And for those who didn't bring sufficient food, Rustin had on hand eighty thousand box lunches packed by volunteers from the National Council of Churches. At Rustin's request, the telephone company installed four hundred pay phones around the march area.

And then there was the sensitive question of where important people were to sit. To address that, Rustin's office produced long lists of who was to sit on the platform behind the speakers, and who was to sit in front below them.

But what about women?

Rustin thought of everything—except the role of women, whom he neglected entirely in his planning for the march. The civil rights movement was surprisingly unenlightened about women—listening to them, or appreciating their roles—and Rustin was no exception. The pioneering Black lesbian lawyer Pauli Murray had coined, or at least publicized in the 1940s, the term "Jane Crow" to describe this sexism. Anna Hedgeman, another veteran activist who had been involved in some of the planning for the march, met with two other women to draft a letter of protest to Randolph, stating that "it is incredible that no woman should appear as a speaker." Rustin made partial amends—several women who had contributed would be asked to stand and be recognized. But there still would be no female speaker, because, Rustin decided, it simply would cause too much trouble. A follow-up memorandum explained that it was too difficult to select "a single woman to speak without causing serious problems vis-à-vis other women and women's groups."

Wednesday, August 28, 1963

As the day of the march approached, white Washington worried. A front-page headline in the *Los Angeles Times* stated, "Washington Gets Jittery Over March." The *New York Herald Tribune* printed an editorial titled "The March Should Be Stopped," and the *Washington Star* denounced the entire effort as "misguided." The great concern was that it would turn violent. In hindsight, that may seem overblown. Yet, at the time, nothing like this had happened before. The prospect of a quarter of a million people, most of them Black, massing in the nation's capital was a new and frightening phenomenon for many whites. This would be a huge and unknown crowd, not a small band of disciplined nonviolent marchers. Who were all these people descending on Washington? What would happen if some radicals lit a match and threw it on the tinder? The District of Columbia's government ordered liquor stores to close for the day and cleared its jails in case space was needed. The Army stationed troops near the city on alert. On the morning of August 28 itself, many whites who worked in the thousands of federal offices that lined the Washington Mall stayed home.

And so the march began. The crowd that assembled from all over the country sprawled eastward on the Mall at least halfway from the Lincoln Memorial to the Capitol. It clearly numbered at least two hundred thousand, and it kept growing. Most of the crowd was Black, but tens of thousands of whites attended—in large part because of the efforts of Anna Hedgeman working with the National Council of Churches—indicating a healthy white support for the goals of the day.

The formal ceremonies began at the Lincoln Memorial at 1:30 in the afternoon with the singing of the national anthem. At 2:00, A. Philip Randolph strode to the microphone and began by saluting those assembled as "the largest demonstration in the history of this nation." He then addressed that most important of questions, the beginning of strategy: Who are we? "We are not a mob. We are the advanced guard of a massive, moral revolution for jobs and freedom." The first step in self-liberation is not allowing others to define who you are.

Randolph did not hold back. He criticized valuing private property over human rights—and reminded his listeners that Black Americans who were enslaved had been valuable "property." "It falls to the Negro," he said, " to reassert this proper priority of values, because our ancestors were transformed from human personalities into private property."

And why are we here, Randolph asked, staging the biggest demonstration in the nation's history? Because gradualism and legal challenges had been slow and often ineffective. (Take that, Roy.) "The plain and simple fact," he continued, "is that until we went into the streets the federal government was indifferent to our demands. It was not until the streets and jails of Birmingham were filled that Congress began to think about civil rights legislation. It was not until thousands demonstrated in the South that lunch counters and other public accommodations were integrated."

Randolph expressed impatience with those who thought Black Americans were moving too fast or becoming too radical, who simply wanted peace and order. Echoing the criticism of King's Birmingham jail letter, he said, "Those who deplore our militance, who exhort patience in the name of a false peace, are in fact supporting segregation and exploitation. They would have social peace at the expense of social and racial justice."

And where do we go next? "When we leave," Randolph said, "it will be to carry on the civil rights revolution home with us into every nook and cranny of the land."

Then, as a result of the protest led by Anna Hedgeman, the women of the Movement were recognized, among them Rosa Parks, Myrlie

Evers (the widow of Medgar Evers), and Diane Nash. Nash was surprised—no one had told her about the planned recognition, and she had decided to stay home in Birmingham because she was tired.

Roy Wilkins vs. John Lewis

Again like Charles de Gaulle, Roy Wilkins was persistent even when he was wrong. He fought a rearguard action into the day of the march itself. Even as the speeches were being delivered, Wilkins argued with John Lewis backstage over some militant passages in Lewis' planned speech. The two were seen shaking fingers at each other. Wilkins accused Lewis of being a double-crosser. Lewis responded that he was speaking for the people in SNCC, the Mississippi Delta, and the Black Belt. "You haven't been there, Mr. Wilkins," he said. "You don't understand." Randolph, his speech finished, came back and intervened, pleading with Lewis to compromise for the sake of unity. It was a request the young man simply could not refuse to a revered leader three times his age.

Lewis excised much of the incendiary material. Out went the fiery reference to the Movement marching across the South like General Sherman. Deleted, too, was the criticism of politicians in Congress for having "betrayed the basic principles of the Declaration of Independence." Lewis even dropped a mention of the need "to protect our people from police brutality." The final version of his speech was weak and unmemorable. In the heat of the moment, and the need for unity, it was a missed opportunity for SNCC. But declawing the speech did serve the larger strategic need, that of the civil rights movement to present itself that day to the American people as made up of decent, nonthreatening people standing together in their cry for simple justice. What was best for SNCC and Lewis was not necessarily, on this day and in this place, what was best for the Movement as a whole.

Ironically, even Roy Wilkins wound up sounding more militant than Lewis on this one day as he denounced the federal government for failing to protect its citizens from police abuse. "We are," Wilkins said in his own speech, "beaten, kicked, maltreated, shot, and killed by local and state law enforcement officers."

However, Martin Luther King, Jr., still had not spoken.

"I Have a Dream" as a speech—and as a strategy

A bit before 4:00, Dr. King began, as the last speaker of the day. He delivered the most memorable talk of his life, known today as the "I Have a Dream" speech. It is, most of all, an awe-inspiring public poem, biblical in its phrasing, mesmerizing in its repetitions.

But inside the magnificent phrases, King also addressed the basic strategic questions: Who are we? What are we trying to do? How are we going to do it? And when? Some of it was familiar stuff—but this was the first time that many people in the country were seeing and hearing him, with all three American television networks of the time carrying the day's proceedings live and then recapping them on the evening news.

King began by greeting the crowd stretched out before him, in the heart of the nation's capital, as "the greatest demonstration for freedom in the history of our nation." Exploring that theme of American history, and standing before the statue of Abraham Lincoln, he consciously reached back to that president's Gettysburg Address, delivered a century earlier: "Five score years ago, a great American, in whose symbolic shadow we stand, signed the Emancipation Proclamation." Then he reached even further back, to the Declaration of Independence and the Constitution, depicting them as promises made but not yet fulfilled.

Next, he rejected "cooling off"—that great desire of the Kennedy administration—and gradualism. Rather, he said, let us focus on "the fierce urgency of now. . . . Now is the time to make justice a reality for all of God's children." For white America, he had a warning: "There will be neither rest nor tranquility in America until the Negro is granted his citizenship rights."

For Black America, he had an admonition to adhere to the strategy of nonviolence:

In the process of gaining our rightful place, we must not be guilty of wrongful deeds. Let us not seek to satisfy our thirst for freedom by drinking from the cup of bitterness and hatred. We must forever conduct our struggle on the high plane of dignity and discipline. We must not allow our creative protest to degenerate into physical violence. Again and again we must rise to the majestic heights of meeting physical force with soul force.

James Lawson's teachings in Nashville echo in this paragraph, especially the last sentence.

The repetition of "now" a few minutes earlier was matched with a burst of negatives. "We cannot be satisfied and we will not be satisfied as long as a Negro in Mississippi cannot vote and a Negro in New York believes he has nothing for which to vote."

Interestingly in personal terms for King's journey of the previous ten years, he said, "No, no, we are not satisfied, and we will not be satisfied until justice rolls down like water and righteousness like a mighty stream." This was the same reference to Amos 5:24 that had been the high point of his first speech to the Movement, nearly a decade earlier at the beginning of the Montgomery bus boycott: "Let judgment run down as waters, and righteousness as a mighty stream."

That was where King himself came from. Now he told the people before him that he also knew where they came from, some "fresh from narrow jail cells." Knowing that, he said it was time to face imprisonment again, if necessary. He sent them back: "Go back to Mississippi, go back to Alabama, go back to Georgia, go back to Louisiana, go back to the slums and ghettos of our northern cities, knowing that somehow this situation can and will be changed."

And, he said, when you do, go back holding this dream. Eight times he said, "I have a dream." He named Georgia, Mississippi, and Alabama as places he dreamed of seeing transformed. But most memorably, he said, "I have a dream that my four little children will one day live in a nation where they will not be judged by the color of their skin but by the content of their character." He topped the eight uses of "dream" with eleven invocations of "let freedom ring." Here he began nationally, with the hilltops of New Hampshire and the peaks of California, but he ended regionally, with Stone Mountain in Georgia, Lookout Mountain in Tennessee, and the molehills of Mississippi.

Finally, he ended with a prayer, that one day, Americans would be able to join hands "and sing in the words of the old Negro spiritual: 'Free at last! Free at last! thank God Almighty, we are free at last!'" It was a stunning moment, perhaps the most memorable American speech of the century.

Then the crowd went home, peacefully. In the entire day, only four people were arrested, none of them participants in the march. By sundown, most of the marchers were on buses and trains, or in cars, and the Washington Mall in front of the Lincoln Memorial was not only empty but clean. Rustin had seen to that also. The entire day had been a logistical triumph.

Until the March on Washington, the Movement could be seen by many white Americans as a distant rumbling in the South. Now they had seen its face and heard a message they could and would remember. The message had surprised some. A white journalist, flying back to Atlanta, had a conversation with a white stewardess. "I haven't been for this civil rights stuff and I've never liked King," she said. "But I watched him on TV, and after it was over I was proud of the Negro and proud of America. I thought they were just going to criticize us white people. He made my country seem so beautiful I felt like I wanted to shake his hand." As the historian Harvard Sitkoff puts it, "To the extent that any single public utterance could, this speech made the black revolt acceptable to white America."

In the context of this book, King's speech that day was a model of strategic rhetoric—defining the Movement, setting forth its goals, and describing how it planned to achieve them. As a speech, it stands by itself. It does not resemble the overblown oratory of nineteenth-century

America. Nor it is much like other twentieth-century political rhetoric, because it is steeped in language that feels biblical. Yet in taking a grand overview of American history, and in staking the claim that the civil rights movement had become a national phenomenon, it is unlike a church sermon. It was a notice to the nation.

A message to the nation

On that day, the Movement had stepped onto the national stage. It had held one of the largest political rallies in American history, just a short walk from the White House. The march also was the largest integrated event the nation had ever seen, with a final turnout of at least 250,000, and perhaps far more.

The nation had seen Bull Connor's America four months earlier. Now the Movement had presented its own deeply different vision of the country, under the gaze of the statue of Lincoln. King said in a television interview that evening that the march was part of "a quest to get into the mainstream of American society." It was a fine way to summarize what had proved to be a very polite day, depicting the Movement as responsible people making reasonable demands. The FBI, looking at the march and King's speech from the other end of the telescope, came to a very different conclusion, deciding that King was now "the most dangerous Negro of the future in this Nation from the standpoint of communism, the Negro and national security."

In sum, the Movement's message had gone national in the best possible way. The march presented to the American people an idea that had been expressed earlier by one participant in the Birmingham protests: "The movement represented courage. It was black people standing up saying, 'I'm a human being, I have a right to be treated like a human being.'"

King emerged from the march showing a new confidence in his methods and approach. With its demonstration of "peace, love, and no finger pointing," he said at a staff conference in Dorchester, Georgia, held just over a week later, it had "helped immeasurably to involve hundreds of thousands of people who before were indifferent," and so was "one of the best examples of the non-violent approach to change."

John Lewis, decades later, mainly agreed with that assessment. "Yes, the march was a failure in terms of specifics, in terms of prompting meaningful action on the part of the government," he wrote in a memoir. "But it was a truly stunning spectacle in terms of showing America and the world the size and strength and spirit of our movement."

Not everyone now counts the march so successful. Manning Marable, a Marxist historian, argued that by making itself acceptable to white America, the Movement inadvertently had alienated its own left wing. "The march's relative conservativism was in part responsible for the breakdown within the Black leadership several years later," Marable wrote. "It probably did more to divide and retard the Black Freedom movement than any other single mobilization between 1960 and 1966." Perhaps. But the split at the march itself was as much between moderates, with Wilkins and King at odds, as it was between the center and the left. The movement's divisions had many causes, as we will see.

Sparking the women's movement

Conflicts often carry surprising social side effects. One notable example is that the French and Indian War, also known as the Seven Years' War, increased the debt load on the French state, and so likely spurred the French revolution. Meanwhile, Britain's attempt to pay for its side of that war by taxing American colonials helped spark the American Revolution.

So, too, did the civil rights movement have long-ranging unintended consequences. One significant result of the march, albeit an accidental one, was that it led women to ask hard questions that led to the founding of the modern, second-wave women's liberation movement, following the first wave of feminism in the nineteenth century. "I've never seen a more immovable force," said Dorothy Height, president of the National Council of Negro Women, referring to the attitudes of the march organizers. "We could not get women's participation taken seriously." Late in 1963, the brilliant lawyer Pauli Murray called the omission of women at the event "bitterly humiliating."

The following year, an anonymous memorandum distributed to members of SNCC noted that women were essential to running the organization yet were "not given equal say-so when it comes to day to day decision making." SNCC's Casey Hayden and Mary King renewed the challenge a year after that, stating, "The caste system perspective dictates the roles assigned to women in the movement." The emerging New Left—in which Casey Hayden's ex-husband, Tom Hayden, was prominent—also exhibited a strong and persistent streak of machismo. Finally, in 1966, a group of women met in Washington, D.C., and founded the National Organization for Women (NOW). Among its organizers were Pauli Murray and Anna Hedgeman, the latter of whom had led the protest to A. Philip Randolph about the exclusion of women from speaking at the March on Washington.

8.
LATER BIRMINGHAM, FALL 1963
Counter-Escalation Against Children

At 10:22 on the morning of Sunday, September 15, 1963, just a few weeks after the ebullience of the March on Washington, nineteen sticks of dynamite planted by Ku Klux Klan members detonated against the eastern wall of the Sixteenth Street Baptist Church, which had been the headquarters of the civil rights campaign in Birmingham. Four girls inside, preparing for a youth service at 11:00, were blasted to death. Three of them were fourteen years old, the fourth was eleven. More than a dozen other people were wounded. All but one of the church's stained-glass windows were blown out. It was the city's twenty-ninth bombing since 1951.

The church's minister, the Reverend John Cross, Jr., digging with members of his congregation, soon found the bodies. "They were all stacked in a pile, like they clung together," he said years later. "Their bodies were so mutilated I couldn't recognize any one of them, as well as I knew these girls. It was like looking at strangers." He picked up a bullhorn and, though sobbing, began reciting the part of Psalm 23 about walking through the valley of the shadow of death. He would dream about that day two or three times a week for the rest of his life.

The bombing was a murderous crime, but it was also a stupendous blunder. Bombing churches and killing children was exactly the wrong step for the segregationists to take. The perpetrators may not have realized it, but they were operating under a national and even global spotlight. Blowing up little girls in a place of worship showed that the two sides could not be considered morally equivalent, as so many Americans outside the South had been inclined to do. Instead, it now was clear that the Movement was demanding that Blacks be permitted their rights as citizens, and that a portion of the white South was responding with bitter violence.

Still, the effect of the church bombing was crushing for those in the Movement. Even Martin Luther King, Jr., fell into a crisis of faith. "It was symbolic of how sin and evil had blotted out the life of Christ," he later said, noting that a stained-glass window portraying Jesus had literally been shattered. "I can remember thinking that if men were this bestial, was it all worth it? Was there any hope? Was there any way out?" There was a hint of this desolation in his funeral eulogy for the girls, in which he tried to see the good that would come out of it, but conceded, "Life is hard, at times as hard as crucible steel"—a simile that went to the heart of Birmingham, a city that had been built on making steel. What kind of crazed system, he asked, produces people who think it right to murder little girls in a church? King also noticed that no white officials were present at the funerals.

At the same time, noted Bayard Rustin, the Black people of Birmingham "did not take to the streets and raise hell. They said, We're still going to be nonviolent. This deeply touched the hearts of the American people." Rustin drew a powerful strategic conclusion from the event: "We were bombed because we were winning, not because we were losing."

The Kennedy administration's response

The Kennedy administration's response was hapless. First the president met with some Black ministers and other leaders from Birmingham, and four days later with a white delegation from the city. One of the whites suggested that the girls in the church had accidentally detonated dynamite being hidden there. When the Birminghamians complained about King, President Kennedy told them to worry more about SNCC, saying, "They're gonna get tougher."

Then, for reasons that are not clear, Kennedy decided to dispatch an inquiry team to Birmingham that consisted of a former secretary of the Army, Kenneth C. Royall, and a former West Point football coach, Earl "Red" Blaik. Sending in the coach may have seemed odd, but the choice of Royall was even more puzzling. He was best known for having been forced out of his leadership position in 1949 under President Truman after "publicly and pugnaciously" opposing the executive order desegregating the military. Royall and Blaik wandered around the town, did not seem to learn much, and never produced a report. Once again, the executive branch seemed insincere and flat-footed, failing to do the necessary research and preparation.

The FBI as a federal foe

The other response of the Kennedy administration was even more astonishing. On October 10, 1963, Robert Kennedy authorized the FBI to put a wiretap on King's home telephone in Atlanta.

That FBI request marked the beginning of an extraordinary episode in American history. When stated clearly, this simple fact is stunning and scandalous: a federal agency secretly declared war on a peaceable domestic political figure and campaigned zealously against him for years. It stands out less, however, because it was hardly J. Edgar Hoover's first abuse of power.

It is one of the paradoxes of the civil rights movement that while its leaders were trying to influence the federal government to help their cause, one part of that government, Hoover's FBI, was at the same time fighting a dedicated campaign against one of those very leaders and some of those around him. Hoover may also have taken advantage of the turmoil that followed the assassination of John F. Kennedy in November. On December 22, 1963, with a new president still settling in, the FBI's Division 5, its domestic intelligence agency, convened a daylong meeting in Washington, D.C. The topic of the day was "neutralizing King as an effective Negro leader." They emerged that day with a plan. To achieve that stated goal of bringing down King, the FBI would have agents across the country use wiretaps, surveillance microphones, and informants to collect material on King's sexual activities and then "expose King" as a "fraud" and "Marxist." They would operate in his home, his offices, and his hotel rooms on his endless travels.

Soon the FBI had a tape recording of King supposedly participating in an alleged sex party at the Willard Hotel in Washington, D.C. "This will destroy the burrhead," FBI director Hoover reportedly exclaimed.

But the agency's effort would go well beyond the passive collection of information. The FBI took wide-ranging active measures to undercut King and the SCLC. The agency urged the Internal Revenue Service to develop a tax fraud case against King. Hoover expressed disappointment when the tax office reported back that it had not detected any violations. When the FBI learned that Nelson Rockefeller was contemplating donating $250,000 to the SCLC, it asked a former agent to try to dissuade him. It did the same when a large grant was being considered by the Ford Foundation. It also tried to persuade colleges not to award King honorary degrees, warning them that there was derogatory information on him. The FBI even sought, unsuccessfully, to sabotage a meeting between King and Pope Paul VI.

In October 1964, when King was awarded the Nobel Peace Prize, Hoover blew a gasket. Soon afterward, the director escalated and told reporters on the record that King was "the most notorious liar" in America. King was stunned by the statement, recalled Dorothy Cotton, a longtime SCLC staff member. "That was the first time I saw him cry," she said. She and Andrew Young sat with him. "Andy and I had to comfort him because it was just so painful for him."

The FBI followed up with an elaborate scheme under which it sent an anonymous letter to King and his wife, encouraging him to commit suicide. The letter was accompanied by a tape with excerpts of the sex party in which King supposedly had participated. Hoover also decided that King did not deserve to be warned about death threats against him that the FBI had learned about, writes Taylor Branch.

Having accrued much power over the decades he had headed the FBI, Hoover effectively was an independent power within the federal government, feared for the secrets he had gathered on politicians and others, especially in the national capital. One indicator of his reach was a present he gave to John F. Kennedy, a man with several embarrassing secrets in his past. Hoover's gift was a glass ashtray engraved with Kennedy's own fingerprints. Kennedy kept it on his desk.

There are few analogies for this situation in conventional modern Western military history. Rather, Hoover operated like a medieval warlord, both an ally of the sovereign and a danger to him, someone who provided useful political intelligence but who controlled his own independent force and so had to be watched and placated. Hoover operated largely autonomously, a potential threat to those to whom he ostensibly reported.

Complicating the matter for the Movement, the Kennedys themselves were not reliable allies. Fred Shuttlesworth had an insight into the Movement's standoff with the Kennedy administration: the goals of the two were inevitably at odds. "The government always wanted to calm things down," Shuttlesworth said, "and we wanted to keep things at attention—create attention, Martin called it—in order to get people to address the problems."

Diane Nash boiled it down even more. She said of the Kennedys, "It was like they were playing." Shuttlesworth and Nash were both correct.

Diane Nash rebukes the Movement's leaders

On Wednesday, September 18, when Diane Nash attended the funeral for three of the four girls killed in the church bombing, she sensed the psychic energy roiling the city. One example: When Freeman Hrabowski

III went to sign out of school in order to attend the funeral—one of the
girls had been a friend of his—the principal removed his own necktie
and put it on the young man, telling him that he would be representing the entire high school. Nash was dismayed, perhaps angered, by
the failure of movement leaders to stay with the crowd and lead it,
that is, to capture the energy of the moment and turn it to positive
ends. Almost all of the leaders who attended followed the hearses to
the cemetery, leaving behind them an emotional crowd of perhaps five
thousand. The people stood for a spell and then began singing. Then,
despite the lack of any planning, they tried to start a march. Action
without preparation was not the Movement way. "The group marched
in one direction for half a block, and then it turned around and they
marched back half a block," Nash recalled. She saw it as a seething, di-
rectionless crowd heading toward wary police. She and others worried
about where the situation was going, so they stopped the march and
urged people to go home.

The U.S. Army's *Ranger Handbook* carries one of the rules supposedly promulgated in 1759 by Major Robert Rogers during the French
and Indian War: "Tell the truth about what you see and what you do.
There is an army depending on us for correct information."

Similarly, one of the lessons Nash had taken away from participating in sit-ins was that it was absolutely essential to report ground
truth accurately. "When you're really honest with yourself, and honest
with other people, you give yourself and them the opportunity to solve
problems, using reality, instead of lack of reality. That makes problem
solving much more efficient." And so Nash wrote a scathing memo to
King, Shuttlesworth, and the others. She told them they should not
have left the crowd to its own devices. "No one knew where they were
marching," she reprimanded them. "Indeed, it began in one direction
and started again in the opposite direction." You should never just leave
your people hanging like that, she admonished. "The crowd was in no
mood to take any insults or brutality from the police. I felt that when
the police attempted to block the crowd that bloodshed would result."

This had been a leadership failure, she continued. "People were highly aroused, frustrated, and sad, eager to do something, but no one knew what to do." They had been left in the lurch. The absence of leadership had undercut the strategy of nonviolence. Nash continued, "You can tell people not to fight *only* if you offer them a way by which justice can be served without violence. . . . Just to tell people not to fight after children are murdered and leave it at that is wrong and you are expecting and appealing to them to be less than men."

Here she returned to a key principle she had been taught and had been passing along for years: "Turn the energy of violence, that was perpetuated against us, into advantage." That is what she and her comrades had done in Nashville a few years earlier when the Black lawyer and city council member Z. Alexander Looby's house had been bombed—they had met, marched, confronted the mayor, and changed the city.

That had not happened here. "This energy could have been channeled, into a constructive, disciplined soul force aimed at creatively using this energy to achieve a concrete gain instead of just suppressing it." Here she was reaching back to Lawson's teachings about the need for "creative protest." Likewise, in combat, there is always a good deal of chaos present. Effective leaders don't try to stop it—that would be a fool's errand—but they do try to work with it. The last thing they should do is turn their backs on it.

Nash and Bevel devise a response

The bombing plunged Nash and her husband, James Bevel, into their own agonizing crisis of faith. They had pledged their lives to nonviolence. They had preached it in churches and practiced it in the streets. But for them, the bombing of the children raised a painful and fundamental question: Could the moment have come when it was necessary to abandon nonviolence? "I was thinking about killing people," Bevel confessed to an interviewer. "My mind turned murderous." He and Nash considered whether they should resign their posts in the SCLC and dedicate themselves to tracking down and executing the bombers.

"We felt confident that if we tried, we could find out who had done it, and we could make sure they got killed," Nash said. "And we considered that as a real option."

Ultimately, as they thought through the situation, their deep training in nonviolence reasserted itself, and they began to think about a different course—quite militant, but still nonviolent. They drafted a two-page paper that called for a massive but nonviolent military-style campaign of resistance to besiege and shut down the state government of Alabama. First, a base would be established in Montgomery to conduct training in nonviolent strategy and tactics. There would be "marching and drills in command and coordination of battle groups." The recruits also would be instructed in how to live in jail—how it works, how to get along, how to practice cooperation or noncooperation as needed, and how to behave when on trial. A separate focus would be on maintaining and gauging "group morale while imprisoned."

There also would be two forms of combat training: "Drill in dealing with fire hoses, dogs, tear gas, cattle prods, police brutality, etc.," and "Practice in blocking runways, train tracks, etc." They were contemplating obstructing all transportation into the capital of Alabama. Mass meetings would fill the downtown streets every night. "This is an army," Nash advised, adding, "Develop a flag and an insignia or pin or button." She wanted to see thousands of recruits trained in nonviolence lay siege to the state capitol in Montgomery, severing its communications and blocking roads, railroads, and runways. Telephones into the capitol would be jammed by constantly "calling and talking about freedom." Segregationists had talked about "massive resistance," but Nash and Bevel wanted to show them what that really looked like.

She presented the proposal to King, but he was distracted. He had just preached a funeral sermon over the caskets of three of the girls murdered in the church bombing. Half his mind was on that, the other half on a trip to Washington the next day. His travel plan irked Nash because experience had taught her that "you have your meeting with your own folks first." That is, get their reactions and views of the way forward before going to meet with outsiders. But King was not interested in Nash's memo. "Doctor King's initial reaction," she recalled, was "'Oh, Diane, get real.'"

"I did not feel that our conversation was fruitful," Nash noted drily.

So for the moment, the Nash plan went nowhere. But it would develop and would eventually lead to the Selma campaign. Nash and Bevel decided to go ahead and take the first steps by themselves, using a few staffers Bevel controlled as the SCLC's organizer for direct action. "When we drew up our plans, it wasn't for Selma," Nash noted. But when activists in Selma asked for help, Bevel and Nash saw a new path. They thought that they could plant some seeds there and that eventually the locals would invite King and the SCLC to intervene. They had buttons made with the word "GROW," which stood for "Get Rid of Wallace," Alabama's white-power governor.

Bevel buttonholed King repeatedly about this statewide Alabama operation. King had a lot of respect for Bevel, but in this case he eventually ordered him to drop the idea.

Yet Bevel and Nash were not the type to let an idea slip away just because the initial reception to it was cool. They thought and planned. In the fall of 1963 Nash wrote a pamphlet she titled "Handbook for Freedom Army Recruits," a kind of basic-training document for new activists. Her notion was that the SCLC should recruit volunteers to sign up for one year of active service. Under this plan, in the spring of 1964 they would be told to "report for duty." In a section with the heading "Our Weapon," she described nonviolent direct action and said, "It is not a weapon for the weak, for it takes a stronger person to use nonviolence well, than it does to fight. . . . Nonviolence begins by remembering that the people who oppose us are human beings, in spite of the way they act sometimes. With this attitude in us, we treat our opponents as humans, showing them good will, even when we oppose them." Seeing the humanity of a foe is good strategy, for it lays some of the groundwork for possible eventual reconciliation.

Next in Nash's booklet came an eleven-point "Code of Discipline," mandating, "We will never retaliate or inflict suffering on another person." Putting a finer edge on that, the sixth item in the code stated, "In the course of the struggle if anyone insults or attacks a policeman or any segregationist, we will protect him from insult or attack even at the risk of our lives." This was indeed a high standard. She went on to provide helpful hints about how to survive and even thrive in jail. Most notably, she recommended a daily routine that included "group worship," "individual meditation," "discussions on . . . segregation and nonviolence," "cleaning up" the cells, and "recreation."

Bevel, meanwhile, was pushing King to step up training in nonviolence. As a result of the gains of the civil rights movement, he argued in a memo, Blacks had lost their sense of fear, but many were acting without any sense of the principles of nonviolence. The result, he worried, had been "demonstration for the sake of demonstrating, and resorting to Brinkmenship tactics." So he recommended that the SCLC abandon "splinter" projects and instead focus its time and energy on training Alabama Blacks in the theory and tactics of nonviolent resistance. There is no indication that King responded to this recommendation. But he may have been pondering the newly militant perspective that Nash and Bevel were taking. In a speech around this time, he awkwardly invoked the analogy himself, stating, "When General of the Armies Douglas MacArthur was repelled in a just campaign during World War II, he fell back. . . . But I serve notice tonight, that *I will return* to Birmingham, unless, by a certain date . . ." It was, however, notes Taylor Branch, "a tinny echo."

Similarly, the lesson that Fred Shuttlesworth took away from the aftermath of the murderous church bombing was that training and discipline were essential. Events would have gotten out of hand, he argued, but for preparation that the Movement had given its volunteers. He also expressed this in military terms: "There were times people wanted to fight, . . . but you have to drill into people that this is a movement, and it's amazing how much discipline people can exercise when they realize they must do it this way in order to gain an appointed end." Historians do not frequently discuss the civil rights struggle in terms of discipline, but it is clear that its leaders understood that it was key. Shuttlesworth's larger point is significant: working toward self-discipline in operations was the way to achieve the strategic goal, and it was imperative to train volunteers to understand and remember that. Indeed, self-discipline mattered more in the Movement than it does in military life, because the Movement lacked the military's authority to enforce behavior and punish lapses. Keeping everyone's eyes on the prize was a way to reinforce self-discipline.

Eventually, the Bevel-Nash plan morphed into what they called the Alabama Project. When translated into on-the-ground action, however, it would not be a statewide effort. Instead, it would be based in Selma, and eventually it would lead to a march to Montgomery that would shut down the capital. Indeed, more than a year later, it would become the last great battle of the 1960s civil rights movement, growing from that bitter seed planted by the bombing of the Sixteenth Street Baptist Church.

Another shock

But 1963 had one more major shock in store. On November 22, President Kennedy was shot in Dallas. King, watching television at home in Atlanta, was deeply disturbed, both by what the murder said about the state of America and about his own fate. "This is what is going to happen to me," he told his wife, Coretta. "This is such a sick society." The thought stayed with him. A couple of years later, Abby Mann, a movie producer interested in making a biopic about King's life, lightly asked King how such a film would conclude. "It ends with me getting killed," King responded.

Two days after the assassination, Kennedy's supposed killer, Lee Harvey Oswald, was shot while television cameras showed him being moved from police headquarters to a jail. Taylor Branch notes, "Millions of NBC viewers had just witnessed the first murder ever broadcast on live television." Civil rights activists already were familiar with the

American capacity for violence. Now the technology of television, with its new capacity for real-time transmission of events, was changing how Americans experienced violent moments.

The end of Birmingham

The outcome of the Birmingham campaign was a victory for the Movement but it carried hidden costs. "Not until the colossus of segregation was challenged in Birmingham did the conscience of America begin to bleed," King said later. The American mood was shifting, and that would lead not just to civil rights legislation with teeth but also to a general change in attitudes.

But for the city, through its own faults, the campaign effectively was an economic disaster. Birmingham's mishandling of the fight against segregation had a devastating long-term effect. Years after the events of 1963, an Alabama newspaper editor observed that every time a corporate executive in the North would tell his wife that he was thinking of moving the company headquarters to either Birmingham or Atlanta, "She began thinking about fire hoses, police dogs, and church bombings. And she said, 'I'm not moving to Birmingham.'" In 1950, Atlanta and Birmingham were about the same size; by the early twenty-first century, the greater Atlanta area was the tenth-largest population cluster in the United States, with 5.8 million people, while the greater Birmingham area was the forty-ninth, with 1.1 million. Much of Birmingham's relatively slow population growth had to do with the decline of the steel industry on which the city's economy had been built. But it also was caused by Atlanta's leadership being more enlightened, not just about race but also about investing in building a major airport.

But in the winter of 1963–64, for the civil rights movement, the question was what to do next. "Finally, after Birmingham, the country was alive," commented Bob Moses. "The problem has, all of a sudden, become a national problem." So how should civil rights leaders respond to the changed context of their movement?

The SCLC was in an odd phase. For months, the organization's leadership had been debating where to go for the next campaign. Finally, King chose to support a burgeoning anti-segregation movement in St. Augustine, a small town in northern Florida where some Black citizens had been protesting the town's failure to enforce laws requiring that schools be integrated. The choice was almost by default, because for a variety of reasons, other possible locations looked unpromising. The move into St. Augustine in May 1964 was noteworthy for a tactical change: most of the marches there took place at night. It isn't clear why the marches were moved to evenings. It may just have been to avoid the heat of the Florida day in May and June. Whatever the reason, marching at night was provocative. It is always more difficult to control crowds in the dark, or to see who is attacking them. In military operations, night operations tend to be messy affairs.

Ultimately, however, St. Augustine developed into a two-month-long sideshow. It was ill-considered, perhaps. But it served the strategic purpose of keeping the issue of racial discrimination in the headlines as the Civil Rights Act was being debated in Congress. It also kept King out of Mississippi during an increasingly dangerous time—which, to speculate for a moment, may have been part of the purpose. An official of the Florida branch of the NAACP denounced the St. Augustine effort as self-aggrandizement by King based on "the yearning to demonstrate for the sheer sake of demonstration"—ironically, the very charge that Bevel had raised about others in his internal memo a year earlier. In military terms, St. Augustine may best be classified as a "holding action," an attack to engage with the enemy while the main event was going on elsewhere—in this case, in the U.S. Senate.

Interestingly, James Bevel, despite being an important SCLC staff member, also kept his distance from the entire campaign in St. Augustine, considering it a "waste of time." He thought it highlighted genuine problems, but that those were about to be addressed by the pending federal civil rights bill, the tough one proposed by the late President Kennedy the previous June. When the bill finally became law in July 1964, he said, the violations could be addressed through lawsuits. "I'm not going to be involved in this kind of shenanigan," he recalled saying. "You guys are just gaming. I'm going back to Alabama, and we'll be ready when you decide to join us." Wyatt Walker asked King to dismiss Bevel for insubordination. King declined, Bevel recalled.

The more radical SNCC, meanwhile, always more comfortable with taking risks, was contemplating trying to build on Bob Moses' grassroots work in Mississippi. If Birmingham had been the worst city in the South, Mississippi was the worst state, notorious for its violent repression and disenfranchisement of Black citizens. In fact, it was the most racially dangerous state in the entire nation. It led the South in known lynchings, with some 578 having been committed between 1882 and 1959. SCLC leaders advised SNCC against going into Mississippi. Andrew Young recalled, "We were all Southerners and we knew the depth of depravity of Southern racism. We knew better than to take on Mississippi."

But in fact the very hardness of Mississippi was part of the attraction of the state to the younger, more daring members of SNCC. As Bob Moses told a SNCC meeting in Atlanta, the state "offers SNCC an opportunity to move where no one else is willing to attack." Moses later would elaborate on that thought, writing, "For a short while we had the field to ourselves, access to people that other people and organizations did not have, simply because they were not willing to run the risks we were."

It was at about this time that Nina Simone wrote the song with the memorable title "Mississippi Goddam":

Alabama's gotten me so upset
Tennessee made me lose my rest
And everybody knows about Mississippi goddam

9.
OXFORD, OHIO, JUNE 1964

SNCC Prepares to Assault a State

The summer of 1964 brought three major changes to the shape and face of the civil rights movement. First, the scope broadened, as SNCC, assisted by CORE, launched an ambitious statewide assault in Mississippi with the idea of challenging the state's entire white supremacist structure. Second, the nature of the troops in the field changed, as those two organizations recruited hundreds of white college students from the North to be deployed into the state. Third, while the SCLC was bogged down in an inconclusive effort in St. Augustine, Florida, SNCC would seize the national lead in the Movement.

SNCC's 1964 invasion of Mississippi is of particular interest for the purposes of this book because it was as close as civil rights leaders ever came to conducting a large, almost conventional military operation. It follows that the experience of the volunteers who went to the state that summer was eerily similar to that of foot soldiers in ground combat, both during it and afterward. Those volunteers began the process in a two-week training session held that June at a small college in Oxford, Ohio.

Time for a blitzkrieg

For two years, Bob Moses, small, bright, brave, and bespectacled, had quietly been preparing the battlefield as he led SNCC workers in a small voter registration campaign in Mississippi. He had an effect. Fannie Lou Hamer would recall that until she heard it from Moses and the SNCC executive secretary James Forman, she didn't know that Blacks even *had* the right to vote in Mississippi. Thus informed, she went down with seventeen others to the courthouse in Indianola on August 31, 1962, to register. That same day, W. D. Marlow, the owner of the cotton plantation where Hamer worked, fired her from her job as his recordkeeper and evicted her from the house where she had lived for eighteen years. "We are not ready for that in Mississippi," Marlow told her. Hamer briefly moved into the home of friends in the nearby town of Ruleville; ten days later, the bedroom she had used there was perforated by sixteen bullets.

Hamer was unusually brave and strong, and her determined effort was exceptional. The concrete results of the registration drive had been disappointing and even frightening to members of SNCC. "We had been weaving, trying to weave, a network of people who could work to change the system," recalled Casey Hayden. "But it was so slow and so many people were getting picked off one by one, the local leaders were getting murdered, people were being evicted." After years of work, there were several counties in Mississippi that still had not a single Black voter registered. And even Blacks who did manage to register often were turned away from voting, sometimes at the point of a gun. The hard fact was that after two years of struggling, Bob Moses was desperate—and ready to try a radically different approach.

The enigmatic Moses is one of the more interesting field commanders of the civil rights movement. One military figure he brings to mind is Orde Wingate, the brilliant but eccentric British special operator of World War II. Wingate's specialty was leading missions deep behind enemy lines in the jungles of Burma. Moses was similar—a quiet and courageous young man who on his own volition went deep into rural Mississippi for the first time in 1960. Ella Baker told him to go to Cleveland, Mississippi, and look up Amzie Moore, the hardened activist who had developed a quiet network of contacts across the state. Moses soon learned that the entrepreneurial Moore did not care much about integrating lunch counters or schools. Rather, he wanted the vote and the political power that it would bring. Undereducated but wise, Moore was pleasantly surprised by his dealings with Moses. "Bob's approach to me was entirely different from what I thought his approach would have been, coming from Harvard, you know," Moore recalled. "He wasn't a jiver. He was just a straightforward man." At another point, Moore said of Moses, "He . . . didn't do much talking, usually presented his ideas and let you think on them."

Moses, following Moore's lead, would spend years in that violent, repressive state, sometimes alone, working for civil rights, focusing mainly on voter registration. It was essentially a combat situation for him, a young Black man who previously had been teaching mathematics at Horace Mann, an expensive prep school in New York. "When you're out there in a really rural area with no electricity, no radio, no running water, everything moves very slowly and you really have time to go into yourself," Moses wrote later, sounding very much like an old infantryman. "I used to think, Pick one foot up and step forward, put it down and pick the next one up. You get down to that level of reality if you're doing canvassing in those dangerous areas."

In Mississippi, Moses was assaulted and jailed repeatedly, sometimes simply for speaking to white people as equals. One day in 1961, Moses was accompanying two men to register at the courthouse in Liberty, in far southwestern Mississippi. Three white men asked Moses where they were going. Moses told them, and in response they beat him. SNCC then called a meeting in the nearby town of McComb. James Bevel, who with Diane Nash soon would move into Amzie Moore's house, began the gathering with impassioned oratory. Bevel was the SCLC's field secretary in Mississippi, an interesting position given that the organization was chary of working in that state.

Following Bevel at the McComb meeting, Moses stood up and said softly, "The law down here is law made by white people, enforced by white people, for the benefit of white people. It will be that way until the Negroes begin to vote." A reporter for the *McComb Enterprise Journal* who was at the gathering wrote, apparently with some surprise, that "the Negroes might be serious."

One night in 1963, Moses and two other organizers were driving toward Greenville, Mississippi, when a Buick with no license plates pulled up alongside them and sprayed their car with thirteen .45-caliber bullets from a submachine gun. Two of them hit Jimmy Travis, the driver, in the neck and shoulder. Moses leaned over, grabbed the wheel, and stepped on the brake. He then rushed to the county hospital. Travis survived and soon returned to his work with the Movement.

Moses, the son of a janitor and the nephew of a college professor, had many gifts, but one of the most unusual was the ability to provide strategic assessments. This might have been in part because he also possessed a leadership skill that should be more widely appreciated. He was, said a Black Mississippi minister who observed him, "one of the great listeners of the world." Emma Allen, who was involved in the Movement in Greenwood, Mississippi, simply said, "Bob didn't do too much talking." Even Stokely Carmichael, known for his energetic sloganeering, praised Moses for taking the opposite approach: "Bob always listened . . . far more than he ever spoke. And whenever he did speak—whether in a meeting or from a platform—it was softly and thoughtfully, almost haltingly, as though he were deliberately screening all emotion and rhetorical flourish out. I cannot remember hearing Bob ever utter a slogan of any kind."

Robert Coles, a Harvard psychiatrist acting as a kind of therapist for SNCC members, was even more impressed with Moses. "There was . . . a certain charismatic quality about him, and it is an interesting kind: it is low key," Coles said years later, adding that Moses had "a youthful almost cat-like tension in him. . . . His silences were extremely powerful." Coles also thought that Moses possessed extraordinary qualities as a leader: "He had imagination, and moral intelligence, as well as some plain old every day intelligence. He was able to work with a range of people from self-important intellectuals to ordinary people in neighborhoods. He was very patient and he was brave."

What's more, Coles discerned in Moses a rare "capacity for reflection and distance from the thing that you are very much in the midst of and even leading." Coles did not say so, but that ability to gain the psychological detachment to reflect on action is a talent of many effective leaders. James Mattis, one of the best American generals in our recent wars, made a habit of carrying in his combat knapsack a copy of the works of Marcus Aurelius. Reading that Roman emperor and Stoic philosopher for a half hour at night, he explained, helped him gain some mental distance from the battlefield.

Moses' actions spoke louder than his words. "Bob Moses was a little bitty fella," recalled Unita Blackwell, a sharecropper in Sunflower County, Mississippi. "And he stood up to this sheriff and Bob said, 'I'm from SNCC.' I had never saw that happen before. From that day on, I said, 'Well, I can stand myself.' People remember them people. SNCC went where nobody went. They was about the nuttiest ones they was. Ended up in some of the most isolated places and drug people out of there to vote." In 1976, Blackwell would become Mississippi's first Black female mayor, in the town of Mayersville.

For all his efforts, Moses had hit a dead end. In a memo to SNCC leadership written late in 1963, he stated simply, "It is not possible for us to register Negroes in Mississippi." He later explained that "the staff was exhausted and they were butting up against a stone wall, no breakthroughs for them." He concluded that "we were just like sitting ducks . . . people were just going to be wiped out." Indeed, Amzie Moore passed word that the Klan was looking to assassinate Moses, Fannie Lou Hamer, CORE's Dave Dennis, the NAACP's Aaron Henry, and himself—that is, every prominent civil rights leader in the state.

Moore's intelligence was solid. We now know that Sam Bowers, imperial wizard of the White Knights of the Ku Klux Klan, the strongest Klan organization in the state, had developed a plan to handle the civil rights invasion. They would leave to others the daylight confrontations in the streets, the ones that were covered by newspapers and television stations. At a meeting in Raleigh, Mississippi, he said, "When the black waves hit our communities, we must remain calm and think in terms of our individual enemies rather than our mass enemy. We must roll with the mass punch which they will deliver in the streets during the day, and we must counterattack the individual leaders at night."

SNCC decided to respond with massive escalation. As Casey Hayden put it, "The white power structure was so strong that it really seemed like we needed an enormous amount of outside support to punch a hole in the whole system of segregation." That effort would take the form of Freedom Summer, a campaign, she said, "to break Mississippi open. It was a kind of blitzkrieg."

White lives matter

The shape of that summer's campaign took its inspiration from a smaller operation in the fall of 1963 by Allard Lowenstein, a wheeling and dealing political operative who had been an administrator at Stanford and also had connections at Yale. Lowenstein had brought in eighty volunteers from those two colleges to work with SNCC in Mississippi for two weeks. One of the notable lessons that emerged from the effort was that "the press would respond to the beating of a Yale student as it simply would not do to the beating of a local Negro," noted one activist. Lowenstein proposed repeating that effort, but on a far larger scale, the following summer. What was required, he argued, was "a massive effort inside and outside Mississippi." Both Moses and Lowenstein were New Yorkers—indeed, Lowenstein had attended the Horace Mann School, where Moses later taught—but Lowenstein was a remarkable character, abrasive and uncollegial, and Moses could not stand working with him. He soon assigned a subordinate to handle all interactions with him.

Despite that personal friction, Lowenstein's idea caught fire. Just as including children had altered the battlefield equation in Birmingham a year earlier, SNCC and CORE now contemplated sending hundreds, perhaps thousands, of white youths into Mississippi. They did this knowing that Mississippi was "a closed society," as Moses described it, and that the appearance of white activists from outside the state would result in violence, and that some of those whites could be killed. There was also a hope, recalled Hollis Watkins, a Black from Mississippi who had been working with Moses, that bringing in white outsiders might deter some white Mississippians from inflicting violence on Black civil rights workers.

At the end of December 1963, SNCC's executive committee met in Atlanta to make plans for the coming year. The problems it hashed through in discussions over the course of five days would be familiar to anyone who has sat through a meeting of senior commanders in wartime. Transportation was a nagging issue. People in the field were wearing out, causing discipline problems. The headquarters staff was acting high-handed and pushing around the people doing the heavy lifting on the front lines.

John Lewis, the chairman of the organization, argued for a "saturation program" that would pour mainly white student volunteers into rural Mississippi and might "force a physical showdown between the federal and local governments." He was supported by Marion Barry, another veteran of the Nashville sit-ins and the future mayor of Washington, D.C.

No one said so at the meeting, according to SNCC records, but they knew they were putting the lives of white volunteers on the line. "We recognized that the results might be great pain and sorrow, but we were not asking that whites do any more than we had done," recalled SNCC's James Forman, the organization's executive secretary from 1961 to 1966. And, Forman knew, white parents would look at Mississippi differently when it was their own children who were there being beaten with truncheons, shot at on roads, and abused in jails. Some of those anxious parents, he also knew, would contact their congressional representatives. Every incident of violence against the white volunteers could have repercussions across the nation. "That's cold," said Dave Dennis of CORE, "but that was also in another sense speaking the language of this country. . . . We didn't plan any of this violence. But we just wanted the country to respond to what was going on."

Their simple but straightforward calculation was that Black suffering wasn't news, but white suffering was, especially when it was inflicted by Mississippi officials on middle-class college students from the North. And so SNCC decided, John Lewis wrote, to bring "an army of Northern college students into Mississippi." Yes, the state was deadly— the SNCC workers understood that in their very souls. "Our people were essentially being slaughtered down there," Lewis continued. "If white America would not respond to the deaths of our people, the thinking went, maybe it would react to the deaths of its *own* children."

Bob Moses sounded tense as he contemplated the looming confrontation. "That whole question about what will happen rests very heavy, because nobody really knows what might happen," he said in an April 1964 speech at Stanford. Moses, who had a master's degree in philosophy from Harvard, was pondering his own responsibility for the September 1961 death of Herbert Lee, an NAACP member murdered in cold blood before twelve witnesses in Amite County, in southern Mississippi. Moses had encouraged Blacks in that county to try to register to vote, though none had been allowed to do so during the twentieth century. Lee, a successful dairy farmer with nine children, had helped Moses by sometimes giving him rides. On the same day of the murder, an all-white coroner's jury acquitted the shooter of any wrongdoing. At Lee's funeral, his widow pounded on Moses' chest and yelled, "You killed my husband."

"Herbert Lee was killed . . . just as surely because we went in there to organize, as rain comes because of clouds," Moses said in his Stanford speech. "If we hadn't gone in there, he wouldn't have been killed." So, he said in a poignant last line, "when you come to deal with it personally, it still rests very heavy."

Moses had found it necessary to go to Stanford because of problems caused by Lowenstein, who was undercutting Moses with some of the recruits, telling them that Moses was too casual about allowing communist-influenced people to be involved. Lowenstein's criticisms had led the Stanford delegation to consider withdrawing from the project. Moses flew out to persuade them that their loyalty should not be to Lowenstein, or indeed to Moses, but to the people of Mississippi. Lowenstein also began operating in Boston without even contacting the local SNCC office there.

Lowenstein also was deciding on his own whether or not the recruits were fit for service in Mississippi. Moses thought those approvals should come only from SNCC staff working in the state. This was not just a power struggle; it also had to do with Moses' concern that the white students would come down and use their self-confidence, education, and sense of entitlement to take over the project, only to leave it a few months later to go back to college. He told recruiters he wanted people who would follow "strict discipline" and not try to be heroes on their own. Recipients of rejection letters were urged to stay active where they were, with Moses emphasizing that "no revolution can continue without its supply base or support troops."

Mississippi braces

Meanwhile, Mississippi's dominant caste was girding for the looming battle. On one night in February 1964, the White Knights of the KKK burned crosses in sixty-four counties. This was a form of boasting, because the White Knights were strong in only about ten counties. But a Klan recruiting drive across Mississippi reportedly brought in thousands of new members. Firepower increased in other ways, some quite literal. The city of Jackson, Mississippi, hunkering down for the expected civil rights invasion, acquired two hundred new shotguns, expanded its police force from 390 people to 450, and issued gas masks for the entire force. It also bought a 13,000-pound armored vehicle from which machine guns and tear gas could be fired. When a voter registration case came before the federal judge Harold Cox, a Kennedy appointee, he repeatedly referred to those trying to register as "a bunch of niggers." Cox also asked, "Who is telling these people they can get

in line and push people around, acting like a bunch of chimpanzees?"
Cox's appointment to the bench, the first judicial appointment of the
Kennedy administration, supposedly was the result of a deal between
Senator James Eastland and the Kennedy brothers, under which Cox,
a college friend of Eastland's, was given the appointment in exchange
for Eastland not blocking the nomination of Thurgood Marshall to a
federal appellate judgeship.

With the murders and beatings of civil rights workers, and a power
structure dedicated to preserving white supremacy, "it was time for a
confrontation," said Joyce Ladner, a SNCC activist in Mississippi. "I
mean everything was just slowly building up. You could either retreat
forever or make the final push for the big one." In military terms, the
civil rights struggle in Mississippi was reaching a culminating point.

Meeting Moses in Ohio

To prepare for the looming confrontation, some eight hundred volunteers attended training sessions at the Western College for Women in
Oxford, Ohio, in June 1964. The first one-week session was for those
going to work on voter registration, while the second was for those going
to start and operate Freedom Schools, meant to teach children the things
that Mississippi's schools wouldn't.

The first morning of the first session began with a Movement song
of resolution—"Ain't Gonna Let Nobody Turn Me 'Round"—followed
by a quick overview of the ground rules of orientation. Then Moses, age
twenty-nine, stood before the fresh-faced volunteers in the clothing of
a Mississippi farmer—white T-shirt and blue denim overalls. This was
just before the era of proletarian chic, so his appearance alone made an
impression. He began to speak, "very softly, very slowly," about what
they were getting into in Mississippi, noted Ellen Barnes, a graduate
student from nearby Miami University. He used surprisingly emotional
terms about the "sense of aloneness, isolation, and despair felt by the
Mississippi Negro."

He let that sink in. "Maybe we're not going to get very many people to register to vote this summer," Moses said in his quiet voice as the room went silent. "Maybe we're not going to get very many people into the Freedom Schools. Maybe all we're going to do is live through this summer." In other words, they sometimes would be conducting what the U.S. Army calls "presence missions," showing the flag and making the point that they were there, despite the threats of enemies. He paused. But living through the summer would be an achievement in itself, Moses concluded. "In Mississippi, that will be so much!" Indeed, survival was more than all of them could reasonably hope for.

Moses' quiet intensity captured the hearts and minds of his audience. "He immediately won the position of undisputed father figure for the volunteers," wrote one of them, Mike Yarrow, a graduate of Antioch College. They adored him. Paul Cowan called Moses "the embodiment of the America for which I had been searching." Cowan, in turn, was exactly the sort of person SNCC wanted to deploy to Mississippi that summer. Like President Kennedy, he was a graduate of the elite prep school Choate and of Harvard. He lived on Park Avenue in Manhattan. His father had created the quiz show *The $64,000 Question* and had then become president of the CBS television network. A third volunteer elevated Moses to "more or less the Jesus of the whole project, not because he asks to be, but because of everyone's reaction to him." It was a lot to put on one embattled young man.

That afternoon the volunteers broke down into sections to discuss the implications of Moses' assessment of the hazards they faced. They had a lot to learn. "The week of intense preparation and training in Oxford was mind-blowing for me," recalled one young woman, Carole Colca, who had just graduated from the University of Iowa. "I had no idea when I signed up just how dangerous this work might be. I had read and heard about black people in the South being beaten and arrested and even lynched. . . . But surely nobody would dare hurt white student volunteers from the North."

The talk of dangers had an effect. The record is unclear, but it appears that one or two people decided to withdraw.

The dangers ahead

On day 2 of the training camp in Oxford, SNCC's James Forman told the volunteers that the overarching goal of the summer project would be "to restore the right of the Negro to vote and to bring a return to Constitutional government. To do this we must dramatize the problem; make the nation aware of what it means to live in Mississippi." It was a good delineation of the strategic goal, enabling people to focus on doing things that moved toward it.

Forman emphasized that this would be extraordinarily dangerous. "Mississippi is going to be hell this summer," one student wrote home on June 17. He reported that Forman had told them that "they could all expect to be arrested, jailed, and beaten this summer, and in many cases, shot at. . . . I'd venture to say that every member of the Mississippi staff has been beaten up at least once."

Hollis Watkins, a seasoned comrade of Moses, was similarly emphatic in his talk to the volunteers: "I just told everybody in all of the sessions I attended that if they were coming, that they definitely need to be prepared for three things: . . . to be beaten, to go to jail, and be killed. And if they weren't prepared to accept those three possibilities, those three realities, then they shouldn't come." Some of the volunteers, he thought, understood what they were getting into, but others, he worried, "had the attitudes of, 'Hey, this is a good vacation to do down South.'" SNCC was trying hard to disabuse them of any such notion.

Robert Coles, the SNCC psychiatrist, thought that these harsh warnings were necessary. Many of the volunteers were children of money and privilege, he said, "cocky kids from Harvard, Yale, whatever," both arrogant and ignorant, who "felt that no one would dare touch them." Many came from the wealthier suburbs of the major cities of the North and the West—Chevy Chase and Bethesda, Maryland; Teaneck and Tenafly, New Jersey; Manhattan and New Rochelle, New York; Greenwich and Westport, Connecticut; Shaker Heights, Ohio; Evanston and Winnetka, Illinois; Palo Alto and Beverly Hills, California. Coles preferred the

quieter volunteers from small Lutheran and Catholic colleges in Minnesota and Iowa: "They weren't prancing around and they didn't have
telephone numbers unlisted in the books." Indeed, later that summer,
when one volunteer was hauled into a Mississippi court on trumped-up
charges, the district attorney, pursuing leftist affiliations, asked him to
identify the organizations to which he belonged. The volunteer listed
first the Freedom Summer project, and then Hasty Pudding and the
Spee Club—two Harvard social societies. Both John Kennedy and Robert Kennedy had been members of Spee. People with such exotic connections were bound to give pause to a judge in rural Mississippi.

At the Oxford orientation, a 1961 CBS News documentary about
Mississippi narrated by Walter Cronkite was shown to the volunteers.
There were a few snickers and laughs among them at the thick accent
of the white registrar in one Mississippi county. Later there was gig-
gling as an old Black woman, a bit odd-looking, described her home
being shotgunned after her husband registered to vote. Several SNCC
field workers who also were in the audience bristled at these reactions
and stormed out of the auditorium. After the documentary ended, one
SNCC staff worker stood and, near tears, said to the assembled volunteers, "These are the people that you are going to work with, you cannot
laugh at them because they do not speak like you speak. . . . They are
doing the best they can with what they have, therefore, let's don't play
them off cheap." The civil rights movement was in a very different place
from the days when the Montgomery bus boycott was carried out by the
working-class Blacks of that city. Freedom Summer was deploying a new
kind of formation, and with it would come new tensions.

After each break, the volunteers would return to the auditorium
singing another Movement song, such as "O Freedom."

James Lawson blunders

On day 3, the training turned to the subject of nonviolence. Surprisingly, this would turn out to be the most fraught day of the entire

week. It also would foreshadow divisions in the Movement that would become national news two years later. Part of the problem was that by this point, the white volunteers were beginning to grasp that, as the volunteer Sally Belfrage put it, "they were being sent as sacrificial victims."

James Lawson, the veteran teacher from Nashville, was the morning's speaker. He tried to cram into one hour what had taken him months in 1959 and 1960 to impart to James Bevel, Diane Nash, John Lewis, and others. As a result, his talk was overly abstract, lacking concrete examples. We have a record of it by Ellen Barnes, who was researching comparative techniques of nonviolence, and whose thirty-five pages of typewritten notes from the week are remarkably detailed.

"Nonviolence is not just a technique," Lawson began. "Rather it is a fundamental organizing principle of life." He then made six points: 1. It is based on faith. 2. "The human being is never a means to an end, but an end in itself." 3. The means of protest must be consistent with the goals. 4. "Love is the law of life." 5. "The power of courage" can overpower threats and intimidations. 6. After you take on board all these principles, "you must be prepared to endure self-suffering and even self-sacrifice."

It was all too much, too fast, too intangible. In his desire to be encompassing, Lawson had neglected one of the fundamental rules of teaching, which is that people learn much more from narratives and examples that illustrate principles than they do from simply stating those principles. Scanning the audience as Lawson spoke, Barnes, the graduate student, observed, "Some faces had registered shock, others grew tense, still others suggested growing cynicism." They weren't sure what Lawson was asking them to do, or how to do it—or, indeed, whether they wanted to do it.

A ten-minute break was called. When the volunteers filed back in, no singing of Movement songs occurred. "By this time many had worked up a healthy belligerence," Barnes wrote.

Lawson tried to fix the mess by giving some concrete examples of how to practice nonviolence: "Keep the face visible. Maintain eye contact with as many in the crowd as you can. Try to discover who the leaders are and try to ask them questions. Ask them 'why?'" He also conceded, "When you turn the other cheek, you must accept the fact that you will get clobbered on it."

But it was too little, too late. Lawson asked for questions and got them, as well as some flat-out denunciations. "The questions came so fast that I stopped writing and just listened," Barnes wrote. It was clear, she noted, that among both the volunteers and the staff there were divisions, with many in both groups reluctant to embrace nonviolence completely.

After a lunch break, SNCC's John Lewis stood up before the assembled volunteers along with two other seasoned staffers. "The questions began and they raged on for nearly two hours," Barnes recorded. The essence of the problem, she concluded, was that Lawson spoke on a religious basis, and that the volunteers really did not trust the Christian church or its teachings. Lawson may have made some incorrect assumptions about his audience.

Stokely Carmichael rebuts Lawson

More division was on the agenda. That evening, Stokely Carmichael, now a SNCC staffer despite his run-in with Lawson three years earlier in Nashville, stood to speak in opposition to Lawson. Carmichael argued that nonviolence had worked when the segregationist South was unprepared to face it, and because Lawson had developed a corps of well-disciplined activists. That was no longer the case, he said, adding that the white power structure had adjusted. But he did not seem to have in mind any specific alternative to nonviolent direct action.

Given the extraordinary level of white violence in Mississippi, Carmichael said years later, "the logic of this [nonviolent approach] was just incomprehensible." He estimated that 90 percent of SNCC workers in Mississippi and Alabama were carrying firearms for self-defense by 1963. It's likely that Carmichael's estimate was wildly high. Amzie Moore, with decades of experience in Mississippi, would later say of

SNCC workers, "I admired their wisdom. Nobody carried a gun or knife or nothing." But perhaps Moore had such a tough reputation and was so well armed that people working around him felt protected enough to forgo weapons.

Moses followed Carmichael by again speaking slowly and carefully. If the differences between Lawson and Carmichael were not enough, Moses now laid down some instructions that directly contradicted Carmichael. "In Mississippi we have two ground rules," he said. "No weapons are to be carried or kept in your room," and "If you feel tempted to retaliate, please leave." But Moses was like a circus rider trying to stand on two galloping horses at once. He himself was ambivalent about nonviolence. "Although I myself personally, I could adopt nonviolence," he later recalled, "I couldn't propagate it. I couldn't talk to local people about it."

Mulling the chances

Day 4 focused on law and security. The issue of legal protection in Mississippi was easy to answer, Jack Greenberg of the NAACP Legal Defense Fund informed them, stating bluntly that "for the Negro— and for you—*there is no law.*" So they were told to learn how to protect themselves, with detailed rules about movements. A "Security Handbook" cautioned: "Know all the roads in and out of town. Study the county map." When driving, keep the doors locked—and always keep gas tanks and hoods locked. "Do not travel with names and addresses of local contacts." If followed, take down license plate numbers, as well as make and model of the car. "Cars without license plates should immediately be reported to the project office." At night, sleep in the back of the house, preferably away from windows. Be distrustful of curious strangers. People who failed to follow these rules would be fired from the project.

Volunteer Mike Yarrow was particularly impressed by the advice to pay attention to your unconscious. "If you wake up at night thinking there is danger wake everybody up. There seems to be a very good instinct for preservation," he wrote. Indeed, one of the lessons people learn in combat is that if you sense something is wrong but you don't know precisely what is wrong, act on that hazy sense. For example, a soldier may find that a grassy field seems odd without being able to put a finger on just what is off. If the grass is long but animals aren't grazing in it, that may be because the animals have learned that it is laden with land mines.

One of the major points Yarrow took away from the week was "the increasing weight of fear. The struggle to come to terms with the possibility of death consumes much of our emotional energy."

Those working on voter education and registration were told to be patient, and to listen as well as speak. "Keep in mind that you have just begun to tear down a set of attitudes that has taken three and a half centuries to build," they were taught. "Talk and keep talking. . . . Also keep listening, and remember that fear will often cause words to mask real responses and that you must learn to hear what is beneath the words." Don't expect to succeed in registering large numbers, they were advised. But regard each and every attempt to do so as a victory—any change in the way Black Mississippians thought and acted would increase the pressure on white supremacy.

After the orientation was over, no one could claim they had not been warned. Stuart Rawlings III, a Stanford student from San Francisco's Presidio Heights neighborhood, sat down and calculated that his chances of being killed that summer were about "one in fifty."

10.
THE BATTLE OF MISSISSIPPI, JULY AND AUGUST 1964

Freedom Summer

Ultimately, about one thousand Movement volunteers flowed into Mississippi in the summer of 1964. Around eight hundred were white students, around one hundred were Black students, and the remaining hundred or so were clergy members, teachers, and medical personnel. Sally Belfrage's insightful description of these volunteers could fit pretty much any group of soldiers on the nervous eve of an offensive: "Some were incredibly courageous, some just reckless; most didn't know yet who they were. They found out. An extreme situation is a quick education." Once in Mississippi, Belfrage wrote, it was "all they could do putting one foot ahead of another," the classic task of the wary and weary infantryman. The best protection they had, advised Bob Moses, was to "melt away into the Black population."

Long, hot days . . .

As observed earlier, war has been described as hours of boredom punctuated by occasional random moments of terror. Life for Freedom

Summer volunteers was remarkably similar to that. Those involved in registration spent their days driving from farm to farm on dirt roads, often trying to coax frightened local Blacks just to talk to them. Most voter registration work was grinding drudgery, Moses had warned them. He had described the job as "going around in the hot sun, talking to people, trying to get them to overcome their fear, trying to convince them that nothing would happen to them if they went down [to register], that their houses wouldn't be bombed, that they would not be shot at, that they would not lose their jobs." A volunteer named William Hodes, a student at Harvard, said that he was not alone in finding that after about three hours each day he was fed up with registration canvassing. However, the expected workload was ten hours a day, six days a week.

Others would show more of what soldiers call tactical patience, a willingness to wait and see, to settle in and take things as they come. One woman wrote home about arriving, just before dusk, at a "dark little falling apart house." She was invited in. She was enchanted:

It began to rain. We sat in a small dark room, lighted only by a brief flame in the fireplace where Mrs. Brotherns was cooking dinner. Their three adopted children sat on the floor and read from schoolbooks or counted bottletops, while the two old people looked on with love. The whole scene was from another century—especially because the little boy had a self-made bow and arrow, bent from a stick and tied with some cord. He proudly shot an arrow into the bushes.

The volunteers would drive out to shacks deep in the woods and fields. "We walk up, smile, say howdy, and hold out our hands," the volunteer Robert Feinglass reported in a letter home from Holly Springs, in the northern part of the state. The volunteers would tell their names, and address the Black people as "mister" and "missus," likely the first time in their lives that had happened, Feinglass noted. But, he continued, "This does not necessarily bode well to them; they are suspicious." Feinglass would tell them that the nation was finally interested in their situation. "We talk about taxes, and cotton allotments, and usury, and schools and hospitals and federal agencies. We talk about dignity. People listen, and they wonder. What does it mean when a white man tells them the truth. . . . Why is he here. What does he really want. What will come of it." Another question, of course, was what would happen when the white newcomers went home. If a volunteer was thanked for being there, the standard response was to say something like "We're not really doing anything here, Mr. Wallace; it's you local people who have to do things. . . . We're just here to let you know what we think can be done—by you."

They also had to keep an ear cocked for nuance. When a potential voter said that this wasn't a good time to talk, did that mean they were not interested, or was it really an invitation to come back at night, under cover of darkness?

And so on they went, day after day, averaging about two hundred miles a day of driving through hot pine woods and hotter cotton fields, making sure they always had an instant escape route in the back of their minds.

. . . and fearful nights

After those long days, night brought other fears. The archives of Freedom Summer are voluminous, but little appears evident about precise housing arrangements, perhaps because of the sensitivity of that information. In the wrong hands, a list of where volunteers were staying would have been a guide for attacking both them and the local residents aiding them.

That is not hyperbole. One evening in July, a young Black man walked into the Freedom House in Shaw, Mississippi, to report that he had been offered $40 by four white men to tell them where the house was located. They wanted it bombed. The volunteers posted guards on the roof, stacked the boxes of books for the Freedom School against the front windows, and then filled buckets with water. Len Edwards, who was volunteering in the nearby town of Ruleville, called his father, a congressman from California named Don Edwards, to ask for the FBI to help. No blast came that night. Fear took a toll not just on one's emotions. For the volunteers, as for soldiers, fear could make it difficult to perceive information and process it—that is, to understand what was happening in their environment.

Sometimes, simply making it through an entire night in one piece was noteworthy. Phil Moore, a Chicagoan volunteering in Greenwood, recalled, "I woke in the morning sighing with relief that I was not bombed." But another volunteer told Robert Coles, the SNCC psychiatrist, "I'm *afraid* in the evening; they might dynamite us or snipe at us, but it's shopping I *hate*—meeting the whites and seeing the murder in their eyes."

Southwestern Mississippi, stated one SNCC report, was "a no man's land of violence." McComb, an isolated railroad maintenance town in that area, was one of the toughest locations in the state. The police chief was the head of the local chapter of the extremist group called Americans for the Preservation of the White Race. A white couple who invited a summer volunteer and a visiting minister for a dinner of tamales found their lives turned upside down—they were ostracized, his business selling insurance collapsed, and their pet dachshund was poisoned. Before the year was out, they moved away. A SNCC log reported nine violent incidents in and around McComb in just one month, July 1964. The local civil rights headquarters was bombed, slightly injuring two volunteers, Dennis Sweeney and Curtis Hayes. Zion Hill Free Baptist Church was burned to the ground. Nat McGehee's house was firebombed. Mount Vernon Missionary Baptist Church was damaged by fire. Charles Bryant's house was bombed and fired on. And on and on—churches, homes, and offices. Being involved in an incident that appeared in the daily report became a matter of pride for volunteers, not unlike British officers being "mentioned in dispatches" in wartime.

"It was not an easy time. . . . Each day you would read about a bombing, a house burning, an assault, whatever it was," recalled Cleveland Sellers, a Howard University student from South Carolina who worked that summer on voter registration. When Sellers arrived in Holly Springs, he went first to see the sheriff, in true Gandhian fashion, to inform him of his presence and his plans to work on voter registration. This was partly to establish a relationship but also to deny law enforcement officers the ability to claim they did not know that the civil rights workers were present. Sellers said it was important as well to send a message to the older Black men who often sat outside the courthouse: "You had to go in as a proud, head-up strong individual. When you come out, you come out the same way. . . . They pass that information on and within an hour or two hours it will be all over the county."

Ground combat alters how one views the world. It excites the senses and can exalt the mundane, making small things deeply meaningful. Dry socks, warm showers, and hot food all take on the feel of extravagant luxuries. Being on alert also opens all the senses, especially to novel sounds and smells. Some found the bombardment of perceptions and emotions overwhelming. "I was just seeing too much, feeling too much," reported one volunteer from a suburb of Chicago who cried herself to sleep every night, experiencing waves of sadness, guilt, and anger. Another volunteer was overcome in another way: "Having sex in a field in the countryside where all you see are stars and I don't know, it just blew my mind."

And, as is universally true with soldiers, letters from family and friends became psychologically vital as a comforting link to another, calmer world. "Everyone back home knows how important it is to write to us, to keep our morale up," one volunteer told Robert Coles.

The volunteers also were inspired by having a sense of purpose. Zoya Zeman, a Freedom School volunteer in Clarksdale, Mississippi, wrote in her diary, "Life is interesting. God how good it is to be feeling and living and doing what one loves. Thanks be."

Sally Belfrage, whose perceptive account of Freedom Summer fits into the genre of classic literary war memoirs such as Samuel Hynes' *Flights of Passage* and Keith Douglas' *Alamein to Zem Zem*, missed the luxury of solitary time. "It was impossible to be alone," she wrote. In their houses and offices, there were always other people around, yet it was too dangerous to wander outdoors without company.

Given the volatile situation, maintaining discipline was more critical than ever. Ivanhoe Donaldson, SNCC's project director in Holly Springs, ran a tight ship. One volunteer, Hardy Frye, was working on voter registration in the downtown area when he was arrested by the police chief for supposedly blocking traffic. Frye threw his hands in the air as if in surrender, embarrassing the chief, who ordered him to put his hands down. An hour later, Frye was back in the SNCC office, regaling others with the tale. Donaldson asked him if he was okay. When Frye said he was, Donaldson responded, "Well go back out there and get to work. . . . There were a lot of people watching when you got arrested. We can't let them think that we are afraid. You know that. Go right back to the spot where you were arrested and continue to try to register people. Act as if nothing happened." Donaldson's directive was more than just a simple matter of discipline, of course. He also was consciously creating a context for the arrest, the beginning of a narrative. In doing so he was following a basic rule of insurgency or counterinsurgency: in a war in which the people are the prize, every action should have meaning and send a signal. If it doesn't do that, then carrying it out should be reconsidered. All operations send a message, inadvertently or not. The more political the conflict, the more important it is to keep that in mind.

In Holmes County, lying between the Yazoo and Big Black rivers, Hollis Watkins, who oversaw eight or so Freedom Schools that summer, had nearly thirty volunteers working for him, twenty-three of them white and four or five Black. He imposed strict rules on socialization: "I laid the law down that there would be no drinking or any going out." And when Stokely Carmichael tried to select students from Howard University to run some projects in the county, Watkins said, he and Carmichael "got into a big fight."

Like soldiers, the volunteers generally lived sparingly. One visitor to a Freedom Summer office found that no one had eaten that day, and that previously they had been living on sardine sandwiches. He dug out five dollars. They decided to spend most of it on stamps, which they needed to mail out organizational notices. Moses took the remainder and went out to buy a loaf of bread and a jar of peanut butter. But there were occasional exceptions, especially out in the countryside. One lucky volunteer reported, "The food is unbelievable, the proverbial farmhand's meal with biscuits, eggs, rice, cornbread, sausage for breakfast and so much dinner that no three people could eat it."

Adapting to the situation on the ground led to new ways of moving and talking. Larry Rubin, a SNCC organizer, walked in Mississippi's towns with a wariness that resembled that of an infantryman on patrol. "I acquired the freedom worker's walk," he wrote. "You sort of slouch and walk to one side of the pavement. Your eyes shift from side to side to see who's following. . . . I had learned to make myself inconspicuous."

SNCC's field secretaries likewise developed a distinctive mode of speech. Len Chandler, a singer-songwriter, and so perhaps sensitized to the nuances of sound, noticed that the organization's leaders that summer had a slow, careful way of talking. "There was a pace, a measured thoughtfulness, a SNCC sound," he recalled. Anyone who has been around military leaders in the field will recognize in that comment a hint of the combat command voice, the unhurried tone that many officers learn to use when speaking amid the noise and terror of combat. The point is to stay even and level, never sounding elated or depressed.

Making ink spots

While in military terms more conventional than most civil rights campaigns, the SNCC operation in Mississippi retained some aspects of insurgency. James Forman's concept of the Mississippi operation that summer was informed by the "ink spot" theory of insurgency, in which control begins in various spots and gradually expands. "I think you have to think of it in terms of guerrilla warfare," Forman later explained. "You develop a little base, and then you develop another little base, another little base . . . [and] then you move in, you know, into the stronghold."

Each of the seventy-three SNCC and CORE projects around the state that summer amounted to one of Forman's ink spots. Thirty-three were voter education projects; another forty were Freedom Schools. Every interaction with a community expanded a localized engagement, and also gathered more intelligence, which plays a larger role in insurgency operations than it generally does in conventional war. Zoya Zeman and a colleague, working on a health education project, visited a drugstore, the only local Black doctor, a nursing home, and local welfare officials. They were not telling local people what to do; they were asking how they could be most helpful. What needed to be done? "Our objective was to let these people know of the program we were planning in health education, and to ask their advice about the needs of the community," Zeman noted. This was remarkably different from how the U.S. military operated four decades later in Iraq, where American officials often decided what they would do and then informed Iraqis of their plans. They also would conduct an action and then try to figure out what to say about it. When at its best, the civil rights movement, by contrast, would figure out first by meeting with locals and holding strategy sessions what it wanted to say, and then would figure out what sort of physical action would convey that message. This did not always happen, but it did often, especially when James Bevel was involved in planning.

Registration and political power

The purpose of the voter projects was to inform people that they had the right to vote and that, to secure that right, they needed to register. At night, despite the dangers it brought, the volunteers held public meetings to encourage people to make the effort to get registered. And when people did go the courthouse to try to register, volunteers would accompany them and document the response of officials.

Voter registration represented a lucrative tactical opportunity to the civil rights movement. Casting a vote for political change is both essentially American and inherently nonviolent. If the dominant caste allowed Blacks to register, that was progress, as they would gain the vote and, with it, political power. But it was far more often the case that Blacks seeking to register were turned away, often brutally. When this happened, then the Movement also succeeded, because it once again forced segregationists to show their true, illegal, antidemocratic, un-American face. Also, in the process, the Movement found some new recruits, people with the courage to step forward and be counted. These people were all potential local leaders, the beginnings of a new cadre. Indeed, some of these people years later would go on to run for office—whether as mayors of towns or as members of Congress.

This is the core of good tactics. Executed well, battlefield moves deprive the enemy of options, putting him in a damned-if-you-do, damned-if-you-don't position. Segregationist officials in Mississippi faced a dilemma, defined as two choices in which both are unpalatable. One choice was to resort to violence: they could club Blacks who came to the courthouses, look the other way as the Klan and other white reactionaries burned the houses of Blacks who tried to register, or kill the activists and their local allies. In Mississippi they did all of that—which ultimately was disastrous, as it first generated bad publicity and then brought the federal government down on them. The other choice was to allow Blacks to register, which meant facing the loss of political power.

For the volunteers, registering Black Mississippians involved far more than simply getting people to go down to the county courthouse and sign up. First one had to canvass Black neighborhoods to find people willing to try. Sometimes potential voters needed tutoring in basic reading and writing. Mass meetings were held at night in churches to teach them about the process. Then they had to appear at the courthouse, sometimes miles away, to deal with white officials who often were hostile and even threatening. Sometimes aspiring registrants were turned away without explanation, or kept waiting for hours while whites who appeared were ushered to the front of the queue. Those who were able to apply then were asked to read and interpret a section of the state constitution.

All in all, it was an unnerving experience, Unita Blackwell remembered, "because you know your life is on the line." When she went to

the courthouse in Mayersville, Mississippi, local whites drove in circles around the building, their rifles and shotguns hanging on racks in
their pickup trucks. Sometimes, she added, employers retaliated against
people who registered by firing them or evicting them from plantation-
owned houses.

Those actually able to register often faced more hurdles. To vote,
people had to pay a poll tax of $2 or $3, which today doesn't sound
like much, but back then, it was a substantial sum for subsistence-level
farmers and others. Black women doing domestic work in the houses
of whites in rural Mississippi were taking home just $13 to $17 for a
full workweek.

Voter registration could have cascading effects. Jurors were drawn
from the registration lists, so by keeping those lists all-white, local juries
were kept the same. And, of course, Black voters eventually would elect
some Black officials.

Education and ideological power

The forty Freedom Schools established by SNCC were essentially dedicated to ideological indoctrination. That is a loaded phrase, intention-
ally. In this case, the ideology being imparted was that of the United
States. As the curriculum plan put it, the mission was "to implant habits of free thinking and ideas of how a free society works." The volunteers taught their students that they had the right to grow up and
vote, and that the police should work for them, not against them. They
discussed the Declaration of Independence and the Constitution. They
tried to define what it meant to be free. Students learned that police
officers should not be members of the Ku Klux Klan.

Such instruction may sound innocuous today, but it was flatly revolutionary in Mississippi in the summer of 1964. Cornelia Mack, a
volunteer from Wisconsin, reported that after students at her school in
Palmer's Crossing on the south side of Hattiesburg read the Declaration
of Independence, they decided to write their own, which declared their

separation from "the unjust laws of Mississippi which conflict with the United States Constitution." Following Thomas Jefferson's example, they listed their grievances, which in this case included poor public schools and libraries, unpaved roads in Black neighborhoods, and a lack of Black police officers. These new schools were having an effect.

The Freedom Schools were more popular than expected. The initial plan was to have twenty-five schools across the entire state, with a total of approximately one thousand students. But in Hattiesburg alone, some six hundred students presented themselves on registration day. By early July, some 2,000 students had enrolled across the state, and by the end of the summer, a total of 2,700 Mississippians, including a surprising number of adults, had attended classes in a total of forty-one schools. Altogether they employed 175 teachers. Unexpectedly, those who were professionally trained tended to find it more difficult, because informal methods such as walking and talking outside were more effective than rigid classroom methods. "Most of what we know about teaching must be unlearned or relearned here," reported one trained teacher. Volunteers who were college students tended to do better with the unstructured environment, in which classes were sometimes conducted through conversations.

One of the most innovative classes was Black history, at that time a new subject even in most university or secondary academic programs. University professors gave lectures to Freedom School teachers to bring them up to speed on the subject. Many students also learned basic literacy. Some students did not know the name of the national capital or how many states there were. Afternoons brought special classes, often on subjects requested by students. Some of the most popular were Spanish, French, math, drama, and journalism, most of which were not offered to Black students in the state. Indeed, the superintendent of schools in Bolivar County had ordered that Black schools teach neither civics nor foreign languages. Typing was especially attractive, as it was an employment skill but also promised to be of help in the Movement.

On the first day of classes at the Gluckstadt Freedom School, students read speeches by Frederick Douglass and poems by Langston

Hughes. Two days later they learned about slave revolts. They also had classes in drawing. At the end of the third week, the school was burned to the ground.

Not all schools launched well, especially in isolated areas, but by changing tactics, a poor start could be converted into a success. Early in the summer, Wallace Roberts, a New Jerseyan leading the Freedom School in Shaw, near Ruleville, wrote to Staughton Lynd, a Spelman College historian who was the overall director of the schools project, "I am completely frustrated. Living conditions are so terrible, the Negroes are so completely oppressed, so completely without hope, that . . . running a Freedom School is an absurd waste of time. . . . I really can't stand it here." Indeed, Roberts had attracted almost no students. Alarmed, Lynd paid an emergency visit to Roberts. They decided to begin a second time by turning all their energies to voter registration. That in turn interested local teenagers. Some thirty-five, about one-third of the local Black high school population, then requested instruction in Black history, voting, and other subjects.

Voting and education went hand in hand. Both summer programs—voting registration and the schools—challenged white supremacist beliefs long used to suppress Black Mississippians. One was that the Black Mississippian did not care to vote, and the other that the Black Mississippian was intellectually inferior and could not or would not learn. The two prongs aimed at the same strategic goal. Even remedial literacy classes increased the pride and self-confidence of the students, and that in turn made them more willing to try to vote.

Three go missing

On June 21, 1964, Louise Hermey was at the SNCC office in Meridian, Mississippi, for her first day as a summer volunteer. Michael "Mickey" Schwerner, a CORE activist from New York who ran the Meridian office, told her that he and two other workers—James Chaney, a local Black volunteer, and Andrew Goodman, a white volunteer from New

York—were going to check on Mount Zion, a church near the small city of Philadelphia that had been burned after the parishioners had offered to let it be used as a Freedom School. If he did not call in by 4:00 p.m., he instructed, she should notify the headquarters above them in Jackson. Hermey took the admonition seriously. She watched the clock tick toward four. When it finally hit the hour, she reached for the phone.

At the Western College for Women in Oxford, Ohio, Bob Moses was speaking to the second week's orientation group in the Peabody Hall auditorium when he was called to the side of the stage and quietly told that the three men were missing. He calculated in that moment that they almost certainly were dead. Standing on the stage, he gazed at his feet and waited until Rita Schwerner, the wife of Mickey Schwerner, left the room. Then he told the audience, "If in fact, anyone is arrested and then taken out of jail, then the chances they are alive were just almost zero." Moses was saying that this was the reality of Mississippi.

Robert Coles, at the orientation in his role as SNCC's psychiatrist, was horrified to realize that such violence was an expected part of the summer project. Yes, he said, Moses and the others grieved. But at the same time, Coles said, "I also think that they consciously at the time realized that this [the disappearance of the three] would help this project immeasurably." Coles recalls "being stunned" when he saw this. "They were realizing that they already had succeeded. . . . Because this became cover stories in the news magazines. And the president of the United States was having something to say. So they had won."

We now know that the three activists had been detained at 3:00 p.m. on June 21 by Cecil Ray Price, a Neshoba County deputy sheriff who also was a member of the Ku Klux Klan. He took them to jail, but released them at 10:30 that night. As they drove out of town, he stopped them again and turned them over to the Klan for execution.

"The disappearance of the three civil rights workers in Mississippi was the lead story on television and in newspapers across the country for that entire week," remembered John Lewis. The simple, hard fact was that the American media and public cared more about killings of whites than of Blacks. Black civil rights activists and locals who stood up for their rights were constantly beaten and killed in Mississippi—that was routine stuff, hardly national news. SNCC's hard calculation about white lives mattering more than Black ones had been confirmed. It may have seemed cold, but it was no different from Winston Churchill celebrating the Japanese attack on Pearl Harbor in 1941. The British prime minister was ecstatic because he knew that now the Americans would enter the war. Many Americans would die, he understood, but their entry made an Allied victory inevitable.

As if to prove SNCC's grim assessment, the ensuing police dragnet in Mississippi uncovered Black bodies in rivers and ditches. "They found torsos in the Mississippi River, they found people who were buried, they even found a few bodies of people on the side of the road," recalled Dave Dennis, a former Freedom Rider who had become Bob Moses' deputy for Freedom Summer. It brought home gut-punch hard just how violent a state Mississippi was.

The Mississippi Klan issued a statement denying any involvement in the situation. It added, "We Knights are working day and night to preserve Law and Order here in Mississippi."

J. Edgar Hoover, spurred hard by President Lyndon Johnson, sent 153 of his agents into the state, where they interviewed nearly a thousand Mississippians, among them five hundred members of the Klan. Hoover also gave the governor a list of highway patrol officers who were Klan members, and the governor, taking the hint, fired them. The boosted federal presence also had a side effect of affording a bit of protection to the volunteers. "Here's a switch," Zoya Zeman, working in Clarksdale, wrote in her diary on July 3. "It seems the police might actually be protecting us from violence from whites. . . . This would probably not have come about if the national focus and the federal attention had not followed the tragedy of Mickey and James and Andy." A bit to the south in Shaw, four volunteers were called in by the sheriff, who informed them that "he felt a physical revulsion when he saw us; but he would protect us to the hilt in order to protect the image of his beloved state of Mississippi and of his country."

Even so, more bloodshed did occur that summer. Mississippi was engaged in a small civil war. Between June 15 and September 15, the Movement logged more than six known murders, eighty beatings, thirty-five shootings, thirty-five church burnings, and thirty bombings. That doesn't include daily incidents that did not result in physical injury—a policeman putting his pistol to a volunteer's temple and cocking it, or the noose tightened around a female volunteer's neck and tied to the rear bumper of a car that began moving, or the Black family hosting a volunteer who noticed their car's hood had been opened and then found four sticks of dynamite connected to the ignition coil. One can only wonder how much more intense the violence would have been if the state had not been crawling with nosy FBI agents.

Mississippi that summer had many of the characteristics of a combat environment. And in war, observed Clausewitz, the philosopher of war, even simple things become difficult. This is especially true for the soldier on the front lines, where the most mundane of activities—heating a pot of coffee, trying to communicate with someone else, or even simply defecating—can get a soldier killed. Likewise, in Mississippi in the summer of 1964, for civil rights activists, just walking home after work, driving to another town, or using a pay telephone sometimes had the feel of lethal struggle. Bob Moses spoke of the situation of SNCC workers who "have to ride those roads by themselves, who have already been shot at once, who maybe every time a headlight flashes up behind them when they're riding at night wonder if this is another time when somebody might take another shot at them. They have to come to grips with themselves about some kind of internal balance about that problem of violence."

Moses was describing what specialists in post-traumatic stress disorder refer to as a state of hypervigilance, which is exhausting to both the mind and body. "We studied the faces of pedestrians and police for homicidal tendencies," wrote Belfrage. The brain is flooded with shots of adrenaline. That is an appropriate response to a lethal threat, but repetition ultimately changes the person and can make it difficult for him or her to live normally. Those jolts of adrenaline also can be addictive, making people seek out danger.

Like soldiers in a foreign land, the volunteers also adopted a fatal-
ism about the dangers. "It was just a matter of, you know, whether you
happened to be in the wrong place at the wrong time or something,"
said Sue Thrasher, a volunteer in Biloxi.

Just as soldiers leaving the front lines find the rest of the world to
have an unreal air to it, Thrasher said that a week back home in "a
normal living situation" was dislocating. It was, she explained, "just
extremely difficult for me. . . . My mind and heart were still in Mississippi." Another activist, Pam Parker, said she struggled when she got
home: "I couldn't adjust. I was distant and uncommunicative. It was
especially difficult for my mother." Denise Nicholas said that after leaving Mississippi, she missed "the clarity of the situation, . . . the insan-
ity of it all." Likewise, some returned soldiers long for the clarity of
frontline combat, where life is reduced to simple essentials and no one
worries much about mortgage payments or babysitting arrangements
or other quotidian problems.

The discovery of the bodies of the three missing workers on August
4 put an enormous strain on the entire Movement in Mississippi. The
two white men, Schwerner and Goodman, had each been shot once in
the head with a .38-caliber bullet. James Chaney had been beaten and
shot three times. They had been buried in an earthen dam.

At the funeral service for James Chaney in his hometown of
Meridian, Mississippi, on August 7, 1964, Dave Dennis, Moses' deputy, gave a eulogy that was a staggering departure from the norm. "I'm
going to tell you deep down in my heart what I feel right now," he said,
surveying the mourners. "If you do go back home and sit down and
take it, God damn your souls! . . . I don't want to have to go to another
memorial. I'm tired of funerals, tired of 'em!" He began to weep. A volunteer who was in the pews wrote home, "Dave finally broke down and
couldn't finish and the Chaney family was moaning and much of the
audience and I was also crying." Dennis turned away from the pulpit
and collapsed.

In 1967, seven men would be tried in a federal case for conspiring
to deny the civil rights of the three activists. Presiding over that case was

Septima Clark (left), a trainer at the Highlander School, asked Rosa Parks (right) in August 1955 to think about how to confront segregation. (Library of Congress, Prints & Photographs Division, Visual Materials from the Rosa Parks Papers, LC-DIG-ppmsca-47364)

Amzie Moore in his Army uniform during World War II. He came home from the war to become a key figure in organizing the fight for Black freedom in Mississippi, operating for years like a wartime resistance leader. (Wisconsin Historical Society, Image 32464)

Rosa Parks being fingerprinted after an arrest for participating in the Montgomery bus boycott (Associated Press / Wikimedia Commons)

After Martin Luther King, Jr., emerged as the leader of the Montgomery bus boycott, white authorities harassed him for years. (Archive PL / Alamy Stock Photo)

Whites attacking students conducting a sit-in at a Nashville lunch counter, February 1960 (Jimmy Ellis / © The Tennessean-USA Today network)

Nashville authorities responded by arresting James Lawson, the divinity student who trained a cadre of key civil rights activists. (Nashville Banner Archives, Special Collections Division, Nashville Public Library)

Three of Lawson's trainees—C. T. Vivian, Diane Nash, and Bernard LaFayette, Jr.— led a silent march to Nashville's city hall to protest the bombing of the home of one of the lawyers representing the sit-in students. (Jack Corn / © The Tennessean-USA Today network)

Name: BEVEL, DIANE JUDITH NASH, N/F
DOB 5/15/38, 5'4½", 115½ lbs., green eyes,
brown hair.
Address: 139 Monroe Street, Montgomery,
Alabama
Occ.: S C L C
Arrest: 12/4/61 Contributing to deliquency
of minor.
Organization: Active in Freedom Riders
Movement and demonstrations throughout
Alabama, Georgia, Mississippi, and other
states.
Associates: James Bevel, husband.

Nash would become an important figure in the civil rights movement, coordinating part of the Freedom Rides and later organizing in Selma. Alabama authorities took notice and issued this card to local police to help identify her. (CRMvet.org)

Welcome to Anniston: a Greyhound bus that had carried Freedom Riders burns in northern Alabama (Bettmann / Getty Images)

And welcome to Montgomery: James Zwerg after being beaten
when the Freedom Riders' bus arrived in the Alabama capital
(Bettmann / Getty Images)

Ole Miss after the Kennedy Administration sent in the U.S. Army
(Charles Moore / Getty Images)

James Meredith registering (Bettmann / Getty Images)

James Bevel played a central role in reinvigorating the Birmingham campaign when it flagged—and also two years later in Selma.
(Alabama Department of Archives and History. Donated by Alabama Media Group. Photograph by Ed Jones, *Birmingham News*)

Bevel's opponent, "Bull" Connor, who oversaw the Birmingham police and fire departments (Birmingham, Alabama Public Library Archives)

Tough and determined, Fred Shuttlesworth was a key local ally during the Birmingham campaign. (Alabama Department of Archives and History. Donated by Alabama Media Group. Photograph by Tom Lankford, *Birmingham News*)

Connor responded to Bevel and Shuttlesworth with police dogs and fire hoses. (Top: Alabama Department of Archives and History. Donated by Alabama Media Group. Unknown photographer, *Birmingham News*. Bottom: Charles Moore / Getty Images)

King speaks at the climax of the March on Washington, August 1963, at which he introduced the civil rights movement to the nation. (Bettmann / Getty Images)

June, 1964: SNCC's Bob Moses prepares volunteers to go into Mississippi.
(Steve Schapiro / Getty Images)

The formidable Fannie Lou
Hamer emerged as a political
leader during Freedom
Summer. (Alabama Department of
Archives and History. Photograph by
Jim Peppler, *Southern Courier*)

An Alabama State Trooper clubs John Lewis on Bloody Sunday, March 7, 1965.
(Bentley Archive / Popperfoto / Getty Images)

King came under internal pressure as Stokely Carmichael (shown in a later image) broke with him and issued a call for Black Power.
(Bentley Archive / Popperfoto / Getty Images)

The toll on King was apparent in 1968. (Alabama Department of Archives and History. Photograph by Jim Peppler, *Southern Courier*)

Marchers in Memphis insisted on their humanity. (Bettmann / Getty Images)

Harold Cox, the federal judge who was given to calling Black people "niggers" even from the bench. When a jury found the defendants guilty, Cox issued sentences of three to ten years. He stated, "They killed one nigger, one Jew, and a white man. I gave them all what I thought they deserved."

For some, the triple execution challenged a basic tenet of the Movement. Could the philosophy of achieving social change through nonviolence survive in Mississippi? Some began to feel doubts. The lesson of the summer, Dave Dennis concluded, was that nonviolence was "a waste of good lives. You have to put some injury on your enemy to get respect."

By late summer, wrote Sally Belfrage, the strain was evident in her comrades. "There are incipient nervous breakdowns walking all over Greenwood," she wrote to a friend. Fear shouldn't become a habit, she wrote. Joanne Grant, Belfrage's roommate that summer, said later, "To say that I was frightened most of the time is a bit of an understatement. Yet, as with all of us, it was the best time in my life. I felt we were changing the world."

Having fear as a constant companion often carries long-term physical and psychological consequences. The human mind and body can only take so much. The military analyst James Dunnigan observes about life in the infantry, "Enemy fire and Mother Nature keep everyone dirty, damaged and generally on the verge of a breakdown. . . . It's an eternal truth of warfare that when campaigning, even without deadly contact with the enemy, an army will eventually wear itself out." By the end of the summer, many activists were fraying.

Hamer speaks in Atlantic City

The summer ended on a sour note at the Democratic Party's national convention in Atlantic City, New Jersey. Mississippi's regular Democratic Party, meeting before the convention, had denounced the Civil Rights Act, supported segregation, and called for cleansing the Supreme

Court. SNCC and CORE worked during the summer toward sending to the national convention an alternate, mostly Black delegation called the Mississippi Freedom Democratic Party, under the leadership of the charismatic Fannie Lou Hamer, from Sunflower County in the Mississippi Delta. "One of the most powerful and beautiful things about the Movement was that it enabled people like Mrs. Hamer to emerge," commented Bob Moses.

President Johnson, not wanting to alienate the state's segregationist Democratic Party, busily pulled strings to undermine the alternates' challenge. Hamer's testimony before the convention's credential committee was watched by television viewers across the country. Rarely had a Black person had such a national platform, and never had one delivered so powerful a statement at a party convention. Hamer described being assaulted and evicted for trying to register to vote. In one incident, her jailers compelled Black inmates to beat her: "After the first Negro had beat until he was exhausted, the State Highway Patrolman ordered the second Negro to take the blackjack. The second Negro began to beat and I began to work my feet, and the State Highway Patrolman ordered the first Negro who had beat me to sit on my feet—to keep me from working my feet. I began to scream and one white man got up and began to beat me in my head and tell me to hush."

Her brief statement concluded with a challenge to the nation: "All of this is on account of we want to register, to become first-class citizens. And if the Freedom Democratic Party is not seated now, I question America. Is this America, the land of the free and the home of the brave, where we have to sleep with our telephones off the hooks because our lives be threatened daily, because we want to live as decent human beings, in America?"

Despite that powerful testimony, Hamer's delegation was excluded. Bob Moses relates that he was summoned to a meeting with several party leaders, including Hubert Humphrey, the liberal senator from Minnesota who had become a national figure due to his stirring call for civil rights at the Democratic National Convention in 1948 when he was mayor of Minneapolis. Humphrey, who in 1964 was about to receive the nomination to be the Democratic candidate for vice president, said, "The president will not allow that illiterate woman to speak from the floor of the convention."

Hamer said that the NAACP's Roy Wilkins took her aside near the entrance to the convention hall and said, "You don't know anything, you're ignorant, you don't know anything about politics. I have been in this business over twenty years. . . . Why don't you pack up and go home?" Looking back, Unita Blackwell, who was a colleague of Hamer's in the alternate delegation, drew an important distinction: "We was ignorant. . . . But we were not stupid, and that's the difference."

In the same month, Wilkins showed how much he knew about politics by backstabbing King, the SCLC, and SNCC in a telephone conversation with President Johnson. Talking to the president on August 15, 1964, he mocked CORE and SNCC's plans for the Democratic convention. He also cast doubt on the character of King. "The motivation of King, of course, is known to yourself," Wilkins said. "You know some of the forces behind him." The president responded, "Yup, yes I do." Wilkins didn't offer details, but he appears to have been alluding to the FBI's private allegation that King was controlled by communist agents.

Hamer was reaching for power. Wilkins was desperately trying to keep it from slipping away. The civil rights movement was becoming more political, and that was not a bad thing. It was a sign of success. Politicians can ignore the weak and voiceless, but they cannot ignore those who might challenge them and win.

Internal tensions: Race, region, and gender

In Mississippi in the summer of 1964, another tension within the Movement became evident. This was the division between SNCC workers who were in Mississippi for an indefinite period versus white college students who had come to help out for the summer. "The white volunteers were economically secure, highly educated, sophisticated in the ways of the world. Without conscious intent or malicious motivation, many found it 'natural' to utilize the skills they brought with them to 'take over' tasks previously carried out by Blacks, whether it was writing press releases, running freedom schools, or coordinating logistics," notes one historian. "This was a Black movement and most of the workers in SNCC were there for the duration."

In addition, strains emerged between Black southerners and Blacks from the North, as Hollis Watkins' run-in with Stokely Carmichael's Howard University contingent demonstrated. Years later, Carmichael would remark about SNCC that "it was a southern organization; it was not a national organization, and thus when called to respond nationally to events, it carried a southern mentality with it. This really was its greatest problem."

Some female volunteers also began to step back to consider how their male comrades treated them. Disproportionately, women had been pushed away from voter registration, which was deemed too risky for them, and toward more traditional roles such as teaching and office work. "When compared to the voter registration workers, the Freedom School teachers were second-class citizens," concludes Doug McAdam, author of one of the most thorough histories of the summer project. Their reflections would add to the questions provoked among women by their exclusion from the speakers' platform in the March on Washington the previous year and by the manifesto written by women at SNCC, fueling the emergence of a new feminist critique.

Battle fatigue

Being part of Freedom Summer may have been too much to ask of everyone. An innovative study of breakdowns among infantrymen in World War II found that soldiers tended to have internal limits of how much combat duty they could endure, with the maximum being about two hundred days. By that point, Army research determined, "all men had broken down psychologically." John Appel, the psychiatrist who conducted the study, reported that after four months of combat, "If he had not 'cracked up,' he was so jittery under shell fire and so overly cautious that in addition to being ineffective as a soldier, he demoralized the newer men." Medical officers told Appel about "old sergeant syndrome," in which seasoned veterans of demonstrated valor who had been decorated for courage under fire suddenly become incapacitated. Another Army study found that even "the sturdiest and most stable" soldiers began to crack up after experiencing about 180 days of combat.

Students operating in Mississippi in the summer of 1964 also suffered from "battle fatigue," reported Robert Coles, the Harvard psychiatrist who worked with SNCC. They showed signs of "exhaustion, weariness, despair, frustration and rage." One patient of his sounded like many combat veterans when he said, "They say I'm jittery, but who isn't?" Another who once had gone to jail happily now found himself "terrified" by that prospect, telling Coles, "I dream I'm going to be hurt, you know, kicked and manhandled by those jailers. Sometimes I wake up in a cold sweat, and I remember that I've actually dreamed that the whole movement was arrested." Coles concluded, "In many ways these young civil rights workers are in a war and exposed to the stresses of warfare."

John Lewis would later say, "I think for many of us that summer in Mississippi was like guerrilla warfare." Dave Dennis, who like Lewis had been on the front lines in the Freedom Rides and then, three years later, in Freedom Summer, agreed. Every morning, Dennis said, you looked at your fellow activists and "you didn't know whether you were going to see them again or not as they went out on different assignments." There was, he said, "just so much you could take. We just reached the end of the ropes." As noted, Dennis himself had broken down at the funeral of James Chaney.

Other people began hitting their own limits. Mary King, who that summer worked in communications for SNCC in Jackson, Mississippi, dreamed that she led her closest friends in the Movement on a visit to a cold, dark morgue. Once inside it, she heard her younger brother weeping. In the dream, she was trying to lift her own body from a box on the floor to a mortuary shelf. She awoke distraught.

Moses and other organizers also made a fundamental mistake in letting volunteers depart without some kind of general meeting and debriefing akin to the orientation session in Oxford, Ohio, that had kicked off the summer. Jonathan Shay, an expert on military cohesion, observes that "the single most important preventative psychiatry move for the military is to keep people together: train them together, send them into danger together, and bring them home together."

Instead, the volunteers arrived home alone, often seeing only un-comprehending faces, a situation that can be terribly disorienting. "I've been depressed since I've returned," wrote one volunteer, in a typical comment. Pam Parker, from Bucks County, Pennsylvania, wondered if she would "ever relax fully again." Another volunteer, back home in the suburbs of New York City, was irked to be asked by people, "What was it like?" and then to find them "start talking before I can answer." This is an eternal complaint of soldiers, angering them because they, like this volunteer, realize that the questioner not only doesn't know what it was like but also really doesn't want to know. They are wrenched, having come from a place where truth mattered because life and death hovered close by, and suddenly are back in a world where insincerity is commonplace and accepted. A teacher who had spent the summer in Mississippi reported that his wife repeatedly complained, "You're not the person I married"—a comment all too familiar among trauma-tized combat veterans. The teacher concluded, "She was right." They divorced.

And then there was the guilt about the people they left behind in Mississippi. One volunteer wrote to a friend, "What am I going to do sitting in the halls of Chicago reading taxation and corporate cases when I hear that one of the people I have lived with and fought with and loved has been shot?"

At a November staff retreat, James Forman, the executive secretary of SNCC, announced that he was taking a leave of absence of at least three months, partly to write, but mainly to try to regain his health. "I'm in bad shape," he confessed. "My dues are overpaid."

Moses departs

Looking back years later, Sam Block, who worked almost undercover as a stealthy activist in Greenwood, Mississippi, before Freedom Summer, said simply that of everyone he ever met in the Movement, he respected Bob Moses the most. But in retrospect, he added, everyone asked too much of him. "All the organizational skills and strategies seemed to come from Bob," he recalled. "Everything was put on Bob. . . . If we wanted anything to be done, and we needed something, if it wasn't but fifteen dollars, we would look to Bob. And he tried. He would never say no. He never said no."

In the winter that followed that extraordinary Freedom Summer, everyone around him noticed that Moses' behavior was changing. Many were rattled by it. Barney Frank, a summer volunteer from Bayonne, New Jersey, who seventeen years later would become a congressman from Massachusetts, recalled a bit tartly that Moses "went off and self-immolated." Frank's assessment is probably excessive, because Moses' next move can also be seen as an act of self-preservation, a stepping back from the Movement after many years of laboring in Mississippi.

Part of the problem for Moses was that the SNCC leader James Forman began to perceive Moses as a promising vehicle for fundraising, in the way that King had become for the SCLC. Moses was appalled by the idea of becoming a symbolic moneymaking machine. "I indicated to him that I was not available for such a projection," he said decades later. "My name had been in a sense projected some, and so it might have been something that could have been easily done, to build up this figure. We discussed, and I expressed to him my disagreement about this."

In reaction, Moses took the radical step of telling his colleagues that he would henceforth be known as Robert Parris, using his middle name as his last. "It was clear to me that they couldn't make me into such a figure if they couldn't use my name," he said. Perhaps. But the manner in which he unveiled the change shocked his colleagues. Cleveland Sellers remembered it came one night in Atlanta. After a long meeting, Moses walked to the front of the room and announced that he was dropping his portentous last name. He talked for a bit about the mental problems suffered by both his parents. He said that SNCC's leaders were becoming creatures of the media and needed to step down.

Then this new un-Moses took up a wine bottle and a chunk of cheese. "I want you to eat and drink," he said, in what appeared to be a surreal Movement version of the Eucharist. The bottle was empty, but people went along with the act. He was, perhaps, trying to put down the messianic role that some had assigned to him. But Charles Marsh, a professor of theology at the University of Virginia, wrote in an innovative study of religion on both sides of the civil rights war that the strange incident held larger meaning. "Everyone present seemed to recognize that *this* SNCC had taken its last supper together," Marsh concluded. The spirit of Nashville was gone. "SNCC as a reconciled brotherhood and sisterhood, sharing a common cause, celebrating shared and sacred hopes, had come to an end."

Yet the psychological isolation of Moses was only beginning. As John Lewis put it later, not unsympathetically, "You could see him almost starting to crack under all these pressures."

His colleagues were growing concerned. In the spring of 1965, a meeting of SNCC's executive committee dwelled on the Moses problem—not just his withdrawal but also the effects of it on staff still working in Mississippi. "When Moses left, there was a vacuum," said one participant in the meeting. "People used to be able to go to him with their problems, now they have no one." Moses and his wife, Dona Richards, had moved to Birmingham, Alabama, but were out of touch with SNCC. Moses had remained on salary but apparently had not informed anyone of his work or plans. "Someone should find out what they are doing," argued Ruby Doris Smith, a tough-minded veteran of the Freedom Rides who had spent time in the prison at Parchman Farm.

Marion Barry, a veteran of the Nashville sit-ins who fourteen years later would become mayor of Washington, D.C., agreed, saying, "If it was anybody else, we'd be raising hell." Smith, at the time SNCC's administrative secretary, commented that Moses seemed to resent her efforts to find out about his plans. "It is true that we would be up in arms about anyone else," she said.

But Moses, it would develop, had at the "last supper" gathering attended his last SNCC meeting.

Moses was, apparently, struggling with some basic questions about life. "We're not heroes," he said in a talk around this time. "We're trying very hard to be people and that is very hard." He then added a comment that would resonate with any veteran of infantry combat: "What we have to do is to see how you can move even though you are afraid." Moses was, in the jargon of combat soldiers, "done" or "used up." He was about to embark on a long physical and psychological journey. He would live under a false name in Canada, divorce his first wife and marry a second, and eventually live in Africa for years.

His withdrawal deepened. "By the spring of 1966, he was in a state of mind where he wasn't answering my phone calls and my letters," recalled Staughton Lynd, who had directed the Freedom Schools.

What the project achieved

Had Freedom Summer failed? If its goal was to end segregation in Mississippi, then clearly it fell short. But if it was to crack open the door of a closed society, to let in some light, and force the rest of America to peek in, then it succeeded. Massive resistance ended, and the use of terror to control the Black citizens of the state began to decline. "We were actually, with that summer project, trying to open up the state, and I think we did," Moses concluded. Some seventeen thousand Black Mississippians had tried to register to vote, and a bit less than 10 percent had been successful. Within two years—and after the passage of the 1965 Voting Rights Act, spurred in part by the high rejection rate—thousands more of them had registered. "These kids . . . treated us like we were special," said Fannie Lou Hamer. "We trusted 'em, and I can tell the world those kids done their share in Mississippi."

Just three years later, in 1968, there were 250,000 Black citizens of Mississippi registered to vote, an extraordinary change that altered the state's politics. Race-baiting ceased to be a favored tool in election campaigns, replaced by work in Black neighborhoods, such as graveling the roads and erecting street signs. And in 1976, twelve years after Freedom Summer, it was the Black vote in Mississippi that gave that state to Jimmy Carter and clinched his victory over an incumbent president. Carter had many to thank for that triumph—but especially Bob Moses and Fannie Lou Hamer, as well as James Chaney, Andrew Goodman, and Michael Schwerner.

The melancholy of a battle won

Yet combat is a volatile thing, carrying extensive and unforeseen consequences. The volunteers had looked into the abyss of Mississippi's system of violent apartheid, but it had stared back into them. If SNCC and its leaders had altered Mississippi, the organization and its members had been altered by the experience. McAdam's systematic analysis of post–Freedom Summer attitudes found that the volunteers had ventured south generally as Kennedy-esque kids not unlike those flocking to the Peace Corps. They returned a few months later often radicalized into the vanguard of the New Left, seeing the federal government not as part of the solution, but as part of the problem.

Another unexpected ricochet was the effect of the national media on SNCC. In Mississippi, SNCC had deftly used the media, but in doing so, the organization also had been changed. Bob Moses worried, "If you let it, the news media will tell you who your leaders are instead of you telling the media who your leaders are." In addition, he thought, the media glare had an allure that attracted people, moth-like, to the detriment of the grassroots movement. "It is a magnet," he said. Once they had been in the journalistic spotlight, he explained, "it isn't easy for people to return to what they were before," to those long steamy days of crossing remote farmland to try to persuade people to try to register to vote.

Indeed, in the years after Freedom Summer, the image of the civil rights worker inexorably shifted from the low-key voting rights organizer to the angry activist shouting into a microphone in front of a camera. Moses said of Stokely Carmichael that he became "a national media figure, and the organizers stopped organizing because it was more glamorous to do what Stokely was doing." At about the same time, Malcolm X, having split with the Black Muslims, became a national figure while lacking any organization at all. "For the media, you don't need even an organization, all you need is a charismatic personality," Moses commented years later. He noted that Jesse Jackson rose to prominence in a similar way: "He is a genius at exploiting the media." Meanwhile, SNCC's field operations dwindled, and it became a group less focused on organizing and more on speaking. SNCC might have been able to deal with these problems better if its people were not so worn out by their time on the front lines of the civil rights movement.

War is cruel, exhausting, and wasteful, even when one prevails. The Duke of Wellington wept after his epochal victory over Napoleon in the battle of Waterloo in 1815, rocking back and forth with emotion as he listened to the casualty list read aloud. He later wrote to a friend, "Believe me, nothing except a battle lost can be half so melancholy as a battle won." Similarly, SNCC's Mary King would write about Freedom Summer, "Like Selma, the project brought concrete breakthroughs and justified attention; in addition, again like Selma, it left chaos, frustration, confusion, and deflation." Yet the Movement's leaders and ground troops together were changing America.

11.
SELMA, 1965

Victory—and Factionalization

Just after the presidential election in November 1964, the SCLC's
leaders convened at the Gaston Motel in Birmingham. The organization, after drifting for much of the year, was refocusing on Alabama. On the table was the question of what to do with the Bevel-Nash
plan, their Alabama Project. James Bevel himself argued for starting in
the rock-hard segregationist stronghold of Selma. Amelia Boynton, a
veteran activist from that town—as well as the mother of Bruce Boynton, the law student who had been the subject of *Boynton v. Virginia*,
the case that inspired the Freedom Rides—also was at the meeting. She
invited the SCLC to intervene, saying, "Well, listen, we're under this
crazy injunction saying that no more than three people can gather on a
street corner, and if you all want to start someplace, we want to be the
place for you to start."

Selma, located in central Alabama, fifty-four miles to the west of
Montgomery, was a perfect target. It had a population of twenty-nine
thousand. The majority was Black yet entirely lacking in political power.
There were fifteen thousand Blacks of voting age in Dallas County, of
which Selma was the county seat. Of them, fewer than two hundred

had been allowed to register to vote. Many others had been turned away as unqualified, including twenty-eight who were college graduates.

The local white power structure was divided and vulnerable. The Dallas County sheriff, a volatile man named Jim Clark, was as bull-headed as Birmingham's Bull Connor yet less competent. On top of that, Selma's white leaders lacked internal cohesion. Both the city's mayor and its police chief disliked Clark's ham-fisted approach, but they didn't have control over him. Rather, as a county official, Clark reported to a bitterly segregationist state circuit judge, James Hare, who in turn reported to Governor George Wallace. As one astute Selma Black man put it, Clark served as the overseer on Hare's plantation.

Wallace wasn't as evil as his rhetoric, Andrew Young calculated, but he believed Clark was. "Jim Clark was a near madman," Young thought. Clark had supplemented his force of deputies with a posse, mainly drawn from the membership of the local White Citizens' Council. It consisted of 66 mounted members and 350 footmen. Clark had used it as a kind of private army, deploying it around the state to help put down civil rights demonstrations in Montgomery, Birmingham, Gadsden, Tuscaloosa, and Tuskegee. All in all, Selma's white establishment violated the basic military principle of unity of command.

SNCC had been working in Selma for two years. It had made Black citizens in the area aware of their right to vote, but beyond that had not made much progress. That stalling out was one reason Boynton invited the SCLC to join the fight. James Bevel and Diane Nash, who both had close friends in SNCC, soon were sent to the town as the SCLC's representatives. Bevel was extremely good at assessing a situation, devising a response, and then talking King into executing it. "Almost all of Dr. King's and my conversations consisted of an ongoing dialogue about principles, plans, strategies, tasks, and tactics," Bevel recalled. "As each project ended he and I would complete it between ourselves with an evaluation." He added that much of what the SCLC did "was based on this continuous discussion." That's a large claim to make, but the evidence supports it. Interestingly, Bevel noted that he and King were not close friends. "I generally don't have friendships," he explained, "and am not really a friendly person."

Some historians of the civil rights movement might argue that the account offered in this book overstates the impact Bevel had. Yet there was a pattern in the SCLC's operations: when he was present, campaigns seemed to be more dynamic and actions more effective than when he was not. Bevel brings to mind Napoleon's supposed comment that he preferred to use generals who were lucky. In the first half of the 1960s, Bevel was good at making luck. Bernard LaFayette, who knew him well from their days together in Nashville, later wrote that Bevel "viewed himself as one of King's apostles, perhaps even a prophet. Dr. King described Bevel as a genius, a convincing and persuasive orator, and he often followed Bevel's recommendations and advice. Bevel was a key leader in making certain decisions." That certainly would be the case in Selma.

There had always been a tension in the Movement about aims. The overarching goal, of course, was to be treated as equal citizens. In some places, this led to efforts at integration—equal access to schools, public transportation, motels, and restaurants. The Civil Rights Act of 1964 appeared to address much of this agenda, although enforcement would remain an issue. In other places, the emphasis had been more on voting rights—that is, access to the ballot box. Remember, for example, that Mississippi's Amzie Moore had told Bob Moses he was far more interested in getting the vote than in getting the right to sit next to white people in a restaurant. The 1964 act, while quite significant, did little to address that. Thus, even after passage of the Civil Rights Act, being able to register remained a major problem for Blacks in many parts of the South. "The Selma movement was to address the specific problem of disenfranchisement," said James Bevel. "It wasn't asking for an accommodation, it was asking for a basic constitutional right."

Selma would bring together all aspects of civil rights campaigning. Like Montgomery, the effort involved widespread participation, but Montgomery had been a boycott, while the main focus in Selma would be direct action aimed at registering to vote. And it would begin with more overall community involvement than had been seen in Birmingham. As King would later put it, "Where Birmingham depended largely upon students and unemployed adults, Selma has involved fully forty percent of the Negro population in active demonstrations."

Moreover, the people of Selma had been inspired by the example of what had happened in Birmingham. They would meet one another, recalled the Reverend F. D. Reese, a minister, educator, and civil rights activist, and say, "Did you see Shuttlesworth on TV? He was on TV!" His was a familiar face. Before moving to Birmingham, Shuttlesworth had been a minister in Selma, and he returned to the town to clear the way for King. "It took us a long time to get a church that would even let us have a mass meeting," recalled J. L. Chestnut, a Black lawyer in Selma. "Shuttlesworth was invaluable. . . . Shuttlesworth undermined a lot of opposition that Martin would have had . . . from Black preachers and all that. Those who were not going to participate, at least they would shut up." Thus the Blacks of Selma would be able to present a more unified front than could the city's whites.

The lessons of Birmingham and, before that, of Albany, Georgia, made Selma look ripe to movement planners. "We were laying a trap," said SNCC's Forman. "We were very conscious about what we were doing in Selma, Alabama." Restated in military terms, the Selma campaign was similar to Yorktown, the last major battle of the American Revolution, in which a hubristic enemy found itself outmaneuvered by the American rebels and their French allies, and wound up trapped on the battlefield. Selma likewise would be the last big Movement campaign for voting rights.

King begins the campaign

King came to Selma fresh from a journey to Norway to collect the Nobel Peace Prize, which had given him new prestige and celebrity around the world. He kicked off the SCLC's new campaign on January 2, 1965, with a speech that stands as a classic nonviolent statement of intentions. "Today marks the beginning of a determined, organized, mobilized campaign to get the right to vote everywhere in Alabama," he boomed out to seven hundred Black listeners at the town's Brown Chapel African Methodist Episcopal (AME) Church, which would become the headquarters of the effort. "Give us the ballot! We are not asking. We are demanding the ballot. To get the right to vote, we must be ready to march. We must be ready to go to jail by the thousands. We will bring a voting bill into being on the streets of Selma." He disclosed also that Selma had been targeted because it was "a symbol of bitter-end resistance to the civil rights movement."

Bevel took charge of the SCLC's preparatory operations in Selma. There were still tensions between SNCC and the SCLC, but Bevel's presence generally helped. Despite his eccentricities, he was an SCLC official with his roots in SNCC, which helped him coordinate activities. Diane Nash began sending pairs of workers, one from the SCLC, the other from SNCC, into Black neighborhoods to spread the word and begin compiling lists of possible participants. Two of Bevel and Nash's old comrades from Nashville, John Lewis and Bernard LaFayette, also came to represent SNCC and to help organize.

In one inspired moment, LaFayette, speaking in a church, admonished the audience not to harass the white deputies sent to monitor the meeting. Take down the tinfoil hung to interfere with the lawmen's walkie talkies, he ordered. "These officers have to do their jobs," he said. "These deputy sheriffs have to work overtime here at the mass meeting and we know they're not getting paid overtime. When we get the right to vote, we're going to make sure that they get paid for the jobs they do, equal justice for all. They need their money to buy food for their families, shoes for their children." LaFayette was not just following the moral principle of treating your opponents like human beings; he was also laying the groundwork for drawing them away from hard-line positions and toward less vigorous enforcement of Sheriff Clark's brutal orders. It is almost always wise to encourage divisions among one's foe.

The Selma campaign had a relentless, driving quality that is best captured by looking at it day to day. This was the civil rights movement at its most effective, led by veterans who paid close attention to the strategic situation. They continually assessed how the foe reacted and how the mood and morale of the people changed. James Lawson once observed, "A movement is a living organism." Each evening they would tend to the state of the Movement, asking what had happened that day and what that meant for tomorrow. They did not always agree, but that is not a negative comment. In the fog and confusion of a movement, the meaning of events will not always be immediately clear. Often clarity can be reached only through vigorous, honest discussion.

THURSDAY, JANUARY 7, 1965

Organizers began with workshops on voter registration in each of Selma's five wards. Bevel was speaking to about fifty people in the Ward IV meeting at Brown Chapel when Clark's deputies entered. Bevel, more confrontational than LaFayette, told them to leave. One of the lawmen began to take a photograph. Bevel told him to stop and get out. It was both a bold move and a classic opening gambit in the Movement to publicly confront the dominant caste's law enforcement officials, and to show both them and the Black community that there was a new moral force in town. Bevel knew what he was doing: his move would be the talk of the town the next day.

TUESDAY, JANUARY 12

Ward meetings elected block captains, who were useful not just in bringing out people to try to register but also in organizing and running marches.

One of the lessons applied constantly in Selma was the importance of organization. This wasn't just about who would march and what would be said. As always in military operations, support efforts were crucial. To succeed, the Movement needed marchers, who in turn needed babysitters, needed to be reminded of the day, and needed food when they got back to the churches for post-march rallies. SNCC had two leaders for each of the five wards in the city where Blacks lived, and under them a designated captain for each block. And of course everything needed to be monitored for potential follow-up moves. For example, in Ward IV, it developed, "the block captains have to be pushed," according to SNCC staff meeting notes. This probably meant they were slow in knocking on doors and compiling and delivering their lists of marchers and other volunteers.

THURSDAY, JANUARY 14

Because the Movement had experienced operatives on the ground in Selma, King was able to come and go from the city to go on fundraising trips and meet other organizational duties. On this day he returned to the town and announced that the first major march to register to vote would be held the following Monday. About this time, the SCLC and SNCC began conducting small reconnaissance patrols, seeing how demonstrators would be received in motels and restaurants. Desegregating these places wasn't the primary focus of the campaign, but it still had a purpose. "The main thing is to keep the police busy," meeting notes stated. The Movement knew by now to avoid yielding the initiative—keep moving, keep the other side off-balance, zig when they expect you to zag. Run the other guy ragged.

MONDAY, JANUARY 18

The campaign unfolded with new events almost daily. King, Bevel, and those around them had learned to maintain a steady operational tempo. Though it flagged on occasion, it never threatened to come to halt.

On this day, King and John Lewis led about three hundred marchers out of Brown Chapel to the county courthouse, which held the office of the voting registrar. The city authorities kept the county's Sheriff Clark from interfering with the march, which on the face of it was a small victory for the city—while the marchers had also established their presence and their desire to register to vote.

TUESDAY, JANUARY 19

John Lewis and Hosea Williams, an SCLC veteran, led another march to the courthouse. It is unclear precisely what day Lewis had a tart exchange with Sheriff Clark, but it might have been this day. Lewis found his way blocked by the sheriff, who told him to go back down the steps. Lewis responded that the courthouse was a public place and he had the right to go inside.

"Did you hear what I said?" Clark asked, and again told Lewis to turn around.

"Did you hear what *I* said?" Lewis said. "We are not going back."

Inside this verbal volley, there was a message: times had changed. Lewis was saying that Clark's whims no longer carried the force of law. Clark could still impose physical pain—and he would, repeatedly. But his power was draining away inexorably. John Lewis would be heard. His words embodied the new attitude that SNCC encouraged the people of Selma to take: As Bernard LaFayette put it, "The sheriff is not after you; you are after the sheriff." This was a transformative new way of thinking. The moment also provides a good illustration of the difference between passive resistance and nonviolent direct action. There was nothing passive about Lewis' response to Clark. It was a challenge.

Lewis and Williams were the first two to be arrested that day, followed by sixty-five others. Most notably, Clark grabbed Amelia Boynton by the collar of her dress coat and manhandled her into a police car.

Wilson Baker, Selma's public safety director—a new post created by the mayor in order to limit Sheriff Clark's reign—told reporters that Clark was "out of control." Baker would say later that the civil rights movement manipulated Clark "just like an expert playing a violin."

WEDNESDAY, JANUARY 20

Three waves of marchers headed toward the courthouse. Each was arrested, for a total of two hundred that day.

FRIDAY, JANUARY 22

For the first time, Selma's Black educators marched. There were 110 of them, amounting to most of the Black schoolteachers in the town. Because they were on the public payroll, they were vulnerable to being dismissed. This was significant, marking a new level of citizen commitment and participation. Teachers had never marched as a group in Birmingham. That Friday, they appeared on the streets of Selma in their Sunday best—women in gloves and flowered hats, the men in dark suits and shined shoes.

Some held aloft their toothbrushes, to signal that they were ready to be jailed. They marched up the steps of the courthouse to demand the right to register. Clark's waiting deputies jabbed billy clubs in their stomachs to push them back down. They walked up again, and again were jabbed back down. And then a third time. After that, Andrew Young and others leading the march instructed the teachers to march back to Brown Chapel. As they did, their students gathered on the sidewalks to applaud them.

Every march should have a point, civil rights activists were taught. The teachers' demonstration made a particularly sharp one: If, as some whites claimed, Blacks were turned away from registering to vote because they were too unschooled to vote, then why were schoolteachers also rejected? And if Blacks were content, why were those on government payrolls and so economically vulnerable willing to risk their livelihoods by presenting themselves to try to register? The impact on the town's Black citizenry was "simply electrifying," writes the historian J. Mills Thornton.

MONDAY, JANUARY 25
One constant in the Selma campaign was that Jim Clark could be relied on to do the wrong thing. On January 25, the sheriff was under pressure again. He and his men pushed the would-be registrants away from the courthouse. Clark shoved Annie Lee Cooper, a 235-pound woman who had been fired the previous fall from her job at a nursing home for trying to register to vote and then had gone to work at Selma's Black-owned Torch Motel. Cooper was not an adherent to nonviolence. "She came right back and punched the sheriff in the head, sending him reeling," recalled John Lewis. "Clark looked out of his mind with anger." The sheriff raised his billy club but hesitated a moment, what with all the protesters and journalists watching.

The fifty-three-year-old Cooper was being held down by several deputies but remained defiant. "I wish you would hit me, you scum," she shouted. Clark then swung his club down on Cooper's head, the impact audible to witnesses. Cooper was led away in handcuffs with blood dripping down her face. A photograph of the clubbing would appear on the front page of the next day's *New York Times*.

Perhaps wary of that incident, Bevel at a mass meeting warned that the adversary was trying to "make discipline break down."

Selma's law enforcement apparatus also was tiring. Clark asked for reinforcements, and Governor Wallace dispatched fifty Alabama state troopers under the command of Colonel Al Lingo, who effectively was head of Wallace's private army.

Despite all the marching and arrests, in the entire month of January, only fifty-seven Black people had been allowed to even try to register— and all had been rejected. In a meeting in Atlanta, King and his counselors decided that it was time for him to make a statement by being jailed once again, despite the risk that carried of him being abused or even murdered, and also despite his profound loathing of being behind bars.

MONDAY, FEBRUARY 1

King led about 250 people on a march to Selma's downtown. He and Ralph Abernathy were arrested for violating a city ordinance banning large demonstrations. By prearrangement, the arrests were made by Wilson Baker, the public safety director, keeping them out of the hazardous hands of Sheriff Clark. When King and Abernathy entered the jail, the regular, non-Movement prisoners broke into applause. Abernathy read aloud to them Psalm 27, which says, in part, "When the wicked, even mine enemies and my foes, came upon me to eat up my flesh, they stumbled and fell."

Leaders can't keep sending the same people into the same situation every day without showing visible progress. People get tired, and that can erode morale and discipline. "Selma needed a break," wrote Andrew Young. To offer relief, King expanded demonstrations to Perry

County, just to the northwest of Selma. On February 1, six hundred people marched in Marion, the county seat. By the end of the month, this move would carry profound consequences for the entire campaign.

Meanwhile, Ramsey Clark, who had just become the deputy attorney general of the United States, visited Selma and met with Young. He was sympathetic to the civil rights cause, but he told Young that it would be impossible to get a voting rights act passed by Congress in 1965.

TUESDAY, FEBRUARY 2

The SCLC's Hosea Williams led 120 adults in a march to the courthouse, and all were arrested. Then 400 students marched and also were taken into custody, for a day's total of 520 arrests.

WEDNESDAY, FEBRUARY 3

Three hundred children demonstrated in Selma and were arrested for violating an injunction by Judge Hare against demonstrations. More than 500 protesters were arrested in Marion and held in inhumane conditions. A SNCC report stated that "400 men were put in a 50 x 16 cubicle. The toilet wouldn't flush. They had to sleep on the concrete floor and the heat was turned off."

THURSDAY, FEBRUARY 4

Two SNCC workers invited Malcolm X, who was traveling in Alabama, to speak in Selma, which he did. Malcolm's speech that evening at Brown Chapel was received politely but not with great enthusiasm, which could have been because of his cool, northern manner of speaking. He was almost subdued, perhaps because he was conscious of being an outsider. "Doctor King wants the same thing I want—Freedom!" he stated.

Afterward, Diane Nash sat in the chapel office and apologized to him for the criticisms leveled at him by local ministers who said he was betraying nonviolence. Nash knew better than others that genuine adherents of nonviolence never tried to force it on others.

Marches were suspended for the day while leaders assessed the impact of various orders by judges. From his jail cell, King chided Andrew

Young for not staging a Thursday march. "We have the offensive," he wrote. "It was a mistake not to march today." King's military terminology was hazy—he meant that the Movement held the initiative—but his instincts were good. When you are winning, don't let up. Maintaining pressure on the other side forces them to make mistakes, which leads to more victories, and so on.

FRIDAY, FEBRUARY 5

Some five hundred marchers were arrested by Clark at the county courthouse. A group of fifteen northern congressmen visited the town and later became vocal about the need for a law protecting voting rights.

MONDAY, FEBRUARY 8

Tensions increased. At the courthouse, James Bevel was arrested and "badly beaten and had to be taken to the hospital," an internal SNCC document reported. He also was suffering from the flu. Sheriff Clark allowed Bevel to moved out of the jail but ordered that he be chained to his hospital bed, according to SNCC records.

Despite the excitement of the Selma campaign, Bevel and Nash's marriage had been deteriorating. Disgusted with his continual sexual infidelity, Nash had a lawyer serve Bevel with divorce papers. When the lawyer reported back to her that Bevel was severely ill and shackled to his bed, she put aside her anger and worked the phones to federal officials and, through their intervention, got the locks taken off him.

WEDNESDAY, FEBRUARY 10

Other authorities in Selma leaned on Sheriff Clark to show restraint. He would try for a time but was unable to stay calm for long. On February 10, around 160 students marched toward the courthouse. Some carried crayoned signs asking for their parents to be allowed to vote. One sign stated, "Jim Clark is a cracker." On this day, Clark unveiled a surprise. His deputies put the students under arrest and were marching them along Alabama Avenue toward the jail, but instead of taking the students there, the deputies began to prod them and order them to start running, pushing them right past the jail. They were made to trot and run three miles southeast out of town. Wilson Baker drove two SNCC workers to the spot so that they could coordinate having the children brought home by Black-owned taxicabs.

A Movement meeting late that night at the Torch Motel amounted to a strategic assessment of the campaign so far. The first question on the agenda was "Where are we going in Selma?" The second was "How far can Selma take us on the right to vote?" This was exactly the kind of council of war that should be held, rising above the tactical questions of the day to look at the bigger picture.

"Selma has been carrying load of right to vote since January 18th," King began, according to the SCLC's record of the session. "People need a rest." Thus the question, he said, was "how do we wrap up Selma." In the meantime, the SCLC members decided that they needed a big march on Monday to show that the campaign was not running out of steam.

THURSDAY, FEBRUARY 11

Some four hundred adults marched to the courthouse in response to Clark's forced run of the children the previous day. Selma's white newspaper criticized Clark's "comedy of errors," showing another crack in the monolith of white power.

MONDAY, FEBRUARY 15

Sheriff Clark was hospitalized with chest pains. This was one of just two days in the month when the voter registration office in the county courthouse was officially open. Wilson Baker, perhaps taking advantage of Clark's absence, ignored the various injunctions and issued a march permit, with the promise that marchers wouldn't be arrested. This helped bring out the largest march yet, numbering some 1,500 people. The marches roared back also in the nearby towns of Marion and Camden.

TUESDAY, FEBRUARY 16

Now the pace of events quickened. It began when the Reverend C. T. Vivian, a veteran of the Nashville sit-ins and the Freedom Rides, walked up the courthouse stairs to confront Sheriff Clark, who was back on the job. Clark turned away from him. Vivian shouted out at him, "You can turn your back on me, but you can't turn your back on justice."

Clark wheeled. He or one of his deputies slugged Vivian in the face—just who did it is a bit unclear—knocking the protest leader down the stone stairs. Clark said years later, "I don't remember all everything he called me, and I did lose my temper then and it seemed that a red skim came over my eyes and the next thing I knew he was . . . at the bottom of the steps picking himself up. . . . I don't remember even hitting him but I went to the doctor and got an x-ray and found out I had a linear fracture in a finger on my left hand."

Vivian, shaken and bleeding, stood. The attack was captured by television cameras and broadcast nationally. "What kind of people are you?" Vivian shouted up the stairs to Clark and his deputies. "What do you tell your children at night? What do you tell your wives at night?"

Vivian had posed a powerful question, at once human and strategic: Who are you? The civil rights movement was founded on trying to answer that question, and now Vivian was asking it of the opposition. Had Clark been thinking strategically, he might have thought to himself: I am defending a system of white supremacy that is weakening rapidly in the United States of 1963, nine years after the Supreme Court ruled against segregation in public schools, and as television cameras show the world how we use violence to oppress American citizens. But Clark was not thinking strategically. He was reacting emotionally, lashing out—and that was making his side enormously vulnerable.

WEDNESDAY, FEBRUARY 17

Under movement doctrine, Clark's sudden violence could not go unanswered. "You do not walk away from that," Vivian said. "You do not allow nonviolence to be destroyed by violence." So on the day after he was slugged, Vivian spoke to hundreds of people at Zion Methodist Church, just across the street from the Perry County courthouse in nearby Marion, Alabama. After he finished, the audience left the church to begin a march to the Marion courthouse. At this point, Alabama state troopers turned off the streetlights and attacked the crowd. They were staging a law enforcement riot.

A white man in a suit—his identity not quite clear—stuck a shotgun in the stomach of Willie Bolden of the SCLC, who was at the front of the march. "You're the nigger from Atlanta, aren't you?" the man said. Bolden said he was. The man ordered him to cross the street. There Bolden told the sheriff that he and the others were exercising their rights under the Constitution. "You don't have any constitutional rights in my town," the sheriff said. He thrust a .38-caliber snub-nose pistol into Bolden's mouth, the muzzle against Bolden's palate. Then he cocked the pistol—but did not pull the trigger. Bolden was beaten and arrested and taken across the street to the jail.

While lying in a cell, Bolden heard shots. That gunfire in Marion would lead to the Selma campaign's major turning point. One family, the Jacksons, fleeing the police crackdown, took refuge in Mack's Café, immediately behind Marion's Zion Methodist Church. Rampaging troopers pursued them inside. Jimmie Lee Jackson, a young deacon at a local church who worked as a woodcutter, and who had tried five times to register to vote, saw his mother cudgeled to the floor. She screamed. He lunged to protect her. A blow to the face knocked him down as well. One trooper picked him up and threw him against a cigarette machine. A second trooper, James Fowler, shot him twice in the stomach at point-blank range. Jackson staggered out of the restaurant while troopers continued to pummel him with batons.

This police riot in Marion was more violent than the far more famous attack on the marchers at the Edmund Pettus Bridge three weeks later. But it happened in the dark, with news cameras suppressed—someone was spraying black paint on their lenses, and journalists were being attacked—so it did not get the national attention it deserved. "They turned all the lights out, shot the lights out, and they beat people at random," recalled a local civil rights activist named Albert Turner. "They didn't have to be marching. All you had to do was be black." The *Alabama Journal* denounced the Marion incident as "a nightmare of State Police stupidity and brutality." It was the kind of event, at once unpredictable but expectable, that transforms movement campaigns. Shooting an unarmed man trying to protect his mother in front of witnesses—that was galvanizing for those in and around Selma.

SUNDAY, FEBRUARY 21

Malcolm X, who had been in Selma two weeks earlier, was assassinated in New York City by hit men from the Nation of Islam.

MONDAY, FEBRUARY 22

King visited the dying Jimmie Lee Jackson in the hospital.

As he was thinking about leading a march that night in Selma, King was contacted by officials from the FBI and the Justice Department who said they had credible information that a death squad planned to kill him during the march, with a two-pronged plan first to attack marchers in the middle in order to draw police away, and then to attack him at the head of the march. King responded skeptically. He was accustomed to receiving threats. A short time later the attorney general, Nicholas Katzenbach, called him to emphasize the seriousness of this threat.

That night, speaking at Brown Chapel, King announced that he was considering a motorcade to the state capitol in Montgomery.

THURSDAY, FEBRUARY 25

At their room in the Torch Motel, Diane Nash had two major pieces of information for James Bevel. She told her husband that Jimmie Lee Jackson was at death's door. And she confronted him directly over his womanizing. According to her account, Bevel, who had been such an eloquent advocate of nonviolence, and who was steeped in Gandhism, hit her in the face. She shouted, "How dare you, lie to me and then hit me!" Bevel, for his part, later wrote, "I tried to leave, and she blocked my way. I roughly shoved her away from me and she fell onto the bed."

The Torch was on Vine Street at the northeastern edge of Selma, with a scrubby field and forest behind it. Bevel stood outside in the dark, roiled with emotion. "I started walking across the lawn and the field, making wide circles" around the motel, Bevel recalled. "And I began to pray. I felt physical pain, and also emotional pain over my violence towards Diane. I also knew our movement was in pain." He also worried about the effects of Jackson's looming death. Would it provoke an irrational outbreak of violence by Blacks? "You've got to give a redemptive response to an injury," he thought. In his nocturnal walk, he eventually decided, "We should march to Montgomery. We should just get up, start walking, and go see Governor Wallace."

FRIDAY, FEBRUARY 26

Jimmie Lee Jackson died. James Bevel and Bernard LaFayette drove to his family's little shotgun shanty on a creek outside Marion. They gathered in the rear of the three-room house, around the kitchen table. Police-inflicted injuries were still evident on the bodies of the family members. Bevel asked them what should be done about marching. Keep going, they said. Can you come lead the next one? Bevel asked. Cager Lee, Jimmie Lee Jackson's eighty-two-year-old grandfather, said, "Oh, yeah." Bevel began crying. LaFayette recalled, "They were sad, and they were bruised, but their spirit was not broken. And that was amazing."

Bevel and LaFayette hurried from there to a rally in Jimmie Lee Jackson's memory. Bevel's particular skill was dreaming up novel and notable ways in which nonviolence could be used to respond with great effect. At the rally, he found many in the crowd toting guns and ready to fight. "They wanted to shoot people," he recalled.

Bevel stood on the podium and began to speak. He wanted to recast the destructive energy he sensed pulsing in the room. "The death of that man is pushing me kind of hard. The blood of Jackson will be on our hands if we don't march," he began. He continued:

Did Governor Wallace order it? Did he? Well, I've got to go talk to him about that. I've got to have a serious talk with George Wallace. But I need some time to think of exactly what I want to say to him. In order to give myself that time, I think I'm going to take a walk to Montgomery.

Anybody here want to join me?

Members of the audience shouted out that yes, they would. Bevel then said, "Well, okay, rather than fighting, shooting folks, and creating a riot, let's put down our guns and go see the governor." Thus the idea of everyone driving to Montgomery was transformed into something far more memorable. Bevel didn't say it, but there was something not quite right about that notion of going in cars. After all, Gandhi did not conduct a Salt Motorcade. He marched, one step at a time, like a foot soldier, a pace that enabled him to look people in the eye.

Bevel's later reflection on the concept of a march to lay the grievance at the feet of the state governor is worth quoting at length. The energy in the air needed to be channeled by Movement leaders. Simply letting it find its own course would be dangerous.

When you have a great violation of the people, and there's a great sense of injury, you have to give people an honorable means and context in which to express and eliminate that grief, and speak decisively and succinctly back to the issue. Otherwise your movement will break down in violence and chaos. So agreeing to go to Montgomery was that kind of tool that would absorb a tremendous amount of energy and effort, and it would keep the issue of disenfranchisement before the whole nation. . . . It was like, we need time to educate all of America to this problem and by walking from Selma to Montgomery, that would give us the five or six days we need to address the nation.

This was Movement leadership at its best, dealing with everything from emotions to politics in a thoughtful, strategic manner.

SUNDAY, FEBRUARY 28

On the Sabbath, Bevel stood up in the pulpit of Zion's Chapel Methodist Church in Marion to speak to the family, friends, and neighbors of the late Jimmie Lee Jackson. First he talked about the passage in Acts 12 describing how King Herod killed James and arrested Peter, two of

Jesus' disciples. Then he turned to Esther 4:8: "Also he gave him the copy of the writing of the decree that was given at Shushan to destroy them, to shew it unto Esther, and to declare it unto her, and to charge her that she should go in unto the king, to make supplication unto him, and to make request before him for her people."

The Black people of Alabama must protest their destruction, he said. It was time, he said, to move. "We must go to Montgomery and see the king!"

TUESDAY, MARCH 2

Dr. King chose this day to make his first public statement against the growing American involvement in the fighting in Vietnam. Speaking at Howard University in Washington, D.C., he said, "The war in Vietnam is accomplishing nothing."

WEDNESDAY, MARCH 3

King returned to Selma and spoke at another funeral service for Jimmie Lee Jackson. Bevel told reporters that the march to Montgomery would be held on the coming Sunday and would be led by King. The campaign was reaching its climax. King then headed to New York City, where on Thursday he held a war council with some of his closest advisers.

FRIDAY, MARCH 5

King met with President Johnson at the White House to discuss voting rights, and then flew home to Atlanta.

Also in Atlanta, the leadership of SNCC, which had been fragmenting, met and split over whether to participate in the march to Montgomery. The feeling of the majority was that it was the SCLC's grandstanding once again, that it was Bevel's idea and King's show. According to the executive committee's records of the session, "Many people on the committee were opposed to the march because they felt that the dangers to the local people were much greater than any possible achievements."

John Lewis took a different view. He argued that SNCC, under its philosophy of following the will of the communities in which it worked, was obliged to support what the Blacks of Selma wanted. "If these people want to march, I'm going to march with them," he said.

The SNCC leadership met again on Saturday. Then, after midnight, Lewis and two friends got in a white Dodge and made the four-hour drive to Selma. Arriving there, Lewis slipped into a sleeping bag on the floor of SNCC's house there and fell asleep. He would walk at the head of the march, not as the chairman of SNCC but as an individual—a distinction perhaps meaningful to the organization, but one that would be lost on the rest of the world. And in fact the organization would remain deeply involved Sunday's march.

King decided not to return to Selma to lead the next day's march. One theory is that he was told, once again, that there would be violence, perhaps to be used as a cover to assassinate him. Another is that his staff did not quite tell him about the threat but still dissuaded him.

In Alabama, George Wallace announced that the planned march to Montgomery would not be permitted because it would not be "conducive to the orderly flow of traffic and commerce within and through the state of Alabama. . . . Such a march cannot and will not be tolerated."

Bloody Sunday: March 7

This cold, gray day was the culmination of the Selma campaign, and arguably of the entire southern civil rights movement.

When word arrived that King would not be in Selma that day, Hosea Williams, James Bevel, and Andrew Young flipped coins to see who would represent the SCLC alongside John Lewis at the head of the march. Williams lost. He and Lewis walked out of Brown Chapel into an air of menace that day, leading a narrow column of approximately six

hundred marchers, walking in ranks of two along the streets of a volatile town on edge. Williams was no stranger to this kind of tension—he
was a World War II veteran and had been wounded in combat.

It has been emphasized throughout this study that organization and
discipline were key to the success of the civil rights movement. Indeed
they were, most of the time. But on this Sunday, there were major
shortfalls in both areas. Lewis was there against the wishes of his divided organization. And planning for the march was minimal. Lewis
and Williams had no idea of what would happen if Alabama authorities
let them lead the march down Highway 80 toward the state capitol
in Montgomery. "There had been . . . nowhere near the preparation
and logistics necessary to move that many people in an orderly manner
down fifty-four miles of highway," Lewis confessed in a memoir.

Lewis and his comrades possessed audacity. That alone was not
enough most of the time, but on March 7, 1965, as the civil rights
campaign reached its decisive point, it was sufficient. Sometimes who
dares, wins. The enemy, paralyzed in its thinking, would take the bait.

For a young organization, SNCC was remarkably good at record-
keeping—a sign of good training and discipline, especially in an outfit that lacked resources. All that day, it maintained what the military
calls a battle log: staffers in the field called in reports to the organization's headquarters in Atlanta. Each entry in SNCC's log for the day
notes who is calling, where they are located, and what they are seeing.
On March 7 at 2:00 p.m., Central Time, Willie Emma Scott, a young
SNCC volunteer from Selma, reported from Brown Chapel in Selma
that leaders were organizing the marchers "into companies and squads,
with company commanders and squad leaders." The companies consisted of groups of about fifty to one hundred local people, each led
by a SNCC staffer. The squads, of about twenty-five each, consisted of
people from the same block. This was a thoughtful way to assemble the
marchers, because having people walk alongside their own neighbors
helps them maintain their own confidence and fosters cohesion. As
battlefield leaders have long known, having familiar faces around also

discourages acts of cowardice and desertion. It is one thing to turn and run when surrounded by strangers, and quite another when facing people you see every day.

They headed into downtown Selma, and then, for the first time, the civil rights marchers turned and began to walk out of the town—and into the jurisdiction of the county and its vicious sheriff. Those at the head of the march walked up the steep arch of the Edmund Pettus Bridge, named for a Confederate general and Ku Klux Klan leader. Diane Nash worked at the tail end of the march, moving up stragglers and trying to keep the ambulances connected to the march despite police interference. At 3:00 p.m., Lafayette Surney, still in his early twenties but already a veteran SNCC organizer in Mississippi, called from his post at a telephone booth near the bridge to report, "They are on the bridge now." Lewis and Williams were leading the equivalent of a frontal attack into the enemy lines. Conducting such a direct assault is never appealing, because it is almost always extremely bloody. But when it succeeds, the payoff can be remarkable, even deciding the outcome of a campaign, as it would here.

Reaching the apex of the span, Lewis and Williams saw below them, waiting just beyond its eastern base, a phalanx of hundreds of state troopers, some mounted, and a group of Sheriff Clark's angry white "posse men," who formed little more than an armed mob. The troopers stretched across the four lanes of highway in three ranks. Lewis and Williams walked forward and then stood at the eastern end of the bridge in silent prayer. The words going through his mind, Lewis said later, were "You keep your eyes on the prize, and you keep moving toward the goal."

"Troopers, advance," commanded Major John Cloud of the Alabama State Police. His troopers and Clark's men charged, assaulting the marchers with bullwhips, clubs, tear gas, and rubber tubes wound with barbed wire. "They showed no mercy towards marchers," recalled one of those attacked, Elizabeth Fitts.

At 3:16, Surney, still at his post in the telephone booth near the bridge, reported, "Police are beating people on the streets. Oh, man, they're just picking them up and putting them in ambulances. People are getting hurt pretty bad." Fay Powell was on the other end of the line, in SNCC's Atlanta office. "We could hear people screaming and sirens blaring; it sounded like a soundtrack from a war movie," she recalled.

Amelia Boynton, who had invited the SCLC to come to Selma, was clubbed into unconsciousness. As she lay on the pavement, a state trooper dropped a tear gas canister in front of her face.

About fifteen men on horses trampled prone marchers. Willie Bolden recalled seeing people knocked off the bridge by the animals, or jumping off it to avoid being run over. The lawmen continued to pummel the people retreating back up the bridge and then for nearly a mile back to Brown Chapel into the Black part of town. "The police were riding along on horseback beating people, and the tear gas was so thick you couldn't get to where people were," said Andrew Young, who was about two blocks behind the vanguard of the march. Some of the mounted men even spurred their horses up the steps of the chapel. Young thought, "Beating us back into our community was like forcing us back into the concentration camp, back into the physical and psychological boundaries erected by the white power structure." Posse men banged their billy clubs on the hoods of cars driven by Blacks, shouting, "We want all the niggers off the streets." That angry order summarized the white supremacism they were seeking to preserve.

Brown Chapel became a makeshift field hospital. Lewis recalled, "I don't know to this day how I made it back to the church." At 3:40, Willie Emma Scott called to report, "About two or three busloads of possemen are in front of the church beating people, throwing tear gas, beating children and adults. They have about twenty people on horseback. I don't know how many's been carried to the hospital. John Lewis has a small hole in his head. I tried to do something for it, but he wouldn't let me." A medical examination would find that Lewis' skull had been fractured. All in all, some 140 Blacks were injured in the police riot, half of them severely enough to require hospitalization. And this was simply because they were asking to be allowed to exercise the most basic right of American citizenship: to vote. Of course, treating

Blacks like equal citizens would undermine the white supremacist basis on which the South had been operating for centuries.

The triumph

John Lewis and Hosea Williams emerged with a victory. That awful moment at the eastern approach of the Edmund Pettus Bridge had been the death spasm of a defeated system. After a year in which churches and houses had been dynamited and civil rights workers murdered, what made the day memorable for the nation was that it was captured on film. That night, the ABC television network interrupted its programming to show fifteen minutes of footage—clouds of nausea-inducing gas wafting through the scene, and horses charging marchers amid shouts of "Get the niggers."

With that, the civil rights movement had won. The American public had been made aware, Bevel said, "in the most graphic way possible, that a sheriff in Alabama was beating law-abiding citizens whose only offense was asking for the right to vote."

Indeed, attuned first by the events in Birmingham and now pondering what it saw from Selma, the nation was now ready to decide that segregation and disenfranchisement were doomed. The subsequent march from Selma to Montgomery would be a victory march—albeit one still plagued by occasional segregationist snipers. As the historian David Garrow summarizes it, "While the voting rights bill had been drafted prior to that now famous afternoon, there is little doubt that the attack of March 7 and the news coverage it received ensured that the bill would be enacted into law." And, contrary to what Ramsey Clark had said, it would pass through Congress quickly.

TUESDAY, MARCH 9

People from across the country flocked to Selma to join the subsequent demonstrations. The Sunday march had consisted of six hundred people. Two days later, on March 9, about two thousand followed

King to the base of the Pettus bridge. He led them in prayer and then turned around. This puzzled some of those behind him, but King had a good reason: his formal request to march from Selma to Montgomery was still pending, and he did not want to antagonize the federal judge considering that request. Some mocked King's reversal as Turnaround Tuesday, but in strategic terms it made sense. King had made his point: he had obeyed the federal order, and he had not led his people into needless violence or into a march toward Montgomery for which no preparations had been made. As he turned around, the state troopers, in a surprise move, cleared the way, opening the road to Montgomery. But King did not take that bait, which amounted to an invitation from Governor Wallace to violate the federal judge's order. Less noticed, King the field commander had also demonstrated superb tactical control of his followers. He had not briefed them on his decisions, and so had no guarantee they would turn with him. But they did.

However, King's solution, while the right move, failed to take into account the bursts of emotion roiling the marchers behind him. They had gone to the bridge expecting to put their bodies on the line, to offer a sacrifice even of their lives. Instead they ended the day restless with energy, confused and angry with King. Hardy Frye, a veteran of Freedom Summer, remembered sitting on the first floor of a funeral home where upstairs SNCC's leaders confronted the SCLC's James Bevel and Andrew Young. "There was a shouting match, it was an argument we could hear from downstairs," Frye said. Many did not understand why the day's march had been called off.

In the room upstairs, Bevel recalled, the disappointed SNCC activists screamed, "You sold out!" He continued: "They were just very irrational people who didn't understand strategy and despised white folks." He thought they were too focused on one day's demonstration and had taken their eyes off the prize: the right to vote. They did not understand that the Movement had won.

Then, at around ten o'clock that same night, as the arguments curled into the air, word came that James Reeb, a white Unitarian minister and civil rights activist then making his home in Boston, had been attacked in downtown Selma by a baseball bat or pipe section being swung into his skull. Diane Nash, working in Amelia Boynton's insurance office, which also served as the SCLC's local office, arranged for an ambulance to take Reeb to a Birmingham hospital and raised $150 to get him admitted once there. He died soon after.

Activists noted a bit bitterly that Reeb's murder captured far more national attention than had the one a few weeks earlier of Jimmie Lee Jackson. President Johnson dispatched an Air Force C-140 passenger jet to collect Reeb's body and his widow and fly them back to Boston. By contrast, remembered Andrew Young, "It was almost as if Jackson's death was to be expected, nothing unusual."

Later that week, James Bevel stood before an audience that must have delighted him: white clerics had flocked to Selma from around the country in response to the killing of Reeb. "You white ministers are all thinking of going home to preach on Sunday," he told them. "Now you just stay here. It will do your congregations much more good for you to be absent." He instructed them in the ways of white southerners: "If it requires letting them beat us, then we'll have to let them beat us, because this is the only way left open to us to communicate with them."

Meanwhile, the adversary in Selma was in disarray. In one incident, the mayor was standing on a Selma street when a state trooper jabbed him in the stomach with a billy club and told him to "move out of here." A nearby reporter informed the trooper that this was the mayor. The trooper didn't care. Also around this time, Jim Clark and Wilson Baker—that is, the county sheriff and the town's top law enforcement official—had an angry personal confrontation. Clark told Baker that if he interfered again with his deputies, he would arrest him. Baker responded that before that happened, he would kill Clark. The mayor, doing his best to peaceably maintain segregation, dived in and separated them.

MONDAY, MARCH 15

A few days later, President Johnson went before Congress to give a speech carried on national television. He cast the Selma march in terms of a centuries-old American search for freedom, citing two foundational wars. "So it was at Lexington and Concord. So it was a century ago at Appomattox," the president said. "So it was last week in Selma, Alabama." He then stated that the government was duty-bound to enforce the basic premise that, "Every American citizen must have an equal right to vote. There is no reason which can excuse the denial of that right." With that, he submitted a bill that would strike down literacy tests and all other restrictions that had been used to deny the vote to Black Americans.

"We shall overcome," Johnson vowed, using the Movement's best-known slogan and thus implicitly allying himself with the cause.

In Selma that night, Martin Luther King, Jr., was watching television with several other members of the Movement in the living room of a Selma dentist. When the president said, "We shall overcome," some of the people in the room cheered. King remained quiet. C. T. Vivian looked over at him and saw him shed a tear of joy and relief. "It really was the final breakup of segregation, as we knew it in the Old South," Vivian said. Bevel thought that at the moment, "We've solved the problem."

The emerging hard-liners at SNCC had a sharply different reaction. James Forman and the SNCC people watching the president's speech with him "felt extremely alienated and we felt it was insincere, . . . a mockery, . . . it just wasn't real." Stokely Carmichael said that Johnson's use of "We shall overcome" made him feel "like vomiting." These wildly varying reactions were signs that the Movement was rapidly losing cohesion, and that SNCC was moving in a radically different direction from the SCLC.

The problems of success

Success in war inevitably unleashes a new set of problems. As the end of a struggle comes into sight, bonds between allies begin to fray. This is not just a failing of human nature, though festering personal grievances, feelings rubbed raw in the friction of war, often are part of the cause. There are realistic political reasons as well. As the danger presented by the enemy recedes, allies lose much of the incentive they have had to submerge their differences. Instead they begin to focus on them, as happened with the United States and the Soviet Union in the closing months of World War II. As Winston Churchill said midway through that war, "The problems of victory are more agreeable than those of defeat, but they are still no less difficult."

Also, the prospect of imminent victory can be nettlesome, because it poses a new series of questions: What actually constitutes victory? Is the struggle really over, and has the goal truly been achieved? Is a partial victory sufficient? And in this case: Have you really won when the president adopts your movement's slogan, or have you been co-opted?

On top of that, as resolution nears, leaders necessarily begin to contemplate the next task, and because of their differences they often disagree about what that should be. For the civil rights movement, a set of questions arose: Once voting rights are secured, what is our next step? Is it to go into elective politics, seeking offices high and low, and living with the compromising life that requires, making deals with politicians who once were our foes? Or is it to remain outside the system, pressuring it with demonstrations and remaining ideologically purer? Should it be to go north and try to improve life in the Black slums? Or is it time to pivot to foreign policy and oppose the U.S. involvement in the Vietnam War, despite President Johnson's vocal support for civil rights? As Malcom Hooks, a participant in the Birmingham campaign, put it, "I feel like a boy standing at the train platform waiting for a train to let him in. Every day he waits until integration finally allows him on the train, but once on the train, he asks, 'Where is this train going?'"

All these centrifugal pressures worked on the Movement during the Selma campaign. And so by its end, old comrades began to look at each other in new and more critical ways.

Marching from Selma to Montgomery

The march from Selma to Montgomery was, at last, approved by the federal judge. It would carry some dangers, but it was more a celebratory parade than a protest. One sign of this is the number of people, many of them powerful or famous, who asked to be included—which was a problem because the judge had ruled that on the narrow part of the highway, where it shrank to two lanes, only three hundred people could participate. To its credit, the SCLC reserved about 250 of those slots for the people who had already been marching in Selma and the surrounding area. Renata Adler of the *New Yorker* magazine deemed the march "ceremonial—almost redundant."

Even so, the SCLC's Andrew Young reminded a group of parade marshals of the rules they needed to enforce. "Keep women and children in the middle," he said. "If there's a shot, stand up and make the others kneel down. Don't be lagging around, or you're going to get hurt. Don't rely on the troopers, either. If you're beaten, crouch and put your hands over the back of your head. Don't put your arm up to ward off a blow. If you fall, fall right down and look dead. Get to know the people in your unit, so you can tell if somebody's missing or if there's somebody who shouldn't be there. And listen! If you can't be non-violent, let me know now." These were classic pre-march instructions that could have been issued at any SCLC action in the previous several years.

On March 21, it got under way. It began with three thousand people, then dropped to three hundred (to stay within the federal order), and finally, on the outskirts of Montgomery, it swelled to twenty-five thousand people. "It was enjoyable and it was tension-filled all at the same time," Ralph Abernathy said. "We knew that victory was in sight." John Lewis felt the same way. "I knew the ending was just a matter of time," he recalled, "that we would get the Voting Rights Act."

Oddly, given the parade-like atmosphere, the march would be one of the most thoroughly militarized episodes of the entire civil rights era. The walkers were protected on the ground by federalized units of the Alabama National Guard. Army jeeps accompanied them. Spotters scanned the tree lines for potential segregationist snipers. Army helicopters clattered overhead, followed on occasion by an Army observation plane. At night, the Guards formed an outer perimeter around the marchers' tents, which were erected only after the campground had been checked by Army minesweepers.

Conditions impinged on the celebratory mood. The longer the march went on, the farther the food had to be driven from kitchens in Selma, with the result that the pork and beans and the spaghetti were often ladled out congealed and cold. Rain poured down at the second night's campsite, turning it into a morass. There were glorious photographs of happy people, Pam Parker recalled, but she added, sounding like many seasoned soldiers through the centuries, "Here's the truth of it, it was muddy and cold."

Still, it was a time of triumph. As the march neared the Montgomery city line, recalled Harris Wofford, King said, "We have a new song to sing tomorrow. We *have* overcome."

On March 25, in the final stage of the march, from the western side of Montgomery to the state capitol downtown, perhaps as many as fifty thousand people walked past the landmarks of the King family's lives and of the Movement. They began at St. Jude Hospital, where Coretta Scott King had given birth to her and Martin's first two children. They saw the Holt Street Baptist Church, where King had begun his role as a civil rights leader, a seeming lifetime ago. They passed through Court Square, where Rosa Parks had gotten onto a bus ten full years earlier, and a few steps from where some of the Freedom Riders were beaten four years earlier. Then they marched past King's old church, Dexter Avenue Baptist. Finally, they stopped in front of the state capitol. It was the largest civil rights march the South had ever seen. All three national television networks covered it live. Perhaps no one noticed it, but the action proposed by Diane Nash and James Bevel after the 1963 Birmingham church bombing had been achieved: the Movement had shut down the capital of Alabama in an entirely nonviolent manner.

They sang "The Star-Spangled Banner," and then King spoke. As usual, he was good at setting the context at the outset, placing the given moment in the larger sweep of history. "It is not an accident that one of the great marches of American history should terminate in Montgomery, Alabama," he said. He then reviewed the history of the Movement, the losses it had seen. But he was there to announce another demise, he said: "I stand before you this afternoon with the conviction that segregation is on its deathbed in Alabama, and the only thing uncertain about it is how costly the segregationists and Wallace will make the funeral."

He concluded not with a passage from the Bible but with one of the most powerful songs of the victorious side of the Civil War:

Mine eyes have seen the glory of the coming of the Lord;
He is trampling out the vintage where the grapes of wrath are stored;
He has loosed the fateful lightning of his terrible swift sword;
His truth is marching on.

It was a surprising choice, perhaps, but appropriate for the end of a long and victorious march.

When King's speech ended, Andrew Young walked over to the Dexter Avenue Baptist Church, went into the men's room, locked the door, and wept. C. T. Vivian, that veteran activist, recalled that he woke up one morning just after Selma and thought, "The movement as we have been doing it is over."

Less than five months later, on August 6, 1965, the president signed the Voting Rights Act. In the year after the bill was passed, the number of Blacks registered to vote in Alabama almost doubled. In just four years, Black voter registration in Mississippi shot from 7 percent to 59 percent. The Deep South began to send Blacks to Congress for the first time since Reconstruction. By 2011, there would be more than ten thousand Black officials holding elective office across the nation. By 2019, there were fifty-two Black members of the House of Representatives, giving them for the first time in U.S. history a representation proportional to their share of the American population. The Department of Justice would call the Voting Rights Act "the single most effective piece of civil rights legislation ever passed by Congress." And in Selma itself, in 1966, Wilson Baker would run against Jim Clark for sheriff and win—but only after a judge ordered that Black votes be tallied. Six years later, Amelia Boynton, the woman who had invited the SCLC to Selma in 1964, and who had been dragged by Sheriff Clark and then knocked out and tear-gassed at the Edmund Pettus Bridge on Bloody Sunday, was elected to the city council.

After this exquisite moment, the Movement fractured. But the lesson of Selma, Andrew Young concluded, was that nonviolence worked. "Change didn't come through confrontation and violence," he said. "Change came through sustained disciplined action on the part of the Black community." Others in the Movement felt differently, however, and soon began to say so, loudly.

What next?

Uncharacteristically, James Bevel did not seem to recognize the moment for what it was. In strategic terms, it almost certainly was a moment to step back, regroup, and consolidate the victory, perhaps with local political campaigns to elect Black mayors and sheriffs. But Bevel's instinct was to keep charging, going for bigger and more explosive goals. He proposed that the next step for the SCLC should be to lead a national boycott of Alabama products. According to the historian Adam Fairclough, Bevel wanted the SCLC to "insist on the immediate participation of blacks in the government of Alabama; . . . [and] to expose Wallace and the legislature as an undemocratic and illegitimate regime, forcing the federal government to supervise new state elections on the basis of a free and universal franchise." It was almost as if he wanted to match SNCC's statewide assault on Mississippi the previous summer.

King at first endorsed Bevel's proposal. Just a week after the end of the Montgomery march, he said on national television:

> I think that it is necessary for the nation to rise up and engage in a massive economic withdrawal program on the State of Alabama. To put it another way, I think the time has come for all people of goodwill to join in an economic boycott of Alabama

products. So I am, in a few days, planning to call on the trade unions to refuse to transport or use Alabama products. I hope to call on all Americans to refuse to buy Alabama products.

The reaction to this idea was almost universally harsh. Unions couldn't support it without violating contracts. Newspaper editorials labeled it vindictive. Northern governors held it at arm's length. Bayard Rustin called it stupid. Most piercing of all was a letter from King's longtime confidant Stanley Levison, who wrote, "The casual manner of proposing [the] boycott, and the impression that this was your central program caused deep disquiet. . . . It was not the best selection of alternatives for action, and it was not logical to emerge from a struggle for voting rights."

King soon backed away from the notion of conducting a nationwide boycott of Alabama. A few weeks later, he suggested at an SCLC staff meeting that "enough progress" had been made in Alabama not to go forward with the plan. "Bevel had seriously misjudged the mood of the Blacks of Alabama," concludes Charles Fager, author of one of the best histories of the Selma campaign. They were elated but exhausted, he writes, and "they were by no means ready to put on their marching shoes again."

Bevel at this time may have been becoming a bit mentally unbalanced. Dismayed, he took a leave of absence from the SCLC. Diane Nash had withdrawn her suit for divorce. She and Bevel moved to Chicago, where they would separate again, then finally end the marriage a few years later. There in Chicago, Bevel began mulling the Movement's next step.

12.
CHICAGO, 1966

A Bridge Too Far

Ten or eleven years is a very long time for an American war to last. The Civil War, the Mexican War, and the Korean War ended in about four years or less, as did the American involvement in the two world wars.

When he spoke on March 25, 1965, at the end of the Montgomery-to-Selma march, by contrast, Martin Luther King, Jr., had been campaigning for a decade. The writer James Baldwin wrote of encountering a "very tired" King one night at a fundraiser in Los Angeles: "We had first met during the last days of the Montgomery bus boycott—and how long ago was that? It was senseless to say, eight years, ten years ago—it was longer ago than time can reckon."

King had been worked hard by the Movement—leading, speaking, fundraising—all while enduring harassment by the FBI and a daily drumbeat of death threats. His marriage was suffering. He was worn down. "I need more time to think through what is being done," he said early in 1965, "to take time out from the mechanics of the movement, to reflect on the meaning of the movement." This is an indication that he knew he was losing his sense of the strategic direction of the Movement, which had been so clear for him at the outset, back in his first great speech in Montgomery on December 5, 1955. He knew there were deep internal tensions in the Movement that eventually could fracture it. He also knew that he desperately needed time off—not a week or two but perhaps a full year. One day he sat in a rocking chair in the Atlanta living room of his close friend Dorothy Cotton and mused, "Maybe I should take a sabbatical." But if he was gone that long, fund-raising for the SCLC might come to a near halt. He must have felt trapped.

What do you do after you achieve your goals? It is one of the hardest questions a war or political movement can pose, and answers can be exceedingly hard to find.

We can only wonder how King's life might have unfolded had he been able in 1966 or 1967 to withdraw to rest and reflect, and to restore himself. He had as an example Gandhi's withdrawal after the Chauri Chaura incident of 1922, in which a march that began as a nonviolent protest turned lethal. Police fired on the demonstrators, who in turn burned their station, killing twenty-two policemen. In response, Gandhi suspended his independence movement, which had been accelerating in strength. Telling the authorities that he was guilty of training his followers insufficiently, he went to jail for two years, during which time he penned an autobiography. "I must undergo personal cleansing," he wrote. "I must become a fitter instrument able to register the slightest variation in the moral atmosphere about me."

Imagine the possibilities if King had found a year of near solitude, of quiet contemplation, of recalibration. It would have given him the chance to make sense of the journey of the previous ten years, and also perhaps gain some perspective on American society. What kind of vision might he have developed? In his absence, the SCLC may well have collapsed. But that might not have been a terrible outcome. The organization perhaps had done what it could do, even if it had not achieved the goal of ending second-class citizenship for Black Americans. If he had disappeared for twelve or more months, he might have been able to come back a different man, and so might have needed a new organization as his vehicle, one more national in orientation, probably less aligned with ministers and more with labor and political entities, and more consistent with his emerging view that the United States needed a fundamental restructuring in order to become a healthy, just society.

But, as we know, King did not step aside. Among King's shortcomings was a nagging failure to take care of himself, physically and mentally. He was under enormous stress, and he worked almost nonstop and then relaxed in unhealthy ways. In this sense he resembled Dwight Eisenhower in World War II, who kept himself going with four packs of cigarettes and as many as fifteen cups of coffee a day, as well as an intimate relationship with his attractive female driver. But Eisenhower's war lasted only a few years, while King's lasted for more than a decade. And, as noted, King fully expected his life to be cut short by an assassin. As the veterans' counselor Jonathan Shay notes, it is not uncommon for soldiers to ask, "When the future isn't real, why take care of your body?" It is unclear whether anyone could have done better than King. Even so, the lack of self-care hurt both him and the Movement. Rest and relaxation are essential to clear thinking, especially on the level of strategy. Not getting sleep and not getting time alone to think are failures of intellectual discipline. And with the passage of time, especially in 1966, King's grasp of strategy seems to have become less certain.

The last three years of King's life would be the saddest. He was looking for what to do next. He developed two answers: oppose the Vietnam War, and attack the unfairness of the American economy. Both these efforts would bring him more critics and antagonists.

But first, he would launch a quixotic effort to transform one of the biggest cities in the United States.

A foray into the North

What to do next was the subject of intense debate in the SCLC's leadership circle. Go north, go national? Or stay in the South, on familiar turf? "We really didn't know what our direction should be after Selma," Andrew Young said. He thought the SCLC should stay focused on the South. "We had been successful in Alabama," he reasoned, "because we knew everybody, we understood the culture and the people, white and Black." In military terms, this meant operating on terrain you understand.

But King was looking to the North. Even before Selma, King had been mulling how "the nonviolent movement . . . can give other movements the lifeblood necessary to deal with such problems as poverty."

Over two days in August 1965, the leadership of the SCLC argued this out at a Hilton hotel near the Atlanta airport. King laid out the rationale. After the March on Washington, he said, the organization had begun receiving invitations to go north. He was especially worried by the lack of understanding in the North about nonviolence. He had been asked to visit Chicago the following month. "We must not ignore their call," he said. He wanted to see whether the Movement had something to offer northern cities.

The minutes of the meeting are hazy about just who said what in response, referring to "some conclusions and suggestions," but it is clear that many top staff members had serious reservations about this plan. "We must not get involved in what cannot be attained," one person said, according to those minutes. Another person, also not identified, asked, "Are we qualified to give leadership in the North in nonviolence as in Birmingham?"

Despite such concerns, the leaders finally decided the move was necessary: "We will do intensified work in the North, using Chicago as a pilot project." The notes provide no details on how that decision was reached, suggesting that King had made up his mind before the meeting.

Diane Nash, who was from Chicago, was not present at that staff meeting. She later stated that she opposed the SCLC moving north. "We weren't finished in the South—there was a lot of work to be done," she said. And Bayard Rustin claimed that he warned King against taking on Chicago mayor Richard Daley, whom Rustin described as a savvy politician who had Black allies. He said he told King, "You won't beat Daley on his home ground, and you'll come away with nothing meaningful for all your efforts."

But King thought that, with riots breaking out in the big northern cities, it was essential to offer to try nonviolent methods there. Yes, money was an issue. But, he noted, one of the SCLC's most successful fundraisers had been held in Los Angeles, also well outside the South.

Moreover, Bevel, whose advice had proved essential in both Birmingham and Selma, was urging King to take aim at Chicago. Bevel took a leave of absence from the SCLC to work in Chicago for the West Side Christian Parish, a religious social reform organization. "The real estate dealers in Chicago are the equivalent to Wallace and Jim Clark in the South," he argued in one talk. That is, they were the leading edge of enforcing segregation, declining to sell or even show houses in white neighborhoods to Black buyers. Target those intermediaries, Bevel thought, and you can bring change.

Bevel's path

James Bevel had always been brilliant but unsteady. As a strategist, he had to think in big ways. But in late 1965 and early 1966, he appears to have been drifting into vast thoughts that were not grounded in reality. He talked about raising a "nonviolent army"—the phrase was Gandhi's—of more than one hundred thousand young Chicagoans. The SCLC's task in Chicago, Bevel wrote, would be nothing less than "getting rid of the slums." They were aiming "not to patch up the ghetto, but to abolish it." This was verbose grandiosity.

In the past, Bevel's flights of thought had been anchored by concrete actions, such as marches. But his plan for Chicago in 1966 rocketed straight into the ether. First, in just a few months, he said, he would raise his army through block-by-block education and organizing. Then, around March 1, a community consensus would arise about what to target. Third, two months later, some form of "massive action" against that target would emerge. Bevel's plan was basically that something would come up. Bevel explained the hazy nature of the plan as necessary: because Chicago officials might accommodate some demands, "we must be prepared to concentrate our forces around any and all issues." This sounds like a plan to be flexible, but it also violates the military maxim that to be prepared for any eventuality is to be prepared for none well. Frederick the Great, the Prussian king and military theorist, stated, "He who defends everything defends nothing." Historians fault Hitler for neglecting that dictum during World War II: he kept large numbers of troops in Italy, Norway, and the Balkans, and repeatedly demanded that his generals fight to the end rather than retreat and regroup.

At times Bevel simply stopped making sense. Was the timeline six months, two years, or many years? At different points he gave different answers. When a strategic plan is not rooted in concrete realities, the descent from effective planning to misleading nonsense can be swift indeed.

King, reviewing Bevel's proposal, should have either put his foot down or encouraged a more levelheaded aide, such as Andrew Young, to step forward and pull it back to earth. But that takes time and energy. King may simply have been too worn down to rein in Bevel. It is one thing to try to chart a future course of action while well rested, with no phone ringing, and with plenty of time for quiet reflection. It is something altogether different to try to map out the way forward while aides are passing urgent messages, funds need raising, the FBI is attacking you, you are physically and psychologically spent—and your most adept strategist may be losing his grasp on reality.

Into Chicago

On Sunday, September 10, 1944, following the Allied breakout from Normandy, the top British field commander, Field Marshal Bernard Law Montgomery, proposed to his ostensible boss, Dwight Eisenhower, that the next step was to make a quick thrust across the Rhine and charge on a narrow front hundreds of miles across northern Germany to Berlin. Eisenhower was weary of Montgomery's constant and condescending criticisms, and so agreed to try his plan. The Americans and British launched Operation Market Garden, as it was called, just a week later, with glider landings and paratrooper drops behind enemy lines in southeastern Holland. The attacks quickly degenerated into a disaster. The attack was simply too narrow, and through bad luck, it ran into two German Panzer divisions that were resting in the area. The Allies pulled back, and the entire assault came to be known with regret as "a bridge too far."

The SCLC's Chicago campaign, announced in January 1966, would prove similarly disappointing. The signature of this operation would be King moving his family into a freezing apartment in the city's slums. Like changing into demonstration clothes three years before, this was another tactic of Gandhi's: In 1946, the Indian activist, aghast at the impending partition of the subcontinent into India and Pakistan, had moved into an abandoned house in a Calcutta slum where Hindu refugees from East Bengal were crowding in on uneasy Muslim shanty-dwellers, leading to riots. Bevel had selected for King a third-floor flat at 1550 South Hamlin Avenue in the West Side neighborhood of North Lawndale. Coretta King was not taken with the urine-soaked ground-floor entrance.

In March, King kicked off the Chicago campaign with a speech that endorsed Bevel's approach, vowing that it would "remove gargantuan structures of injustice in the north." It was, he said, a "movement to end slums." How? The plan was as vague as the ambitions were large. "Time will not permit me to outline our program of action," King prestidigi-tated. "But it is clear to me that we must organize this total community into unities of political and social power."

It was in Chicago, King told people, "that the grapes of wrath are stored." But in that city his nonviolent sword was neither terrible nor swift. The overwhelming fact that Bevel and King had not addressed was that, for the SCLC, Chicago was foreign turf in several ways. In 1966, the city's population was more than twenty times that of Birmingham. In Chicago, King and his circle would learn one of the harder lessons of military operations, which is that operating in large cities requires large amounts of soldiers and supplies. "Cities are sponges that soak up troops," commented David Kilcullen, an Australian military expert. They badly underestimated the number of staff organizers and the amount of money required. As the historian Adam Fairclough puts it, "With never more than fifty staff members in the city, Chicago overwhelmed SCLC's resources."

On top of that, the goals King and Bevel set for Chicago were wildly ambitious. In a move resembling his post-Montgomery effort to launch a Citizenship Crusade to double Black voter registration in the South almost overnight, King overpromised on what might be achieved in his first foray in the North. "We're going to organize to make Chicago a model city," King vowed at one Chicago rally.

Moreover, the religious ground was quite different, and contained several minefields. King's SCLC was an organization of southern Black Protestant ministers mounting an operation in a city with a sizable white Catholic population, not something it had encountered before. Also, along with Detroit, Chicago was one of two major outposts for the Black Muslim movement, which was skeptical of King's approach. Even within the realm of Protestantism, Chicago's Black Baptist church harbored hostility to King: it was the bastion of J. H. Jackson, the powerful leader of the National Baptist Convention, and a bitter rival of King since King had tried to oust him from his post in 1961.

The city also had an uneven record on political activism. In the 1940s, campaigns to punish companies that did not employ Blacks had succeeded in several northern cities, but the one in Chicago fizzled out because, as two historians put it, organizers found "Chicago blacks unenthusiastic about boycotting and picketing." Indeed, King received only lukewarm local support. By May, some Chicago activists suggested that Bevel and another SCLC worker, Al Sampson, leave the city. A rally in July at Chicago's Soldier Field, which then had a capacity of about 100,000, attracted a crowd perhaps half that amount.

The stadium event was supposed to kick-start the action phase of the operation. "This day we must decide that our votes will determine who will be the next mayor of Chicago," King told the audience. "We must make it clear that we will purge Chicago of every politician, whether he be Negro or white, who feels that he owns a Negro vote." But he knew the campaign was sputtering.

One hot summer day, Chicago teenagers opened fire hydrants so they could play in the spray. The city turned off the hydrants, and some of the teenagers then rioted. J. H. Jackson blamed King and Bevel for that reaction. "I believe our young people are not vicious enough to attack a whole city," Jackson said at a press conference, standing alongside Mayor Daley. "Some other forces are using these young people."

King was hoping and waiting for a misstep by Daley. At a mass meeting, referring to the successes in the South, he said, "Our movement won not only because of ingenuity and because of our ability to organize . . . but it won as much because of the mistakes of our opponents." So, he went on, "we will welcome any mistake our opponents are willing to make in Chicago." But Daley was an adroit and powerful politician who scrambled to offset King's initiatives with his own programs to clean up slums and eradicate rats. Bevel had aimed to recruit 300,000 members for a Chicago "tenant union." He managed to find 10,000.

King's retreat

As was noted earlier, one military axiom holds that one should never reinforce failure—that is, don't pour troops and treasure into a defeat, and know when to cut your losses. Do not let pride get in the way. To King's credit, he understood the need to find a way to end the Chicago campaign. In August, Mayor Daley asked King to sit down for a settlement discussion. Daley also was embarrassed by the racist responses to movement marches into Chicago's all-white neighborhoods, which gave him an incentive to offer King a way out. "We were trying to find a way to wind it up," Andrew Young recalled.

After two long and intense sessions with Daley, King emerged with a statement saying that Chicago's real estate agents would try to reduce segregation and that the city government would keep an eye on them and enforce existing fair housing rules. "All in all, the Summit Agreement amounted to little more than various pledges of nondiscrimination," concludes the historian Adam Fairclough. It wasn't much, but it was enough to allow King to leave town in an orderly retreat. Knowing when to stop and try something different is an underappreciated virtue.

King spoke at the meeting's close as if he had triumphed. "This must be interpreted, this agreement, as a victory for justice and not a victory over the Chicago Real Estate Board or the city of Chicago," he insisted. And then he got out of Dodge. Despite the magnanimous rhetoric, King's exit did not look good. Soon after King left town, Daley was reelected, receiving impressive support from Black areas. The historian Manning Marable notes, "To most political observers, the King campaign was less than ineffectual; the Daley machine controlled the Black community more strongly than ever before." Indeed, after he was reelected, Daley let it be known that he did not consider the August agreement with King to be binding.

Bevel would later claim that King had secured a secret agreement with Daley that fair housing ordinances would be much more rigorously enforced. But because that couldn't be disclosed, he said, "Our movement looked like it had ended prematurely."

At a staff retreat in Frogmore, South Carolina, a few months later, King noted that there was "a great deal of confusion in the air." He admitted that the way forward looked unclear. "I think we would all agree that a lot of people are frustrated, a lot of people have lost their way. I guess a lot of us wonder where we are going." This was normal, he counseled, as all revolutions have their ups and downs. He also took a hard whack at the new cry of "Black Power," which was gaining popularity that year among younger activists. He called it a slogan, not a program, and a bad one at that—a cry of pain that was a show of weakness.

King knew that the Chicago campaign had been messy. "In all frankness, we found the job greater than even we imagined," he said later. Still, he must have been staggered by an unforgiving note he received from Timuel Black, a veteran organizer of Black labor in Chicago. Black had helped bring King to Chicago to speak in 1956. Over the years, King had come to call the Chicagoan "Brother Black," and Black in turn called him "Doc." Black had helped organize the Chicago contingent that went to the 1963 March on Washington. Black tartly wrote to King that the SCLC's abortive foray into Chicago had been hugely counterproductive, breaking the back of the city's civil rights movement and leaving it holding empty promises. "Take a long, hard look at the Chicago scene," he advised. "Whatever your future ventures are, I hope they will be better planned and more successful than those of last year."

When Hosea Williams visited the remnants of the Chicago campaign at the end of 1966, he found morale problems not unlike those that would plague the U.S. Army as it became bogged down in Vietnam. "Many of SCLC's regular staff members were doing little more than laying around their rooms all day, playing cards, drinking and smoking pot," Williams reported to King.

Nowadays, some revisionist historians argue that the rise of Barack Obama from Chicago community organizer in 1985 to president of the United States in 2009 can be traced to the changes that began in part with the SCLC's foray into the city in 1966. It is a pleasant notion, but it seems a stretch, at best, given the ample evidence that the SCLC intervention in the city had a negative effect.

Bevel departed Chicago and took a leave of absence from the SCLC to work full-time against the Vietnam War. His psychological decline continued. Early in 1967, King retreated to Ocho Rios, Jamaica, to rest and work on a book. Bevel followed him there, showing up unannounced and uninvited to try to persuade King to join an antiwar march planned for that spring in New York. King agreed. But we know from the FBI wiretap that he also called Andrew Young at this time to worry that "Bevel sounds like he's off his rocker and needs a psychiatrist."

Others developed similar worries. In a note that spring, the historian Lawrence Reddick, a longtime friend and adviser to King, recorded that one of King's confidants, the Wall Street lawyer Harry Wachtel, worried to him that "Bevel perhaps needed psychiatric commitment." Bevel was telling people that he had had a vision in which a man told him to mobilize against the Vietnam War. Hosea Williams, a longtime rival of Bevel's within the SCLC, wrote a memorandum to King stating, "Our staff problems are unbelievable," and accusing Bevel of being the root cause.

Meredith's march—June 1966

In the same year, King unexpectedly was pulled in yet another direction, by the shooting of James Meredith. Characteristically, Meredith had veered through life since graduating from Ole Miss. He had considered running for Congress, had accepted and then abandoned a postgraduate fellowship in Nigeria, and had enrolled at Columbia University's law school.

Then, on June 5, 1966, he set out on a small "March Against Fear" from Memphis to Jackson, Mississippi. In this new endeavor, as at Ole Miss in 1962, Meredith operated almost entirely alone. This may have antagonized Movement leaders, but it also made him, for the second time, a one-man monument to the strength of the human will.

The next day, Monday, June 6, as his march took Meredith near Hernando, Mississippi, a white man from Memphis fired three 16-gauge shotgun loads of number 4 birdshot at him. Even though Meredith was an outsider, it was in keeping with the principles of the Movement that such violence could not go unanswered. King, CORE's Floyd McKissick, SNCC's Stokely Carmichael, and the NAACP's Roy Wilkins converged on Memphis to discuss the response. They met at James Lawson's church. The SNCC people drove away Wilkins, mocking him and telling him it was time for him to retire. According to Carmichael's sympathetic biographer, Carmichael "started to scream and curse" at Wilkins and the Urban League's Whitney Young.

King and Carmichael would march together in Mississippi along Meredith's planned route, followed at first by hundreds, then thousands. At one point, state troopers pushed them off the pavement. Carmichael gestured as if to counterattack, and King restrained him. Lawson critiqued Carmichael for lacking a clarity of purpose. Because Carmichael was ambivalent about nonviolence, Lawson said, "When you get shoved you get confused."

As Lawson's tart observation showed, even as King and Carmichael walked together, they were mentally out of step. The media was there because King was there. Carmichael used that platform to criticize nonviolence and advertise the emerging slogan of "Black Power." Carmichael had a point: Until 1966, the civil rights movement had been about using protest to appeal to those holding power. Now he and others were talking instead about winning and wielding power. "We're not a protest movement," Carmichael insisted. On the other hand, by rejecting exotic Gandhian nonviolence and embracing the use of force and threats, Carmichael arguably was becoming not more radical but more conventionally American.

King asked him to be quiet about Black Power, but Carmichael declined. Carmichael explained that his view was that King was too powerful to take on and depose, so the task was "to see where we can use him." When he admitted this plan to King, the older man responded, with apparent resignation, "Well, Stokely, I've been used before." But he was less accepting when he got home to Atlanta, telling a friend there that he doubted he could continue to work with SNCC.

One night in Greenwood, Mississippi, Carmichael told a crowd, "Every courthouse in Mississippi ought to be burned tomorrow to get rid of the dirt." In a moment that captured the old movement versus the emerging one, James Lawson, appalled, confronted Carmichael. The minister of nonviolence argued that the Movement had achieved a lot nonviolently, and now had the backing of all three branches of the federal government. He argued that Carmichael's new slogan threatened to undermine nonviolence and alienate white supporters, who sometimes interpreted "Black Power" to mean "Black violence."

In response, Carmichael just shrugged. In his view, King and Lawson had been courageous but quickly were becoming voices of the past. It was a new day. Carmichael had pushed out John Lewis as chairman of SNCC just a month earlier, and he was setting a new course for the organization. "The system had learned how to contain nonviolent demonstrations," he said. "Having learned how to contain them, it was not necessary for them to respond to them. Thus, King was not failing as much as the white establishment was no longer responding to him. . . . Alternative methods were therefore necessary." Others noted that Carmichael didn't specify what those new methods were, or what progress had been achieved through their use.

"Stokely Carmichael's cry for Black Power in '66 was a cry of frustration," Lawson said later. "It did not have planning behind it, and in some ways I feel Stokely—whom I loved, whom I liked a good bit personally in 1960 when I first met him—betrayed the movement."

The question of the use of force and the advocacy of Black Power was complex. Charles Sims, the head of the Deacons for Defense, an organization of armed Black vigilantes based in Bogalusa, Louisiana, a rough lumber-mill town on the Mississippi border, was also present for the Meredith march, providing security. Yet he opposed the slogan, saying that it "didn't do a damn thing but hurt the Movement." He added, "I don't wanna live under Black Power. I don't wanna live under white power. I want equal power."

Perhaps supporting that position, Andrew Young offered a provocative regionalist interpretation of the coming of Black Power: it wasn't so much moderates versus radicals, he argued, as it was northern versus southern. "The Black Power movement was more an attempt to take SNCC from the Southerners" than it was a challenge to King's approach, he wrote. "There's a complete difference in the way we were brought up in the South and they were brought up in the North."

James Bevel's son Enoch agreed: "My father was a southern boy. He knew the South. But the North was a lot different."

Unseen in all this infighting was James Meredith himself, who had left his Memphis hospital bed, fainted while trying to give a statement to the press, and then flew home to New York City, wary of being associated with the march he had started. He returned later to take a look at the march after the Mississippi State Police attacked and teargassed one of the marchers' encampments in Canton, Mississippi. He joined the march's final day, when fifteen thousand people walked into the state capital, Jackson. It was the largest civil rights gathering in the state's history.

King goes antiwar

King had one more major departure to make. "Over the last few months I've gone through a lot of soul-searching and agonizing moments," he told an interviewer in March 1967. Among his conclusions was, "Some of the old optimism was a little superficial and now it must be tempered with a solid realism." There were difficult days ahead, he warned. And, he said in the same interview, he was increasingly appalled by the Vietnam War. Critics responded that he was out of his area in doing so, a view he utterly rejected.

So, on April 4, 1967, King mounted the pulpit at Riverside Church in New York City to deliver a sustained, clear blast against the war. We need to admit, he said, "that we have been wrong from the beginning of our adventure in Vietnam, that we have been detrimental to the life of the Vietnamese people." Most notably, he called the American government "the greatest purveyor of violence in the world today." He concluded by reaching back to his first great speech, at the start of the Montgomery boycott twelve years earlier: "If we will but make the right choice, we will be able to speed up the day, all over America and all over the world, when justice will roll down like waters, and righteousness like a mighty stream."

His old friend James Lawson would call this address "his most important and creative speech from the point of view of spiritual understanding. It is his most prophetic speech." But, as Lawson noted, "The reaction in the press and the reaction in Washington was intense hostility." That summer King and Lawson were at a retreat at the Penn Center, in South Carolina. King asked Lawson to walk with him to discuss the pressures he was feeling. "He told me the death threats at home and in the office multiplied," Lawson recalled.

King also was beginning to doubt the entire American system. "The movement must address itself to the question of restructuring the whole of American society," he stated in 1967. "It means ultimately coming to see that the problem of racism, the problem of economic exploitation, and the problem of war are all tied together. These are triple evils that are interrelated." It was an ambitious critique, tied together by his belief that in each case, the answer was nonviolence: "We must come to see that peace is not merely a distant goal we seek, but that it is a means by which we arrive at that goal."

This was a strategic insight. As he put it in a sermon later that year, "We must pursue peaceful ends through peaceful means." He was pointing toward an alternate path that the country did not take in the following decades but that has remained alluring to many Americans— living in a way that does less violence to other people, and also to the Earth itself.

It was a hard time across the Movement. SNCC had ousted Lewis and edged away from nonviolence. Finally, in May 1967, the organization's leadership segregated itself, deciding that "the whites should be put off staff and work with us on a strictly volunteer or contractual basis." The stout-hearted Fannie Lou Hamer resigned in protest of that action. Some of the more callous staff members had dismissed her as a rube. An organization that had started as a dynamic but peaceful force for integration was now a declining entity that seemed to endorse violence and was officially segregated by race. At the same time, Carmichael was replaced as SNCC's leader by H. Rap Brown, who announced that "SNCC is moving from rhetoric to program"—which was the opposite of what really had happened within the organization over the previous few years.

The Black Panthers adopt a military pose

SNCC's leaders talked about merging with the nascent Black Panther Party, which had been formed in late 1966 by Huey P. Newton and

Bobby Seale in Oakland, California. But the combination didn't work out, mainly because the Panthers' leaders found SNCC too factionalized. "There was Rap Brown running on one end with James Forman directing things and Stokely on the other end, directing his own thing," recalled Seale. SNCC soon dwindled into oblivion.

The case of the Black Panthers is worth pausing to consider, especially in the context of this book. They had a military air, wearing a uniform of black leather jackets, blue shirts, and black berets. They carried shotguns and rifles as an innovative form of promoting their party. "We have the guns," Newton, the party's "minister of defense," explained, "because we're instituting a new organization, a revolutionary organization." In 1970, Newton became "supreme commander" of the party. They appointed three field marshals. They stated that their goal was "the total destruction of the racist decadent imperialist American society."

At the grassroots level, the Panthers launched some ambitious programs to feed breakfast to children and provide some health care. More controversially, and with a good deal of courage, they also shadowed police patrols in some cities, carrying firearms and law books as they did. They sometimes engaged in shouting matches on sidewalks with police officers who were stunned to find constitutional arguments being hurled at them angrily by Black men jacking shells into their shotguns. They were, to use a twenty-first-century term, performatively militaristic.

It was nervy actions like the monitoring of police, plus the revolutionary rhetoric, that captured media attention and then public interest. "I started seeing these images of Panthers on TV and in the newspaper just about every day," recalled Charlotte O'Neal. "Seeing the brothers in their black leather and their shades and their berets, they looked really good. Then, when I started hearing about the community service programs, that just about clinched it for me." She joined the party's Kansas City chapter.

In May 1967, thirty members of the Panthers, many of them carrying shotguns and pistols, strode into the California capitol in Sacramento to protest pending legislation that had been aimed at them—a law against carrying loaded weapons in public. It is indicative of the Black Panthers' bold but reckless approach that they did not conduct any preliminary reconnaissance of the California capitol before executing their mission there—something that CORE, SNCC, and the SCLC certainly would have done. Instead, Bobby Seale, leading the group that day, parked and asked bystanders for directions to the assembly's chambers. California governor Ronald Reagan soon signed into law the measure to curtail the carrying of loaded weapons in public.

In fact, despite their militaristic appearance, the Panthers never developed the institutional practices and strengths that actually make military organizations effective, such as training, doctrine, unit discipline, logistics, and strategic planning. Carolyn Foster, a Panther in New York, lamented in her diary, "The cadre doesn't relate to door-to-door section work." Indeed, as this book tries to show, the major nonviolent civil rights organizations that engaged in direct action—the SCLC, SNCC, and CORE—were in their operations very much like military forces, and certainly more so than the Panthers.

Part of the problem for the Panthers was that they grew so quickly that it was hard for anyone to actually oversee the organization or to vet recruits. After the Sacramento episode, Huey Newton wrote, "We had more members than we could handle. From all across the country calls came to us about establishing chapters and branches; we could hardly keep track of the requests. In a matter of months we went from a small Bay Area group to a national organization." In retrospect, he said, "The party grew much too rapidly, because many of the young people were . . . very enthusiastic about the guns and about the berets but they knew little about the community programs that really are our reason for existing."

It may be wrong to primarily assess the Panthers as a political organization, looking at training, planning, and effectiveness. The historians Judson Jeffries and Ryan Nissim-Sabat write, "The BPP [Black Panther Party] was not merely an organization; it was a cultural happening." To take that formulation another step, the party was more a cultural phenomenon than it was an organized party. So it probably should be understood in more organic terms—in terms of how it grew, multiplied, mutated, and divided.

Killing the Panthers—and imitating them

At any rate, the American security establishment responded to the Panthers viscerally. In September 1968, the FBI director J. Edgar Hoover declared that the Panthers were "the greatest threat to the internal security of the country."

The Panthers were an ideal adversary for the FBI—fragile, overwhelmed, and sufficiently frightening to many white people that not a lot of questions were asked at the time by politicians about how law enforcement agencies dealt with them. Civil rights groups—from the Montgomery bus boycotters to the Freedom Riders to the Selma marchers—tended to be stronger and more resilient than they looked. Even the schoolchildren marchers of Birmingham were backed up by training, organization, planning, and reconnaissance. By contrast, the Panthers were less capable of handling challenges than their fierce appearance suggested. They were particularly lax about counterintelligence, notes Ahmad Rahman, a former Panther who went on to become a professor of history at the University of Michigan-Dearborn.

Most of all, their primary recruiting tool could be turned against them. When Huey Newton called the firearm the basic tool of liberation, praising "the power of the gun," he was using the language of force and violence, a tongue the FBI and many local police departments spoke well. From late 1968 on, the FBI worked with police forces to destroy the struggling organization. A congressional investigation found that the FBI used "lawless tactics" and in fact sought to foment violence. For example, one of the agency's field offices reported, as a positive, that its work had resulted in "shootings, beatings, and a high degree of unrest in the area of southeast San Diego."

Of 295 actions launched by the FBI against Black political organizations under its anti-leftist Counter Intelligence Program (COINTEL-PRO), some 233 targeted the Panthers. Most memorably, before dawn on December 4, 1969, the Chicago police raided the apartment of Fred Hampton, head of the Panthers in Illinois, and shot him dead as he lay in bed. Chicago authorities claimed at the time that the police were returning fire from the Panthers, but a subsequent federal grand jury investigation concluded that the police had fired eighty-two times while the Panthers had only shot once. In Chicago, as in Detroit and Los Angeles, the Panthers' local chief of security was actually an FBI informant. In New York, three members of the chapter's security force also were cooperating with the FBI. Between 1968 and 1971, American law enforcement officials reportedly killed forty members of the party, while scores more were jailed. It is likely that the true scope and reach of the FBI-led assassination campaign against the Panthers has not been fully revealed even now.

In certain respects, American law enforcement officials seemed to be taken with the Panthers' performative aspect. Partly in response to the party's public posture, police departments began fielding specially uniformed SWAT teams—often wearing all-black garb, helmets, body armor, and kneepads—which made them appear far more militarized than regular police. One respected police department told academic researchers that a key aspect of its use of tactical teams was "the ostentatious display of weaponry"—a page taken, of course, from the Panther playbook. Los Angeles often led the way in fielding these new paramilitary units. Indeed, the first major use of that city's newly created SWAT team was against the local branch of the Panthers, in December 1969, just two days after the murder of Fred Hampton in Chicago.

King on the verge

Martin Luther King, Jr., was flagging. Septima Clark, old and wise, sent him a note in June 1967 warning him to take better care of his health.

"May God help you to help yourself," she wrote. But relief was not on the way. Coretta Scott King remembered that during this time, King was physically drained and deeply depressed. He would tell her, "I don't feel like speaking to people. I don't have anything to tell them."

A few months later, in September 1967, at an SCLC staff retreat at Airlie House, a conference center in northern Virginia, King sat through a long, paralyzing staff debate about whether to continue focusing on civil rights, to work for economic change, or to switch and work on opposing the Vietnam War. At the end of that hard day, he retreated alone into his room with a bottle of whiskey, fatigued and frustrated. He was heard to shout out, with no one else present, "I don't want to do this anymore. I want to go back to my little church." Young and Abernathy went to him, took away his whiskey, and put him to bed.

At a similar meeting that December, FBI surveillance reported, "King was visibly angry at Bevel" for mocking the notion of working to address American poverty rather than throwing everything into opposing the war.

We can only wonder what might have happened if King, who had given so much and labored for so long, had somehow been able to follow up on his impulse to go back to his church. Instead, many months later, he went to Memphis.

13.
MEMPHIS, 1968
The Costs of It All

If you miss me from the Movement
And you can't find me nowhere,
Come on over to the graveyard
And I'll be buried there.

—MOVEMENT-ADAPTED SPIRITUAL

On March 18, 1968, Martin Luther King, Jr., was in Memphis to lend support to a strike by the city's Black garbagemen. James Lawson, who had done so much to instruct the civil rights movement in effective nonviolence, was now ministering in Memphis, and he had reached out to King for help in rallying support for the strikers, who wanted equal treatment with white coworkers and recognition of their nascent union.

King ended his speech that day not with his customary rhetorical flight, but with a very specific proposal that the Blacks of Memphis launch a general strike. "You know what? You may want to escalate the struggle a little bit," he told his audience of Memphians. "You let that day come, and not a Negro in this city will go to any job downtown."

King's proposal was novel and innovative, combining his concerns about racial equality with those about economic justice but remaining within the context of nonviolent action. As the labor historian Michael K. Honey notes, until this point, no one in the civil rights movement had proposed a general strike by Blacks. Such massive actions were exceedingly rare in the twentieth century in the United States, Honey adds, coming only at points of extraordinary tension—Seattle in 1919, San Francisco and Minneapolis in 1934, Oakland in 1946. But the tactic was one that Gandhi had favored in India as he pushed for independence from Britain. He called it a *hartal*, using the Gujarati phrase for closing down shops.

King had been pondering the issue of poverty in America. "One of the things he said to me at the time was that 'you are doing in Memphis what I want to do,'" Lawson recalled. "Mainly, tie up this question of economic justice with racism. I think this is where a lot of people miss the whole meaning of his last days."

So, perhaps, in Memphis—and back in the familiar South—King began to see a way forward after hitting a dead end up north in Chicago. More than many people outside the region realize, Memphis is the capital of the Deep South, dominating the space between Dallas and Atlanta, and serving as the business and cultural center for much of Arkansas, the northern parts of Louisiana and Mississippi, the western chunk of Tennessee, and even a portion of Alabama. The city has had an outsized impact on American music, producing an array of greats from W. C. Handy and Jimmie Lunceford to Elvis Presley, Johnny Cash, Charlie Rich, Jerry Lee Lewis, and Al Green.

Yet there was a countervailing problem, one that King did not see. One of the most dangerous things in warfare is assumptions. Assuming that the enemy is not present in an area can get you killed. Guessing that the road has not been mined will do the same. This is the reason that combat leaders at all levels constantly probe and double-check: Did we send out a patrol? Is that machine gun nest still there? On a larger scale, before World War II, everyone assumed that bombers were unstoppable. That belief was incorrect. Likewise, American officials assumed before the 2003 invasion of Iraq that the people there overwhelmingly would welcome the American presence.

On March 28, King returned to Memphis for what was supposed to be a quick visit. Andrew Young recalled that King said, "Jim Lawson has been around for so long, and here are garbage workers on strike. He just wants me to come in and make a speech and lead a march in the morning. And I'll be right back."

King was preoccupied with planning a "Poor People's March" on Washington for that spring, in order to highlight the persistence of hunger and poverty in America, just as the civil rights movement had spotlighted racism. He called for full employment and a guaranteed income plan, also known as a "negative income tax." But despite his intensifying focus on economic justice, he felt obliged to come to the aid of Lawson, who had done so much for the Movement.

King was exhausted and depressed, however—a dangerous way to go into a campaign. He and those around him may have been task-saturated, too busy to think and too tired to stop and examine the situation they were entering. Going into Memphis, King's party assumed that any march led by Lawson, the old master of nonviolent direct action, would sport all the hallmarks of a Movement operation. That is, those participating would have been prepared with instruction in nonviolence, told they must maintain self-discipline, and reminded while marching to act in a dignified and restrained manner. They might even have engaged in some role-playing and then signed pledge cards, as the marchers in Birmingham had done. To ensure that the parade went smoothly, trained marshals would walk along each section, setting the pace and keeping an eye on possible troublemakers.

A King march turns violent

But none of that happened, and so the march of about five thousand participants went badly wrong, veering off into dangerous territory.

The crowd was rowdy and tired of waiting for King, who as usual was tardy. Even before he arrived, two liquor stores had been looted. When he got to the march in a white Lincoln Continental borrowed from a funeral home, the crowd pressed against it so much that it took at least ten minutes before he could get out of the car. When he finally emerged, he said, "The people were trampling over my feet . . . crowding around me." Years of marching had attuned his senses to gauging a crowd, and he didn't like what he was sensing that day. "The atmosphere was just wrong," he said.

These were worrisome signs that this march had not been organized with the care and discipline traditional in SCLC campaigns. "It was just a mass of people," said Bernard Lee, King's personal assistant. "I don't think the leadership in the march was ever in control."

The march finally started. King and his entourage were walking alongside Lawson on Beale Street in downtown Memphis when they heard glass shattering behind them. Some marchers were breaking store windows. They may have been paid provocateurs—if so, that was something that parade marshals were supposed to spot and stop. Looters then began entering the stores.

Unfortunately, the ministers who were supposed to be regulating the parade instead had clustered up front, near King, Abernathy, and Lawson. "Those assigned to marshal the participants were not trained in leading such a demonstration," recalled a rueful Andrew Young. "I assumed that Lawson was as well organized in Memphis as he had been in Nashville. That assumption proved inaccurate." The rear of the march, he added, was left "completely unsupervised."

Accounts differ on just what happened next. According to Ralph Abernathy, King turned to Lawson and said, "Jim, call off this march right now. Call it off right now!" Abernathy's recollections are not always reliable, but in this case, they are supported by King himself, who said in a press conference the next day, "I told Reverend Lawson, who had the bullhorn, to call it off and turn the people back, and he did."

However, Lawson himself recalled that he alone made the decision to stop the march. "I consulted nobody," he stated. Indeed, he added that King and Abernathy initially balked at his order, but then agreed, and then began walking down McCall Street toward Front Street, where they flagged down a pickup truck whose driver gave them a ride to the Holiday Inn–Rivermont.

Behind them, the parade degenerated into 280 arrests, 60 injuries, and 1 death by police gunfire. Looters ransacked stores along Main and Beale streets: Hardy's Shoes, York Arms, Federal Clothiers, Main Liquor, Adams Hats, Uncle Sam's Pawn Shop, Paul's Tailoring, American Loan Company pawnshop, Pape's Men's Store, Quality Liquors. By the account of Honey, which is credible, the rank and file of the Memphis police responded to the initial violence with a full-scale law enforcement riot, sending flying wedges into groups of marchers, clubbing people indiscriminately, and firing tear gas canisters. Police operating under the gaze of their commanders generally were restrained, but smaller detachments farther away from such supervision whirled through the streets in a frenzy, attacking Blacks in parking lots, outside churches, and even huddled in offices. Black teenagers responded by throwing rocks and bottles.

Postmortem

At the Holiday Inn–Rivermont, King began to sort through the implications of the day's events. It was one thing to be a figurehead if a protest followed King's philosophy of nonviolence. It was another thing to be there if what he stood for was being violated. It was the first time that King had seen violence by Blacks participating in a march he was leading. He had stated at the March on Washington in his most famous speech, "We must not allow our creative protest to degenerate into physical violence." Yet precisely that had just happened.

It was his last march.

In his somber post-march analysis, Lawson essentially said that he had underestimated the pull on the public that King had developed by 1968, which meant that the day's event was much bigger than previous ones in Memphis had been. There were parade marshals available, but so many people had come that the streets and the sidewalks were full, making it difficult for the marshals to move up and down the sides of the march. "Not having had that big of a march, we did not work hard enough on disciplining and training our marshals," he noted years later. Because the previous marches had been smaller and peaceful, "Their experience was limited." In addition, he said, it was a mistake to have signs on sticks, because people began using the sticks offensively.

King's staff was irate over the events of the day, and was looking at Lawson with pained disappointment. "We should have had some intelligence work done before we came here," Bernard Lee said during a postmortem. "We walked right into this thing." Lawson wanted to hold another march the next day to reassert the principle of nonviolence, but King's team had lost much confidence in him.

The deterioration of the march enormously complicated King's plans. He had been assuring all concerned that the Poor People's March would be nonviolent, that he had over a decade of experience in organizing such endeavors. But now, he told Lawson at the Rivermont, he had been at the head of a smaller and simpler demonstration that had gone off the tracks. "One of the things he said there was that he could see a lot of critics now saying we can't have any more nonviolent marches and that we couldn't come to Washington," Lawson recalled. There would need to be another Memphis march, but it would be held on King's terms. He told Lawson that he needed to lead and stage a peaceful march in the city "because if we didn't have one then he would find it almost impossible to have one in Washington."

Sitting in Suite 801, King stayed awake until dawn, stewing over the situation and making telephone calls. The FBI listened in as King talked to a confidant about what the critics would say—"Martin Luther King is dead. He's finished. His nonviolence is nothing, no one is listening to him."

King said at a press conference that the march had been poorly planned, lacked adequate numbers of trained marshals, and suffered from faulty communications with some youth groups. "Our demon-

strations have been planned in a totally different atmosphere altogether," he said. Lawson then held his own press conference to refute
that assertion. The Movement, once so skilled at dividing its enemies,
now itself was in disarray, with internal differences being aired publicly.

King was correct about how the chaos of the day had changed his
situation. Rather than simply visiting Memphis for a day, he had become enmeshed in the sanitation workers' strike. There were echoes of
the problems of the Albany Movement here, but now the consequences
were catastrophic. On the day after the march, he and Abernathy flew
back to Atlanta and had dinner together, along with their wives. "He
was more depressed that night, I believe, than I'd ever seen him," recalled Juanita Abernathy.

The NAACP rarely missed a chance to snipe at King, and he had
presented a large target. Alfred Lewis, the organization's treasurer, said
at a rally in Virginia, "The Reverend Martin Luther King, Junior, must
bear the blame for racial rioting in Memphis, Tennessee, because he
exerts no discipline over his followers."

"Take My Hand, Precious Lord"

On April 3, King returned to Memphis for the promised second march.
Of course, it never happened.

Soon after arriving in the city, he delivered a speech that was at once
meditative and soaring. "I'm just happy that God has allowed me to
live in this period to see what is unfolding," he said. He summed up
the Movement's philosophy: "We aren't engaged in any negative protest
and in any negative arguments with anybody. We are saying that we
are determined to be men. We are determined to be people." He also
reminded his listeners that the Movement's tactics had led to success,
again and again: "We are masters in our nonviolent movement in dis-
arming police forces; they don't know what to do."

He concluded, perhaps from a premonition, "I've been to the mountaintop. . . . Like anybody, I would like to live a long life—longevity

has its place. But I'm not concerned about that now. I just want to do God's will. And He's allowed me to go up to the mountain. And I've looked over, and I've seen the Promised Land. I may not get there with you. But I want you to know tonight, that we, as a people, will get to the Promised Land."

The next afternoon, at 6:00 p.m., King was standing on a balcony of the Lorraine Motel, outside Room 306, getting ready to go out to dinner with a group of his friends and assistants. He saw a musician who was going to appear at the dinner and requested that he include his favorite song in the set—Thomas Dorsey's "Take My Hand, Precious Lord." A moment later, at 6:01, a sniper's bullet from a Remington Gamemaster hunting rifle hit King at the base of his face. The power of firearms is astonishing to those who do not spend time around them. The metal-jacketed .30-06 bullet traveling at about 1,800 miles per hour blasted off much of his chinbone, passed through his neck, and severed his spine. Part of his face later was found adhered to the ceiling of the balcony.

Ralph Abernathy, his old colleague from the Montgomery days, knelt by King's side. "I was the first person to get to him and I comforted him and cuddled him in my arms and said to him, 'Martin, don't worry, it will be all right, it will be all right.' And his eyes were staring and turning in he could not utter a word, but he was upset, but finally he heard me. I'm convinced he heard me and he knew that it would be all right."

James Bevel had been standing on the pavement below the balcony. He instinctively prepared for great pain, on the instantaneous assumption that whoever was shooting would try to hit the people around King. When that didn't happen, he ran up the stairs to the balcony, where he found King on the floor, suddenly without a chin. "I could see right down into his mouth and neck," Bevel recalled.

Within hours, rioting broke out in dozens of cities across the country. A total of fifty-five thousand Army and National Guard troops would be deployed. When it was all over, some forty-six people had been killed and thousands more injured.

The remains of the Poor People's Campaign

Pursuing a strategy of aggressive nonviolence, brilliantly and persistently, King had compelled the nation to look at the realities of segregation. He had hoped to expose poverty in the same way, to make Americans look at it straight on. But he would not be there to do that. Ralph Abernathy was chosen to succeed him as head of the SCLC. This was understandable, but it was a mistake for the organization. Abernathy had played the role of King's buddy wonderfully, but he was not the person to fill King's shoes. It probably would have been impossible for anyone to do that—King was a unique figure.

Andrew Young's memories of the Poor People's Campaign, which culminated with building a plywood encampment called Resurrection City in the center of Washington, D.C., were of squabbling among demoralized staffers disappointed with Abernathy. "James Bevel and Jesse Jackson wasted time and energy expressing their dissatisfaction with Ralph's leadership," Young wrote.

In retrospect, they were all in emotional shock, with King's assassination coming on top of years of severe stress. "I was in a daze, functioning on autopilot," Young wrote. He had a telling insight: "I remember thinking that there was no way I was going to jail with this crew. . . . I had no desire to spend time in jail with people bickering and fighting with one another. I had never felt so despondent." At one point, Young jumped over a conference table to attack Hosea Williams, whom he considered a loudmouthed bully. If cohesion and trust are lost, carrying out an existing campaign becomes difficult. Executing a new campaign to focus America on poverty was just about impossible. Then Robert Kennedy was murdered in June 1968, after greatly redeeming himself in the eyes of Black leaders. After that, Young continues, "I sank into a depression so deep it was impossible for me to go on." A few weeks later, Washington, D.C., police tore down the sadly named Resurrection City.

It was at almost the same time that A. Philip Randolph gave a speech that almost amounted to a eulogy for the Movement, which he saw being pulled apart by centrifugal forces: "The Civil Rights Revolution is a bourgeois democratic revolution which is definitely limited in the range, power and area of action. History has not designed the Civil Rights Revolution to solve the problems of jobs, housing and education. These are social problems that can only be solved by a social revolution." Randolph was warning that the Movement had reached its natural limits.

Combat stress and the civil rights movement

Specialists in combat stress have concluded that there are limits to how much time anyone can spend in fighting. As noted earlier, the expert consensus is that most sane people are psychologically exhausted after about two hundred days of living on the front lines. The leaders of the Movement in fact had spent years with fears of being bombed, shot, beaten, arrested and mistreated in jail. The sad fact is that waging a campaign like theirs carries a high physical and mental toll. "A year in the Movement was about five years of normal life," Bob Moses once commented. Lawrence Guyot, a Black Mississippian who had led the work in Hattiesburg during Freedom Summer, had found his left side temporarily paralyzed one evening that summer. In 1968, he stopped working in Mississippi because of his health—he was suffering from high blood pressure and heart trouble. He was then twenty-nine years old. "I've always felt that many people who participated in the movement became wounded," commented Thomas Armstrong, a 1961 Freedom Rider.

Years of extravagant stress and wracking uncertainty combined with moments of pain and terror amounts to a recipe for post-traumatic stress disorder (PTSD). That is perhaps the best way to understand both King's chronic depression and some of the sexual adventurism and abuse of alcohol attributed to him. Jonathan Shay writes in *Odysseus in America*, a study of the psychic weight that combat veterans carry when they return home, that while some troubled former soldiers fall into using drugs and alcohol, others become sex addicts, looking for release and relief in constant erotic encounters, especially intense and varied ones. He cites a veterans' counselor who reported that "for some vets, orgasm functions as a form of 'shock treatment' for their depression." Shay also notes that Odysseus, that great archetype of the soldier who has a hard time getting home, spent eight of the ten years of his long homeward voyage wallowing in sex, first with Circe and then with Calypso.

The theory of PTSD developed as a diagnosis of soldiers' dislocating experiences in the Vietnam War, so it is itself a kind of child of the 1960s. Indeed, the clinical understanding of PTSD grew out of "rap group" meetings of veterans that, David Morris notes, were themselves inspired by group talk sessions developed by the modern women's liberation movement, which in turn was partially a result of the civil rights movement.

Deepening its connection to the sixties, the symptoms of PTSD also can be found in many veterans of the Movement. "I think the people who believed change was possible, but expected it to happen the next day, burnt out first," observed Ivanhoe Donaldson, a veteran of Freedom Summer and later director of SNCC's New York office. "They just got frustrated. They freaked out. Some people freaked out from the violence. Some people were battle weary, you know, battle fatigue. They went into shock." Some were afflicted by what we now call post-traumatic stress effects. "Once you've had a bad experience physically, where you've been mauled or beaten or brutalized or hit with a bullet or had some broken bones," Donaldson explained, "that fear is always in you." He described seeing old comrades drifting through their post-movement lives: "You're just out there. Maybe you become a cab driver in San Diego, an all-white community, or you become an airplane mechanic." Donaldson himself ran into another sort of trouble. He managed the rise of Marion Barry, another SNCC vet, in the political world of Washington, D.C., in the 1970s. Then, in 1985, Donaldson pleaded guilty to embezzling $190,000 in city funds and was sentenced to seven years in prison.

In the mid-1970s, Dave Dennis, who had been one of the leaders of Freedom Summer, was checking out a book at the University of Michigan's law library when he recognized the desk clerk. He realized she was a former Freedom Summer volunteer who had been tortured by policemen in Natchez—they had held a pistol to her head and played Russian roulette. He later learned that the library job was part of a work-release therapy program at the insane asylum where she resided.

"I just thank the Lord I'm still in my right mind," said Hezekiah Watkins, who participated in the 1961 Freedom Rides while he was still in high school. "That's not true for so many people who were in the movement."

There is a sadness in many Movement vets, even those who recovered or came through relatively unscathed. Their words reflect the costs of their campaigning, and also how much more there is to do. They carry grief in their hearts—for their fallen comrades, for their half-realized goals, for their own pains and sacrifices, and for their country. The patriotic clichés that grew up around Vietnam veterans—that "all gave some but some gave all," or that they only wanted their country to love them as much as they loved it, as the character Rambo put it in a bitter 1985 film—also apply to these less visible frontline troops of the civil rights era. Indeed, James Baldwin said it twenty years before Rambo, stating in 1965, "It comes as a great shock around the age of five or six or seven to discover the flag to which you have pledged allegiance, along with everybody else, has not pledged allegiance to you." Unfortunately, veterans of the civil rights movement are not entitled to the care of VA hospitals.

Even at the time, there were people who had to leave the Movement because of the psychological pressure. Septima Clark, one of its secular saints, who had trained people in literacy and nonviolence for decades, acknowledged that it could be overwhelming for some. "They just couldn't take the movement," she said. "It was just too much for them."

Others stayed but paid psychic costs. "I don't think they were really aware of it," said Constance Curry, a SNCC member in the early 1960s. "And as it emerged I think it was a terrible, terrible toll. I mean, look at what it did to Bob Moses. It just made him into a—it broke his heart."

The odyssey of Bob Moses

Bob Moses eventually emerged from his crash. Through some combination of luck, determination, and reflection, he managed to have rich and productive second and third acts in his life.

Like many others in the mid-1960s, Moses became interested in opposing the Vietnam War. And like many of those activists, he soon found himself facing a draft notice. He fled to Canada, where he assumed a false identity and spent two years working odd jobs. He was a night watchman, he sold newspaper subscriptions, he filled food trays for airlines. In 1968 he and a new wife traveled to Africa without much money and found themselves stuck in Cairo for nine months, lacking the necessary papers to travel on. Finally, they landed teaching jobs in Tanzania, where they remained for six years. In rural Tanzania, Moses built a new life. He focused on teaching mathematics but especially on raising his daughters. "I've always felt that was a blessing," he told the journalist John Blake, who traveled around the country visiting children of movement leaders and martyrs, and also interviewing some of their parents. "Tanzania turned out to be a good choice to recuperate and also to pay attention to family and to get ready, as it turns out, to re-enter."

Thus prepared, Moses and his family returned to the United States in 1976. He did not set foot in Mississippi again until he traveled there in 1982 for the funeral of Amzie Moore, the grizzled World War II vet who had become his mentor back in 1960. In a sense, Moses' adulthood, or at least his mission in life, had begun when he met Moore in Mississippi.

Moses, after years of uncertainty and recovery, rediscovered his mission. He became interested in using the old Freedom School methods to teach mathematics. A decade later, Moses started The Algebra Project, an effort to prepare poor Black students for college-level math classes and generally to stress quality in education. In 1991, this brought him back again to Mississippi, where he reconnected with Dave Dennis, his old deputy from the Freedom Summer. The two began working on their new project in Indianola. Moses, whose psychological journey may have been one of the longest anyone in the Movement experienced, seemed to come out the other side surprisingly healthy. At the age of sixty-nine, he had the love of his daughters and also swam more than a mile a day. "He exudes tranquility," wrote Blake, the newspaper reporter. Moses died in July 2021, at the age of eighty-six, as this book was being written.

Similarly, after splitting with James Bevel, Diane Nash went on to a quiet and normal life in Chicago, raising their two children on her own. She knocked around a variety of jobs, working briefly for the Nation of Islam newspaper *Muhammad Speaks*, for Western Union, and for some community service organizations. She eventually became a real estate investigator, tracking down legal documents that might affect transactions. Then, in her middle age, she was pleased to find herself receiving requests to speak about her role in the Movement. "There is a satisfaction," she stated. "It's a satisfaction that has to do with the fact that—this isn't modest, but—with the fact that my living has made a difference on this planet. And I love that. I really do."

Some of the oddest second and then third acts in life happened to Hank Thomas, who had been one of the first group of Freedom Riders, and who was clubbed in the head with a baseball bat after stumbling out of the burning Greyhound bus in Anniston, Alabama. He was drafted into the Army, was trained as a medic, and in November 1965 found himself dealing with mass casualties at the battle of Ia Drang, the Army's first major battle in the Vietnam War against the North Vietnamese army—later the subject of the movie starring Mel Gibson titled *We Were Soldiers*. Thomas later was shot in the hand. After leaving the Army, he moved to Atlanta and opened a laundromat. Entrepreneurial and successful, he became wealthy, acquiring a Dairy Queen outlet and, eventually, six McDonald's franchises and eight hotels.

Dying young

In reviewing the post-Movement lives of its participants, one fact that stands out is how many of them died relatively young. In the context of exposure to combat, however, these early demises become more understandable: the civil rights movement was a small-scale, regional civil war. The harsh fact is that people who have been in combat tend to lead shorter lives than those who have never experienced war firsthand. A study of a group of World War II veterans found that of those who had been exposed to heavy combat, 56 percent were dead or chronically ill by the age of sixty-five.

And so it was with the Movement. Ralph Abernathy, for example, died in 1990 at the age of sixty-four. Bernard Lee, King's personal assistant and traveling companion, died of heart failure a year later at the age of fifty-five.

A potential replacement for Abernathy at the SCLC had been the Reverend Jesse Jackson. Septima Clark recalled that in the 1960s she had considered Jackson "a worthwhile fellow" with promise. But in 1971, she added, she was in Chicago and saw him at a meeting wrapping himself in "great glory." At that moment she thought to herself, "Well now, here's a guy who's turned. He's becoming a god, also." In that same year, Jackson, having feuded with Ralph Abernathy and been suspended by the SCLC over his handling of finances, left the organization and founded his own, People United to Save Humanity (PUSH). His landmark presidential campaigns and other future efforts would exhibit his signal strengths as well as some surprising lapses.

Stokely Carmichael left the United States behind. In 1969, he publicly resigned from the Black Panthers, calling its actions "dishonest and vicious," and about this time also moved abroad, though he would occasionally return on speaking tours. Like Moses, he chose a new identity—in his case, taking the name Kwame Ture, which he kept permanently. He died of prostate cancer in Guinea in 1998, just fifty-seven years old.

Sometimes the deaths were violent. Allard Lowenstein, who helped conceive the Freedom Summer campaign and recruit for it, was elected to Congress, where he served a single term. He was shot and killed in 1980 by Dennis Sweeney, a former volunteer in Mississippi who had been bombed there back in 1964. Sweeney, who had been briefly married to fellow SNCC activist Mary King in the 1960s, wobbled into a world of schizophrenic hallucinations during the following decade, filing down his teeth in the belief that the CIA was controlling him through them.

Cordell Reagon, who had been one of the young SNCC leaders of the Albany Movement, was killed in California in 1996 at the age of fifty-three in an incident that remains unsolved.

Even the irrepressible Fannie Lou Hamer emerged from the Movement era feeling shortchanged, according to her husband. "My wife loved people, but people didn't love her," Pap Hamer reported. For years, she always had a hot meal and a dollar bill for those who knocked on her door, he said. But, he continued, "They wore her down. She raised lots of money and she would come back and give it to people. And when she died, she didn't have a dime." She passed in 1977 at the age of fifty-nine.

Not all went so fast, and many went on to have wonderful lives. C. T. Vivian lived to be ninety-five, and John Lewis to be eighty. As of this writing, Andrew Young and James Lawson are still with us. Interestingly, all four held divinity degrees. David Morris, author of *The Evil Hours*, one of the best studies of post-traumatic stress, comments, "Broadly speaking, religious belief tends to serve as a 'protective factor' against the development of PTS."

It would be wrong to see civil rights activists as victims. Generally, "they came through in fine style," concludes the historian John Dittmer. They fought well and hard, and scores went on to become respected leaders of communities and organizations. One interesting example: Freeman Hrabowski III, who as a child had confronted Bull Connor in Birmingham, grew up to become president of the University of Maryland, Baltimore County, and has been nationally recognized for his dynamic and innovative leadership. Another example is

Pauli Murray, who after helping organize the National Organization for Women in the 1960s went on a decade later to be ordained the first Black woman priest in the Episcopal Church—a fitting move for a person who had been inspired and counseled by Howard Thurman, the Black theologian, in the 1940s. Today a college at Yale is named for her. Murray, who sometimes dressed in men's clothing, also is seen by some as a transgender pioneer.

Bevel's descent

And others fell far from grace. The most shocking post–civil rights life was that of James Bevel. Already mentally fragile at the time of King's death, he was despondent after it, his son Enoch Bevel recalled. "My mom says he was on the verge of suicide," he said.

The Army's study of combat-exhausted soldiers in World War II found that the loss of a comrade or of a trusted leader "may constitute a wound more painful than that of a bullet through the body." John Lewis thought the killing of King pushed Bevel over the edge. Bevel always had been forceful, but now he began to scare people. Bevel, in turn, felt misunderstood. He wrote, "SCLC's Executive Board misdefined my intensity as either violence or as mental illness. They then spent their time worrying about what to do with me rather than working with me."

In mid-1969, Bevel was alone at a house in Atlanta listening to an Aretha Franklin record when Martin Luther King, Jr., appeared to him in a vision. This apparitional King took him on a journey, first to Hell, "where Judas was on trial for Jesus' murder. . . . I had to help get him acquitted." Next they spoke with the baby Jesus, who told them, "Each person must be directed from within." Then King took him to a morgue where King's body lay.

The following summer, at Paschal's Motor Hotel in Atlanta, Bevel had a breakdown, according to accounts by John Lewis and Andrew Young. Bevel angrily denied the accounts the two gave in their books, telling his writing collaborator, Randy Kryn, "That weekend was like all my other meetings. . . . There was nothing unusual about it." In any case, the SCLC let him go.

Bevel drifted rightward and wound up working on the American political fringe with right-wing extremist Lyndon LaRouche. In 1995, he helped Louis Farrakhan stage the Million Man March in Washington, D.C. One of his daughters, Bacardi Jackson, said he frequently compared himself to Zeus and Jesus. It was at about that time that another of Bevel's daughters, Chevara Orrin, went to see her father speak in an Atlanta church. As she sat in the front row, Orrin, whose mother was white, heard Bevel begin preaching that white women were useful only as slaves and sex pets. She was horrified. "I wanted to stand up and shout to him, 'How dare you? Here I am your own daughter, the result of a relationship between you and a white woman.' I was just devastated."

There was, unfortunately, more—much more. The most disturbing aspect of Bevel's thought was that he believed that incest was natural. In a 1971 interview, he argued that "a man who is totally concerned about the intelligent, wholesome development of his daughter" should be allowed to "teach her the rudiments of sex." The interviewer responded that Bevel's view sounded like an advocacy of incest. Bevel replied, "I don't make categories about who and why and when folks should participate in sex." In November 2005, ten of his children, born to several different women, gathered at his home in Selma, Alabama, to confront him. There was a ten-year-old daughter living in the house, and they wanted her to move away from him. He declined, so his children went public with the charges and filed suit. In 2008, Bevel was found guilty of committing incest upon a teenage daughter about fifteen years earlier. He died of cancer before that year was out and was buried in a seventeen-foot canoe in Eutaw, Alabama.

Some of his children clearly inherited his intelligence and drive. His daughter Bacardi made it to Yale Law School. Another child, Enoch, grew up partly in the headquarters of the Blackstone Rangers, a powerful Chicago street gang. (Years earlier, his father had been the SCLC's liaison to the gang.) There he slept on the floor, cocooning himself in a blanket to keep off the rodents. He never learned to read until he was eleven years old, he recalled in a conversation. He eventually ran away and was taken in by an older sister. He later worked as an intern in President Obama's White House, while supporting himself by working as a waiter at Le Pain Quotidien, just off Dupont Circle. He got himself through Georgetown University and then law school at the University of Maryland.

"He was my best friend," Enoch Bevel said of his father. "He was the guy I wanted to be like." But James Bevel also brought his son one of the hardest moments of his life. As an undergraduate at Georgetown, Enoch took a course in the history of America in the 1960s. He had explained to the professor that he wanted to learn more about the civil rights movement because of his father's participation in it. One day a woman came to talk about the Freedom Rides, and noted that she had been told that James Bevel's son was in the room. Enoch Bevel was the only Black person there. Unfortunately, it was just weeks after James Bevel had been arrested for incest. Enoch recalled that students on his left and right googled "James Bevel" and "the screens started popping up with my father in an orange jumpsuit. It was the hardest time, a painful time. There was a lot of trauma."

Children of the Movement

It was not easy being a child of the Movement. That is painfully evident in the lives of the children of Martin Luther King, Jr., and his wife, Coretta. John Blake, the reporter who interviewed children of leaders and martyrs of the Movement, found that some were leading productive lives, while others felt somewhat crippled by the prominence of their fathers and mothers. He wrote with evident sadness about Martin Luther "Little Marty" King III, who was elected president of the SCLC in 1997 but whose tenure was controversial. Little Marty was suspended at one point, and resigned in 2004. His sister Bernice King was elected president of the organization in 2010, but a year later decided against taking the position. The surviving King children fell out, with Bernice and Martin suing Dexter King over money. They eventually reconciled. They also took legal action against Henry Hampton, producer of *Eyes on the Prize*, the essential documentary series on the Movement, for its use of King's image.

Ralph David Abernathy III led a star-crossed life. He was elected to the Georgia state senate but later was convicted of defrauding the state in his expense accounts. He had a scad of other legal troubles, including a swindling charge, before dying of cancer in 2016 the age of fifty-six.

Andrew Young's son, Andrew "Bo" Young III, seems to have set out to be the opposite of his diplomatic, conciliatory father. In his teen years, he recalled, "I went out of my way to make sure I could be as bad a kid as I could be." He racked up multiple arrests on drug, alcohol, and weapons charges. Then, as an adult, he set his eyes on becoming rich. "Bo wants to be a millionaire," his father told a reporter. "Not only do I not understand it, I don't believe in it, and it's somewhat offensive to me." The son's response: "I want to integrate the money."

It is difficult to pursue a normal life after being touched by fire. Jonathan Shay, a veterans' counselor and a psychiatrist specializing in combat trauma, observes that in those life-and-death moments that combat brings, people gaze for a moment upon the divine. But, he adds, humans are not meant to do so, which is why the ancients often draped a face veil on their statues of gods. Ministers like to sermonize that meeting God is neither safe nor easy. One glimpse of the divine can shock both body and soul. It is too much for the human system to take—yet that jolt can also be addictive. And when the thrill is gone, regular daily life can feel very mundane indeed, and even close relatives are somehow kept at arm's length. James Zwerg, who was badly beaten in Montgomery, Alabama, during the first Freedom Rides in 1961, found that the emotional damage ran deeper than the physical. "One of the things that I have discovered since, after having had a chance to really talk with several of the others, is that almost all of us had some form of real emotional problems with family or personally, in one way or another," he said.

The story of the Black American struggle for freedom isn't over, but we can stop to rest in many places. One of them is near where it began, with Martin Luther King, Jr., and James Lawson, two men who, like Gandhi, held fast to nonviolence all their lives. Lawson loved King, yet he forgave James Earl Ray, the man convicted of shooting him. This was in part because he believed Ray was simply a pawn in a larger game, and likely had not carried out the killing by himself. He visited Ray in prison. When Ray decided to marry a woman who had been communicating with him, Lawson agreed to perform the ceremony.

EPILOGUE

The Good War Today

This book covers only one phase in a very long struggle for civil rights, albeit a crucial one. As the Movement veteran Charles E. Cobb, Jr., who is credited with conceiving the Freedom Schools, claims, "We live better because of it. Not perfectly, but better."

The transformations brought about by the Movement have hardly gone uncontested. Since the 1960s, there have been three substantial backlashes against equality for Black Americans. The first, which came late in that decade, was embodied by George Wallace. The second came under the presidency of Ronald Reagan, who kicked off his 1980 campaign at a fairground just outside Philadelphia, Mississippi, with a speech in which he emphasized, "I believe in states' rights." A third wave, less restrained and uglier, emerged in recent years under Donald Trump.

America's demographics and values are changing, with more Blacks, Hispanics, Asians, and women holding positions of power, and greater acceptance of openly gay and transgender people, and that is causing older white heterosexual men too often to react with anger and resentment. As the United States becomes more of a multiethnic, multicultural democracy, their traditional positions of privilege are eroding.

Most notably, they are losing the authority to define by themselves what is "normal" in American society, and that has been a shock for some, leading them to react with political extremism and violence, amid talk of "taking back America." More subtly, right-wing American oligarchs have poured money into politics, effectively undercutting the power of the vote.

Meanwhile, a polarized America has developed three distinct accounts of the classical Movement, as seen by the mainstream right, center-liberals, and the left. The right has come belatedly to venerate King as a hero of color blindness, the man who called for a nation where people would be judged not "by the color of their skin but by the content of their character." In this view, the Movement achieved reforms that were in retrospect necessary and went far enough.

The center-left recognizes we must do more than the Movement did, but believes we can do so by working to deepen America's foundational commitments and to expand existing institutions. As Barack Obama put it in his speech at the 2020 Democratic National Convention, the U.S. Constitution included "a North Star that would guide future generations; a system of representative government—a democracy—through which we could better realize our highest ideals. Through civil war and bitter struggles, we improved this Constitution to include the voices of those who'd once been left out. And gradually, we made this country more just, more equal, and more free."

Well to the left of that stands the view that there has been almost no real progress since the 1960s because America is a white supremacist country through and through, with a race structure reinforced by grinding capitalism. Related to this is the academic criticism that pursuing integration rather than voting rights and political power destroyed Black businesses and undercut Black professionals, especially teachers. In this context, it is worth noting that critical race theory—the real school of thought, not the symbol attacked by the right—first evolved as a critique of mainstream Movement thinking on the value of integration.

Amid these contending visions, a strong if embattled civil rights movement still exists, just in different forms. Its exponents are focused on a range of causes, including reparations for slavery and segregation and the ending of mass incarceration. Most notably, the Movement to-day addresses itself to two familiar causes made necessary by the endur-ance of systemic racism: preserving voting rights and ending oppressive police behavior.

Protecting the vote

The right to vote was the question in Selma, Alabama, in 1965, and, dismayingly, remains under attack today. Stacey Abrams, a Black fe-male lawyer and Georgia politician, is now the most prominent leader of the fight for voting rights. All the methods by which minority voters are disenfranchised nowadays bear a strong resemblance to the tools employed by the white supremacist South a lifetime ago. The registrar's office in Selma was open only two days a month. Abrams notes that in our own time, Sauk City, Wisconsin, has been even worse, making voter ID cards available only on the fifth Wednesday of every month— that is, about five times a year or so. Along the same lines, Republicans in several states have pushed for "Exact Match" rules that require a precise match in spelling and punctuation between voting rolls and a driver's license or other identity card. These rules disproportionately affect people who have unusual names or spellings or spaces in their names, such as La'Tasha or Pai-Ling, Abrams writes. Or voting loca-tions are moved to places less reachable by public transport, which of course has more of an effect on people who don't own cars. After "souls to the polls" campaigns that urged Black parishioners to go directly from church to cast early votes, North Carolina cut back on early vot-ing on Sundays. And then there are "poll purges," which ostensibly aim at cleansing the voting rolls of the names of voters who have died or moved, but also sometimes remove those who simply have not voted for a while. A federal appeals court noted with disapproval that one set of North Carolina voting provisions "target[ed] African Americans with almost surgical precision."

Individually, each of those restrictive steps—and dozens of others—may seem like typical political gamesmanship. But when added together, Abrams concludes, they amount to an effort to restrict the votes of minorities so much that they can change the outcomes of elections. Not only is that unfair and illegal, but it is unpatriotic and un-American, because the right to vote is the basic building block of the American system.

Abrams works inside the tent, trying to secure the votes that are the path to political power in our society Her efforts resemble those of the NAACP and, to a degree, the SCLC. "Give us the ballot!" Dr. King demanded in 1957, and Abrams pursues that same goal now. Her efforts were key to electing Raphael Warnock to the U.S. Senate in January 2021. Warnock, the first Black Democrat elected to the Senate from the old Confederacy, is also the senior pastor at King's home church, Atlanta's Ebenezer Baptist—and, to take us back to the beginning of this book, the son of a Black Army veteran of World War II.

Tackling police abuse

The second major problem is that American police culture has proved extraordinarily resistant to reform, generally lagging behind cultural and political changes in the workplace and elsewhere. Officers all too often escalate when they should try to pacify situations. Departments fail to investigate police shootings, or even report them to the FBI, with the result that only half of all police shootings may be actually counted by that agency. Police departments generally lack transparency and stubbornly resist outside investigations.

The vigilante killing in 2012 of Trayvon Martin, an unarmed Black seventeen-year-old, and the jury acquittal of his killer a year later, was the first great shock that spurred the Black Lives Matter movement.

The nationwide fallout from the Martin case brings to mind the effect that the lynching of Emmett Till had on the sit-in generation half a century earlier. Alicia Garza, then a young organizer and activist living in Oakland, California, was sitting in a bar with a friend when the jury's finding was announced. "I can't breathe. NOT GUILTY?!?!?!?!?!" she tweeted at 7:04 p.m. Ten minutes later, she added, "Where those folks saying we are in post-racial America?" To that question she appended an inspired hashtag: "#blacklivesmatter." Later that evening, she explained in a third tweet, "I continue to be surprised at how little Black lives matter."

Then came more deaths: Michael Brown in Ferguson, Missouri; Eric Garner in New York City; and Tamir Rice in Cleveland, Ohio, all three in 2014. Freddie Gray in Baltimore, Maryland, and Jeremy McDole in Wilmington, Delaware, both in 2015. Philando Castile in St. Anthony, Minnesota, in 2016. Emantic Bradford, Jr., in Hoover, Alabama, in 2018. Breonna Taylor in Louisville, Kentucky; George Floyd in Minneapolis, Minnesota; Rayshard Brooks in Atlanta, Georgia; Daniel Prude in Rochester, New York; and Jonathan Price in Wolfe City, Texas, all five in 2020. Dominique Williams and James Johnson in Takoma Park, Maryland, and Daunte Wright in Brooklyn Center, Minnesota, all in 2021.

A poll conducted in April 2021 showed that two-thirds of white Americans approve of how police operate; two-thirds of Black Americans do not.

Black Lives Matter, whose organizers are more rambunctious and turbulent than Stacey Abrams, stands outside the tent, making it today's counterpart of SNCC. It is focused less on gaining power through the vote and more on confronting how power currently is exercised against minorities. So it should be no surprise that in August 2014, after police in Ferguson, Missouri, killed the eighteen-year-old Michael Brown, the digital-era activist Nicole Carty sat down to pick the brain of none other than James Lawson himself, who had done so much half a century earlier to organize the Nashville sit-in movement that produced some of SNCC's early leaders. One of the thoughts that Carty took away from her meeting with the venerable Lawson was, "It's easy to be reactive—something bad happens, you take to the streets. The real craft is in the planning, the strategizing. Having an entire sequence of tactics in mind—if I do this, then this, how do I ultimately win?"

The fact that Carty met with an essential figure from the early civil rights movement was no accident. To be sure, there are some major differences between then and now—after all, BLM exists in a different time. It is national, rather than regional. It has kept its distance from many Black churches, but not all. And unlike the Movement of the King era, BLM is female-centered, notes the historian Barbara Ransby, who adds that this gender shift reflects "the gendered nature of state violence," with male hands delivering most of the mistreatment. Also, Black Lives Matter emerged when a Black person was president of the United States, which was not the case in the 1950s. However, in some ways, Barack Obama was an obstacle to BLM, making it necessary to argue that, despite his election, the United States was far from becoming a post-racial society. Some people saw Obama's political compromises as a tragic necessity for a Black man wielding power; others saw them as betrayals.

Despite those differences, the parallels are even more striking. In both instances, advances in technology enabled the undertaking. The civil rights movement took advantage of the coming of television, which beamed images of segregationist violence into homes across the nation. Likewise, the advent of cell phones with cameras made it possible for citizens to record instances of police brutality. The resulting images often offer persuasive evidence that runs counter to official accounts. Moreover, the explosion of social media has decentralized distribution of those images. Activists no longer need to depend on reporters from large media organizations being present at a demonstration for it to make an impact. News of controversial police killings of Black people rockets instantly across Facebook, Twitter, and other platforms.

BLM's critique of American capitalism echoes some of the concerns Martin Luther King, Jr., expressed in the last years of his life. Like the civil rights movement, BLM regards America as a sick society. King had a difficult time conveying that message. It remains to be seen whether BLM will do better. But it does seem that the time is ripe for a thoroughgoing critique of the excesses of American capitalism, as we experience a new Gilded Age in which the rich dominate politics, take for themselves an unfair share of the economy, and think their business success makes them social gurus.

Takeaways for today

So what can the classical civil rights movement of more than half a century ago tell us about today? One of the major points of this book has been that there are clear and concrete lessons we can take from it, especially from its focus on discipline and organization. But we need to be careful about how to present those. Judy Richardson, a veteran of SNCC and later one of those who created the wonderful *Eyes on the Prize* documentaries, observed, "Movement people will sometimes say, 'You young people just aren't doing diddly squat and da da da.' Young folks don't need to hear that. What they need to hear is, this is how we did stuff. This is how we got started. These were the difficulties that we had."

The scholar Erica Chenoweth, who directs Harvard University's Nonviolent Action Lab, has identified four key elements present in successful nonviolent movements around the world: "numbers, defections [from security forces], tactical innovations, and discipline." Similarly, I would say that the civil rights movement succeeded as much as it did because of several aspects common to most of its campaigns:

- *Training.* Volunteers generally were subjected to intense training in how to prepare for demonstrations, how to maintain self-control in a demonstration, and how to act afterward, whether in jail or on the streets. All this kept them one step ahead of their opponents.
- *Discipline.* This word may sound strange to outsiders to a freedom movement, but not to anyone who is familiar with Gandhi,

or who has read this book. Protesters needed to be held to their training. Internal observers especially would monitor marches and try to stop anyone deviating into violence, which was essential to maintaining public support. This is also useful in deterring provocateurs working for the foe.

- *Support structures.* These ranged from employing those observers to compiling lists of potential marchers who needed babysitters. There was little spontaneous about the civil rights movement, and that was a good thing. Logistics was the key—if unseen—aspect of much of the Movement.

- *Planning.* As James Lawson told Nicole Carty, you need to think through consequences. If we do this, and they do that, what do we do next? This is harder than it sounds.

- *Strategy.* They kept their eyes on the prize, the ultimate goal. But, of course, that goal first had to be identified through intense discussions that brought to the surface internal differences and examined them.

- *Reconciliation.* Making this the final step changes everything that precedes it. The goal is not to crush your opponents but to change them, to find a way to live together down the road. Reconciliation may not be comfortable, but it does show a way forward. This may be the hardest step to grasp and implement.

Applying the app

The preceding list can be viewed as a "civil rights app." The question now is to what degree today's movements have made use of this app. The evidence here is mixed, and still developing. At its core, BLM, with its interracial protests and efforts to change the behavior of police forces, is remarkably similar to some of the most effective actors of the classical civil rights movement. Deva Woodly, a professor of politics at the New School and author of a thorough study of the Black Lives Matter movement, concludes that the purpose of political organizing is to help people "start to think about themselves . . . as the kind of people who can act" to bring about democratic change. That is what was happening, she says, with the millions of people who demonstrated against police brutality in 2020. It also, of course, was a major purpose of the Freedom Summer in Mississippi in 1964.

So it is no surprise that the Movement for Black Lives—a coalition of more than fifty groups, including the Black Lives Matter Global Network Foundation—features on its website a section about Freedom Summer, stating that it "laid the foundation for the electoral-justice and political-organizing efforts of progressive organizations today." Nor is it a shock that Bob Moses, the key leader of Freedom Summer, attended a BLM conference in New York in the summer of 2015 and was generally supportive of BLM efforts before his death in 2021. Woodly traces the roots of BLM's approach back to the Highlander Folk School, the embattled outpost in rural Tennessee that was so crucial in the lives of Movement stalwarts such as Septima Clark, Rosa Parks, and Andrew Young, and also touched the lives of others such as James Bevel and John Lewis.

Dewey Clayton, a political scientist of the University of Louisville, argues that a major difference between the civil rights movement and BLM is that "Black Lives Matter has struggled with a message of inclusion—many see their message as exclusive, specifically as anti-police." By contrast, he says, the Movement was seen as more inclusive, and also more forgiving, and so was better able to appeal to mainstream America. However, the classical Movement also had trouble with inclusion at times.

Omar Wasow, a political scientist at Pomona College, advances a related concern. He says that BLM and its allies need to do a better job of framing their arguments and so capturing the narrative. One of the lessons of the 1960s, he found, was that the use of violence alienated public opinion, whether it was employed by white police or Black rioters. "Activists picked places like Birmingham and Selma because there were these police chiefs with a hair trigger for violence who would engage in brutal repression in front of cameras," he observes. "That would

shock the conscience of these otherwise indifferent or even hostile actors outside the South. It changed public opinion." So, he continues,
"If you're an activist on the ground thinking about and angry about this
injustice against George Floyd and a long history of police violence in
this country against African Americans, if you want to put that at the
center of the national conversation, it's important to be thinking about
this: Is what we are doing on the ground elevating the justice frame or
elevating the riots frame?" Having the discipline to emphasize justice,
Wasow says, expands the base of support, while violence tends to drive
away the wavering. This would argue for BLM not just renouncing
violence but also denouncing it whenever it occurs. Taking that stance
also helps protect an organization against acts by provocateurs.

Indeed, recent research indicates that nonviolent movements carry
an inherent strategic advantage, in part because they find it easier to
gather and retain mass support.

Erica Chenoweth studied 627 resistance movements around the
world, from the Philippines at the end of the nineteenth century to
Montenegro in 2019, and concluded that nonviolent campaigns
succeeded nearly twice as often as violent ones. Not surprisingly,
Chenoweth counts James Lawson as a mentor. Moreover, she and a
coauthor found that the regimes established in the wake of nonviolent
turnovers tend to be more peaceful, stable, and democratic than those
that achieve power through violence.

BLM's achievements

There is some evidence that BLM is more attentive to the lessons of
its predecessors than it has been given credit for, and in particular understands that taking to the streets without adequate preparation and
organization is a road to failure. It also has sought to downplay individual personalities, with some of its components using the motto "High
impact, low ego." Woodly, the New School political scientist, who in
her recent book on BLM devoted an entire chapter to questions of

organization, concludes, "The Movement for Black Lives has a semi-federated kind of leadership. . . . The movement is highly adaptive and is very attentive to the history of movements, so it is no mistake that they have this form. They are studied, and are very interested in how you have the coordinating capacity of a large organization without being stultified the way that a large organization can become."

Woodly also argues that BLM has been more effective in controlling its narrative than the classical Movement was. BLM has astutely used social media to convey and explain its views and goals. As a result, she says, BLM developed broader public support than the Movement ever did in the 1950s and 1960s. In addition, she notes, BLM has produced a variety of concrete results. In cities where it has demonstrated, killings by police generally have declined. BLM activists also have developed new tools, such as running electoral campaigns that target prosecutors who are tolerant of police brutality. BLM also has helped stir a national discussion about policing, and whether the money spent on city police forces might better go to social programs to reduce homelessness and domestic violence. They have not always been successful, but they have changed the terms of debate, and not just about police actions. Of course, these efforts have prompted furious backlashes, especially in a time of rising homicide rates around the country.

Alicia Garza, who started the #BlackLivesMatter hashtag, is a seasoned activist with a serious, unromantic sense of the hard work that is required to get people to strive for social change in a sustained way. She writes, "Hashtags don't build movements. People do." She also has learned that putting people in the streets is the least of it. She sounds a bit like a veteran SNCC field secretary at, say, Selma, when she explains, "Protests are never enough to build a movement. Protests need planning and preparation. Outreach and attendance. Follow-up. Security and safety plans. Messaging and targets. Demands. Cultural components."

The real test of BLM will be whether it can maintain a sustained presence and develop sufficient power to force major changes in American police behavior. The best way to do that may be to threaten to vote out political leaders who fail to bring about those changes and to vote in those who will. To achieve that outcome, the two wings of social activism—those around BLM and those doing work akin to Stacey Abrams'—may need to work more closely with each other.

To return to the core theme of this work, in military terms, BLM has the organization not of a hierarchy such as the U.S. Army, but rather that of a distributed network, which makes it more resilient and so both sustainable and adaptive. It is useful here to remember that the internet began as a U.S. military project to ensure that communications would be possible after a nuclear clash between superpowers. Perhaps BLM may prove sustainable because of this survival-oriented structure. On the other hand, winning sides tend to have clearly established leaders.

Can America do it?

For the last several years, it's often seemed the United States has been running backward into the past. We've had demonstrators waving Confederate flags, just as Klan members did during the 1960s, and politicians thinking it clever to reduce access to the vote. We suffered a right-wing attack on the U.S. Capitol in an attempt to block the peaceful transfer of power. Even the most ardent white supremacists never sank to that depth in the 1950s or 1960s.

There were moments as I wrote this book that I felt that this country was locked in a downward spiral. Yet there were other times when—having looked at the insight of James Lawson, the tenacity of Diane Nash, the dignity of Fannie Lou Hamer, the resolve of Bob Moses, the humanity of John Lewis, the strategic acuity of James Bevel, the perseverance of Martin Luther King, Jr., and the abiding courage of them all—I saw that the country had succeeded once and felt that we can do it again.

If we are able to reverse our direction and complete a second civil rights movement—or a third reconstruction, as some call today's racial

justice efforts—I think it will be the result of a focused effort to organize, train, plan, and reconcile. Leaders emerge from such an approach,
as we have seen in this book. As Gandhi put it, "There certainly will be
no mass response where the ground has not been previously tilled, ma-
nured and watered." For the sake of all Americans, I hope that the wa-
terings of today and tomorrow across the nation eventually will merge
and grow into a mighty stream of righteousness.

NOTES

Epigraph

vii Erik H. Erikson, *Gandhi's Truth: On the Origins of Militant Nonviolence* (W. W. Norton, 1969), 408.

Preface

xiii *A Different Angle*: This preface reflects the thinking and words of my friend Karin Chenoweth, who read the first draft of this book and offered an extensive and rigorous commentary about how to better frame the subject. I am grateful for her help.

xiv *"public fable"*: Jeanne Theoharis, *A More Beautiful and Terrible History: The Uses and Misuses of Civil Rights History* (Beacon Press, 2018), 33.

xv *a new generation of scholars*: See, for example, recent works by Peniel Joseph; Christopher Lebron; Yohuru Williams; Omar Wasow; Eddie S. Glaude, Jr.; and Hasan Kwame Jeffries.

xv *major league sports*: See, for example, Louis Moore, *We Will Win the Day: The Civil Rights Movement, the Black Athlete, and the Quest for Equality* (Praeger, 2017).

xv *the role of food*: See Frederick Opie, *Southern Food and Civil Rights: Feeding the Revolution* (History Press, 2017).

xvi *"Protracted struggle is a moral struggle"*: James M. Lawson, Jr., with Michael K. Honey and Kent Wong, *Revolutionary Nonviolence: Organizing for Freedom* (University of California Press, 2022), 47.

xvi *"It was a war"*: Interview with Charles Sherrod, conducted by Blackside, Inc., December 20, 1985, for *Eyes on the Prize: America's Civil Rights Years (1954–1965)*, Washington University Libraries, Film and Media Archive, Henry Hampton Collection, transcript, repository.wustl.edu/downloads/tx31qk696.

xvi *"It was almost like a shorter version"*: Interview with Cleveland Sellers by Joseph Sinsheimer, March 30, 1985, Civil Rights Movement Archive, crmvet.org/nars/js_sellers.pdf, 31.

xvi *victory at Ulm in 1805*: James Marshall-Cornwall, *Napoleon as Military Commander* (Penguin, 2002), 138.

xvi *America's "good war"*: Peter Onuf to author, email, June 28, 2021.

xviii *"struggle—disciplined, thoughtful, creative struggle"*: Charles E. Cobb, Jr., *This Nonviolent Stuff'll Get You Killed: How Guns Made the Civil Rights Movement Possible* (Basic Books, 2014), 250.

xviii *"Those of us who love peace"*: Martin Luther King, Jr., "The Casualties of War in Vietnam," speech, February 25, 1967, Los Angeles, California, Investigating U.S. History, investigating history.ashp.cuny.edu/module11D.php.

xix *"There is no civil disobedience possible"*: M. K. Gandhi, *Non-Violent Resistance (Satyagraha)* (1961; repr. Dover, 2001), 56.

Introduction

3 *"war made the state"*: Charles Tilly, "Reflections on the History of European State-Making," in *The Formation of National States in Western Europe*, ed. Charles Tilly (Princeton University Press, 1975), 42.

3 *about 10 percent of Black males*: Gilles Vandal, "The Policy of Violence in Caddo Parish, 1865–1884," *Louisiana History* 32, no. 2 (Spring 1991): 166.

4 *more than 370,000 Black men served*: Anthony Siracusa, *Nonviolence Before King: The Politics of Being and the Black Freedom Struggle* (University of North Carolina Press, 2021), 21.

4 *Whites rioted against Blacks*: See Cameron McWhirter, *Red Summer: The Summer of 1919 and the Awakening of Black America* (Henry Holt, 2011).

4 *In 1921, armed Black vets*: Patricia Sullivan, *Lift Every Voice: The NAACP and the Making of the Civil Rights Movement* (The New Press, 2009), 101.

4 *"a turning point"*: James Baldwin, "Letter from a Region in My Mind: November 17, 1962" [later collected and reprinted as "The Fire Next Time"], reprinted in *The Matter of Black Lives: Writing from The New Yorker*, ed. Jelani Cobb and David Remnick (Ecco, 2021), 27.

4 *one million returning Black veterans*: Henry Hampton and Steve Fayer, *Voices of Freedom: An Oral History of the Civil Rights Movement from the 1950s Through the 1980s* (Bantam Books, 1990), xxiv.

4 *"we are not going to put up with this anymore"*: Interview with Bayard Rustin, conducted by Blackside, Inc., October 26, 1979, for *Eyes on the Prize: America's Civil Rights Years (1954–1965)*, Washington University Libraries, Film and Media Archive, Henry Hampton Collection, transcript, repository.wustl.edu/downloads/2r36v024m.

4 *"to help defeat domestic enemies back home"*: Charles Dryden, *A-Train: Memoirs of a Tuskegee Airman* (University of Alabama Press, 1997), 139.

4 *he was amazed to see that German prisoners of war*: Dryden, *A-Train*, 176.

4 *"I think it was World War II"*: "Charlie Cobb Discusses the Freedom Movement," discussion held at the Museum of the African Diaspora, San Francisco, February 22, 2009, Civil Rights Movement Archive, crmvet.org/disc/0902moad.htm.

5 *"We had a terrible idea"*: "Oral History with Mr. Amzie Moore, Black Civil Rights Worker," Center for Oral History and Cultural Heritage, University of Southern Mississippi, 38, 23, 19, 10.

5 *he refused to put up "White" and "Colored" signs*: "Charlie Cobb Discusses the Freedom Movement."

5 *"the father of the Movement"*: Interview with Sam Block by Joseph Sinsheimer, November 12, 1986, Civil Rights Movement Archive, crmvet.org/nars/js_block_oh-r.pdf, 43.

5 *the feel of a successful regional chief of the French Resistance*: Karin Chenoweth to author, email, July 6, 2021.

5 *The victims were shot a total of sixty-six times*: Richard Gergel, *Unexampled Courage: The Blinding of Sgt. Isaac Woodard and the Awakening of Harry S. Truman and Judge J. Waties Waring* (Farrar, Straus & Giroux, 2019), 35.

6 *"Up until George went in the army"*: Quoted in John Egerton, *Speak Now Against the Day: The Generation Before the Civil Rights Movement in the South* (Alfred A. Knopf, 1994), 369.

6 *The first big postwar fight erupted in Columbia, Tennessee*: The account of this incident relies

mainly on Gail O'Brien, *The Color of the Law: Race, Violence, and Justice in the Post–World War II South* (University of North Carolina Press, 1999), 7–10. See also Dorothy Beller, "Race Riot in Columbia, Tennessee, February 25–27, 1946," *Tennessee Historical Quarterly* 39, no. 1 (Spring 1980); and Oliver Harrington, *Terror in Tennessee: The Truth About the Columbia Outrages* (National Committee for Justice in Columbia, Tennessee, n.d.), NAACP files, ProQuest History Vault.

6 *Sergeant Isaac Woodard*: Gergel, *Unexampled Courage*, 4.

7 *"I can't approve of such goings on"*: Gergel, *Unexampled Courage*, 155–56.

7 *"dominant caste"*: See, for example, Isabel Wilkerson, *Caste: The Origins of Our Discontents* (Random House, 2020), 6, 23, 48.

7 *"I remember 1949 as a very bad year"*: Rosa Parks with Jim Haskins, *My Story* (Puffin Books, 1992), 94.

7 *lynched for whistling at a white woman*: Some historians have questioned whether Emmett Till did in fact whistle, but a recent overview of the case concludes that he did. See Wright Thompson, "His Name Was Emmett Till," *The Atlantic*, September 2021.

7 *"This is supposed to have led"*: Interview with Rosa Parks, November 14, 1985, *Eyes on the Prize*, repository.wustl.edu/downloads/0v8382275.

8 *Blacks made up 68 percent of the population*: Neil McMillen, *The Citizens' Council: Organized Resistance to the Second Reconstruction, 1954–64* (University of Illinois Press, 1994), 19.

8 *In some parts of Mississippi*: William Doyle, *An American Insurrection: James Meredith and the Battle of Oxford, Mississippi, 1962* (Anchor, 2003), 22.

8 *By this point*: This paragraph was drafted by my daughter, Molly Ricks, a historian, as part of her critique of the first draft of the manuscript of this book.

8 *the Supreme Court rejected*: Rawn James, Jr., *Root and Branch: Charles Hamilton Houston, Thurgood Marshall, and the Struggle to End Segregation* (Bloomsbury Press, 2010), 232.

9 *"That was almost like getting religion again"*: Interview with Rev. Fred Shuttlesworth, November 7, 1985, *Eyes on the Prize*, repository.wustl.edu/downloads/k643b305j.

9 *"It takes massive organization to overcome massive resistance"*: Quoted in John M. Glen, *Highlander: No Ordinary School, 1932–1962* (University Press of Kentucky, 2014), 152.

1. Montgomery, 1955–1956

12 *"I have a great belief"*: Quoted in Katherine Mellen Charron, *Freedom's Teacher: The Life of Septima Clark* (University of North Carolina Press, 2009), 354.

12 *"What do you want to do?"*: Charron, *Freedom's Teacher*, 223. Italics inserted.

12 *the session Rosa Parks attended at Highlander*: Jeanne Theoharis, *The Rebellious Life of Mrs. Rosa Parks* (Beacon Press, 2013), 35.

12 *Highlander's teachers found Parks shy*: John M. Glen, *Highlander: No Ordinary School, 1932–1962* (University Press of Kentucky, 2014), 136.

12 *"Had you seen Rosa Parks (the Montgomery sparkplug)"*: Charron, *Freedom's Teacher*, 235.

12 *"Desegregation prove[s] itself by being put in action"*: "Rosa Parks Notes, School Desegregation Workshop, Highlander Center, July 24–August 8, 1955," Civil Rights Movement Archive, crmvet.org/docs/5507park.htm.

13 *"At Highlander, I found out"*: Quoted in Myles Horton, with Judith Kohl and Herbert Kohl, *The Long Haul: An Autobiography* (Doubleday, 1990), 149–50.

13 *She literally was a Sunday school teacher*: Douglas Brinkley, *Rosa Parks* (Viking, 2000), 72.

13 *"I was quite tired"*: "Mrs. Rosa Parks Reports on Montgomery, Ala., Bus Protest," Highlander Folk School, March 1956, Civil Rights Movement Archive, crmvet.org/disc/5603_parks_mbb.pdf.

14 *none of the four moved*: Interview with Rosa Parks, conducted by Blackside, Inc., November 14, 1985, for *Eyes on the Prize: America's Civil Rights Years (1954–1965)*, Washington University

Libraries, Film and Media Archive, Henry Hampton Collection, transcript, repository.wustl .edu/downloads/0v8382275.

15 *"Baby, we've got a case"*: Interview with E. D. Nixon, 1979, *Eyes on the Prize*, repository.wustl.edu /downloads/2514nn211.

15 *surreptitiously mimeographed*: Interview with Jo Ann Robinson, August 27, 1979, *Eyes on the Prize*, repository.wustl.edu/downloads/8s45qb646.

15 *watched with his wife out their front window*: Martin Luther King, Jr., *Stride Toward Freedom: The Montgomery Story* (1958; repr. Beacon Press, 2010), 41–42.

15 *Bus drivers complained that day*: Jo Ann Gibson Robinson, *The Montgomery Bus Boycott and the Women Who Started It* (University of Tennessee Press, 1987), 59.

15 *"We had never seen a crowd like that before"*: Interview with Rev. Ralph Abernathy, November 6, 1985, *Eyes on the Prize*, repository.wustl.edu/downloads/vx021g754.

15 *"You know something, Finley"*: Quoted in Taylor Branch, *Parting the Waters: America in the King Years* (Simon & Schuster, 1988), 139. I want to say at this first citation of Branch's classic work that reading it inspired me to write this book, and that its influence is reflected throughout.

16 *"to redeem the soul of America"*: Martin Luther King, Jr., to Johnnie Goodson, August 29, 1960, King Papers, Stanford University.

16 *"We are here this evening"*: This and subsequent passages from this speech are from Martin Luther King, Jr., "MIA Meeting at Holt Street Baptist Church," December 5, 1955, in *The Papers of Martin Luther King, Jr.*, vol. 3: *Birth of a New Age, December 1955–December 1956* (University of California Press, 1997), 71–74.

16 *Jesus was providing the spirit*: Martin Luther King, Jr., "Pilgrimage to Nonviolence," in *The Papers of Martin Luther King Jr.*, vol. 5: *Threshold of a New Decade, January 1959–December 1960*, ed. Clayborne Carson (University of California Press, 2005), 423.

17 *"fired up"* and *"began to read all the books on Gandhi"*: Quoted in David Varel, *The Scholar and the Struggle: Lawrence Reddick's Crusade for Black History and Black Power* (University of North Carolina Press, 2020), 138.

17 *"a persecuted religious minority"*: Anthony Siracusa, *Nonviolence Before King: The Politics of Being and the Black Freedom Struggle* (University of North Carolina Press, 2021), 67.

17 *"Jesus is still unknown in this land"*: Quoted in Siracusa, *Nonviolence Before King*, 60.

17 *"implicit in the Christian message"*: Howard Thurman, "Judgment and Hope in the Christian Message," in *The Christian Way in Race Relations*, ed. William Nelson (1948; repr. Books for Libraries Press, 1971), 229.

17 *asked him why American slaves*: Howard Thurman, *With Head and Heart: The Autobiography of Howard Thurman* (Mariner, 1981), 132.

17 *"it may be through the [American] Negroes"*: Howard Thurman, "With Our Negro Guests," March 14, 1936, in *The Papers of Howard Washington Thurman*, vol. 1: *My People Need Me, June 1918–March 1936*, ed. Walter Earl Fluker (University of South Carolina Press, 2012), 337.

17 *"A civilization is to be judged"*: Louis Fischer, *The Life of Mahatma Gandhi* (HarperCollins, 1997), 527.

17 *"survival kit"*: James Lawson, quoted in Siracusa, *Nonviolence Before King*, 164.

17 *"people who stand with their backs against the wall"*: Howard Thurman, *Jesus and the Disinherited* (1949; repr. Beacon Press, 1996), xix.

17 *a Christian face on Gandhi's philosophy*: This sentence grew out of a conversation with the documentarian Jim Gilmore on March 31, 2021.

19 *He did it all in just sixteen minutes*: Stephen Oates, *Let the Trumpet Sound: The Life of Martin Luther King, Jr.* (Harper & Row, 1982), 71.

19 *"the first actual massive uprising"*: Interview with Rev. Fred Shuttlesworth, November 7, 1985, *Eyes on the Prize*, repository.wustl.edu/downloads/k643b305j.

19   *the boycotters' initial demand was not for full integration*: Thomas Thrasher, "Alabama's Bus Boycott," in *The Walking City: The Montgomery Bus Boycott, 1955–1956*, ed. David Garrow (Carlson Publishing, 1989), 61.

19   *King would go on to lead an insurgency*: The thinking behind this paragraph was provoked by the use of the word "insurgency" in Jonathan Rieder, *The Word of the Lord Is Upon Me: The Righteous Performance of Martin Luther King, Jr.* (Belknap, 2008).

20   *"If there had been any violence at all"*: Interview with Bayard Rustin, October 26, 1979, *Eyes on the Prize*, repository.wustl.edu/downloads/2r36v024m.

20   *"does not mean meek submission"*: M. K. Gandhi, *Non-Violent Resistance (Satyagraha)* (1961; repr. Dover, 2001), 134.

21   *the true face of oppression*: This sentence was influenced by one in Erica Chenoweth, *Civil Resistance: What Everyone Needs to Know* (Oxford University Press, 2021), 35.

21   *"Many think that non-violence is not an active force"*: M. K. Gandhi, "Letter to Lord Irwin," in *Gandhi in India: In His Own Words*, ed. Martin Green (University Press of New England, 1987), 117.

21   *"Your violent opponent wants you to fight"*: Richard B. Gregg, *The Power of Non-Violence* (1934; repr. Cambridge University Press, 2018), 102.

21   *The nonviolent arsenal*: Joan Bondurant, *Conquest of Violence: The Gandhian Philosophy of Conflict* (Princeton University Press, 1988), 26, 126.

21   *"the capability of maneuver"*: Quoted in "Protests in Perspective: Civil Disobedience & Activism Today, with Erica Chenoweth & Deva Woodly," *Carnegie Council Transcripts and Articles*, November 16, 2020, 4.

22   *Montgomery's Black population besieged the city*: I first saw the Montgomery campaign described as a siege in David L. Chappell, *Waking from the Dream: The Struggle for Civil Rights in the Shadow of Martin Luther King, Jr.* (Random House, 2014), 176.

22   *their ministers used their pulpits*: See, for example, King's report to the Forty-Seventh Annual NAACP Convention, June 27, 1956, in *Papers of Martin Luther King, Jr.*, 3:302.

22   *When strange voices telephoned*: Robinson, *The Montgomery Bus Boycott*, 56, 61.

22   *"Don't ride the bus 'til you hear from us"*: E. D. Nixon interview, in Garrow, *The Walking City*, 547.

23   *a transportation committee was formed*: Information in this and the next paragraph is from King, *Stride Toward Freedom*, 61–66.

23   *hired about eight dispatchers*: This and subsequent details are from J. B. Simms interviews, in Garrow, *The Walking City*, 578, 581.

23   *required about $5,000 a month*: Martin Luther King, Jr., to Arthur James, *Papers of Martin Luther King, Jr.*, 3:287.

23   *out-of-state banks, most of them Black-owned*: Thomas Gilliam, "The Montgomery Bus Boycott of 1955–1956," in Garrow, *The Walking City*, 230.

23   *Two Black-owned properties*: Rufus Lewis interview, in Garrow, *The Walking City*, 540.

24   *the organization of white ministers*: King, *Stride Toward Freedom*, 204.

24   *"The most pervasive mistake I have made"*: "*Playboy* Interview: Martin Luther King, Jr.," January 1965, in *A Testament of Hope: The Essential Writings and Speeches of Martin Luther King, Jr.*, ed. James Melvin Washington (1986; repr. HarperCollins, 1991), 345.

24   *"dirty crackers"*: Simms transcript, in Garrow, *The Walking City*, 579.

24   *"At the beginning of the protest"*: This and subsequent details about the meetings are from King, *Stride Toward Freedom*, 72–75.

24   *"The mass meetings were so stimulating"*: Rufus Lewis interview transcript, in Garrow, *The Walking City*, 541.

25   *"If we granted the Negroes these demands"*: Quoted in King, *Stride Toward Freedom*, 100–101.

25   *the bus company halted service*: Robinson, *The Montgomery Bus Boycott*, 84.

25 *"prominent Negro ministers"*: King, *Stride Toward Freedom*, 115–16. For details on this odd incident, see also Robinson, *The Montgomery Bus Boycott*, 118.

26 *"Did they think we were fools?"*: Johnnie Carr interview transcript, in Garrow, *The Walking City*, 530.

26 *"tired of pussyfooting around"*: Quoted in "Statement of Attorney Fred D. Gray," Hearings Before the Subcommittee on Constitutional Rights, Senate Judiciary Committee, February 14–March 5, 1957, 827.

26 *"Nigger, we are tired of you"*: Brinkley, *Rosa Parks*, 149.

26 *"Don't get panicky"*: Quoted in Robinson, *The Montgomery Bus Boycott*, 132.

26–27 *his greatest moment of fear*: "Interview at Bennett College," February 11, 1958, in *Papers of Martin Luther King, Jr.*, 4:367.

27 *"He listened a lot and thought a lot"*: Erna Dungee Allen interview, in Garrow, *The Walking City*, 523.

27 *about $10,000 a month*: Gilliam, "The Montgomery Bus Boycott," in Garrow, *The Walking City*, 230.

27 *fifteen new station wagons*: King, *Stride Toward Freedom*, 66.

28 *"They were used to seeing"*: Ralph David Abernathy, *And the Walls Came Tumbling Down: An Autobiography* (Harper & Row, 1989), 160.

28 *"The threats on his life"*: James Lawson testimony, *Coretta Scott King v. Loyd Jowers*, King Library, 4:367.

28 *so elated he began shouting*: Interview with James Lawson by Joan Beifuss and David Yellin, January 21, 1969, "Sanitation Strike Tapes," Memphis and the Mid-South Files, Rhodes College Digital Archives, dlynx.rhodes.edu/jspui/bitstream/10267/33928/4/SS269_transcript.pdf.

28 *"The definition that most Americans have of nonviolence"*: Interview with James Lawson, January 21, 1969, "Sanitation Strike Tapes."

29 *"an instrument of aggression"*: This and the subsequent quotation are from Krishnalal Shridharani, *War Without Violence: A Study of Gandhi's Method and Its Accomplishments* (Victor Gollancz, 1939), 240, 15.

29 *"a growing commitment to the philosophy of non-violence"*: Martin Luther King, Jr., to Bayard Rustin, September 20, 1956, "Montgomery Bus Boycott," in Bayard Rustin Papers, ProQuest History Vault.

29 *"The experience in Montgomery"*: Martin Luther King, Jr., "Pilgrimage to Nonviolence," in *Papers of Martin Luther King, Jr.*, 5:423.

29 *letters of advice by every American liberal*: See, for example, Harris Wofford to King, April 25, 1956, and Hazel Foster to King, April 29, 1956, in *Papers of Martin Luther King, Jr.*, kinginstitute.stanford.edu/king-papers/documents/harris-wofford and kinginstitute.stanford.edu/king-papers/documents/hazel-e-foster.

29 *a rivalry developed*: William Robert Miller to Martin Luther King, Jr., and King to Miller, in *The Papers of Martin Luther King, Jr.*, vol. 4: *Symbol of the Movement*, ed. Clayborne Carson (University of California Press, 2000), 142, 181.

30 *"The glorious thing"*: "Reminiscences of Bayard Rustin, 1987," Oral History Archives, Columbia University, 4–138.

30 *"acted as if King were a precious puppet"*: Harris Wofford, *Of Kennedys and Kings: Making Sense of the Sixties* (Farrar, Straus & Giroux, 1980), 115. For a somewhat different view of how and when King was influenced by Gandhi, see Gary Dorrien, *Breaking White Supremacy: Martin Luther King Jr. and the Black Social Gospel* (Yale University Press, 2018), 263–68.

30 *"it is usually forgotten"*: Gene Sharp, *Gandhi as a Political Strategist* (Porter Sargent Publishers, 1979), 8.

31 *"They had backed us up"*: *"Playboy* Interview: Martin Luther King, Jr.," 343.

31 *"We have discovered"*: Martin Luther King, Jr., "Facing the Challenge of a New Age," December 3, 1956, in *Papers of Martin Luther King, Jr.*, 3:452.

32 *"It thus had the strength of unity"*: Bayard Rustin to Martin Luther King, Jr., December 23, 1956, in *Papers of Martin Luther King, Jr.*, 3:492–93.

32 *"a nation within a nation"*: E. Franklin Frazier, *The Negro Church in America* (1964; repr. Schocken Books, 1971), 44.

32 *"consumed by trivialities"*: Richard Kluger, *Simple Justice: The History of* Brown v. Board of Education *and Black America's Struggle for Equality* (Alfred A. Knopf, 2004), 100.

32 *the churches had become the command posts*: This sentence was inspired by a note that Professor Adrian Lewis of the University of Kansas sent to me on June 20, 2021.

32 *"Adept at the internal politics"*: Andrew Young, *An Easy Burden: The Civil Rights Movement and the Transformation of America* (Harper, 1996), 176.

33 *Dwight Eisenhower tried to focus*: Thomas E. Ricks, *The Generals: American Military Command from World War II to Today* (Penguin Press, 2012), 48.

33 *"walk for another week or two"*: King, *Stride Toward Freedom*, 159.

33 *"I believe you are Reverend King"*: King, *Stride Toward Freedom*, 163–64.

35 *"It felt as if the Earth had just erupted"*: "James Roberson," in Horace Huntley and John W. McKerley, eds., *Foot Soldiers for Democracy: The Men, Women, and Children of the Birmingham Civil Rights Movement* (University of Illinois Press, 2009), 112.

35 *"At that moment, all fear was taken from me"*: For this and the subsequent two quotations from this incident, see Interview with Rev. Fred Shuttlesworth, *Eyes on the Prize*.

35 *a moonshiner turned minister*: Andrew Manis, *A Fire You Can't Put Out: The Civil Rights Life of Birmingham's Reverend Fred Shuttlesworth* (University of Alabama Press, 2002), xvi.

35 *"an extremely disciplined person"*: Interview with Andrew Young, in Peter W. Kunhardt, dir., *King in the Wilderness* (Kunhardt Film Foundation, 2018), transcript, kunhardtfilmfoundation.org /featured-interviews/andrew-young.

36 *"It created a sense of hope, a sense of optimism"*: Interview with John Lewis, May 14, 1979, *Eyes on the Prize*, repository.wustl.edu/downloads/sn00b0587.

2. Nashville, 1960

37 *"The idea was to understand the power"*: Interview with C. T. Vivian, conducted by Blackside, Inc., January 23, 1986, for *Eyes on the Prize: America's Civil Rights Years (1954–1965)*, Washington University Libraries, Film and Media Archive, Henry Hampton Collection, transcript, repository .wustl.edu/downloads/br86b5432.

38 *Crusade for Citizenship*: John D'Emilio, *Lost Prophet: The Life and Times of Bayard Rustin* (The Free Press, 2003), 269.

38 *"to double the number"*: "Proposed Plans for Kick-Off Meetings/Crusade for Citizenship," Bayard Rustin files on SNCC, ProQuest History Vault, 1.

38 *"I have come to the conclusion"*: Martin Luther King, Jr., to Mordecai Johnson, July 5, 1957, King Papers, Stanford University.

38 *He was eventually found not guilty*: Stephen Oates, *Let the Trumpet Sound: The Life of Martin Luther King, Jr.* (Harper & Row, 1982), 152–55.

39 *"we are losing the initiative"*: "Memorandum to M. L. King, Jr. from Ella J. Baker," July 16, 1958, Bayard Rustin papers, ProQuest History Vault.

39 *"gave him the devil"*: "Notes by Lawrence Dunbar Reddick on SCLC Administrative Committee Meetings on 2 April and 3 April 1959," King Papers, Stanford University.

39 *"fading away"*: Martin Luther King, Jr., to Theodore Brown, October 19, 1959, *The Papers of Martin Luther King, Jr.*, vol. 5: *Threshold of a New Decade, January 1959–December 1960*, ed. Clayborne Carson (University of California Press, 2005), 312.

39 *"The fact remains"*: Martin Luther King, Jr., to Simeon Booker, October 20, 1959, *Papers of Martin Luther King, Jr.*, 5:314.

39 *more than two hundred speeches in 1958 alone*: For number of speeches, see Alan Westin and Barry Mahony, *The Trial of Martin Luther King* (Crowell, 1974), 30.

39 *"While the voting drive still holds"*: Martin Luther King, Jr., "Recommendations to SCLC Committee on Future Program," October 27, 1959, *Papers of Martin Luther King, Jr.*, 5:316.

40 *Lawson had recorded that his was "human"*: Barry Everett Lee, "The Nashville Civil Rights Movement: A Study of the Phenomenon of Intentional Leadership Development and Its Consequences for Local Movements and the National Civil Rights Movement" (PhD diss., Georgia State University, 2010), 78.

40 *"[We] found ourselves to be very much in sync"*: Some accounts state that the meal King and Lawson talked over was lunch, but Lawson states that it was dinner in an interview by Joan Beifuss and David Yellin, January 21, 1969, "Sanitation Strike Tapes," Memphis and the Mid-South Files, Rhodes College Digital Archives, dlynx.rhodes.edu/jspui/bitstream/10267/33928 /4/SS269_transcript.pdf. See also James Lawson testimony, *Coretta Scott King v. Loyd Jowers*, King Library, 4:362–64.

40 *Vanderbilt University, which had begun admitting*: Lee, "The Nashville Civil Rights Movement," 82, 118.

41 *"The first step was investigation"*: Quoted in Fred Powledge, *Free at Last?: The Civil Rights Movement and the People Who Made It* (Little, Brown, 1991), 233.

41 *"Their exercises lack none of the vigor"*: Quoted in J. E. Lendon, *Soldiers and Ghosts: A History of Battle in Classical Antiquity* (Yale University Press, 2005), 235.

41 *contributed a prologue to an American edition*: Martin Luther King, Jr., to Richard Gregg, May 1, 1956, King Papers, Stanford University. For King's recommending Gregg's volume to others, see Joseph Kosek, "Richard Gregg, Mohandas Gandhi, and the Strategy of Nonviolence," *Journal of American History* 91, no. 4 (March 2005): 1318.

42 *"When there are more than twelve"*: This and quotations in the next paragraph are from Richard B. Gregg, *The Power of Non-Violence* (1934; repr. Cambridge University Press, 2018), 177–78.

42 *the "primary group" of about a dozen people*: This sentence was inspired by James Dunnigan, *How to Make War: A Comprehensive Guide to Modern Warfare* (William Morrow, 1988), 293.

43 *"special ingredient"*: Benjamin Houston, *The Nashville Way: Racial Etiquette and the Struggle for Social Justice in a Southern City* (University of Georgia Press, 2012), 85.

43 *"a laboratory for demonstrating nonviolence"*: Wesley Hogan, *Many Minds, One Heart: SNCC's Dream for a New America* (University of North Carolina Press, 2007), 17.

43 *the first of what he called "workshops"*: Lee, "The Nashville Civil Rights Movement," 133.

43 *"You have to have a common discipline"*: Lee, "The Nashville Civil Rights Movement," 161.

43 *had been puzzled as a boy*: John Lewis, *Walking with the Wind: A Memoir of the Movement* (Simon & Schuster, 2015), 36.

43 *"Those Tuesday nights"*: Lewis, *Walking with the Wind*, 76.

43 *Tuition cost him $42 a semester*: David Halberstam, *The Children* (Random House, 1998), 65.

44 *"He thanked the man who spat on him"*: James Bevel with Randy Kryn, "Declaring Peace: James Bevel's 1960s Movements and Strategies; A Practical History and Guide to Nonviolence" (unpublished manuscript, 1988–2004), 14–15.

44 *"I left Highlander on fire"*: For an account of this visit to the Highlander School, see Lewis, *Walking with the Wind*, 79–82.

44 *"They have a sense of rightness"*: Bevel with Kryn, "Declaring Peace," 141.

45 *The first step in the workshops*: Interview with C. T. Vivian, *Eyes on the Prize*.

45 *"When you don't retaliate with a personal insult"*: Quoted in Hogan, *Many Minds, One Heart*, 28.

45 *"We will not injure you"*: This and the following quotation from Lawson are from James Lawson testimony, *Coretta Scott King v. Loyd Jowers*, King Library, 4:422–23.

46 *"take the blows"*: Interview with C. T. Vivian, *Eyes on the Prize.*

46 *"If one person was taking a severe beating"*: Interview with Diane Nash, November 12, 1985, *Eyes on the Prize*, repository.wustl.edu/downloads/7m01bn67n.

47 *"Non-violence demands the strictest honesty"*: Quoted in Louis Fischer, *The Life of Mahatma Gandhi* (HarperCollins, 1997), 470.

48 *"part of a focusing in"*: Quoted in Hogan, *Many Minds, One Heart*, 32.

48 *"We had a nonviolent academy"*: Quoted in Lee, "The Nashville Civil Rights Movement," 168.

48 *"If it is possible to know"*: Quoted in Howell Raines, *My Soul Is Rested: Movement Days in the Deep South Remembered* (Penguin Books, 1983), 78.

48 *"I mean, it was like a flash fire"*: This and following quotations from Sellers are from "An Oral History with Cleveland Sellers Jr.," North Mississippi Oral History and Archives Program, Center for Oral History and Cultural Heritage, University of Southern Mississippi, 2, 4.

49 *"The picture of Emmett Till sticks"*: "Junius W. Williams Oral History Interview Conducted by Joseph Mosnier in Newark, New Jersey, 2011 July 20," U.S. Civil Rights History Project, transcript, 5, loc.gov/item/2015669136.

49 *Some five hundred showed up*: Lewis, *Walking with the Wind*, 92–93.

49 *"If you asked us to wait until next week"*: Quoted in Lee, "The Nashville Civil Rights Movement," 174.

49 *"There was no stopping this thing now"*: Lewis, *Walking with the Wind*, 93.

49 *"traveled constantly and . . . traveled light"*: Lewis, *Walking with the Wind*, 202.

49 *"Protracted struggle is a moral struggle"*: James Lawson with Michael Honey and Kent Wong, *Revolutionary Nonviolence: Organizing for Freedom* (University of California Press, 2022), 50.

50 *Lawson deployed observers*: A. W. Martin, "The Lawson Affair, the Sit-ins, and Beyond," *Tennessee Historical Quarterly* 75, no. 2 (Summer 2016): 145.

50 *"We had white people who stayed"*: Interview with Rev. James Lawson, December 2, 1985, *Eyes on the Prize*, repository.wustl.edu/downloads/n870zs44k.

51 *"Niggers, go home"*: Lewis, *Walking with the Wind*, 96.

51 *"Oh, nigras everywhere!"*: Diane Nash, "Inside the Sit Ins and Freedom Rides: Testimony of a Southern Student," in *The New Negro*, ed. Matthew H. Ahmann (Biblo and Tannen, 1969), 48.

51 *"Sir, do you have a handkerchief?"*: Brad Schmitt, "After a White Man Spit in His Face, Civil Rights Protester Saw a Flash of Humanity," *Nashville Tennessean*, January 15, 2018.

51 *"When they knocked me out of the chair"*: Larry Isaac et al., "'Movement Schools' and Dialogical Diffusion of Nonviolent Praxis: Nashville Workshops in the Southern Civil Rights Movement," in *Nonviolent Conflict and Civil Resistance*, ed. Sharon Nepstead and Lester Kurtz (Emerald Group Publishing, 2012), 173.

52 *asked the mayor of Nashville*: Lee, "The Nashville Civil Rights Movement," 177.

52 *John Lewis wrote up a list*: "Rules of Action Proposed by Sit-in Participants," The Rhetoric of the Civil Rights Movement, Center for Democratic Deliberation at Penn State, sites.psu.edu /civilrightsrhetoric/rules-of-action-for-sit-in-participants/. Also reproduced, with details about the production, in Lewis, *Walking with the Wind*, 98.

53 *"On this Saturday, very suddenly"*: Interview with James M. Lawson, Jr., March 17, 1964, Robert Penn Warren's Who Speaks for the Negro?: An Archival Collection, Vanderbilt University Library, whospeaks.library.vanderbilt.edu/interview/james-m-lawson-jr.

53 *"insulting us, blowing smoke in our faces"*: Paul LaPrad, "Nashville: A Community Struggle," in *Sit Ins: The Students Report* (CORE, 1960).

54 *"The principle should always"*: J. A. Gilbert, *An Exposition of the First Principles of Grand Military Combinations and Movements* (T. Egerton, 1825), 19.

54 *"No matter what they did"*: Interview with Diane Nash, *Eyes on the Prize.*

54 *"[It] was the first time that I was arrested"*: Interview with John Lewis, May 14, 1979, *Eyes on the Prize*, repository.wustl.edu/downloads/sn00b0587.

55 *"There were many Blacks who were arrested"*: Interview with Dr. William G. Anderson, November 7, 1985, *Eyes on the Prize*, repository.wustl.edu/downloads/5h73px82v.

55 *"The social terrain had now begun to shift"*: Lee, "The Nashville Civil Rights Movement," 180.

55 *"If you dare to pray such prayers"*: Oral History Interview with James Lawson, October 26, 2011, Boston University School of Theology, Buniverse, bu.edu/buniverse/view/?v=2KTPFUqK.

55 *"We created our own church services"*: Interview with C. T. Vivian, *Eyes on the Prize*.

55 *"cheerful acceptance of jail discipline"*: M. K. Gandhi, *Non-Violent Resistance (Satyagraha)* (1961; repr. Dover, 2001), 63.

56 *"the best prisoners I've ever had"*: Quoted in Jeff Kisseloff, *Generation on Fire: Voices of Protest from the 1960s* (University Press of Kentucky, 2007), 12.

56 *Nashville's adults began to make more donations*: Houston, *The Nashville Way*, 15.

56 *the sit-ins stopped being the action of students*: Houston, *The Nashville Way*, 15.

56 *"The city fathers"*: Interview with C. T. Vivian, *Eyes on the Prize*.

56 *"We learned that asking for change"*: Bevel with Kryn, "Declaring Peace," 21.

56 *"It marked one of the earliest instances"*: Lewis, *Walking with the Wind*, 106.

57 *"where the law was used simply to oppress people"*: Lee, "The Nashville Civil Rights Movement," 184.

57 *"It was essential to keep the sit-ins"*: Roy Wilkins, *Standing Fast: The Autobiography of Roy Wilkins* (Da Capo Press, 1994), 270.

58 *"direct action did not form a significant part"*: August Meier and Elliott Rudwick, *Along the Color Line: Explorations in the Black Experience* (University of Illinois Press, 1976), 344.

58 *"a century of litigation"*: "Interview by Zena Sears on 'For Your Information,'" in *The Papers of Martin Luther King, Jr.*, 5:545. The exact Cook quotation, slightly less certain than the way King tended to formulate it, can be found in several books, such as Tomiko Brown-Nagin, *Courage to Dissent: Atlanta and the Long History of the Civil Rights Movement* (Oxford University Press, 2012), 312.

58 *"Sometimes I get awfully tired"*: Quoted in Richard Kluger, *Simple Justice: The History of Brown v. Board of Education and Black America's Struggle for Equality* (Alfred A. Knopf, 2004), 324.

59 *"A lot of the younger people"*: Quoted in Eric Etheridge, *Breach of Peace: Portraits of the 1961 Mississippi Freedom Riders* (Atlas, 2008), 153.

59 *"I wanted to participate in my own struggle"*: Quoted in Etheridge, *Breach of Peace*, 197.

59 *"reveals the state of mind"*: James Baldwin, "The Dangerous Road Before Martin Luther King," in *The Price of the Ticket: Collected Nonfiction, 1948–1985* (St. Martin's Press, 1985), 261.

59 *"I have refused to fight back"*: "To Jackie Robinson," June 19, 1960, in *Papers of Martin Luther King, Jr.*, 5:477–78.

60 *"This is a new stage in the struggle"*: Quoted in David Garrow, *The FBI and Martin Luther King, Jr.: From "Solo" to Memphis* (W. W. Norton, 1981), 20.

60 *"everyone should be involved in his own liberation"*: Coby Smith, quoted in Michael K. Honey, *Going Down Jericho Road: The Memphis Strike, Martin Luther King's Last Campaign* (W. W. Norton, 2007), 374.

60 *"The movement had a way of reaching inside me"*: Interview with Diane Nash, *Eyes on the Prize*.

61 *"The students managed to move so fast"*: Interview with Diane Nash, *Eyes on the Prize*.

61 *"We just moved so fast"*: Interview with Diane Nash, July 7, 1983, David Garrow Research Files #832, 9. Courtesy of David Garrow and Jonathan Eig.

61 *"to keep the movement as creative as possible"*: Interview with James M. Lawson, Jr., Robert Penn Warren's Who Speaks for the Negro?

61 *"We Shall Not Be Moved"*: John M. Glen, *Highlander: No Ordinary School, 1932–1962* (University Press of Kentucky, 2014), 148.

61 *singing together was a primary way*: Gregg, *The Power of Nonviolence*, 185.

62 *"made you bigger"*: "Selma & the March to Montgomery: A Discussion, November–June, 2004–2005," Civil Rights Movement Archive, crmvet.org/disc/selma.htm.

62 *"I don't know the song but I know the note"*: Bernard LaFayette, Jr., and Kathryn Lee Johnson, *In Peace and Freedom: My Journey in Selma* (University Press of Kentucky, 2013), 40.

62 *"there were no marshals"*: Andrew Young, *An Easy Burden: The Civil Rights Movement and the Transformation of America* (Harper, 1996), 260.

62 *one hundred towns across the South*: Glen, *Highlander*, 145.

63 *"heard this big boom"*: Interview with Diane Nash, November 12, 1985, *Eyes on the Prize*, repository.wustl.edu/downloads/7m01bn67n.

63 *The blast nearly destroyed his house*: Halberstam, *The Children*, 229.

63 *"We decided to respond that day"*: Lee, "The Nashville Civil Rights Movement," 213.

63 *They maintained silence, a sign of resolve*: Larry Isaac, "Performative Power in Nonviolent Tactical Adaptation to Violence," in *Social Movements, Nonviolent Resistance, and the State*, ed. Hank Johnston (Routledge, 2019), 36.

63 *"Everyone was very intense"*: Lewis, *Walking in the Wind*, 109.

63 *"a turning point"*: Interview with C. T. Vivian, *Eyes on the Prize*.

64 *"the best organized and most disciplined"*: *Papers of Martin Luther King Jr.*, 5:466n.

64 *"the most dangerous man in all Nashville"*: Quoted in Halberstam, *The Children*, 230.

64 *alienate the courts*: Patricia Sullivan, *Lift Every Voice: The NAACP and the Making of the Civil Rights Movement* (The New Press, 2009), 326.

64 *"While a series of legal shifts"*: Anthony Siracusa, *Nonviolence Before King: The Politics of Being and the Black Freedom Struggle* (University of North Carolina Press, 2021), 157.

64–65 *King wanted to hire Lawson*: Siracusa, *Nonviolence Before King*, 168.

65 *bank account had increased*: Lee, "The Nashville Civil Rights Movement," 196.

65 *"A general feeling of dignity and self-respect"*: C. T. Vivian, speaking on Track 8 of *The Nashville Sit-In Story*, Folkways Records, 1960.

65 *"Throughout the Southland, we took that movie"*: Quoted in Lee, "The Nashville Civil Rights Movement," 220.

65 *"It was rare enough"*: Young, *An Easy Burden*, 125, 129.

65 *"somebody was doing something"*: Robert P. Moses, "Speech on Freedom Summer at Stanford University," April 24, 1964, American Radio Works, americanradioworks.publicradio.org/features/blackspeech/bmoses.html.

66 *"This movement is not only against segregation"*: Quoted in Adam Fairclough, *To Redeem the Soul of America: The Southern Christian Leadership Conference and Martin Luther King, Jr.* (University of Georgia Press, 1987), 63.

66 *Visiting their offices in Alabama and Mississippi*: Howard Zinn, *SNCC: The New Abolitionists* (Beacon Press, 1964), 12.

3. The Freedom Rides, 1961

68 *"The Doolittle Raid"*: Adrian Lewis to Thomas E. Ricks, email, June 20, 2021. Craig Symonds, in *The Battle of Midway* (Oxford University Press, 2011), 131, states, "The Doolittle Raid did not trigger the Midway expedition. . . . It did, however, remove any doubts the [Japanese] Army had about backing the operation."

68 *"We somehow had to cut across state lines"*: Quoted in Howell Raines, *My Soul Is Rested: Movement Days in the Deep South Remembered* (Penguin Books, 1983), 109.

69 *his first formal address as the attorney general*: Patricia Sullivan, *Justice Rising: Robert Kennedy's America in Black and White* (Belknap, 2021), 99.

69 *"If one man's rights are denied"*: Quoted in Philip Goduti, Jr., *Robert Kennedy and the Shaping of Civil Rights, 1960–1964* (McFarland, 2013), 59.

69 *"something new"*: Interview with Colonel Floyd Mann, conducted by Blackside, Inc., February

18, 1986, for *Eyes on the Prize: America's Civil Rights Years (1954–1965)*, Washington University Libraries, Film and Media Archive, Henry Hampton Collection, transcript, repository.wustl .edu/downloads/mg74qn81m.

70 *Gaither had been one of the people*: "Oral History Interview: Tom Gaither," September 12, 2011, Civil Rights Movement Archive, crmvet.org/nars/gaithert.htm.

70 *His task was to travel the planned route*: Raymond Arsenault, *Freedom Riders: 1961 and the Struggle for Racial Justice* (Oxford University Press, 2007), 96–97.

70 *"troops with above average combat skills"*: James Dunnigan, *How to Make War: A Comprehensive Guide to Modern Warfare* (William Morrow, 1988), 274.

70 *CORE held preparatory meetings*: Derek Catsam, *Freedom's Main Line: The Journey of Reconciliation and the Freedom Rides* (University Press of Kentucky, 2009), 84.

70 *one volunteer dropped out*: Arsenault, *Freedom Riders*, 108.

71 *"It was like the Last Supper"*: Interview with John Lewis, 1979, *Eyes on the Prize*, repository.wustl .edu/concern/videos/vt150m28q.

71 *"it is never the numbers that count"*: M. K. Gandhi, *Non-Violent Resistance (Satyagraha)* (1961; repr. Dover, 2001), 87.

71 *Gandhi restricted his column to seventy-eight people*: Peter Ackerman and Jack Duvall, *A Force More Powerful: A Century of Nonviolent Conflict* (St. Martin's Press, 2000), 85–86.

71 *"I was like a soldier in a nonviolent army"*: Interview with John Lewis in *American Experience: Freedom Riders*, dir. Stanley Nelson, PBS, season 23, episode 12, aired May 16, 2011.

72 *White toughs waiting there*: Arsenault, *Freedom Riders*, 122.

72 *"about blacks being taken out of southern jails"*: Catsam, *Freedom's Main Line*, 131.

72 *Ivory, who used a wheelchair*: August Meier and Elliott Rudwick, *Along the Color Line: Explorations in the Black Experience* (University of Illinois Press, 1976), 369.

72 *"He didn't have to tell me twice"*: Catsam, *Freedom's Main Line*, 131.

73 *"You will never make it through Alabama"*: Quoted in John Lewis, *Walking with the Wind: A Memoir of the Movement* (Simon & Schuster, 2015), 140.

73 *A crowd of whites led by the local Klan leader*: Arsenault, *Freedom Riders*, 143–44.

73 *"Across the highway, in a state patrol car"*: Albert Bigelow, "Committee of Inquiry Testimony," May 25, 1962, Civil Rights Movement Archive, crmvet.org/riders/6205_core_coi_bigelow.pdf, 2.

73 *"Let's burn the niggers alive"*: Quoted in *American Experience: Freedom Riders*.

74 *The man then swung a baseball bat*: Halberstam, *The Children*, 263. A similar account is in Arsenault, *Freedom Riders*, 145.

75 *"The Freedom Rides didn't really come"*: Interview with Burke Marshall, November 4, 1985, *Eyes on the Prize*, repository.wustl.edu/downloads/v405sc266.

75 *"The military value of a partisan's work"*: John S. Mosby, *Mosby's War Reminiscences, and Stuart's Cavalry Campaigns* (1887; repr. Dodd, Mead, 1898), 44.

75 *some three hundred people*: Taylor Branch, *Pillar of Fire: America in the King Years, 1963–1965* (Simon & Schuster, 1998), 54.

75 *"They used my husband's head"*: James Farmer, *Lay Bare the Heart: An Autobiography of the Civil Rights Movement* (Texas Christian University Press, 1998), 202.

75 *"Doggone, it looks like"*: Farmer, *Lay Bare the Heart*, 202.

76 *"I ain't seen a thing"*: Arsenault, *Freedom Riders*, 150.

76 *"By God, if you are going to do this thing"*: FBI Birmingham office, "RE: CONGRESS OF RACIAL EQUALITY," May 12, 1961, FBI memoranda file, Birmingham Public Library Digital Collections, 1–2.

76 *"one passenger was knocked down"*: Quoted in Lewis, *Walking with the Wind*, 142.

76 *"too tired to care"*: Interview with James Peck, October 26, 1979, *Eyes on the Prize*, repository .wustl.edu/downloads/ww72bd261.

76 *W. W. "Red" Self called the Klan*: J. Mills Thornton III, *Dividing Lines: Municipal Politics and the*

Struggle for Civil Rights in Montgomery, Birmingham, and Selma (University of Alabama Press, 2002), 248.

77 *"This is the greatest thing"*: Quoted in Arsenault, *Freedom Riders*, 161.

77 *"Can't you get your goddamned friends off those buses?"*: Quoted in Arsenault, *Freedom Riders*, 164.

78 *this initial group of Riders formally disbanded*: "Chronology," ii, in "Special Report: The Freedom Ride," May 1961, Southern Regional Council, crmvet.org/riders/61_src_fr-may-r.pdf.

78 *"one of the most basic tenets"*: Lewis, *Walking with the Wind*, 143.

78 *"The message would have been sent"*: Interview with Diane Nash in *American Experience: Freedom Riders*.

78 *"That was a very dangerous thing to happen"*: Interview with Diane Nash, November 12, 1985, *Eyes on the Prize*, repository.wustl.edu/downloads/7m01bn67n.

78 *"The nonviolent strategy understands"*: Interview with Diane Nash, *Eyes on the Prize*.

79 *"We were fresh troops"*: Interview with Diane Nash in *American Experience: Freedom Riders*.

79 *"How do you want your body buried?"*: This and the subsequent Bevel quotations in this passage are from James Bevel with Randy Kryn, "Declaring Peace: James Bevel's 1960s Movements and Strategies; A Practical History and Guide to Nonviolence" (unpublished manuscript, 1988–2004), 38.

80 *"If you're in any type of leadership position"*: Quoted in Terry Gross, "Former Marine Says the Contradictions of War Can Make You Feel Insane," *Fresh Air*, NPR, November 11, 2021.

80 *"That's how prepared they were"*: Interview with Diane Nash, *Eyes on the Prize*.

80 *"Who the hell is Diane Nash?"*: Interview with John Seigenthaler in *American Experience: Freedom Riders*.

80 *a twenty-one-year-old college dropout*: Halberstam, *The Children*, 269.

80 *"people are going to be killed"*: Interview with Diane Nash in *American Experience: Freedom Riders*.

80 *if the initial Nashville Riders were killed*: Arsenault, *Freedom Riders*, 183.

80 *she had more volunteers on hand*: Arsenault, *Freedom Riders*, 185.

80 *"If you want to know"*: Harry Belafonte with Michael Shnayerson, *My Song: A Memoir of Art, Race and Defiance* (Vintage, 2011), 235.

81 *"She is going to get those people killed"*: Quoted in Lewis, *Walking with the Wind*, 145.

81 *the first and most important task*: Carl von Clausewitz, *On War*, ed. and trans. Michael Howard and Peter Paret (Princeton University Press, 1976), 88.

81 *"We were going to be rid of segregation"*: Interview with Diane Nash in *American Experience: Freedom Riders*.

81 *"Every one of you should"*: Quoted in Louis Fischer, *The Life of Mahatma Gandhi* (HarperCollins, 1997), 480.

81–82 *"IF YOU THINK FREE, YOU ARE FREE"*: "Ruby Doris Smith (Robinson)," SNCC Digital Gateway, snccdigital.org/people/ruby-doris-smith-robinson/.

82 *"Since we agreed"*: Bevel with Kryn, "Declaring Peace," 24.

82 *"like being at war"*: Interview with Diane Nash, *Eyes on the Prize*.

82 *when their Greyhound arrived*: Arsenault, *Freedom Riders*, 187.

83 *to wear down their opponents*: This paraphrases a comment by Diane Nash in "Non-Violence and the Quest for Civil Rights," March 29, 2003, JFK Library Symposium, 21.

84 *"And then, all of a sudden"*: Interview with Frederick Leonard, November 3, 1985, *Eyes on the Prize*, repository.wustl.edu/downloads/gx41mk838.

84 *"The moment we started"*: Interview with John Lewis, *Eyes on the Prize*.

84 *He tasted his own blood*: Halberstam, *The Children*, 31.

84 *"Everything turned white"*: Lewis, *Walking with the Wind*, 156.

84 *reciting Psalm 27*: John Blake, *Children of the Movement* (Lawrence Hill Books, 2004), 24–27.

84 *"You're going to get hurt"*: Quoted in Goduti, *Robert Kennedy and the Shaping of Civil Rights*, 77.

85 *"The president was mad"*: Interview with Burke Marshall, *Eyes on the Prize*.

85 *Robert Kennedy ordered a detachment*: Arsenault, *Freedom Riders*, 220. There is some difference in accounts about whether the federal marshals were being assembled before the attack on Seigenthaler, with Burke Marshall stating that the order came before the attack. But there appears to be no doubt that the attack moved the Kennedys toward direct intervention.

85 *Hearing the weapon's report*: Arsenault, *Freedom Riders*, 215.

85 *"I just put my pistol"*: Interview with Floyd Mann, *Eyes on the Prize*.

85 *a federal judge would conclude*: Catsam, *Freedom's Main Line*, 226.

85 *the Montgomery movement had been church-based*: Andrew Young, "And Birmingham," *Drum Major* (SCLC magazine), Winter 1971, 22.

86 *"I thought they were going to burn down the church"*: Quoted in Kisseloff, *Generation on Fire*, 29.

86 *"They began to throw tear gas"*: Interview with Floyd Mann, *Eyes on the Prize*.

86 *"It was a horrible night"*: Interview with Wyatt Walker by Andrew Manis, April 20, 1989, Oral Histories, Birmingham Public Library Digital Collections, transcript, bplonline.contentdm.oclc.org/digital/collection/p15099coll2/id/69.

86 *The English author Jessica Mitford*: Arsenault, *Freedom Riders*, 233.

87 *"Farmer was determined to share the spotlight"*: Arsenault, *Freedom Riders*, 225.

87 *"Please tell the attorney general"*: Farmer, *Lay Bare the Heart*, 206.

87 *"example of strong courageous action"*: Martin Luther King, Jr., "Address at Freedom Riders Rally at First Baptist Church," May 21, 1961, in *The Papers of Martin Luther King, Jr.*, vol. 7: *To Save the Soul of America, January 1961–August 1962*, ed. Clayborne Carson (University of California Press, 2014), 230–31.

88 *"Every human being has some defects"*: "Reminiscences of Bayard Rustin, 1987," Oral History Archives, Columbia University, 205.

88 *Heroes especially tend*: Jonathan Shay, *Odysseus in America: Combat Trauma and the Trials of Homecoming* (Scribner, 2002), 242.

88 *"I am very imperfect"*: Quoted in Fischer, *The Life of Mahatma Gandhi*, 464.

88 *"unacknowledged textual appropriations"*: Martin Luther King, Jr., Papers Project, "The Student Papers of Martin Luther King, Jr.: A Summary Statement on Research," *Journal of American History* 78, no. 1 (June 1991): 31.

88 *"chronic plagiarism"*: David Lewis, "Failing to Know Martin Luther King, Jr.," *Journal of American History* 78, no. 1 (June 1991): 81–85. For what it is worth, Patrick Parr makes it clear repeatedly in his study of King's years at seminary school that King frequently engaged in plagiarism during that phase in his education. Parr concludes that King's professors were not bothered by the obvious lifting of phrases, sentences, and even paragraphs. See Patrick Parr, *The Seminarian: Martin Luther King Jr. Comes of Age* (Lawrence Hill, 2018).

88 *"Jail is depressing"*: Martin Luther King, Jr., "Albany Jail Diary from 10 July–11 July 1962," in *Papers of Martin Luther King, Jr.*, 7:515.

88 *"almost paralyzing fear"*: Andrew Young, *An Easy Burden: The Civil Rights Movement and the Transformation of America* (Harper, 1996), 175.

89 *placed him in a straitjacket*: David Garrow, *Bearing the Cross: Martin Luther King, Jr., and the Southern Christian Leadership Conference* (William Morrow, 1986), 146.

89 *"He just broke down and cried"*: Quoted in Garrow, *Bearing the Cross*, 148.

89 *"a palace"*: Quoted in Fischer, *The Life of Mahatma Gandhi*, 542.

89 *"I am quite at peace"*: Quoted in Fischer, *The Life of Mahatma Gandhi*, 119.

89 *"He talked loud and big"*: The account of this meeting here and in the following paragraphs is largely based on John Lewis, *Walking with the Wind*, 163–64. There are similar accounts in Diane McWhorter, *Carry Me Home: Birmingham, Alabama; The Climactic Battle of the Civil Rights Revolution* (Simon & Schuster, 2012), 238, and in several memoirs of the Movement, such as James Farmer, *Lay Bare the Heart*, 207.

89 *"We'll have Freedom Rides"*: Bevel with Kryn, "Declaring Peace," 40.

90   *"Freedom Riders must develop"*: Quoted in Taylor Branch, *Parting the Waters: America in the King Years* (Simon & Schuster, 1988), 468.

91   *"He was one of the most impressive"*: Stokely Carmichael with Ekwueme Michael Thelwell, *Ready for Revolution: The Life and Struggles of Stokely Carmichael (Kwame Ture)* (Scribner, 2003), 156.

91   *"Several of the Freedom Riders"*: Arsenault, *Freedom Riders*, 255.

91   *In a renowned article*: Edward A. Shils and Morris Janowitz, "Cohesion and Disintegration in the Wehrmacht in World War II," *Public Opinion Quarterly* 12, no. 2 (Summer 1948): 280–315.

92   *six soldiers from the Alabama National Guard*: Halberstam, *The Children*, 332.

92   *"My prayers are with you"*: Farmer, *Lay Bare the Heart*, 3. The account here additionally relies on Lewis, *Walking with the Wind*, 166.

93   *"It was like a death kind of scene"*: Interview with Dave Dennis, November 10, 1985, *Eyes on the Prize*, repository.wustl.edu/downloads/dv13zv94x.

93   *"27 Mixers Jailed on Arrival Here"*: *Jackson (Mississippi) Clarion-Ledger*, May 25, 1961.

93   *"You're a black son of a bitch, aren't you?"*: Quoted in Etheridge, *Breach of Peace*, 213.

93   *"I saw one person"*: Interview with Dave Dennis, *Eyes on the Prize*.

93   *"It became almost a university"*: Interview with Raymond Arsenault in *American Experience: Freedom Riders*.

94   *political seminars, French classes*: Arsenault, *Freedom Riders*, 361.

94   *"You shut yo' mouth, boy"*: This and the other details in this paragraph are from Arsenault, *Freedom Riders*, 352–55.

94   *to hang prisoners from their cell bars by handcuffs*: Branch, *Pillar of Fire*, 117.

94   *"We must identify the traitors in our midst"*: Quoted in Michael Klarman, Brown v. Board of Education *and the Civil Rights Movement* (Oxford University Press, 2007), 321.

94   *The prosecutor offered a deal*: Arsenault, *Freedom Riders*, 372.

95   *fifteen Episcopal ministers*: Arsenault, *Freedom Riders*, 433.

95   *"The president is going abroad"*: Quoted in Goduti, *Robert Kennedy and the Shaping of Civil Rights*, 95.

95   *"You know, they don't understand"*: Quoted in Arsenault, *Freedom Riders*, 275.

96   *Kennedy instead had retreated*: A similar thought is expressed in Glenn T. Eskew, *But for Birmingham: The Local and National Movements in the Civil Rights Struggle* (University of North Carolina Press, 1997), 165.

96   *a petition he filed on May 29*: Arsenault, *Freedom Riders*, 292.

96   *"For all their talents, the Kennedy men"*: William Doyle, *An American Insurrection: James Meredith and the Battle of Oxford, Mississippi, 1962* (Anchor, 2003), 48.

96   *"a signal flare"*: Arsenault, *Freedom Riders*, 374.

96   *all CORE had to do*: Arsenault, *Freedom Riders*, 461–62, 475.

97   *"There won't be any integration in Georgia"*: Quoted in David L. Chappell, "The Divided Mind of Southern Segregationists," *Georgia Historical Quarterly* 82, no. 1 (Spring 1998): 45.

97   *75 percent of southern whites*: Chappell, "The Divided Mind of Southern Segregationists," 48.

97   *"a general immunity from arrest"*: David Chalmers, *Backfire: How the Ku Klux Klan Helped the Civil Rights Movement* (Rowman & Littlefield, 2005), 3.

97   *"Oppressive systems tend to be"*: Erica Chenoweth, *Civil Resistance: What Everyone Needs to Know* (Oxford University Press, 2021), 29.

98   *"outrage the sense of decency"*: Quoted in Arsenault, *Freedom Riders*, 420.

98   *"encouraging disobedience to any law"*: Quoted in Numan V. Bartley, *The Rise of Massive Resistance: Race and Politics in the South During the 1950's* (1969; repr. Louisiana State University Press, 1997), 211.

98   *"to make it difficult, if not impossible"*: Quoted in Neil R. McMillen, *The Citizens' Council: Organized Resistance to the Second Reconstruction, 1954–64* (University of Illinois Press, 1994), 209.

98   *By September, sixteen of them*: McMillen, *The Citizens' Council*, 210.

99   *"White people will be justified"*: Quoted in Garry Boulard, "'The Man' versus 'The Quisling': Theodore Bilbo, Hodding Carter, and the 1946 Democratic Primary," *Journal of Mississippi History* 51 (August 1989): 211.

99   *The first commercial stations*: John Egerton, *Speak Now Against the Day: The Generation Before the Civil Rights Movement in the South* (Alfred A. Knopf, 1994), 350.

99   *"Now you were having"*: Interview with Bayard Rustin, October 26, 1979, *Eyes on the Prize*, repository.wustl.edu/downloads/2r36v024m.

99   *"in the South, in the nonviolent movement"*: Unaired NBC News interview with Martin Luther King, Jr., in Atlanta, Georgia, May 8, 1967, YouTube, youtube.com/watch?v=2xsbt3a7K-8.

99–100   *In 1956, a judge in Alabama*: Patricia Sullivan, *Lift Every Voice: The NAACP and the Making of the Civil Rights Movement* (The New Press, 2009), 425.

100   *"In destroying the NAACP"*: McWhorter, *Carry Me Home*, 92.

100   *"Closing down the NAACP"*: McWhorter, *Carry Me Home*, 90.

100   *"It has been a policy of mine"*: Quoted in Arsenault, *Freedom Riders*, 444.

101   *One of the most notorious examples*: William Stewart, *Admirals of the World: A Biographical Dictionary, 1500 to the Present* (McFarland, 2009), 291.

101   *A Navy panel dominated by battleship admirals*: John Toland, *Infamy: Pearl Harbor and Its Aftermath* (Doubleday, 1982).

101   *the long history of southern white men*: McMillen, *The Citizens' Council*, 29–30.

101   *"The slaveholders had written"*: McWhorter, *Carry Me Home*, 205.

102   *"pick out a nigger girl and a horse"*: Quoted in Kenneth O'Reilly, *Nixon's Piano: Presidents and Racial Politics from Washington to Clinton* (The Free Press, 1995), 207.

102   *"never organized concerted, consistent propaganda"*: Chappell, "The Divided Mind of Southern Segregationists," 68–69.

102   *that cost calculation would begin to change*: This paraphrases a thought in Chappell, "The Divided Mind of Southern Segregationists," 48.

102   *"voluntary repatriation in Africa"*: McMillen, *The Citizens' Council*, 229.

103   *ban a children's book*: Michael Klarman, "Why Massive Resistance?," in *Massive Resistance: Southern Opposition to the Second Reconstruction*, ed. Clive Webb (Oxford University Press, 2005), 25.

103   *Black children in Jackson, Mississippi*: Branch, *Parting the Waters*, 826.

103   *"I felt that I wanted to check them out"*: Interview with Hollis Watkins, November 9, 1985, *Eyes on the Prize*, repository.wustl.edu/downloads/9z903175z.

104   *"It was the first time"*: Interview with Diane Nash in *American Experience: Freedom Riders*.

104   *A study of roll call votes*: Bartley, *The Rise of Massive Resistance*, 150.

105   *"I could see that discipline eroding"*: Lewis, *Walking with the Wind*, 176–77.

105   *a premed student from Howard University*: Carmichael with Thelwell, *Ready for Revolution*, 155.

105   *"outright daring the white hecklers"*: Lewis, *Walking with the Wind*, 177.

105   *"we booted him out of Nashville"*: Interview with James Lawson by Joan Beifuss and David Yellin, January 21, 1969, "Sanitation Strike Tapes," Memphis and the Mid-South Files, Rhodes College Digital Archives, dlynx.rhodes.edu/jspui/bitstream/10267/33928/4/SS269_transcript.pdf.

105   *Carmichael's own recollection*: Carmichael with Thelwell, *Ready for Revolution*, 239–40.

105   *he seriously considered playing the role of a U.S. senator*: Papers of Martin Luther King, Jr., 7:314n4. See also Garrow, *Bearing the Cross*, 169.

4. The Albany Movement, 1961–1962

108   *"I couldn't do anything in Terrell County"*: "The Reminiscences of Charles Sherrod," May 12, 1985, Student Movements of the 1960s, Oral History Research Office, Columbia University, 48.

108 *"They had nothing else to do"*: "The Reminiscences of Charles Sherrod," 50.

108 *"The goals of the Albany movement"*: Aldon D. Morris, *The Origins of the Civil Rights Movement: Black Communities Organizing for Change* (The Free Press, 1984), 241.

108 *"Some of us really didn't think"*: Interview with Charles Sherrod, conducted by Blackside, Inc., December 20, 1985, for *Eyes on the Prize: America's Civil Rights Years (1954–1965)*, Washington University Libraries, Film and Media Archive, Henry Hampton Collection, transcript, repository.wustl.edu/downloads/tx31qk696.

109 *"So when these mass marches started"*: Interview with Laurie Pritchett, November 7, 1985, *Eyes on the Prize*, repository.wustl.edu/downloads/8w32r7368.

110 *Together, these three steps*: This sentence reflects a thought in Adam Fairclough, "Martin Luther King, Jr. and the Quest for Nonviolent Social Change," *Phylon* 47, no. 1 (Spring 1986): 6.

110 *"days and days of uneventful protest"*: John Lewis, *Walking with the Wind: A Memoir of the Movement* (Simon & Schuster, 2015), 320.

110 *"We ran out of people"*: Quoted in Pat Watters, *Down to Now: Reflections on the Southern Civil Rights Movement* (University of Georgia Press, 1993), 206.

110 *While they were out of touch*: Interview with Charles Sherrod, *Eyes on the Prize*.

110 *"We were in a situation"*: Quoted in Morris, *Origins of the Civil Rights Movement*, 242.

110 *He called an old schoolmate*: Morris, *Origins of the Civil Rights Movement*, 243.

111 *"Martin felt like he'd been put in a trick"*: Andrew Young, *An Easy Burden: The Civil Rights Movement and the Transformation of America* (HarperCollins, 1996), 168.

111 *Pritchett told him that the telegram*: Interview with Laurie Pritchett, *Eyes on the Prize*.

111 *the Gandhian principle*: Krishnalal Shridharani, *War Without Violence: A Study of Gandhi's Method and Its Accomplishments* (Victor Gollancz, 1939), 221–22.

111 *Gandhi's followers once had postponed*: Joan Bondurant, *Conquest of Violence: The Gandhian Philosophy of Conflict* (Princeton University Press, 1988), 120.

112 *"a spontaneous appearance"*: Interview with Rev. Andrew Young, October 11, 1985, *Eyes on the Prize*, repository.wustl.edu/downloads/nk322g272.

112 *The city then offered an unwritten "truce"*: Here I follow the account in Morris, *Origins of the Civil Rights Movement*, 246.

112 *King told reporters*: Taylor Branch, *Parting the Waters: America in the King Years* (Simon & Schuster, 1988), 550–51.

113 *"Many people misunderstand your policy"*: Quoted in Watters, *Down to Now*, 205. For similar account, see Branch, *Parting the Waters*, 205.

113 *"a sophisticated segregationist"*: Interview with Ralph Abernathy, November 6, 1985, *Eyes on the Prize*, repository.wustl.edu/downloads/vx021g754.

113 *"a cunning man"*: Lewis, *Walking with the Wind*, 185.

113 *"took the leap"*: Young, *An Easy Burden*, 178.

113 *"I knew that if he stayed in jail"*: Interview with Laurie Pritchett, *Eyes on the Prize*.

113 *"the moral means of nonviolence"*: Martin Luther King, Jr., *Why We Can't Wait* (1964; repr. Signet, 2000), 82.

113 *After that third arrest in Albany*: "Albany Movement," *The King Encyclopedia*, Stanford University, kinginstitute.stanford.edu/encyclopedia/albany-movement.

113 *"In the end, the Albany movement"*: Young, *An Easy Burden*, 181.

114 *"Dr. King vowed to refuse bail"*: Barry Everett Lee, "The Nashville Civil Rights Movement: A Study of the Phenomenon of Intentional Leadership Development and Its Consequences for Local Movements and the National Civil Rights Movement" (PhD diss., Georgia State University, 2010), 280.

114 *"In Albany, we were like firefighters"*: Interview with Wyatt Tee Walker, October 11, 1985, *Eyes on the Prize*, repository.wustl.edu/downloads/7s75df107.

114 *"People who had done the fighting"*: Quoted in Watters, *Down to Now*, 147.

115 *"When Martin left Albany, he was very depressed"*: Interview with Rev. Andrew Young, *Eyes on the Prize*.

115 *"We needed to make certain mistakes"*: Interview with Charles Sherrod, *Eyes on the Prize*.

115 *"We were inexperienced as civil rights activists"*: Interview with Dr. William G. Anderson, November 7, 1985, *Eyes on the Prize*, repository.wustl.edu/downloads/5h73px82v.

116 *"The mistake I made there"*: "*Playboy* Interview: Martin Luther King, Jr.," January 1965, in *A Testament of Hope: The Essential Writings and Speeches of Martin Luther King, Jr.*, ed. James Melvin Washington (1986; repr. HarperCollins, 1991), 343.

116 *"When we planned our strategy"*: Martin Luther King, Jr., "Chapter 16: The Albany Movement," in *The Autobiography of Martin Luther King, Jr.*, ed. Clayborne Carson (Warner, 2001), 168.

116 *"Just think of how much"*: Septima Clark, *Ready from Within: Septima Clark and the Civil Rights Movement* (Wild Trees Press, 1986), 103.

116 *"passion and enthusiasm"*: Young, *An Easy Burden*, 184.

5. Ole Miss, 1962

117 *the son of a Confederate veteran*: Patricia Sullivan, *Justice Rising: Robert Kennedy's America in Black and White* (Belknap, 2021), 133.

117 *"I want to register at the university"*: Quoted in William Doyle, *An American Insurrection: James Meredith and the Battle of Oxford, Mississippi, 1962* (Anchor, 2003), 75. This chapter relies foremost on Doyle's compelling and detailed book.

118 *Thurgood Marshall tried to determine*: Michael Williams, *Medgar Evers: Mississippi Martyr* (University of Arkansas Press, 2011), 218.

119 *"I was at war"*: Doyle, *An American Insurrection*, 34.

119 *"He's got more guts"*: Doyle, *An American Insurrection*, 32.

119 *"I have never made a mistake in my life"*: James Meredith, *Three Years in Mississippi* (Indiana University Press, 1966), 21.

119 *"the romance, the chivalry"*: Charles Eagles, *The Price of Defiance: James Meredith and the Integration of Ole Miss* (University of North Carolina Press, 2009), 18.

120 *"the land of mint juleps"*: Eagles, *The Price of Defiance*, 24.

120 *enrolling there was forbidden*: Doyle, *An American Insurrection*, 24.

120 *Two Black Mississippians had tried before*: Frank Lambert, *The Battle of Ole Miss: Civil Rights v. States' Rights* (Oxford University Press, 2010), 5.

120 *to the state penitentiary*: Lambert, *The Battle of Ole Miss*, 62.

120 *"I'm bluffing. But you wait and see"*: Doyle, *An American Insurrection*, 77.

120 *"He knew that Meredith was going"*: Interview with Burke Marshall, conducted by Blackside, Inc., November 4, 1985, for *Eyes on the Prize: America's Civil Rights Years (1954–1965)*, Washington University Libraries, Film and Media Archive, Henry Hampton Collection, transcript, repository.wustl.edu/downloads/v405sc266.

121 *"I love Mississippi!"*: Doyle, *An American Insurrection*, 113.

121 *"I have to be confronted with your troops"*: Doyle, *An American Insurrection*, 121.

122 *A force of 125 U.S. deputy marshals*: Paul J. Scheips, *The Role of Federal Military Forces in Domestic Disorders, 1945–1992* (Center of Military History, U.S. Army, 2005), 101.

123 *"You have occupied this university"*: Lambert, *The Battle of Ole Miss*, 120.

123 *preparing to order the state highway patrolmen*: Nicholas Katzenbach, *Some of It Was Fun: Working with RFK and LBJ* (W. W. Norton, 2008), 76.

123 *"As soon as the highway patrol drove out"*: Interview with Nicholas Katzenbach, December 10, 1985, *Eyes on the Prize*, repository.wustl.edu/downloads/4m90dx18d.

123 *"Katzenbach decided simply to line his men up"*: Doyle, *An American Insurrection*, 132.

123   *"to get mean and get ugly"*: Interview with John Doar, November 15, 1985, *Eyes on the Prize*, repository.wustl.edu/downloads/s1784n301.

123   *"We were sent in unprepared"*: Quoted in Doyle, *An American Insurrection*, 129.

123   *"a public-address truck"*: Doyle, *An American Insurrection*, 141.

124   *"the scene became a nightmare"*: Quoted in Michael Durham, *Powerful Days: The Civil Rights Photography of Charles Moore* (Stewart, Tabori & Chang, 1991), 17. For more on the scene on the campus at this point, see Eagles, *The Price of Defiance*, 351–52, 354.

124   *the marshals began to respond with tear gas*: Lambert, *The Battle of Ole Miss*, 120.

125   *"Keep it up all night"*: Doyle, *An American Insurrection*, 168.

125   *"Getting the Army from Memphis to Oxford"*: Katzenbach, *Some of It Was Fun*, 78.

125   *Falkner and his little convoy of three jeeps*: This and subsequent details in this paragraph are from Scheips, *The Role of Federal Military Forces in Domestic Disorders*, 105–108.

126   *"I haven't had such an interesting time"*: Quoted in Jonathan Rosenberg and Zachary Karabell, *Kennedy, Johnson, and the Quest for Justice: The Civil Rights Tapes* (W. W. Norton, 2003), 66.

126   *"Damn Army!"*: Rosenberg and Karabell, *Kennedy, Johnson, and the Quest for Justice*, 73.

127   *"had no feeling of elation"*: Interview with John Doar, *Eyes on the Prize*.

127   *Kennedy had General Walker arrested*: Scheips, *The Role of Federal Military Forces in Domestic Disorders*, 118.

127   *The president also contemplated*: Rosenberg and Karabell, *Kennedy, Johnson, and the Quest for Justice*, 83.

127   *"Neither you nor Bobby"*: Katzenbach, *Some of It Was Fun*, 84.

127–28   *"very naïve about the South"*: Andrew Young oral history transcript, June 18, 1970, Lyndon B. Johnson Library, I-3.

128   *a judge in Mississippi*: Taylor Branch, *Pillar of Fire: America in the King Years, 1963–1965* (Simon & Schuster, 1998), 55–56.

128   *the SCLC hired Bevel*: "Press Release, Statement on Intensified Voter Registration Drive," *The Papers of Martin Luther King, Jr.*, vol. 7: *To Save the Soul of America*, ed. Clayborne Carson (University of California Press, 2014), 433–34.

128   *"We waited for the people of Mississippi"*: James Bevel with Randy Kryn, "Declaring Peace: James Bevel's 1960s Movements and Strategies; A Practical History and Guide to Nonviolence" (unpublished manuscript, 1988–2004), 44–46.

129   *"You are witnessing one more chapter"*: Ross Barnett, in "The American Revolution of '63," NBC News special report, September 2, 1963.

129   *"If Congress can make canals"*: Quoted in Thomas E. Ricks, *First Principles: What America's Founders Learned from the Greeks and Romans and How That Shaped Our Country* (Harper, 2020), 289.

130   *"Why doesn't somebody kill him?"*: Quoted in Scheips, *The Role of Federal Military Forces in Domestic Disorders*, 122.

130   *He was generally shunned in the cafeteria*: Eagles, *The Price of Defiance*, 373.

130   *undergraduates would bounce basketballs*: Eagles, *The Price of Defiance*, 387.

130   *The tires on his car were slashed*: Scheips, *The Role of Federal Military Forces in Domestic Disorders*, 129.

130   *"Most of the time, I am perhaps"*: Lambert, *The Battle of Ole Miss*, 138.

130   *the editors of the college yearbook*: Lambert, *The Battle of Ole Miss*, 144.

130   *"prisoner of war"*: Eagles, *The Price of Defiance*, 374.

131   *all three branches would finally focus*: This sentence was inspired by a comment in Harris Wofford, *Of Kennedys and Kings: Making Sense of the Sixties* (Farrar, Straus & Giroux, 1980), 103.

6. Early Birmingham, Spring 1963

133   *"By '63 we were pretty confident"*: Interview with James Bevel, conducted by Blackside, Inc., November 13, 1985, for *Eyes on the Prize: America's Civil Rights Years (1954–1965)*, Washing-

ton University Libraries, Film and Media Archive, Henry Hampton Collection, transcript, repository.wustl.edu/downloads/9306t101z.

133   *Birmingham minister Fred Shuttlesworth*: Glenn T. Eskew, *But for Birmingham: The Local and National Movements in the Civil Rights Struggle* (University of North Carolina Press, 1997), 211–12.

134   *"If you can break the back"*: Quoted in Andrew Manis, *A Fire You Can't Put Out: The Civil Rights Life of Birmingham's Reverend Fred Shuttlesworth* (University of Alabama Press, 2002), 332.

134   *"Some of us are going to lose"*: Quoted in Andrew Young, *An Easy Burden: The Civil Rights Movement and the Transformation of America* (Harper, 1996), 194.

134   *a 1930 ordinance made it illegal*: Manning Marable, *Black American Politics: From the Washington Marches to Jesse Jackson* (Verso, 1985), 76.

134   *"far more learned than Fred Shuttlesworth"*: Interview with J. L. Chestnut by Andrew Manis, December 27, 1989, Oral Histories, Birmingham Public Library Digital Collections, transcript, cdm16044.contentdm.oclc.org/digital/collection/p15099coll2/id/74.

134   *"We believe that if we stand"*: Fred Shuttlesworth, "A Call for Reason, Sanity, and Righteous Perseverance in a Critical Hour," June 5, 1962, in *Rhetoric, Religion, and the Civil Rights Movement, 1954–1965*, ed. Davis Houck and David Dixon (Baylor University Press, 2006), 467–68.

135   *"less than the average railroad worker"*: Eskew, *But for Birmingham*, 95.

135   *The police were regarded*: Horace Huntley and John McKerley, eds., *Foot Soldiers for Democracy: The Men, Women, and Children of the Birmingham Civil Rights Movement* (University of Illinois Press, 2009), 29.

135   *In 1954, a burglary ring*: Eskew, *But for Birmingham*, 96.

135   *A reformist Birmingham police chief*: J. Mills Thornton III, *Dividing Lines: Municipal Politics and the Struggle for Civil Rights in Montgomery, Birmingham, and Selma* (University of Alabama Press, 2002), 179.

135–36 *"The Birmingham Police Department"*: "James Roberson," in Huntley and McKerley, *Foot Soldiers for Democracy*, 113.

136   *One policeman alone, James Albert Hale*: Margaret Burnham et al., "Police Killings in Jefferson County, Alabama, 1930–1970," Civil Rights and Restorative Justice Project (Northwestern University School of Law, 2020), 11.

136   *In 1951, the city's police*: Patricia Sullivan, *Lift Every Voice: The NAACP and the Making of the Civil Rights Movement* (The New Press, 2009), 397.

136   *"terrorized the community"*: "Washington Booker III," in Huntley and McKerley, *Foot Soldiers for Democracy*, 190.

136   *In March 1960, after a handful*: Eskew, *But for Birmingham*, 148–49.

136   *"We planned to go into Birmingham"*: Young, *An Easy Burden*, 202.

137   *The people getting off the bus*: Katherine Charron, *Freedom's Teacher: The Life of Septima Clark* (University of North Carolina Press, 2009), 310–11.

137   *"It is our duty to dress them first"*: M. K. Gandhi, "My Loin-Cloth," in *The Collected Works of Mahatma Gandhi*, vol. 28, BJP e-Library, library.bjp.org/jspui/handle/123456789/597, 369–71. A similar quotation appears in Joseph Lelyveld, *Great Soul: Mahatma Gandhi and His Struggle with India* (Vintage, 2012), 163.

137   *Funded in large part by the Marshall Field Foundation*: Information on funding is from Interview with Dorothy Cotton, Civil Rights History Project, Southern Oral History Program Collection, University of North Carolina at Chapel Hill, 32.

137   *They focused on counties*: Young, *An Easy Burden*, 143.

138   *"What we used to look for"*: Quoted in Eliot Wigginton, ed., *Refuse to Stand Silently By: An Oral History of Grass Roots Social Activism in America, 1921–1964* (Doubleday, 1991), 282.

138   *Soon after arriving at Dorchester*: This and the following four paragraphs summarize the rich

account in Dorothy Cotton, *If Your Back's Not Bent: The Role of the Citizenship Education Program in the Civil Rights Movement* (Atria Books, 2012), 115–37.

139 *Fannie Lou Hamer, who attended a session*: Information on Hamer's attendance and what was taught at Dorchester is from Kay Mills, *This Little Light of Mine: The Life of Fannie Lou Hamer* (University Press of Kentucky, 2007), 53–55.

139 *seven or eight thousand people*: For "seven thousand," see Interview with Dorothy Cotton, Civil Rights History Project. For "eight thousand," see Cotton, *If Your Back's Not Bent*, 112.

139 *"get in trouble with the local authorities"*: Interview with Andrew Young, June 18, 1970, Oral Histories Collection, Lyndon B. Johnson Library, I-7.

140 *"Abernathy was his brother"*: Interview with Wyatt Walker by Andrew Manis, April 20, 1989, Oral Histories, Birmingham Public Library Digital Collections, transcript, bplonline .contentdm.oclc.org/digital/collection/p15099coll2/id/69.

140 *"When people get irrational"*: Interview with Andrew Young, in Peter W. Kunhardt, dir., *King in the Wilderness* (Kunhardt Film Foundation, 2018), transcript, kunhardtfilmfoundation.org /featured-interviews/andrew-young.

140 *"to come down in the middle"*: Interview with Rev. Andrew Young, October 11, 1985, *Eyes on the Prize*, repository.wustl.edu/downloads/nk322g272.

140 *"You had an executive staff"*: Quoted in Howell Raines, *My Soul Is Rested: Movement Days in the Deep South Remembered* (Penguin Books, 1983), 447.

141 *President Kennedy saw a photograph*: Taylor Branch, *Pillar of Fire: America in the King Years, 1963–1965* (Simon & Schuster, 1998), 69–71.

141 *the civil rights bill that Kennedy proposed*: Julian Zelizer, *The Fierce Urgency of Now: Lyndon Johnson, Congress, and the Battle for the Great Society* (Penguin Press, 2019), 41.

141 *Implementing a classic*: This paragraph summarizes Joan Bondurant, *Conquest of Violence: The Gandhian Philosophy of Conflict* (Princeton University Press, 1988), 40–41.

142 *"function as a part of a national network"*: Andrew Young, "And Birmingham," *Drum Major* (SCLC magazine), Winter 1971, 23–24. The quotations from Young in the following two paragraphs are from the same part of this article.

143 *according to Ralph Abernathy*: Diane McWhorter, *Carry Me Home: Birmingham, Alabama: The Climactic Battle of the Civil Rights Revolution* (Simon & Schuster, 2012), 317.

143 *"they were not going to change"*: Young, *An Easy Burden*, 205.

144 *"We just wanna know"*: Quoted in Raines, *My Soul Is Rested*, 156.

144 *"Birmingham is part of the United States"*: "Birmingham Manifesto," April 3, 1963, Civil Rights Movement Archive, crmvet.org/docs/bhammanf.htm.

144 *"secondary targets"*: Interview with Wyatt Tee Walker, October 11, 1985, *Eyes on the Prize*, repository.wustl.edu/downloads/7s75df107.

145 *Of the four hundred Black churches*: Young, *An Easy Burden*, 209. See also Eskew, *But for Birmingham*, 219.

145 *"doggedness, his tenacity"*: Interview with Wyatt Walker by Andrew Manis, Birmingham Public Library Digital Collections.

145 *only sixty-five locals attended*: Alan Westin and Barry Mahony, *The Trial of Martin Luther King* (Crowell, 1974), 67.

145 *parading without a permit*: Thornton, *Dividing Lines*, 292.

145 *King spoke to 125 Black ministers*: Thornton, *Dividing Lines*, 300.

145 *The number of the jailed did not increase much*: Huntley and McKerley, *Foot Soldiers for Democracy*, xxvi–xxix.

146 *"The demonstrations . . . reached rock bottom"*: William Kunstler, *Deep in My Heart* (William Morrow, 1966), 189.

146 *To increase the count a bit*: Interview with Wyatt Tee Walker, March 18, 1964, Robert Penn

Warren's Who Speaks for the Negro?: An Archival Collection, Vanderbilt University Library, tape 3, whospeaks.library.vanderbilt.edu/interview/wyatt-tee-walker.

146 *King's speeches often went unnoticed*: Taylor Branch, *Parting the Waters: America in the King Years* (Simon & Schuster, 1988), 599–600.

147 *In his treatise on guerrilla warfare*: Che Guevara, *Guerrilla Warfare* (University of Nebraska Press, 1998), 82–83.

147 *"The enemy . . . collected and tightly controlled"*: Quoted in Thomas E. Ricks, *The Generals: American Military Command from World War II to Today* (Penguin Press, 2012), 322.

147 *In 1963, he raised some $400,000*: Interview with Wyatt Tee Walker, Robert Penn Warren's Who Speaks for the Negro?

147 *"If you go to jail, we are lost"*: Quoted in Martin Luther King, Jr., *Why We Can't Wait* (1964; repr. Signet, 2000), 81. The quotations from King in this and the next paragraph are from this page.

148 *"not knowing how"*: Interview with Rev. Andrew Young, *Eyes on the Prize*.

148 *Even on this day*: David Garrow, *Bearing the Cross: Martin Luther King, Jr., and the Southern Christian Leadership Conference* (William Morrow, 1986), 242.

148 *"in a nightmare of despair"*: "*Playboy* Interview: Martin Luther King, Jr.," January 1965, in *A Testament of Hope: The Essential Writings and Speeches of Martin Luther King, Jr.*, ed. James Melvin Washington (1986; repr. HarperCollins, 1991), 376.

149 *"Frankly, I have yet to engage"*: Martin Luther King, Jr., "Letter from Birmingham Jail," in *Why We Can't Wait*, 91.

149 *"I have been gravely disappointed with the white moderate"*: King, "Letter from Birmingham Jail," 96–97.

150 *"I have been so greatly disappointed with the white church"*: King, "Letter from Birmingham Jail," 104–107.

150 *"even if our motives"*: King, "Letter from Birmingham Jail," 108.

150 *"I have tried to make it clear"*: King, "Letter from Birmingham Jail," 110.

151 *An assignment editor*: Margalit Fox, "Harvey Shapiro, Poet and Editor, Dies at 88," *New York Times*, January 7, 2013.

152 *"guerilla warriors for preservation of the order"*: Quoted in Raines, *My Soul Is Rested*, 180.

152 *"The pope! How many divisions does he have?"*: For one version of Stalin's question, see Fred Coleman, *The Decline and Fall of the Soviet Empire* (St. Martin's, 1996), 272.

152 *"We attempted to plan our demonstrations"*: Young, *An Easy Burden*, 225.

152 *only ten people volunteered*: McWhorter, *Carry Me Home*, 339.

152 *"We needed more troops"*: Quoted in Stephen Oates, *Let the Trumpet Sound: The Life of Martin Luther King, Jr.* (Harper & Row, 1982), 232.

152 *"We've got to get something going"*: Quoted in Garrow, *Bearing the Cross*, 247.

153 *Historians often depict Bevel*: See, for example, Adam Fairclough, *To Redeem the Soul of America: The Southern Christian Leadership Conference and Martin Luther King, Jr.* (University of Georgia Press, 1987), 125.

153 *"human hurricane"*: John Lewis, *Walking with the Wind: A Memoir of the Movement* (Simon & Schuster, 2015), 79.

153 *"loved nothing more than stirring the pot"*: Lewis, *Walking with the Wind*, 61.

153 *"the seventh son"*: James Bevel with Randy Kryn, "Declaring Peace: James Bevel's 1960s Movements and Strategies; A Practical History and Guide to Nonviolence" (unpublished manuscript, 1988–2004), 7.

154 *"You think these white folks"*: Quoted in Branch, *Pillar of Fire*, 126.

154 *"You know, whenever God's people go to church"*: Bevel with Kryn, "Declaring Peace," 78.

154 *"One should get joy out of making decisions"*: Quoted in Julius Lester, "Political Psychiatry: An Interview with James Bevel," *Evergreen Review* 15, no. 89 (May 1971): 48.

155 *"The act of nonviolent protest"*: Peter Singer to author, email, September 30, 2021.

155 *he began by seeking out two disc jockeys*: McWhorter, *Carry Me Home*, 341–43. Some additional details come from Bevel with Kryn, "Declaring Peace," 62.

155 *"I PLEDGE MYSELF"*: King, *Why We Can't Wait*, 67–68.

156 *"They trained us to understand strategy and discipline"*: Freeman Hrabowski III, *Holding Fast to Dreams: Empowering Youth from the Civil Rights Crusade to STEM Achievement* (Beacon Press, 2015), 38.

156 *required volunteers to sign formal pledges*: Gene Sharp, *Gandhi as a Political Strategist* (Porter Sargent Publishers, 1979), 99.

156 *Every child who marched had been trained*: "Kenneth B. Clark Interview," in *A Testament of Hope: The Essential Writings and Speeches of Martin Luther King, Jr.*, ed. James Melvin Washington (1986; repr. HarperCollins, 1991), 337.

156 *"If we don't do this, we might wind up"*: Bevel with Kryn, "Declaring Peace," 62.

156 *Parents getting wind of their children's plans*: This distinction in parental oversight is discussed in Gisell Jeter-Bennett, "'We're Going Too!': The Children of the Birmingham Civil Rights Movement" (PhD diss., The Ohio State University, 2016), ProQuest Dissertations Publishing, 136.

156 *"a party at the park"*: Manis, *A Fire You Can't Put Out*, 369. See also Don Keith, *Mattie C.'s Boy: The Shelley Stewart Story* (NewSouth Books, 2013), 240.

156 *"They just poured in"*: "Jimmie Lucille Spencer Hooks," in Huntley and McKerley, *Foot Soldiers for Democracy*, 22.

156 *"He still had his doubts"*: Bevel with Kryn, "Declaring Peace," 70.

157 *"flexibility of maneuver"*: See, for example, James Marshall-Cornwall, *Napoleon as Military Commander* (Penguin, 2002), 55.

157 *"You always left with a euphoric feeling"*: "Shirley Smith Miller," in Huntley and McKerley, *Foot Soldiers for Democracy*, 183.

157 *"We were never just sent out"*: "Gwendolyn Sanders Gamble," in Huntley and McKerley, *Foot Soldiers for Democracy*, 145.

157 *Ultimately, more than one thousand children*: Aldon Morris, "Birmingham Confrontation Reconsidered: An Analysis of the Dynamics and Tactics of Mobilization," *American Sociological Review* 58, no. 5 (October 1992): 629.

158 *Bevel also had made*: Interview with James Bevel, *Eyes on the Prize*.

158 *"I have been inspired and moved today"*: Quoted in Eskew, *But for Birmingham*, 265. Eskew's source, interestingly, was a Birmingham police department report on the meeting.

158 *"We were taught to sit down"*: "Annetta Streeter Gary," in Huntley and McKerley, *Foot Soldiers for Democracy*, 120.

159 *"It was very painful"*: "Carolyn Maull McKinstry," in Huntley and McKerley, *Foot Soldiers for Democracy*, 155.

159 *"When they brought the dogs in, we ran"*: "Shirley Smith Miller," in Huntley and McKerley, *Foot Soldiers for Democracy*, 184.

159 *"News photographs of the violence"*: Branch, *Pillar of Fire*, 77.

159 *"We're not going to have violence"*: Interview with James Bevel, *Eyes on the Prize*.

159 *"An injured, maimed or dead child"*: Quoted in "Robert Kennedy Warns of 'Increasing Turmoil'; Deplores Denials of Negroes' Rights but Questions Timing of Protests in Birmingham," *New York Times*, May 4, 1963, 8.

160 *"What do you want, little Nigra?"*: Hrabowski, *Holding Fast to Dreams*, 41.

160 *"I went and stood in front of the girl"*: Quoted in Raines, *My Soul Is Rested*, 146–47.

160 *Swindle did not pass along that instruction*: McWhorter, *Carry Me Home*, 369.

161 *"security force defections"*: Erica Chenoweth, *Civil Resistance: What Everyone Needs to Know* (Oxford University Press, 2021), 100.

161 *"They would ask silly questions"*: "Audrey Faye Hendricks," in Huntley and McKerley, *Foot Soldiers for Democracy*, 211.

161   *"That was pretty frightening"*: Interview with David J. Vann, November 1, 1985, *Eyes on the Prize*, repository.wustl.edu/downloads/qb98mg93f.

161   *Birmingham's first suburban shopping center*: McWhorter, *Carry Me Home*, 364.

162   *Bevel launched Operation Confusion*: Manis, *A Fire You Can't Put Out*, 376–77.

162   *"Let's put some water on the reverend"*: Bud Schultz and Ruth Schultz, *The Price of Dissent: Testimonies to Political Repression in America* (University of California Press, 2001), 183. See also Manis, *A Fire You Can't Put Out*, 378.

162   *"We thought they had killed him"*: "Joe N. Dickson," in Huntley and McKerley, *Foot Soldiers for Democracy*, 75.

162   *"I wish they'd carried him away in a hearse"*: Quoted in McWhorter, *Carry Me Home*, 387.

163   *"You've been Mister Big"*: Quoted in McWhorter, *Carry Me Home*, 397. Similar accounts of this exchange are in Garrow, *Bearing the Cross*, and Eskew, *But for Birmingham*, among other books.

163   *"We had a little confrontation"*: Interview with Rev. Andrew Young, *Eyes on the Prize*.

163   *"Fred took the call"*: Young, *An Easy Burden*, 247.

163   *"All basic disagreements"*: Casey Hayden, "In the Attics of My Mind," in *Hands on the Freedom Plow: Personal Accounts by Women in SNCC*, ed. Faith S. Holsaert et al. (University of Illinois Press, 2012), 386.

164   *"I think conflict can be very healthy"*: Interview with Diane Nash, July 7, 1983, David Garrow Research Files #832, 37–38. Courtesy of David Garrow and Jonathan Eig.

164   *"the ugly situation"*: "News Conference 55, May 8, 1963," John F. Kennedy Presidential Library and Museum, jfklibrary.org/archives/other-resources/john-f-kennedy-press-conferences/news-conference-55.

164   *one should be inflexible in means*: Bondurant, *Conquest of Violence*, 34.

165   *"You know what's the trouble with this country?"*: From "Freedom Now!: Birmingham, Alabama, 1963," Pacifica Radio documentary, Civil Rights Movement Archive, crmvet.org/info/bham63.htm.

165   *"I don't think Fred saw the larger picture"*: Interview with C. T. Vivian by Andrew Manis, December 27, 1989, Oral Histories, Birmingham Public Library Digital Collections, transcript, bplonline.contentdm.oclc.org/digital/collection/p15099coll2/id/66.

165   *"They were doing a lot of talking"*: Quoted in Fred Powledge, *Free at Last?: The Civil Rights Movement and the People Who Made It* (Little, Brown, 1991), 80.

165   *In May 1963, for the first time, the Gallup poll*: Doug McAdam, *Freedom Summer* (Oxford University Press, 1988), 150.

165   *"whilst he is ever ready for fight"*: M. K. Gandhi, *Non-Violent Resistance (Satyagraha)* (1961; repr. Dover, 2001), 278.

166   *"I'm not going to guard him"*: Interview with Laurie Pritchett, November 7, 1985, *Eyes on the Prize*, repository.wustl.edu/downloads/8w32r7368.

166   *"That was just like putting gas on the fire"*: Interview with Sheriff Mel Bailey, November 2, 1985, *Eyes on the Prize*, repository.wustl.edu/downloads/jm214q935.

166   *On May 11, 1963, the Gaston Motel*: "The A.G. Gaston Motel and the Birmingham Civil Rights National Monument," National Park Service, U.S. Department of the Interior.

166   *"We know they were done"*: From "Freedom Now!: Birmingham, Alabama, 1963."

166   *"Dogs can't stop us"*: From "Freedom Now!: Birmingham, Alabama, 1963."

167   *"We heard the motor of the car coming in"*: Interview with Myrlie Evers, November 27, 1985, *Eyes on the Prize*, repository.wustl.edu/downloads/05741t61g.

167   *The bullet . . . had passed through him*: Michael Williams, *Medgar Evers: Mississippi Martyr* (University of Arkansas Press, 2011), 271.

167   *"Just events are making our problems"*: Quoted in Branch, *Parting the Waters*, 828.

167   *Kennedy proposed a new civil rights bill*: The account in this paragraph relies heavily on the account given in Zelizer, *The Fierce Urgency of Now*.

167 *More than 700 demonstrations*: Branch, *Parting the Waters*, 825.
167 *Corporate America threw its weight*: Harvard Sitkoff, *The Struggle for Black Equality* (1981; repr. Hill and Wang, 2008), 144.
168 *"We started with one lunch counter a day"*: Young, *An Easy Burden*, 250.
168 *"he had been thinking"*: Interview with Diane Nash, July 7, 1983, David Garrow Research Files #832, 21–22. Courtesy of David Garrow and Jonathan Eig.
168 *"just like the 1930 march in India"*: Bevel with Kryn, "Declaring Peace," 75.
169 *In January 1963, he had asked his old friend*: William Jones, *The March on Washington: Jobs, Freedom, and the Forgotten History of Civil Rights* (W. W. Norton, 2013), 160–61.
169 *"We are on the threshold"*: Quoted in Garrow, *Bearing the Cross*, 265.
169 *"We are ready to go on a national level"*: Quoted in Branch, *Pillar of Fire*, 102.
169 *"agreed that it would take"*: Branch, *Pillar of Fire*, 102.
169 *King was even thinking about conducting sit-ins*: Jones, *The March on Washington*, 167.

7. The March on Washington, Mid-1963

171 *"Amateurs talk tactics"*: See, for example, Barrett Tillman, *D-Day Encyclopedia: Everything You Want to Know About the Normandy Invasion* (Regnery, 2014).
171 Etappenschweine: David Moore, "Logistics," in *The Oxford Companion to Military History*, ed. Richard Holmes (Oxford University Press, 2001), 515.
172 *"be the spark"*: Quoted in Lucy Barber, *Marching on Washington: The Forging of an American Political Tradition* (University of California Press, 2002), 150.
172 *"They're all getting tough"*: This conversation between the Kennedys is in Jonathan Rosenberg and Zachary Karabell, *Kennedy, Johnson, and the Quest for Justice: The Civil Rights Tapes* (W. W. Norton, 2003), 117, 119.
172 *About 75 percent*: William Jones, *The March on Washington: Jobs, Freedom, and the Forgotten History of Civil Rights* (W. W. Norton, 2013), xviii–xix.
173 *"seemed to me a great mistake"*: Quoted in David Garrow, *Bearing the Cross: Martin Luther King, Jr., and the Southern Christian Leadership Conference* (William Morrow, 1986), 271.
173 *"whispered to me his sympathy"*: Arthur Schlesinger, Jr., *A Thousand Days: John F. Kennedy in the White House* (Houghton Mifflin, 2002), 971.
173 *"I am not involved"*: Quoted in Garrow, *Bearing the Cross*, 273.
173 *NAACP staffers felt that sometimes*: For example, see "Reminiscences of Bayard Rustin, 1987," Oral History Archives, Columbia University, 3–92.
174 *Wilkins told him to resign*: Michael Williams, *Medgar Evers: Mississippi Martyr* (University of Arkansas Press, 2011), 145–46.
174 *Evers complied with that instruction*: Taylor Branch, *Pillar of Fire: America in the King Years, 1963–1965* (Simon & Schuster, 1998), 101.
174 *Andrew Young once noted*: Andrew Young, *An Easy Burden: The Civil Rights Movement and the Transformation of America* (Harper, 1996), 193.
174 *"We couldn't comment on any idea a student has"*: Quoted in Taylor Branch, *Parting the Waters: America in the King Years* (Simon & Schuster, 1988), 830.
174 *capable of maintaining a sustained fight*: Branch, *Parting the Waters*, 831.
174 *his price was that*: This anecdote is related in detail in "Reminiscences of Bayard Rustin, 1987," Oral History Archives, Columbia University, 202.
175 *"I can't say I liked what I saw"*: John Lewis, *Walking with the Wind: A Memoir of the Movement* (Simon & Schuster, 2015), 208.
175 *"No less than 100,000 of us"*: Roy Wilkins, "To: Presidents of Branches, Youth Councils, College Chapters and State Conferences," July 30, 1963, NAACP memorandum, Civil Rights Movement Archive, crmvet.org/docs/6308_naacp_mow.pdf.
175 *"threadbare"*: Jones, *The March on Washington*, 342.

175 *"Martin and the regular civil rights leaders"*: Interview with Ossie Davis, conducted by Blackside, Inc., July 6, 1989, for *Eyes on the Prize: America's Civil Rights Years (1954–1965)*, Washington University Libraries, Film and Media Archive, Henry Hampton Collection, transcript, reposi tory.wustl.edu/downloads/jd4731463.

175 *two thousand buses*: Jones, *The March on Washington*, 171.

175 *Each bus had a designated captain*: Jones, *The March on Washington*, 179.

176 *"create, by example, an atmosphere"*: "Marshals' Manual," March on Washington for Jobs and Freedom, August 28, 1963, Civil Rights Movement Archive, crmvet.org/docs/6308_mow _marshallsmanual.pdf.

176 *"My theory of maintaining order"*: "Reminiscences of Bayard Rustin, 1987," 198.

176 *Rustin invited the Guardians Association*: Jones, *The March on Washington*, 181. Jones calls the New York group the Guardian Association, but other sources, such as the King Papers, use the plural "Guardians."

176 *Rustin brought in three experts to train*: "Reminiscences of Bayard Rustin, 1987," 197.

176 *Rustin announced in early August*: Jones, *The March on Washington*, 172.

176 *Rustin decided to divide the day into two parts*: "Reminiscences of Bayard Rustin, 1987," 235.

176 *Rustin also produced a military-style "Operating Manual"*: Information in this paragraph is from "March on Washington for Jobs and Freedom, Operating Manual No. 1," 1963, March on Washington files, ProQuest History Vault. The "strongly advised" quotation is from page 8 of the manual.

177 *four hundred pay phones*: "Reminiscences of Bayard Rustin, 1987," 199.

177 *The pioneering Black lesbian lawyer Pauli Murray*: Rosalind Rosenberg, *Jane Crow: The Life of Pauli Murray* (Oxford University Press, 2017), 389–90.

177–78 *"it is incredible that no woman should appear"*: Jones, *The March on Washington*, 175.

178 *"a single woman to speak"*: "Proposed Program—Lincoln Memorial," undated memorandum, March on Washington files, ProQuest History Vault.

178 *"Washington Gets Jittery Over March"*: Cited in Jones, *The March on Washington*, 176.

178 *"The March Should Be Stopped"*: Cited in Manning Marable, *Black American Politics: From the Washington Marches to Jesse Jackson* (Verso, 1985), 92.

178 *"misguided"*: Quoted in Marable, *Black American Politics*, 92.

178 *tens of thousands of whites attended*: Jennifer Scanlon, *Until There Is Justice: The Life of Anna Arnold Hedgeman* (Oxford University Press, 2019), 3.

178 *large part because of the efforts of Anna Hedgeman*: Scanlon, *Until There Is Justice*, 168.

179 *"the largest demonstration"*: This and subsequent quotations from Randolph's speech in the following three paragraphs are taken from "A. Philip Randolph's 1963 March on Washington Speech," transcript posted by *Florida Times-Union*, using WGBH tapes of the event.

180 *Nash was surprised*: Interview with Diane Nash, July 7, 1983, David Garrow Research Files #832, 25. Courtesy of David Garrow and Jonathan Eig.

180 *"You haven't been there, Mr. Wilkins"*: Lewis, *Walking with the Wind*, 225.

180 *Lewis excised much of the incendiary material*: Lauren Feeney, "Two Versions of John Lewis' Speech," *Moyers on Democracy*, July 24, 2013.

180 *even Roy Wilkins wound up sounding more militant*: Roy Wilkins speech, March on Washington for Jobs and Freedom, August 28, 1963, WGBH Open Vault.

181 *"the greatest demonstration for freedom"*: Martin Luther King, Jr., speech, March on Washington for Jobs and Freedom, August 28, 1963, WGBH Open Vault.

183 *only four people were arrested*: Branch, *Pillar of Fire*, 132.

183 *"I haven't been for this civil rights stuff"*: Quoted in Jones, *The March on Washington*, 202.

183 *"To the extent that any single public utterance could"*: Harvard Sitkoff, *The Struggle for Black Equality* (1981; repr. Hill and Wang, 2008), 152–53.

184 *a final turnout of at least 250,000*: For estimates on crowd size, see Scott Sandage, "A Marble

House Divided: The Lincoln Memorial, the Civil Rights Movement, and the Politics of Memory, 1939–1963," *Journal of American History* 80, no. 1 (June 1993): 156.

184 *Now the Movement had presented*: This sentence is influenced by Sandage, "A Marble House Divided," 157.

184 *"a quest to get into the mainstream"*: Quoted in Garrow, *Bearing the Cross*, 286.

184 *"the most dangerous Negro"*: Quoted in David Garrow, *The FBI and Martin Luther King, Jr.: From "Solo" to Memphis* (W. W. Norton, 1981), 68.

184 *"The movement represented courage"*: "Washington Booker III," in Horace Huntley and John McKerley, eds., *Foot Soldiers for Democracy: The Men, Women, and Children of the Birmingham Civil Rights Movement* (University of Illinois Press, 2009), 192.

184 *"peace, love, and no finger pointing"*: Quoted in Annell Ponder, "Minutes of Staff Conference Held at Dorchester," September 5–7, 1963, SCLC files, ProQuest History Vault.

185 *"Yes, the march was a failure in terms of specifics"*: Lewis, *Walking with the Wind*, 231.

185 *"The march's relative conservativism"*: Marable, *Black American Politics*, 97.

185 *the French and Indian War*: Charles Tilly, *Coercion, Capital and European States, AD 990–1992* (Blackwell, 1994), 74.

185 *"I've never seen a more immovable force"*: Quoted in Jeanne Theoharis, *A More Beautiful and Terrible History: The Uses and Misuses of Civil Rights History* (Beacon Press, 2018), 171.

186 *"bitterly humiliating"*: Quoted in Scanlon, *Until There Is Justice*, 170.

186 *an anonymous memorandum*: "SNCC Position Paper" (Women in the Movement), November 1964, Civil Rights Movement Archive, crmvet.org/docs/6411w_us_women.pdf.

186 *"The caste system perspective"*: Casey Hayden and Mary King, "A Kind of Memo," November 18, 1965, Civil Rights Movement Archive, crmvet.org/docs/651118_kindof_memo.pdf.

186 *a strong and persistent streak of machismo*: Sara Evans, *Personal Politics: The Roots of Women's Liberation in the Civil Rights Movement and the New Left* (Alfred A. Knopf, 1979), 182, 224.

8. Later Birmingham, Fall 1963

187 *It was the city's twenty-ninth bombing since 1951*: Andrew Manis, *A Fire You Can't Put Out: The Civil Rights Life of Birmingham's Reverend Fred Shuttlesworth* (University of Alabama Press, 2002), 403.

187 *"They were all stacked in a pile"*: Quoted in Matt Schudel, "Rev. John Cross Jr.; Pastor at Bombed Church," *Washington Post*, November 18, 2007.

188 *"It was symbolic of how sin and evil"*: "*Playboy* Interview: Martin Luther King, Jr.," January 1965, in *A Testament of Hope: The Essential Writings and Speeches of Martin Luther King, Jr.*, ed. James Melvin Washington (1986; repr. HarperCollins, 1991), 347.

188 *"Life is hard"*: Martin Luther King, Jr., "Eulogy for the Martyred Children," September 1963, King Papers, Stanford University.

188 *King also noticed that no white officials*: Martin Luther King, Jr., *Why We Can't Wait* (1964; repr. Signet, 2000), 137.

188 *"did not take to the streets and raise hell"*: Interview with Bayard Rustin, 1964, Robert Penn Warren's Who Speaks for the Negro?: An Archival Collection, Vanderbilt University Library, whospeaks.library.vanderbilt.edu/interview/bayard-rustin.

188 *"We were bombed because we were winning"*: Bayard Rustin, "The Meaning of the March on Washington," *Liberation*, October 1963, Civil Rights Movement Archive, crmvet.org/info /mowrust.htm.

189 *"They're gonna get tougher"*: Quoted in Taylor Branch, *Pillar of Fire: America in the King Years, 1963–1965* (Simon & Schuster, 1998), 143.

189 *the choice of Royall was even more puzzling*: Robert Edgerton, *Hidden Heroism: Black Soldiers in America's Wars* (Basic Books, 2001), 165.

189 *"publicly and pugnaciously"*: Patricia Sullivan, *Lift Every Voice: The NAACP and the Making of the Civil Rights Movement* (The New Press, 2009), 360.

189 *Royall and Blaik wandered around the town*: For a contrary view, see J. Mills Thornton III, *Dividing Lines: Municipal Politics and the Struggle for Civil Rights in Montgomery, Birmingham, and Selma* (University of Alabama Press, 2002), 350. Thornton argues that Royall and Blaik actually brought pressure on Birmingham's white establishment to make genuine concessions. However, he does not mention Royall's questionable credentials for the mission.

190 *"neutralizing King as an effective Negro leader"*: David Garrow, *The FBI and Martin Luther King, Jr.: From "Solo" to Memphis* (W. W. Norton, 1981), 102–103. This section of the chapter was influenced heavily by Garrow's impressive work.

190 *"This will destroy the burrhead"*: Garrow, *The FBI and Martin Luther King, Jr.*, 106. See also Branch, *Pillar of Fire*, 207.

190 *The FBI took wide-ranging active measures*: The examples in this paragraph are from Garrow, *The FBI and Martin Luther King, Jr.*, 114, 132, 179, 121, 183.

190 *"the most notorious liar"*: Quoted in Garrow, *The FBI and Martin Luther King, Jr.*, 121. See also "Federal Bureau of Investigation," *The King Encyclopedia*, Martin Luther King, Jr., Research and Education Institute, Stanford University.

190 *"That was the first time I saw him cry"*: Interview with Dorothy Cotton, Civil Rights History Project, Southern Oral History Program Collection, University of North Carolina at Chapel Hill, 47.

191 *Hoover also decided that King did not deserve*: Branch, *Pillar of Fire*, 198.

191 *Hoover's gift was a glass ashtray*: "President Kennedy's Desk," John F. Kennedy Presidential Library and Museum.

191 *"The government always wanted"*: Interview with Rev. Fred Shuttlesworth, conducted by Blackside, Inc., November 7, 1985, for *Eyes on the Prize: America's Civil Rights Years (1954–1965)*, Washington University Libraries, Film and Media Archive, Henry Hampton Collection, transcript, repository.wustl.edu/downloads/k643b305j.

191 *"It was like they were playing"*: Interview with Diane Nash, November 12, 1985, *Eyes on the Prize*, repository.wustl.edu/downloads/7m01bn67n.

192 *the principal removed his own necktie*: Freeman Hrabowski III, *Holding Fast to Dreams: Empowering Youth from the Civil Rights Crusade to STEM Achievement* (Beacon Press, 2015), 46.

192 *"The group marched in one direction"*: Interview with Diane Nash, July 7, 1983, David Garrow Research Files #832, 33–34. Courtesy of David Garrow and Jonathan Eig.

192 *"Tell the truth about what you see"*: U.S. Army Ranger Training Brigade, *Ranger Handbook* (U.S. Army, 2000), ii.

192 *"When you're really honest with yourself"*: Interview with Diane Nash, *Eyes on the Prize*. The Nash quotations in the following three paragraphs are also from this interview.

193 *"I was thinking about killing people"*: Interview with James Bevel, November 13, 1985, *Eyes on the Prize*, repository.wustl.edu/downloads/9306t101z.

193 *"My mind turned murderous"*: James Bevel with Randy Kryn, "Declaring Peace: James Bevel's 1960s Movements and Strategies; A Practical History and Guide to Nonviolence" (unpublished manuscript, 1988–2004), 81.

194 *"We felt confident that if we tried"*: Interview with Diane Nash, *Eyes on the Prize*.

194 *They drafted a two-page paper*: "Proposal for Action in Montgomery," no date or authors listed on original. Accessed at CRMvet.org, at https://www.crmvet.org/docs/6309_nash_actionplan.pdf. Quotations in this paragraph and the next are from this document. Its timing and authorship are discussed in Branch, *Pillar of Fire*, 139–41.

194 *She presented the proposal to King*: Interview with Diane Nash, *Eyes on the Prize*.

194 *"you have your meeting with your own folks first"*: Interview with Diane Nash, July 7, 1983, Garrow Research Files, 31.

195 *"Doctor King's initial reaction"*: Interview with Diane Nash, in Peter W. Kunhardt, dir., *King*

in the Wilderness (Kunhardt Film Foundation, 2018), transcript, kunhardtfilmfoundation.org /featured-interviews/diane-nash. The following Nash quote is also from this interview.

195 *"When we drew up our plans, it wasn't for Selma"*: Interview with Diane Nash, Garrow Research Files, 38.

195 *They had buttons made*: Andrew Young, *An Easy Burden: The Civil Rights Movement and the Transformation of America* (Harper, 1996), 335.

195 *ordered him to drop the idea*: Bevel with Kryn, "Declaring Peace," 84.

195 *"It is not a weapon for the weak"*: The quotations in this and the following paragraph are from SCLC, "Handbook for Freedom Army Recruits," Civil Rights Movement Archive, crmvet.org /docs/64_sclc_freedomarmy.pdf.

196 *"demonstration for the sake of demonstrating"*: James Bevel, "Non-Violent vs. Brinksmenship [*sic*]," undated but filed in SCLC papers under "Bevel, James: 1963," ProQuest History Vault.

196 *"When General of the Armies Douglas MacArthur"*: Quoted in Taylor Branch, *Parting the Waters: America in the King Years* (Simon & Schuster, 1988), 900.

196 *"a tinny echo"*: Branch, *Parting the Waters*, 901.

196 *"There were times people wanted to fight"*: Interview with Rev. Fred Shuttlesworth, *Eyes on the Prize*.

197 *"This is what is going to happen to me"*: Garrow, *Bearing the Cross*, 307.

197 *"It ends with me getting killed"*: Garrow, *Bearing the Cross*, 469.

197 *"Millions of NBC viewers"*: Branch, *Pillar of Fire*, 176.

198 *"Not until the colossus of segregation"*: Martin Luther King, Jr., "How Long? Not Long—Our God Is Marching On!," March 25, 1965, Civil Rights Movement Archive, crmvet.org/info /ourgod65.htm.

198 *"She began thinking about fire hoses"*: Newspaper editor, in conversation with the author, 1982. This conversation occurred when I was a young reporter for the *Wall Street Journal* on my first trip to Alabama.

198 *"Finally, after Birmingham, the country was alive"*: Robert P. Moses, "Speech on Freedom Summer at Stanford University," April 24, 1964, American Radio Works, americanradioworks .publicradio.org/features/blackspeech/bmoses.html.

199 *"the yearning to demonstrate"*: Dan Warren, *If It Takes All Summer: Martin Luther King, the KKK, and States' Rights in St. Augustine, 1964* (University of Alabama Press, 2008), 139.

199 *"waste of time"*: Quoted in Branch, *Pillar of Fire*, 407.

199–200 *"I'm not going to be involved"*: Bevel with Kryn, "Declaring Peace," 88.

200 *Wyatt Walker asked King to dismiss Bevel*: Bevel with Kryn, "Declaring Peace," 163. Walker's move against Bevel also is mentioned in Dorothy Cotton, *If Your Back's Not Bent: The Role of the Citizenship Education Program in the Civil Rights Movement* (Atria Books, 2012), 194.

200 *Mississippi was the worst state*: Alan Draper, "The Mississippi Movement: A Review Essay," *Journal of Mississippi History* 60, no. 4 (Winter 1998): 356.

200 *led the South in known lynchings*: Derek Catsam, *Freedom's Main Line: The Journey of Reconciliation and the Freedom Rides* (University Press of Kentucky, 2009), 137.

200 *"We were all Southerners"*: Pat Watters, *Down to Now: Reflections on the Southern Civil Rights Movement* (University of Georgia Press, 1993), 137.

200 *"offers SNCC an opportunity"*: "Minutes of SNCC Executive Committee Meeting, September 6–9, 1963, Atlanta, Georgia," ProQuest History Vault, 5.

200 *"For a short while we had the field"*: Robert P. Moses and Charles E. Cobb, Jr., *Radical Equations: Math, Literacy and Civil Rights* (Beacon Press, 2002), 80.

9. Oxford, Ohio, June 1964

202 *Fannie Lou Hamer would recall*: "An Oral History with Fannie Lou Hamer," April 14, 1972, Center for Oral History and Cultural Heritage, University of Southern Mississippi, 2, 5–6,

and "Fannie Lou Hamer Deposition," 1964, in *Risking Everything: A Freedom Summer Reader*, ed. Michael Edmonds (Wisconsin Historical Society, 2014), 27. The name of the plantation owner who employed Hamer is sometimes spelled "Marlowe"; see, for example, John Dittmer, *Local People: The Struggle for Civil Rights in Mississippi* (University of Illinois Press, 1995), 137. Dittmer's terrific book influenced the first section of this chapter.

202 *"We are not ready for that in Mississippi"*: "Testimony of Fannie Lou Hamer, Credentials Committee, National Democratic Convention, Atlantic City, New Jersey, August 22, 1964," Civil Rights Movement Archive, crmvet.org/info/fs.htm#fs64_flhac.

202 *Hamer briefly moved into the home*: Dittmer, *Local People*, 137–38.

202 *"We had been weaving"*: Quoted in Henry Hampton and Steve Fayer, *Voices of Freedom: An Oral History of the Civil Rights Movement from the 1950s Through the 1980s* (Bantam Books, 1990), 193.

202 *Blacks who did manage to register*: Dittmer, *Local People*, 3.

203 *"Bob's approach to me was entirely different"*: Interview with Amzie Moore, conducted by Blackside, Inc., March 22, 1980, for *Eyes on the Prize: America's Civil Rights Years (1954–1965)*, Washington University Libraries, Film and Media Archive, Henry Hampton Collection, transcript, repository.wustl.edu/downloads/mg74qn79k.

203 *"He . . . didn't do much talking"*: "Oral History with Mr. Amzie Moore, Black Civil Rights Worker," Center for Oral History and Cultural Heritage, University of Southern Mississippi, 48.

203 *"When you're out there in a really rural area"*: Robert P. Moses and Charles E. Cobb, Jr., *Radical Equations: Math, Literacy and Civil Rights* (Beacon Press, 2002), 55.

203 *James Bevel, who with Diane Nash*: "Robert Moses interview with Clayborne Carson at Harvard University," March 29, 1982, Civil Rights Movement Archive, crmvet.org/nars/820329_moses _carson.pdf, 26.

203 *Bevel was the SCLC's field secretary*: Randall L. Kryn, "James L. Bevel: The Strategist of the 1960s Civil Rights Movement," in *We Shall Overcome: The Civil Rights Movement in the United States in the 1950's and 1960's*, ed. David Garrow (Carlson Publishing, 1989), 2:519.

204 *"The law down here is law made by white people"*: Quoted in Eric Burner, *And Gently He Shall Lead Them: Robert Parris Moses and Civil Rights in Mississippi* (New York University Press, 1994), 52. This paragraph and the previous one were influenced by Burner's book.

204 *"the Negroes might be serious"*: Quoted in Burner, *And Gently He Shall Lead Them*, 52.

204 *One night in 1963*: Howard Zinn, *SNCC: The New Abolitionists* (Beacon Press, 1964), 89–90.

204 *"one of the great listeners of the world"*: Joseph Sinsheimer, "The Freedom Vote of 1963: New Strategies of Racial Protest in Mississippi," *Journal of Southern History* 55, no. 2 (May 1989): 222.

204 *"Bob didn't do too much talking"*: Interview with Emma Allen by Joseph Sinsheimer, May 5, 1986, Civil Rights Movement Archive, crmvet.org/nars/js_allen_oh-r.pdf, 8.

204 *"Bob always listened"*: Stokely Carmichael with Ekwueme Michael Thelwell, *Ready for Revolution: The Life and Struggles of Stokely Carmichael* (Scribner, 2003), 311.

204 *"There was . . . a certain charismatic quality"*: Interview with Robert Coles by Joseph Sinsheimer, November 19, 1983, Civil Rights Movement Archive, crmvet.org/nars/js_coles.pdf, 27–28. The Coles quotations following this one are from the same source.

205 *"Bob Moses was a little bitty fella"*: Quoted in Hampton and Fayer, *Voices of Freedom*, 180.

205 *"It is not possible for us"*: Bob Moses, "Memo to: S.N.C.C. Executive Committee," Civil Rights Movement Archive, crmvet.org/docs/63_sncc_moses_ms.pdf, 2.

205 *"the staff was exhausted"*: "Bob Parris Moses," oral history interview by Anne Romaine, Highlander Center, September 5, 1966, Civil Rights Movement Archive, crmvet.org/nars/66_moses .pdf, II-18.

205 *"we were just like sitting ducks"*: Dittmer, *Local People*, 219.

205 *Amzie Moore passed word*: Mary King, *Freedom Song: A Personal Story of the 1960s Civil Rights Movement* (William Morrow, 1987), 322.

206 *"When the black waves hit our communities"*: Quoted in Charles Marsh, *God's Long Summer: Stories of Faith and Civil Rights* (Princeton University Press, 1999), 66.

206 *"The white power structure was so strong"*: Quoted in Hampton and Fayer, *Voices of Freedom*, 192.

206 *"the press would respond"*: "Notes on Mississippi," late 1963, in Edmonds, *Risking Everything*, 42.

206 *"a massive effort"*: "Minutes of COFO Convention," February 9, 1964, Civil Rights Movement Archive, crmvet.org/docs/6402_cofo_minutes.pdf, 3.

206 *He soon assigned a subordinate*: "Robert Moses interview with Clayborne Carson at Harvard University," 32–34.

207 *"a closed society"*: "Minutes of the Meeting of the SNCC Executive Committee, December 27–31, 1963," Civil Rights Movement Archive, crmvet.org/docs/6312_sncc_excom_min.pdf, 29.

207 *There was also a hope*: Hampton and Fayer, *Voices of Freedom*, 182–83.

207 *"saturation program"*: "Minutes of the Meeting of the SNCC Executive Committee, December 27–31, 1963," 28.

207 *"We recognized that the results"*: Quoted in William Chafe, *The Unfinished Journey: America Since World War II*, 5th ed. (Oxford University Press, 2003), 306.

207 *Some of those anxious parents*: "Jim Forman—November 12, 1965," interview by Howard Zinn, Zinn Interview Transcripts, 1963–65, Howard Zinn Papers, Freedom Summer Digital Collection, Wisconsin Historical Society, content.wisconsinhistory.org/digital/collection/p15932coll2/id/11919, 4.

207 *"That's cold"*: Quoted in Harvard Sitkoff, *The Struggle for Black Equality* (1981; repr. Hill and Wang, 2008), 159.

208 *"an army of Northern college students"*: John Lewis, *Walking with the Wind: A Memoir of the Movement* (Simon & Schuster, 2015), 250.

208 *"That whole question"*: Robert P. Moses, "Speech on Freedom Summer at Stanford University," April 24, 1964, American Radio Works, americanradioworks.publicradio.org/features/blackspeech/bmoses.html.

208 *"You killed my husband"*: Quoted in Taylor Branch, *Parting the Waters: America in the King Years* (Simon & Schuster, 1988), 510.

208 *"Herbert Lee was killed"*: Moses, "Speech on Freedom Summer at Stanford University."

208–209 *Lowenstein's criticisms had led the Stanford delegation*: Dittmer, *Local People*, 232–33. See also Laura Visser-Maessen, *Robert Parris Moses: A Life in Civil Rights and Leadership at the Grass Roots* (University of North Carolina Press, 2016), 193–94.

209 *"no revolution can continue without its supply base"*: Visser-Maessen, *Robert Parris Moses*, 192.

209 *burned crosses in sixty-four counties*: Dittmer, *Local People*, 215.

209 *the White Knights were strong*: Marsh, *God's Long Summer*, 57.

209 *But a Klan recruiting drive*: Taylor Branch, *Pillar of Fire: America in the King Years, 1963–1965* (Simon & Schuster, 1998), 240.

209 *It also bought a 13,000-pound armored vehicle*: "Allen's Army," *Newsweek*, February 24, 1964, 30.

209 *"a bunch of niggers"*: Quoted in Dittmer, *Local People*, 223.

210 *Cox's appointment to the bench*: Kay Mills, *This Little Light of Mine: The Life of Fannie Lou Hamer* (University Press of Kentucky, 2007), 32.

210 *"it was time for a confrontation"*: Interview with Joyce Ladner by Joseph Sinsheimer, May 23, 1986, Civil Rights Movement Archive, crmvet.org/nars/js_ladner.pdf, 30.

210 *"very softly, very slowly"*: Ellen Barnes, "Mississippi Volunteers," Freedom Summer Papers, Wisconsin Historical Society, content.wisconsinhistory.org/digital/collection/p15932coll2/id/33964, 3–5.

211 *"Maybe we're not going to get very many people"*: Quoted in Tracy Sugarman, *We Had Sneakers, They Had Guns: The Kids Who Fought for Civil Rights in Mississippi* (Syracuse University Press, 2009), 14.

211 *"He immediately won the position"*: Mike Yarrow, "Letter re Orientation & Training," June 18, 1964, Civil Rights Movement Archive, crmvet.org/lets/640618_yarrow.pdf, 1.

211 *"the embodiment of the America"*: Paul Cowan, *The Making of an Un-American: A Dialogue with Experience* (Viking, 1970), 31.

211 *He lived on Park Avenue in Manhattan*: "Parents List—Addresses and Names," Civil Rights Movement Archive, crmvet.org/docs/contacts/640000_msfs_parentslist.pdf.

211 *"more or less the Jesus of the whole project"*: Quoted in Elizabeth Martínez, ed., *Letters from Mississippi: Reports from Civil Rights Volunteers & Poetry of the 1964 Freedom Summer*, 50th anniversary ed. (Zephyr Press, 2007), 19.

211 *"The week of intense preparation"*: Carole Colca, "Reflections on a Life-Changing Experience," in *Finding Freedom: Memorializing the Voices of Freedom Summer*, ed. Jacqueline Johnson (Miami University Press, 2013).

212 *"to restore the right of the Negro to vote"*: Quoted in Barnes, "Mississippi Volunteers," 14.

212 *"Mississippi is going to be hell this summer"*: Quoted in Martínez, *Letters from Mississippi*, 10.

212 *"I just told everybody in all of the sessions I attended"*: Interviews with Hollis Watkins by Joseph Sinsheimer, February 13 and 14, 1985, Civil Rights Movement Archive, crmvet.org/nars/js _watkins-r.pdf, I-31, II-3.

212 *"cocky kids from Harvard, Yale, whatever"*: Interview with Robert Coles by Joseph Sinsheimer, 5–6, 9.

212 *Chevy Chase and Bethesda, Maryland*: Most of the towns listed here are from "Parents List—Addresses and Names," while a few are from a similar document, "Volunteers in the State—July 3, 1964," Civil Rights Movement Archive, crmvet.org/docs/contacts/64_msfs_volslist.pdf.

213 *"They weren't prancing around"*: Interview with Robert Coles by Joseph Sinsheimer, 15.

213 *The volunteer listed first the Freedom Summer project*: Martínez, *Letters from Mississippi*, 151.

213 *There were a few snickers and laughs among them*: Sugarman, *We Had Sneakers*, 16.

213 *"These are the people that you are going to work with"*: Interview with Cleveland Sellers by Joseph Sinsheimer, March 30, 1985, Civil Rights Movement Archive, crmvet.org/nars/js_sellers.pdf.

214 *"they were being sent as sacrificial victims"*: Sally Belfrage, *Freedom Summer* (University Press of Virginia, 1990), 8.

214 *"Nonviolence is not just a technique"*: Quoted in Barnes, "Mississippi Volunteers," 18.

214 *1. It is based on faith*: Quoted in Barnes, "Mississippi Volunteers," 18–19.

214 *"Some faces had registered shock"*: Barnes, "Mississippi Volunteers," 20.

214 *"By this time many"*: Barnes, "Mississippi Volunteers," 21.

214 *"Keep the face visible. Maintain eye contact"*: Quoted in Barnes, "Mississippi Volunteers," 21.

215 *"When you turn the other cheek"*: Quoted in Bruce Watson, *Freedom Summer: The Savage Season of 1964 That Made Mississippi Burn and Made America a Democracy* (Penguin Books, 2010), Kindle edition.

215 *"The questions came so fast that I stopped writing"*: Barnes, "Mississippi Volunteers," 22.

215 *"The questions began and they raged on"*: Barnes, "Mississippi Volunteers," 23.

215 *Carmichael argued that nonviolence had worked*: Barnes, "Mississippi Volunteers," 23.

215 *"the logic of this [nonviolent approach]"*: Interview with Stokely Carmichael, May 5, 1986, *Eyes on the Prize*, repository.wustl.edu/downloads/4x51hk606.

215 *He estimated that 90 percent of SNCC workers*: Interview with Stokely Carmichael, November 7, 1988, *Eyes on the Prize II: America at the Racial Crossroads (1965–1985)*, repository.wustl.edu /downloads/jw827g69g.

216 *"I admired their wisdom"*: "Oral History with Mr. Amzie Moore, Black Civil Rights Worker," Center for Oral History and Cultural Heritage, University of Southern Mississippi, 52.

216 *"In Mississippi we have two ground rules"*: Quoted in Barnes, "Mississippi Volunteers," 23.

216 *"Although I myself personally"*: Interview with Robert Moses by Joseph Sinsheimer, April 11, 1984, Civil Rights Movement Archive, crmvet.org/nars/js_moses2-cr5.pdf, 6.

216   *"for the Negro—and for you*—there is no law*"*: Quoted in Barnes, "Mississippi Volunteers," 27.

216   *"Know all the roads in and out of town"*: "Security Handbook," Freedom Summer Papers, Wisconsin Historical Society, content.wisconsinhistory.org/digital/collection/p15932coll2/id/43705 /rec/5, 1–3.

216–17 *"If you wake up at night thinking there is danger"*: Yarrow, "Letter re Orientation & Training," 4.

217   *"the increasing weight of fear"*: Yarrow, "Letter re Orientation & Training," 4.

217   *"Keep in mind that you have just begun"*: "Voter Registration Summer Prospects," in Edmonds, *Risking Everything*, 116.

217   *Stuart Rawlings III, a Stanford student*: Doug McAdam, *Freedom Summer* (Oxford University Press, 1988), 151, 228. Rawlings' neighborhood is derived from "Parents List—Addresses and Names."

217   *"one in fifty"*: Quoted in McAdam, *Freedom Summer*, 71.

10. The Battle of Mississippi, July and August 1964

219   *one hundred were Black*: Eric Burner, *And Gently He Shall Lead Them: Robert Parris Moses and Civil Rights in Mississippi* (New York University Press, 1994), 264.

219   *"Some were incredibly courageous, some just reckless"*: Sally Belfrage, *Freedom Summer* (University Press of Virginia, 1990), xiii.

219   *"all they could do putting one foot ahead of another"*: Sally Belfrage, *Freedom Summer*, xx.

219   *"melt away into the Black population"*: Interview with Bob Moses in *American Experience: Freedom Summer*, directed by Stanley Nelson, PBS, season 26, episode 6, aired June 24, 2014.

220   *"going around in the hot sun"*: Robert P. Moses, "Mississippi: 1961–1962," *Liberation* 14 (January 1970): 15. This article is a transcript of a talk Moses gave in 1962.

220   *after about three hours each day*: Mary Rothschild, *A Case of Black and White: Northern Volunteers and the Southern Freedom Summers, 1964–1965* (Greenwood, 1982), 62.

220   *the expected workload*: Elizabeth Martínez, ed., *Letters from Mississippi: Reports from Civil Rights Volunteers & Poetry of the 1964 Freedom Summer*, 50th anniversary ed. (Zephyr Press, 2007), 81.

220   *"dark little falling apart house"*: Quoted in Martínez, *Letters from Mississippi*, 54–55.

220   *"We walk up, smile, say howdy"*: Robert Feinglass, "Dear Dad," in *Risking Everything: A Freedom Summer Reader*, ed. Michael Edmonds (Wisconsin Historical Society, 2014), 125.

221   *"We're not really doing anything here"*: Quoted in Martínez, *Letters from Mississippi*, 85–86.

221   *When a potential voter said*: "An Oral History with Cleveland Sellers Jr.," North Mississippi Oral History and Archives Program, Center for Oral History and Cultural Heritage, University of Southern Mississippi, 17.

221   *One evening in July, a young Black man*: Wallace Roberts, letter from Shaw, Mississippi, July 13, 1964, accessed at Civil Rights Movement Archive, crmvet.org/lets/640713_roberts-let.pdf.

222   *"I woke in the morning sighing with relief"*: Quoted in Rothschild, *A Case of Black and White*, 59.

222   *"I'm afraid in the evening"*: Quoted in Robert Coles, *Children of Crisis: A Study of Courage and Fear* (Little, Brown, 1967), 196–97.

222   *"a no man's land of violence"*: "The Mississippi Summer Project," unsigned report, 1964, Civil Rights Movement Archive, crmvet.org/docs/640900_sncc_mississippisummer-r.pdf, 12.

222   *A white couple who invited*: John Dittmer, *Local People: The Struggle for Civil Rights in Mississippi* (University of Illinois Press, 1995), 99–100, 266, 305. The detail about serving tamales is from Hodding Carter II, *So the Heffners Left McComb* (1965; repr. University Press of Mississippi, 2016), 9.

222   *A SNCC log reported nine violent incidents*: "Civil Rights Incidents in McComb," 1964, Civil Rights Movement Archive, crmvet.org/info/mccomb1964.pdf, 1.

222   *a matter of pride for volunteers*: Doug McAdam, *Freedom Summer* (Oxford University Press, 1988), 110.

222 *"It was not an easy time"*: Interview with Cleveland Sellers by Joseph Sinsheimer, March 30, 1985, Civil Rights Movement Archive, crmvet.org/nars/js_sellers.pdf, 33.

223 *"You had to go in as a proud"*: Interview with Cleveland Sellers by Joseph Sinsheimer, 31.

223 *"I was just seeing too much"*: Quoted in McAdam, *Freedom Summer*, 88.

223 *"Having sex in a field"*: Quoted in McAdam, *Freedom Summer*, 88.

223 *"Everyone back home knows"*: Quoted in Coles, *Children of Crisis*, 228.

223 *"Life is interesting"*: "Zoya Zeman's Freedom Summer Diary," entry for August 31, 1964, Mc-Cain Library, University of Southern Mississippi, usm.access.preservica.com/uncategorized/IO _9fab1dae-e6e6-45c3-bccc-537d8776508f, 25.

223 *"It was impossible to be alone"*: Belfrage, *Freedom Summer*, 101.

224 *"Well go back out there and get to work"*: Quoted in Cleveland Sellers, *The River of No Return: The Autobiography of a Black Militant and the Life and Death of SNCC* (University Press of Mississippi, 1990), 97–98.

224 *"I laid the law down"*: Interview with Hollis Watkins by Joseph Sinsheimer, February 13, 1985, Civil Rights Movement Archive, crmvet.org/nars/js_watkins-r.pdf, I-31–34.

225 *Moses took the remainder*: Burner, *And Gently He Shall Lead Them*, 130.

225 *"The food is unbelievable"*: Quoted in Martínez, *Letters from Mississippi*, 49.

225 *"I acquired the freedom worker's walk"*: Larry Rubin, "A Walk in Holly Springs, Mississippi, Winter 1964," in *Freedom Is a Constant Struggle: An Anthology of the Mississippi Civil Rights Movement*, ed. Susie Erenrich (Black Belt Press, 1999), 265.

225 *"There was a pace"*: Len Chandler, "A Long Introduction to a Long Poem About the Long Summer of '64," in Erenrich, *Freedom Is a Constant Struggle*, 209.

225 *"I think you have to think of it"*: "Jim Forman—November 12, 1965," interview by Howard Zinn, Zinn Interview Transcripts, 1963–65, Howard Zinn Papers, Freedom Summer Digital Collection, Wisconsin Historical Society, content.wisconsinhistory.org/digital/collection /p15932coll2/id/11919, 6.

226 *"Our objective was to let these people know"*: "Zoya Zeman's Freedom Summer Diary," 14.

227 *"because you know your life is on the line"*: "An Oral History with Honorable Unita Blackwell," Center for Oral History and Cultural Heritage, University of Southern Mississippi, 13, 10, 19.

228 *were taking home just $13 to $17 for a full workweek*: "Oral History with Mr. Amzie Moore, Black Civil Rights Worker," Center for Oral History and Cultural Heritage, University of Southern Mississippi, 37.

228 *"to implant habits of free thinking"*: Quoted in Belfrage, *Freedom Summer*, 90.

229 *"the unjust laws of Mississippi"*: Cornelia Mack, "Dear Family and Friends," in Edmonds, *Risking Everything*, 161.

229 *listed their grievances*: Rothschild, *A Case of Black and White*, 106–107.

229 *The Freedom Schools were more popular than expected*: Rothschild, *A Case of Black and White*, 100–101.

229 *"Most of what we know about teaching"*: Quoted in Rothschild, *A Case of Black and White*, 105–106.

229 *the superintendent of schools in Bolivar County*: Martínez, *Letters from Mississippi*, 106.

229 *On the first day of classes*: Martínez, *Letters from Mississippi*, 125–26.

230 *"I am completely frustrated"*: Quoted in Rothschild, *A Case of Black and White*, 108–109.

230 *Even remedial literacy classes*: Dittmer, *Local People*, 183.

230 *On June 21, 1964, Louise Hermey*: "Oral History Interview with Louise (Hermey) Stanford," September 6, 1989, Oral Histories Collection, Lyndon B. Johnson Library, 18–21.

231 *"If in fact, anyone is arrested"*: Quoted in Henry Hampton and Steve Fayer, *Voices of Freedom: An Oral History of the Civil Rights Movement from the 1950s Through the 1980s* (Bantam Books, 1990), 190.

231 *"I also think that they consciously"*: Interview with Robert Coles by Joseph Sinsheimer, November 19, 1983, Civil Rights Movement Archive, crmvet.org/nars/js_coles.pdf, 7.

231 *We now know that the three activists*: Dittmer, *Local People*, 247.

231 *"The disappearance of the three civil rights workers"*: John Lewis, *Walking with the Wind: A Memoir of the Movement* (Simon & Schuster, 2015), 265.

232 *The British prime minister was ecstatic*: See Thomas E. Ricks, *Churchill and Orwell: The Fight for Freedom* (Penguin Press, 2017), 148–49.

232 *"They found torsos in the Mississippi River"*: Interview with Dave Dennis, conducted by Blackside, Inc., November 10, 1985, for *Eyes on the Prize: America's Civil Rights Years (1954–1965)*, Washington University Libraries, Film and Media Archive, Henry Hampton Collection, transcript, repository.wustl.edu/downloads/dv13zv94x.

232 *The Mississippi Klan issued a statement*: Quoted in Charles Marsh, *God's Long Summer: Stories of Faith and Civil Rights* (Princeton University Press, 1999), 70.

232 *Hoover also gave the governor a list of highway patrol officers who were Klan members*: Dittmer, *Local People*, 251.

232 *"Here's a switch"*: "Zoya Zeman's Freedom Summer Diary," entry for July 3, 1964, 11.

232 *"he felt a physical revulsion"*: Quoted in Martínez, *Letters from Mississippi*, 157.

233 *Between June 15 and September 15*: Lewis, *Walking with the Wind*, 274. Similar numbers are listed in Stephen Oates, *Let the Trumpet Sound: The Life of Martin Luther King, Jr.* (Harper & Row, 1982), 309.

233 *daily incidents that did not result*: McAdam, *Freedom Summer*, 100, 90.

233 *even simple things become difficult*: Carl von Clausewitz, *On War*, ed. and trans. Michael Howard and Peter Paret (Princeton University Press, 1976), 119.

233 *"have to ride those roads by themselves"*: Robert P. Moses, "Speech on Freedom Summer at Stanford University," April 24, 1964, American Radio Works, americanradioworks.publicradio.org /features/blackspeech/bmoses.html.

233 *"We studied the faces of pedestrians and police"*: Belfrage, *Freedom Summer*, 33.

234 *"It was just a matter of"*: Interview with Sue Thrasher by Joseph Sinsheimer, November 11, 1983, Civil Rights Movement Archive, crmvet.org/nars/js_thrasher-cr.pdf, 19.

234 *"a normal living situation"*: Interview with Sue Thrasher by Joseph Sinsheimer, 15.

234 *"I couldn't adjust"*: Pam Parker, "My parents said yes!," in *Finding Freedom: Memorializing the Voices of Freedom Summer*, ed. Jacqueline Johnson (Miami University Press, 2013), 27.

234 *"the clarity of the situation"*: Denise Nicholas, "The Free Southern Theater," in Erenrich, *Freedom Is a Constant Struggle*, 254.

234 *The discovery of the bodies*: Sellers, *River of No Return*, 107.

234 *"I'm going to tell you"*: Dave Dennis, "Address at the Funeral Service for James Chaney," August 7, 1964, in *Rhetoric, Religion, and the Civil Rights Movement, 1954–1965*, ed. Davis Houck and David Dixon (Baylor University Press, 2006), 1:778.

234 *"Dave finally broke down and couldn't finish"*: Quoted in Martínez, *Letters from Mississippi*, 220.

235 *"They killed one nigger, one Jew, and a white man"*: "MIBURN (Mississippi Burning)," Civil Rights Digital Library, University of Georgia.

235 *"a waste of good lives"*: Quoted in Dittmer, *Local People*, 249.

235 *"There are incipient nervous breakdowns"*: Belfrage, *Freedom Summer*, 195.

235 *"To say that I was frightened"*: Quoted in Cheryl Lynn Greenberg, ed., *A Circle of Trust: Remembering SNCC* (Rutgers University Press, 1998), 70.

235 *"Enemy fire and Mother Nature"*: James Dunnigan, *How to Make War: A Comprehensive Guide to Modern Warfare* (William Morrow, 1988), 37.

235 *Mississippi's regular Democratic Party*: Dittmer, *Local People*, 273–74.

236 *"One of the most powerful and beautiful things"*: Robert P. Moses and Charles E. Cobb, Jr., *Radical Equations: Math, Literacy and Civil Rights* (Beacon Press, 2002), 80.

236   *"After the first Negro had beat"*: "Testimony of Fannie Lou Hamer, Credentials Committee, National Democratic Convention, Atlantic City, New Jersey, August 22, 1964," Civil Rights Movement Archive, crmvet.org/info/fs.htm#fs64_flhac.

236   *"All of this is on account of"*: "Testimony of Fannie Lou Hamer."

237   *"The president will not allow that illiterate woman"*: Quoted in Moses and Cobb, *Radical Equations*, 83. See also John Skipper, *Showdown at the 1964 Democratic Convention: Lyndon Johnson, Mississippi and Civil Rights* (McFarland, 2012), 141. Note that Hamer was not illiterate, and as a child had "loved to read," she once told an interviewer; see "Interview with Fannie Lou Hamer by Dr. Neil McMillen, April 14, 1972, and January 25, 1973, Ruleville, Mississippi; Oral History Program, University of Southern Mississippi," in *The Speeches of Fannie Lou Hamer: To Tell It Like It Is*, ed. Maegan Parker Brooks and Davis W. Houck (University Press of Mississippi, 2011), 149.

237   *"You don't know anything"*: Interview with Fannie Lou Hamer by Anne Romaine and Howard Romaine, 1966, Wisconsin Historical Society, Civil Rights Movement Archive, crmvet.org /nars/66_hamer_romaine.pdf, 5.

237   *"We was ignorant"*: "An Oral History with Honorable Unita Blackwell," 16.

237   *"The motivation of King, of course, is known"*: "Telephone conversation #4940, sound recording, LBJ and Roy Wilkins 8/15/1964, 9:50AM," LBJ Library, discoverlbj.org/item/tel-04940, time stamp 7:02.

237   *"The white volunteers were economically secure"*: William Chafe, *The Unfinished Journey: America Since World War II*, 5th ed. (Oxford University Press, 2003), 167.

238   *"it was a southern organization"*: Quoted in Greenberg, *A Circle of Trust*, 167.

238   *"the Freedom School teachers were second-class citizens"*: McAdam, *Freedom Summer*, 110.

238–39   *"all men had broken down"*: John Appel, "Fighting Fear," *American Heritage* 50, no. 6 (October 1999): 22–30.

239   *"the sturdiest and most stable"*: Leo Bartemeier et al., "Combat Exhaustion," *Journal of Nervous and Mental Disease* 104 (July 1946): 308.

239   *"battle fatigue"*: Robert Coles, "Social Struggle and Weariness," *Psychiatry* 27, no. 4 (November 1964): 308.

239   *"exhaustion, weariness, despair"*: Coles, "Social Struggle and Weariness," 308.

239   *"They say I'm jittery, but who isn't?"*: Quoted in Coles, "Social Struggle and Weariness," 311.

239   *"I dream I'm going to be hurt"*: Quoted in Coles, "Social Struggle and Weariness," 310.

239   *"In many ways these young civil rights workers are in a war"*: Coles, "Social Struggle and Weariness," 315.

239   *"that summer in Mississippi was like guerrilla warfare"*: John Lewis, "Freedom Summer Remembered," in Erenrich, *Freedom Is a Constant Struggle*, 318.

239   *"you didn't know whether"*: Quoted in Howell Raines, *My Soul Is Rested: Movement Days in the Deep South Remembered* (Penguin Books, 1983), 275.

239   *"We just reached the end of the ropes"*: Interview with Dave Dennis, *Eyes on the Prize*.

239   *dreamed that she led her closest friends*: Mary King, *Freedom Song: A Personal Story of the 1960s Civil Rights Movement* (William Morrow, 1987), 406.

240   *"the single most important preventative"*: Jonathan Shay, *Odysseus in America: Combat Trauma and the Trials of Homecoming* (Scribner, 2002), 219.

240   *"I've been depressed since I've returned"*: Martínez, *Letters from Mississippi*, 268–69.

240   *"ever relax fully again"*: Quoted in McAdam, *Freedom Summer*, 114.

240   *"What was it like?"*: Quoted in Martínez, *Letters from Mississippi*, 269.

240   *"You're not the person I married"*: Quoted in McAdam, *Freedom Summer*, 197.

240   *"What am I going to do"*: Quoted in McAdam, *Freedom Summer*, 135.

241   *"I'm in bad shape"*: "Text of speech delivered at the staff retreat of the Student Nonviolent Coordinating Committee at Waveland, Mississippi, November 6, 1964, by James Forman,

Executive Secretary," Civil Rights Movement Archive, crmvet.org/info/6411_sncc_forman -waveland.pdf, 5.

241 *"All the organizational skills"*: Interview with Sam Block by Joseph Sinsheimer, December 12, 1986, Civil Rights Movement Archive, crmvet.org/nars/js_block_oh-r.pdf, 35.

241 *"went off and self-immolated"*: Interview with Barney Frank by Joseph Sinsheimer, November 14, 1983, Civil Rights Movement Archive, crmvet.org/nars/js_frank.pdf, 5.

241 *"I indicated to him that I was not available"*: "Robert Moses interview with Clayborne Carson at Harvard University, March 29, 1982," Civil Rights Movement Archive, crmvet.org/nars /820329_moses_carson.pdf, 3–4.

242 *"It was clear to me"*: Quoted in Laura Visser-Maessen, *Robert Parris Moses: A Life in Civil Rights and Leadership at the Grass Roots* (University of North Carolina Press, 2016), 278.

242 *"I want you to eat and drink"*: Quoted in Sellers, *River of No Return*, 138–39.

242 *"Everyone present seemed to recognize"*: Marsh, *God's Long Summer*, 172.

242 *"You could see him almost starting to crack"*: Lewis, *Walking with the Wind*, 305.

242 *"When Moses left, there was a vacuum"*: All quotes in this paragraph are from "SNCC Executive Committee Meeting," Holly Springs, Mississippi, April 12–14, 1965, Civil Rights Movement Archive, crmvet.org/docs/6504_sncc_excom_min.pdf, 1, 12–14.

243 *"We're not heroes"*: "Questions Raised by Moses," April 1965, Freedom Summer documents collection, University of Southern Mississippi.

243 *"By the spring of 1966"*: Interview with Staughton Lynd and Alice Lynd by Joseph Sinsheimer, December 30, 1985, Civil Rights Movement Archive, crmvet.org/nars/js_lynd.pdf, 17.

243 *Massive resistance ended*: The points in this sentence reflect those in Dittmer, *Local People*, 314, 426.

243 *"We were actually, with that summer project"*: Interview with Robert Moses, May 19, 1986, *Eyes on the Prize*, repository.wustl.edu/downloads/j3860870r.

243 *Some seventeen thousand Black Mississippians*: McAdam, *Freedom Summer*, 81.

244 *"These kids . . . treated us"*: Quoted in Raines, *My Soul Is Rested*, 233.

244 *Race-baiting ceased to be a favored tool*: The points in this sentence and the previous one are from Dittmer, *Local People*, 425, 412.

244 *And in 1976, twelve years after Freedom Summer*: David Garrow, *Protest at Selma: Martin Luther King, Jr., and the Voting Rights Act of 1965* (Yale University Press, 1979), vii.

244 *They returned a few months later often radicalized*: McAdam, *Freedom Summer*, 127–28.

244 *"If you let it, the news media"*: Quoted in King, *Freedom Summer*, 473.

244 *"It is a magnet"*: Interview with Robert Moses by Joseph Sinsheimer, December 5, 1984, Civil Rights Movement Archive, crmvet.org/nars/js_moses3.pdf, 13.

245 *"a national media figure"*: Interview with Robert Moses by Joseph Sinsheimer, December 5, 1984, 13.

245 *"For the media, you don't need even an organization"*: Interview with Robert Moses by Joseph Sinsheimer, April 11, 1984, Civil Rights Movement Archive, crmvet.org/nars/js_moses2-cr5 .pdf, 3.

245 *"He is a genius at exploiting the media"*: Interview with Robert Moses by Joseph Sinsheimer, April 11, 1984, 7.

245 *SNCC's field operations dwindled*: Marsh, *God's Long Summer*, 181–82.

245 *"Believe me, nothing except a battle lost"*: John Marius Wilson, *A Memoir of Field-Marshal the Duke of Wellington* (A. Fullarton, 1853), 2:409.

245 *"Like Selma, the project brought concrete breakthroughs"*: Quoted in King, *Freedom Song*, 522.

11. Selma, 1965

247 *"Well, listen, we're under this crazy injunction"*: Interview with Diane Nash, July 7, 1983, David Garrow Research Files #832, 39–40. Courtesy of David Garrow and Jonathan Eig.

247 *fewer than two hundred*: Taylor Branch, *Pillar of Fire: America in the King Years, 1963–1965* (Simon & Schuster, 1998), 63.

248 *Clark served as the overseer on Hare's plantation*: This paraphrases a passage in David Halberstam, *The Children* (Random House, 1998), 494.

248 *"Jim Clark was a near madman"*: Interview with Rev. Andrew Young, conducted by Blackside, Inc., October 11, 1985, for *Eyes on the Prize: America's Civil Rights Years (1954–1965)*, Washington University Libraries, Film and Media Archive, Henry Hampton Collection, transcript, repository.wustl.edu/downloads/nk322g272.

248 *It consisted of 66 mounted members*: J. Mills Thornton III, *Dividing Lines: Municipal Politics and the Struggle for Civil Rights in Montgomery, Birmingham, and Selma* (University of Alabama Press, 2002), 411.

248 *"Dr. King's and my conversations"*: James Bevel with Randy Kryn, "Declaring Peace: James Bevel's 1960s Movements and Strategies; A Practical History and Guide to Nonviolence" (unpublished manuscript, 1988–2004), 138.

249 *"viewed himself as one of King's apostles"*: Bernard LaFayette, Jr., and Kathryn Lee Johnson, *In Peace and Freedom: My Journey in Selma* (University Press of Kentucky, 2013), 121.

249 *The 1964 act, while quite significant*: This sentence paraphrases a passage in David Garrow, *Protest at Selma: Martin Luther King, Jr., and the Voting Rights Act of 1965* (Yale University Press, 1979), 25.

249 *"The Selma movement was to address"*: Interview with James Bevel, November 13, 1985, *Eyes on the Prize*, repository.wustl.edu/downloads/9306t101z.

250 *"Where Birmingham depended"*: Martin Luther King, Jr., "Civil Right No. 1: The Right to Vote," in *A Testament of Hope: The Essential Writings and Speeches of Martin Luther King, Jr.*, ed. James Melvin Washington (1986; repr. HarperCollins, 1991), 187.

250 *"Did you see Shuttlesworth on TV?"*: Interview with F. D. Reese by Andrew Manis, August 1, 1989, Oral Histories, Birmingham Public Library Digital Collections, transcript, cdm16044 .contentdm.oclc.org/digital/collection/p15099coll2/id/60/rec/1, 21.

250 *"It took us a long time to get a church"*: Interview with J. L. Chestnut by Andrew Manis, December 27, 1989, Oral Histories, Birmingham Public Library Digital Collections, transcript, cdm16044.contentdm.oclc.org/digital/collection/p15099coll2/id/74/rec/2, 35.

250 *"We were laying a trap"*: Interview with James Forman, December 11, 1985, *Eyes on the Prize*, repository.wustl.edu/downloads/pr76f520h.

251 *"Today marks the beginning"*: Harvard Sitkoff, *King: Pilgrimage to the Mountaintop* (Hill and Wang, 2008), 149.

251 *seven hundred Black listeners*: Garrow, *Protest at Selma*, 39.

251 *"a symbol of bitter-end resistance to the civil rights movement"*: Garrow, *Protest at Selma*, 39.

251 *"These officers have to do their jobs"*: LaFayette and Johnson, *In Peace and Freedom*, 71.

252 *"A movement is a living organism"*: James M. Lawson, Jr., with Michael K. Honey and Kent Wong, *Revolutionary Nonviolence: Organizing for Freedom* (University of California Press, 2022), 59.

252 *Bevel told him to stop and get out*: Charles Fager, *Selma, 1965: The March That Changed the South* (Charles Scribner's Sons, 1974), 25.

252 *SNCC had two leaders for each of the five wards*: "Staff Meeting Notes," January 7, 1965, Selma file, SNCC, ProQuest History Vault.

253 *"the block captains have to be pushed"*: "Staff Meeting Notes," January 15, 1965, Selma file, SNCC, ProQuest History Vault.

253 *"The main thing is to keep the police busy"*: "Notes from Meeting with Rev. King after Mass Meeting," January 14, 1965, Selma files, SNCC papers, ProQuest History Vault.

253 *The campaign unfolded with new events*: This section of the chapter, up to "Wednesday, March 3" (p. 265), relies heavily on the chronology at "Civil Rights Movement History; 1965:

Selma & the March to Montgomery; Selma Voting Rights Campaign (Jan–Mar)," Civil Rights Movement Archive, crmvet.org/tim/timhis65.htm.

254 *"Did you hear what I said?"*: Quoted in Halberstam, *The Children*, 497.

254 *"The sheriff is not after you; you are after the sheriff"*: LaFayette and Johnson, *In Peace and Freedom*, 42.

254 *"out of control"*: Quoted in Branch, *Pillar of Fire*, 562.

254 *"just like an expert playing a violin"*: Quoted in Howell Raines, *My Soul Is Rested: Movement Days in the Deep South Remembered* (Penguin Books, 1983), 200.

255 *Teachers had never marched*: Andrew Young, *An Easy Burden: The Civil Rights Movement and the Transformation of America* (Harper, 1996), 349.

255 *"simply electrifying"*: Thornton, *Dividing Lines*, 483.

255 *had been fired the previous fall*: Cooper's employment history is from "Annie Lee Cooper," SNCC Digital Gateway, snccdigital.org/people/annie-lee-cooper/.

255 *"She came right back and punched the sheriff"*: John Lewis, *Walking with the Wind: A Memoir of the Movement* (Simon & Schuster, 2015), 323. The details and quote in the next paragraph are from the same source.

256 *"make discipline break down"*: Quoted in Branch, *Pillar of Fire*, 566.

256 *only fifty-seven Black people*: Branch, *Pillar of Fire*, 570.

256 *Abernathy read aloud to them Psalm 27*: Fager, *Selma, 1965*, 52.

256 *"Selma needed a break"*: Young, *An Easy Burden*, 352.

257 *he told Young that it would be impossible*: Young, *An Easy Burden*, 350.

257 *Then 400 students marched*: Adam Fairclough, *To Redeem the Soul of America: The Southern Christian Leadership Conference and Martin Luther King, Jr.* (University of Georgia Press, 1987), 233.

257 *"400 men were put in a 50 x 16 cubicle"*: "February 4, 1965," summary of Prathia Hall's report the previous evening, SNCC papers included in SCLC files, ProQuest History Vault.

257 *"King wants the same thing I want—Freedom"*: Quoted in Robert Pratt, *Selma's Bloody Sunday: Protest, Voting Rights, and the Struggle for Racial Equality* (Johns Hopkins University Press, 2017), 41.

257 *Diane Nash sat in the chapel office*: Branch, *Pillar of Fire*, 579.

258 *"We have the offensive"*: Quoted in Adam Fairclough, "Martin Luther King, Jr. and the Quest for Nonviolent Social Change," *Phylon* 47, no. 1 (Spring 1986): 10.

258 *A group of fifteen northern congressmen*: Pratt, *Selma's Bloody Sunday*, 40.

258 *"badly beaten"*: Betty Garman (northern coordinator, Friends of SNCC), memo, "Student Nonviolent Coordinating Committee project in Alabama," SCLC files, ProQuest History Vault.

258 *ordered that he be chained*: "WATS reports," February 10, 1965, in "Student Nonviolent Coordinating Committee Wide Area Telephone Service Reports," December 1964 through February 1965, ProQuest History Vault.

258 *Bevel was severely ill and shackled to his bed*: Bevel with Kryn, "Declaring Peace," 92.

259 *Wilson Baker drove two SNCC workers*: Fager, *Selma, 1965*, 67.

259 *"Where are we going in Selma?"*: Quotations in this and the following paragraph are from "Wednesday night at the Torch Motel," February 10, 1965, Selma records, SNCC papers in SCLC files, ProQuest History Vault.

259 *Clark was hospitalized with chest pains*: Fager, *Selma, 1965*, 68.

260 *"I don't remember all everything he called me"*: Interview with Sheriff James Clark, February 19, 1986, *Eyes on the Prize*, repository.wustl.edu/downloads/4t64gq249.

260 *"What kind of people are you?"*: Quoted in Halberstam, *The Children*, 502. Another account states that it was not Clark who hit Vivian; see David Garrow, *Bearing the Cross: Martin Luther King, Jr., and the Southern Christian Leadership Conference* (William Morrow, 1986), 391.

260 *"You do not walk away from that"*: Interview with C. T. Vivian, January 23, 1986, *Eyes on the Prize*, repository.wustl.edu/downloads/br86b5432.

261 *"You're the nigger from Atlanta, aren't you?"*: Quoted in Raines, *My Soul Is Rested*, 191–92.

261 *Jimmie Lee Jackson, a young deacon*: The police murder of Jimmie Lee Jackson is covered in every history of the Selma campaign, but my account relies most on Fager, *Selma, 1965*, 74.

261 *"They turned all the lights out"*: Quoted in Fairclough, *To Redeem the Soul of America*, 239.

261 *"a nightmare of State Police stupidity"*: Quoted in Garrow, *Protest at Selma*, 62.

262 *the attorney general, Nicholas Katzenbach*: Fager, *Selma, 1965*, 78.

262 *"How dare you, lie to me and then hit me"*: Taylor Branch, *At Canaan's Edge: America in the King Years, 1965–68* (Simon & Schuster, 2006), 13.

262 *"I tried to leave, and she blocked my way"*: Bevel with Kryn, "Declaring Peace," 93.

262 *"I started walking across the lawn"*: Bevel with Kryn, "Declaring Peace," 93–94.

263 *Can you come lead the next one?*: Branch, *Pillar of Fire*, 599.

263 *"They were sad, and they were bruised"*: Bevel with Kryn, "Declaring Peace," 229.

263 *"The death of that man"*: Quoted in Fairclough, *To Redeem the Soul of America*, 240.

263 *"Did Governor Wallace order it?"*: Bevel with Kryn, "Declaring Peace," 94.

264 *"When you have a great violation"*: Interview with James Bevel, *Eyes on the Prize*.

265 *"The war in Vietnam is accomplishing nothing"*: Quoted in Branch, *At Canaan's Edge*, 23.

265 *Bevel told reporters*: Garrow, *Protest at Selma*, 68.

265 *"Many people on the committee were opposed"*: "A Short Summary of the Executive Committee Meeting, March 5 and 6, 1965, in Atlanta, Ga.," SNCC, Civil Rights Movement Archive, crmvet.org/docs/6503_sncc_excom.pdf.

266 *"If these people want to march"*: Lewis, *Walking with the Wind*, 332.

266 *King decided not to return to Selma*: Garrow, *Protest at Selma*, 73.

266 *"conducive to the orderly flow of traffic"*: Quoted in Fager, *Selma, 1965*, 89.

266 *flipped coins*: Fager, *Selma, 1965*, 93.

267 *"There had been . . . nowhere near"*: Lewis, *Walking with the Wind*, 337.

267 *"into companies and squads"*: "Selma, Alabama—March 7, 1965," in "SNCC Wide Area Telephone Service reports," ProQuest History Vault, 1.

267 *The squads, of about twenty-five each*: Branch, *At Canaan's Edge*, 48.

268 *Nash worked at the tail end*: Branch, *At Canaan's Edge*, 49.

268 *"They are on the bridge now"*: "Selma, Alabama—March 7, 1965, 3 pm," in "SNCC Wide Area Telephone Service reports," ProQuest History Vault, 1.

268 *leading the equivalent of a frontal attack*: Robert Killebrew to author, email, July 5, 2021.

268 *"You keep your eyes on the prize"*: Interview with John Lewis, November 5, 1985, *Eyes on the Prize*, repository.wustl.edu/downloads/kk91fn310.

268 *"They showed no mercy"*: "Elizabeth Fitts," in Horace Huntley and John McKerley, eds., *Foot Soldiers for Democracy: The Men, Women, and Children of the Birmingham Civil Rights Movement* (University of Illinois Press, 2009), 109.

268 *"Police are beating people"*: "Selma, Alabama—March 7, 1965, 3 pm," 1.

269 *"We could hear people screaming"*: Fay Powell, "Playtime Is Over," in *Hands on the Freedom Plow: Personal Accounts by Women in SNCC*, ed. Faith Holsaert et al. (University of Illinois Press, 2012), 477.

269 *a state trooper dropped a tear gas canister*: Fager, *Selma, 1965*, 94.

269 *people knocked off the bridge*: Raines, *My Soul Is Rested*, 209.

269 *"The police were riding along on horseback"*: Interview with Rev. Andrew Young, *Eyes on the Prize*.

269 *"Beating us back into our community"*: Young, *An Easy Burden*, 356–57.

269 *"We want all the niggers off the streets"*: Quoted in Fager, *Selma, 1965*, 95.

269 *"I don't know to this day how I made it"*: Interview with John Lewis, *Eyes on the Prize*.

269 *"About two or three busloads"*: "Selma, Alabama—March 7, 1965," in "SNCC Wide Area Telephone Service reports," ProQuest History Vault, 2.

269   *some 140 Blacks were injured*: Stephen Oates, *Let the Trumpet Sound: The Life of Martin Luther King, Jr.* (Harper & Row, 1982), 348.

270   *"in the most graphic way possible"*: Bevel with Kryn, "Declaring Peace," 96.

270   *"While the voting rights bill"*: Garrow, *Protest at Selma*, 134.

271   *"There was a shouting match"*: "Selma & the March to Montgomery: A Discussion, November–June, 2004–2005," Civil Rights Movement Archive, crmvet.org/disc/selma.htm.

271   *"You sold out!"*: Bevel with Kryn, "Declaring Peace," 96–97.

271   *Then, at around ten o'clock*: Details in this paragraph are from Branch, *At Canaan's Edge*, 79, 81.

272   *"It was almost as if Jackson's death"*: Young, *An Easy Burden*, 362.

272   *"You white ministers"*: Quoted in Fager, *Selma, 1965*, 131.

272   *In one incident, the mayor*: Fager, *Selma, 1965*, 115.

272   *Clark told Baker that if he interfered again*: Fager, *Selma, 1965*, 142–43.

273   *"So it was at Lexington and Concord"*: Lyndon Johnson, "Special Message to the Congress: The American Promise," March 15, 1965, accessed through the LBJ Library, https://www.lbjlibrary.org/object/text/special-message-congress-american-promise-03-15-1965.

273   *"It really was the final breakup of segregation"*: Interview with C. T. Vivian, *Eyes on the Prize*. For a similar account of this scene, see Lewis, *Walking with the Wind*, 354.

273   *"We've solved the problem"*: Interview with James Bevel, *Eyes on the Prize* transcripts.

273   *"felt extremely alienated"*: Interview with James Forman, *Eyes on the Prize* transcripts.

273   *"like vomiting"*: Interview with Stokely Carmichael, May 5, 1986, *Eyes on the Prize*, repository .wustl.edu/downloads/.

274   *"The problems of victory are more agreeable"*: Winston S. Churchill's *Maxims & Reflections* (Barnes & Noble, 1992), 90.

274   *"I feel like a boy standing at the train platform"*: "Malcolm Hooks," in Huntley and McKerley, *Foot Soldiers for Democracy*, 174.

275   *only three hundred people could participate*: Fager, *Selma, 1965*, 145–46.

275   *the SCLC reserved about 250 of those slots*: Branch, *At Canaan's Edge*, 131.

275   *"ceremonial—almost redundant"*: Renata Adler, "Letter from Selma," April 2, 1965, in *The Matter of Black Lives: Writing from The New Yorker*, ed. Jelani Cobb and David Remnick (Ecco, 2021), 272.

275   *"Keep women and children in the middle"*: Quoted in Adler, "Letter from Selma," 273.

275   *"It was enjoyable and it was tension-filled"*: Interview with Rev. Ralph Abernathy, November 6, 1985, *Eyes on the Prize*, repository.wustl.edu/downloads/vx021g754.

275   *"I knew the ending was just a matter of time"*: Interview with John Lewis, *Eyes on the Prize*.

275   *Oddly, given the parade-like atmosphere*: Details in this paragraph are from Fager, *Selma, 1965*, 153–55.

276   *"Here's the truth of it"*: "Selma & the March to Montgomery: A Discussion, November–June, 2004–2005," 82.

276   *"We have a new song"*: Quoted in Harris Wofford, *Of Kennedys and Kings: Making Sense of the Sixties* (Farrar, Straus & Giroux, 1980), 195.

276   *It was the largest civil rights march*: Oates, *Let the Trumpet Sound*, 362.

276   *All three national television networks*: Garrow, *Protest at Selma*, 117.

276   *"It is not an accident"*: Martin Luther King, Jr., "How Long? Not Long—Our God Is Marching On!," March 25, 1965, Civil Rights Movement Archive, crmvet.org/info/ourgod65.htm.

277   *Andrew Young walked over*: Young, *An Easy Burden*, 367.

277   *"The movement as we have been doing it is over"*: Quoted in James R. Ralph, Jr., and Mary Lou Finley, eds., "In Their Own Voices: The Story of the Movement as Told by the Participants," in *The Chicago Freedom Movement: Martin Luther King Jr. and Civil Rights Activism in the North*, ed. Mary Lou Finley et al. (University Press of Kentucky, 2017), 23.

277 *Black voter registration in Mississippi*: Alan Draper, "The Mississippi Movement: A Review Essay," *Journal of Mississippi History* 60, no. 4 (Winter 1998): 362.

277 *The Deep South began to send*: Young, *An Easy Burden*, 369.

277 *By 2019, there were fifty-two Black members*: Anna Brown and Sara Atske, "Blacks Have Made Gains in U.S. Political Leadership, but Gaps Remain," Pew Research Center, January 18, 2019.

277 *"the single most effective piece of civil rights legislation"*: "Introduction to Federal Voting Rights Laws," U.S. Department of Justice, justice.gov/crt/introduction-federal-voting-rights-laws-0.

278 *elected to the city council*: Garrow, *Protest at Selma*, 188.

278 *"Change didn't come through confrontation and violence"*: Interview with Rev. Andrew Young, *Eyes on the Prize*.

278 *"insist on the immediate participation"*: Fairclough, *To Redeem the Soul of America*, 258.

278 *"I think that it is necessary"*: Martin Luther King, Jr., on NBC's *Meet the Press*, March 28, 1965, SCLC papers, ProQuest History Vault.

279 *Northern governors held it at arm's length*: Fairclough, *To Redeem the Soul of America*, 260.

279 *Bayard Rustin called it stupid*: Branch, *At Canaan's Edge*, 200.

279 *"The casual manner of proposing"*: Quoted in Branch, *At Canaan's Edge*, 200.

279 *"enough progress"*: Quoted in Fager, *Selma, 1965*, 168–69.

279 *"Bevel had seriously misjudged the mood"*: Fager, *Selma, 1965*, 168.

12. Chicago, 1966

281 *A Bridge Too Far*: This chapter's subtitle was inspired by a comment made to me over lunch by Christian Cotz of the First Amendment Museum, Augusta, Maine, September 29, 2021.

281 *"We had first met"*: James Baldwin, *No Name in the Street* (Vintage, 1972), 137.

281 *"I need more time to think"*: "*Playboy* Interview: Martin Luther King, Jr.," January 1965, in *A Testament of Hope: The Essential Writings and Speeches of Martin Luther King, Jr.*, ed. James Melvin Washington (1986; repr. HarperCollins, 1991), 372.

282 *"Maybe I should take a sabbatical"*: Quoted in Dorothy Cotton, *If Your Back's Not Bent: The Role of the Citizenship Education Program in the Civil Rights Movement* (Atria Books, 2012), 251.

282 *"I must undergo personal cleansing"*: Mahatma Gandhi, "The Crime of Chauri Chaura," in *Selected Political Writings*, ed. Dennis Dalton (Hackett Publishing, 1996), 33.

283 *he resembled Dwight Eisenhower*: Thomas E. Ricks, *The Generals: American Military Command from World War II to Today* (Penguin Press, 2012), 85.

283 *"When the future isn't real"*: Jonathan Shay, *Odysseus in America: Combat Trauma and the Trials of Homecoming* (Scribner, 2002), 89.

283 *"We really didn't know"*: Andrew Young, *An Easy Burden: The Civil Rights Movement and the Transformation of America* (Harper, 1996), 376.

284 *"We had been successful in Alabama"*: Young, *An Easy Burden*, 381.

284 *"the nonviolent movement"*: "Executive Staff Retreat," SCLC, November 10–12, 1964, Gaston Motel, Birmingham, Alabama, 7.

284 *receiving invitations to go north*: Dorothy Cotton, "Southern Christian Leadership Conference, Executive Staff Meeting, Hilton Inn, August 26–28, 1965," in "Board Meeting" file, SCLC 1965, in SCLC Papers, ProQuest History Vault. The quotations in the following two paragraphs are also from this document.

284 *"We weren't finished in the South"*: Interview with Diane Nash, in Peter W. Kunhardt, dir., *King in the Wilderness* (Kunhardt Film Foundation, 2018), transcript, kunhardtfilmfoundation.org/featured-interviews/diane-nash.

284 *"You won't beat Daley on his home ground"*: Alan Westin and Barry Mahony, *The Trial of Martin Luther King* (Crowell, 1974), 192.

285 *most successful fundraisers*: Interview with Andrew Young, *King in the Wilderness*, kunhardtfilm
     foundation.org/featured-interviews/andrew-young.
285 *"The real estate dealers in Chicago"*: Quoted in David Garrow, *Bearing the Cross: Martin Luther
     King, Jr., and the Southern Christian Leadership Conference* (William Morrow, 1986), 432.
285 *"getting rid of the slums"*: Quoted in Garrow, *Bearing the Cross*, 444.
285 *"not to patch up the ghetto, but to abolish it"*: Quoted in Garrow, *Bearing the Cross*, 452.
286 *"we must be prepared"*: Quoted in Garrow, *Bearing the Cross*, 457.
286 *"He who defends everything defends nothing"*: Quoted, for example, in Antony Beevor, *D-Day:
     The Battle for Normandy* (Viking, 2009), 32. See also Stephen R A'Barrow, *Death of a Nation: A
     New History of Germany* (Book Guild, 2015).
287 *this was another tactic of Gandhi's*: Joseph Lelyveld, *Great Soul: Mahatma Gandhi and His Strug-
     gle with India* (Vintage, 2012), 328.
287 *Bevel had selected for King*: Taylor Branch, *At Canaan's Edge: America in the King Years, 1965–68*
     (Simon & Schuster, 2006), 408, 427.
287 *"remove gargantuan structures of injustice"*: Martin Luther King, Jr., address at the Chicago Free-
     dom Festival, March 12, 1966, Civil Rights Movement Archive, crmvet.org/docs/6603_sclc
     _mlk_cfm.pdf, 1.
287 *"movement to end slums"*: King, address at the Chicago Freedom Festival, 11.
287 *"Time will not permit me"*: King, address at the Chicago Freedom Festival, 8.
287 *"the grapes of wrath are stored"*: Quoted in Branch, *At Canaan's Edge*, 468.
288 *"Cities are sponges that soak up troops"*: "Urban Combat," *The Cipher Brief*, November 6, 2017.
288 *"With never more than fifty staff members"*: Adam Fairclough, *To Redeem the Soul of America: The
     Southern Christian Leadership Conference and Martin Luther King, Jr.* (University of Georgia
     Press, 1987), 288.
288 *"We're going to organize"*: Quoted in Don Terry, "King Led a Crusade from Chicago 3-Flat,"
     Chicago Tribune, January 20, 1986.
288 *the religious ground was quite different*: James R. Ralph, Jr., and Mary Lou Finley, eds., "In Their
     Own Voices: The Story of the Movement as Told by the Participants," in *The Chicago Freedom
     Movement: Martin Luther King Jr. and Civil Rights Activism in the North*, ed. Mary Lou Finley
     et al. (University Press of Kentucky, 2017), 35.
288 *"Chicago blacks unenthusiastic"*: August Meier and Elliott Rudwick, *Along the Color Line: Explo-
     rations in the Black Experience* (University of Illinois Press, 1976), 327.
288 *some Chicago activists suggested*: Garrow, *Bearing the Cross*, 471.
288 *A rally in July at Chicago's Soldier Field*: Young, *An Easy Burden*, 409. However, Garrow, in *Bear-
     ing the Cross*, 492, says that the number may have been larger, as does Fairclough in *To Redeem
     the Soul of America*, 292.
288 *"This day we must decide"*: Quoted in Manning Marable, *Black American Politics: From the Wash-
     ington Marches to Jesse Jackson* (Verso, 1985), 207.
289 *"I believe our young people"*: Quoted in Branch, *At Canaan's Edge*, 504.
289 *"Our movement won"*: Quoted in Garrow, *Bearing the Cross*, 515.
289 *Bevel had aimed to recruit*: Fairclough, *To Redeem the Soul of America*, 328–29.
289 *one should never reinforce failure*: This saying appears in hundreds of works of military history.
     See, for example, J. F. Lazenby, *The Peloponnesian War: A Military Study* (Routledge, 2004),
     169. Winston Churchill generally was a deft military strategist in World War II, but he erred in
     wanting to persist by pouring troops and materiel into the stalemated Italian campaign, and so
     argued against diverting resources from there to support the Allied landings in southern France
     in August 1944, which would prove enormously successful. See Thomas E. Ricks, *Churchill and
     Orwell: The Fight for Freedom* (Penguin Press, 2017), 198–200. A good modern nonmilitary
     example is the long-running and fruitless U.S. government "war on drugs."

289   *"We were trying to find a way"*: Interview with Rev. Andrew Young, conducted by Blackside,
      Inc., October 11, 1985, for *Eyes on the Prize: America's Civil Rights Years (1954–1965)*, Wash-
      ington University Libraries, Film and Media Archive, Henry Hampton Collection, transcript,
      repository.wustl.edu/downloads/nk322g272.

289   *King emerged with a statement*: Stephen Oates, *Let the Trumpet Sound: The Life of Martin Luther
      King, Jr.* (Harper & Row, 1982), 415.

290   *"All in all, the Summit Agreement"*: Fairclough, *To Redeem the Soul of America*, 303.

290   *"This must be interpreted"*: Garrow, *Bearing the Cross*, 523.

290   *"To most political observers"*: Marable, *Black American Politics*, 209.

290   *Daley let it be known*: Branch, *At Canaan's Edge*, 550.

290   *"Our movement looked like"*: James Bevel with Randy Kryn, "Declaring Peace: James Bevel's
      1960s Movements and Strategies; A Practical History and Guide to Nonviolence" (unpublished
      manuscript, 1988–2004), 115.

290   *"a great deal of confusion in the air"*: "Dr. King's speech, Frogmore—November 14, 1966,"
      SNCC Files, ProQuest History Vault.

290   *"In all frankness, we found the job"*: Quoted in Fairclough, *To Redeem the Soul of America*, 329.

290   *Timuel Black, a veteran organizer*: Timuel Black, *Sacred Ground: The Chicago Streets of Timuel
      Black* (Northwestern University Press, 2019).

291   *"Take a long, hard look"*: Garrow, *Bearing the Cross*, 559–60.

291   *"Many of SCLC's regular staff members"*: Quote in Fairclough, *To Redeem the Soul of America*, 323.

291   *the rise of Barack Obama*: See, for example, James Ralph, Jr., "Interpreting the Chicago Freedom
      Movement: The Last Fifty Years," in Finley et al., *The Chicago Freedom Movement*, 93–94.

291   *Bevel departed Chicago*: Mary Lou Finley, "Movement Success: The Long View," in Finley et al.,
      The Chicago Freedom Movement, 412.

291   *"Bevel sounds like he's off his rocker"*: Quoted in Branch, *At Canaan's Edge*, 577. See also Garrow,
      Bearing the Cross, 543.

291   *"Bevel perhaps needed psychiatric commitment"*: L. D. Reddick, "MLK at Strategy Meeting,"
      March 7, [apparently 1967], L. D. Reddick papers, Schomburg Center for Research in Black
      Culture, New York Public Library.

292   *"Our staff problems are unbelievable"*: Quoted in Branch, *At Canaan's Edge*, 584.

292   *fired three 16-gauge shotgun loads*: Aram Goudsouzian, *Down to the Crossroads: Civil Rights, Black
      Power, and the Meredith March Against Fear* (Farrar, Straus & Giroux, 2014), 23.

292   *The SNCC people drove away Wilkins*: Clayborne Carson, *In Struggle: SNCC and the Black Awak-
      ening of the 1960s* (Harvard University Press, 1981), 207.

292   *"started to scream and curse"*: Peniel Joseph, *Stokely: A Life* (Basic Civitas, 2014), 108.

293   *"When you get shoved you get confused"*: Quoted in Fairclough, *To Redeem the Soul of America*,
      310.

293   *"We're not a protest movement"*: Quoted in Branch, *At Canaan's Edge*, 464.

293   *"to see where we can use him"*: Interview with Stokely Carmichael, May 5, 1986, *Eyes on the Prize*,
      repository.wustl.edu/downloads/4x51hk606.

293   *"Well, Stokely, I've been used before"*: Quoted in Goudsouzian, *Down to the Crossroads*, 183.

293   *he doubted he could continue*: Garrow, *Bearing the Cross*, 489. For a similar account, see Goud-
      souzian, *Down to the Crossroads*, 245.

293   *"Every courthouse in Mississippi"*: Quoted in John Dittmer, *Local People: The Struggle for Civil
      Rights in Mississippi* (University of Illinois Press, 1995), 396.

294   *"The system had learned"*: Interview with Stokely Carmichael, November 7, 1988, *Eyes on the Prize
      II: America at the Racial Crossroads (1965–1985)*, repository.wustl.edu/downloads/jw827g69g.
      See also interview with James Lawson by Joan Beifuss and David Yellin, August 21, 1969, "Sani-
      tation Strike Tapes," Memphis and the Mid-South Files, Rhodes College Digital Archives, dlynx
      .rhodes.edu/jspui/bitstream/10267/33762/2/SS248_transcript.pdf.

294 *"Carmichael's cry for Black Power"*: Quoted in Eric Etheridge, "How Stokely Carmichael Betrayed the Movement," *Breach of Peace* blog, May 21, 2010.

294 *"didn't do a damn thing"*: Quoted in Howell Raines, *My Soul Is Rested: Movement Days in the Deep South Remembered* (Penguin Books, 1983), 422.

294 *"The Black Power movement"*: Interview with Andrew Young, *King in the Wilderness*.

294 *"My father was a southern boy"*: Interview with Enoch Bevel by the author, December 27, 2020.

294 *Unseen in all this infighting*: This paragraph is based on Goudsouzian, *Down to the Crossroads*, 45–46, 215, 223, 242.

295 *the largest civil rights gathering*: Joseph, *Stokely*, 120.

295 *"Over the last few months"*: Unaired NBC News interview with King in Atlanta, Georgia, May 8, 1967, YouTube, youtube.com/watch?v=2xsbt3a7K-8.

295 *"that we have been wrong"*: Martin Luther King, Jr., "Beyond Vietnam," April 4, 1967, King Papers, Stanford University. A somewhat different version of this speech, lacking the concluding reference to Amos 5:24, is Martin Luther King, Jr., "A Time to Break Silence," in *A Testament of Hope: The Essential Writings and Speeches of Martin Luther King, Jr.*, ed. James Melvin Washington (1986; repr. HarperCollins, 1991), 231–44.

295 *"his most important and creative speech"*: James Lawson testimony in *Coretta Scott King v. Loyd Jower*, 4:372.

295 *"He told me the death threats at home"*: Lawson testimony in *Coretta Scott King v. Loyd Jower*, 4:377.

296 *"The movement must address itself"*: Martin Luther King, Jr., "Where Do We Go From Here?," August 1967, address to the 11th Annual SCLC Convention, King Papers, Stanford University.

296 *"We must pursue peaceful ends"*: Martin Luther King, Jr., "A Christmas Sermon on Peace," December 24, 1967, King Papers, Stanford University.

296 *"the whites should be put off"*: "Central Committee Meeting Notes and Decisions of May 1967," Selma files, SNCC papers, ProQuest History Vault, 66.

296 *Fannie Lou Hamer resigned in protest*: Dittmer, *Local People*, 408.

296 *Some of the more callous staff members*: Joseph, *Stokely: A Life*, 167.

296 *"SNCC is moving from rhetoric to program"*: Carson, *In Struggle*, 253.

297 *"There was Rap Brown running on one end"*: Quoted in Carson, *In Struggle*, 280.

297 *"We have the guns"*: Quoted in Bobby Seale, *Seize the Time: The Story of the Black Panther Party and Huey P. Newton* (Random House, 1970), 73.

297 *"the total destruction"*: Quoted in *The Black Panther Leaders Speak*, ed. Louis Heath (Scarecrow Press, 1976), 34.

297 *They sometimes engaged in shouting matches*: Joshua Bloom and Waldo Martin, *Black Against Empire: The History and Politics of the Black Panther Party* (University of California Press, 2016), 45–47.

297 *"I started seeing these images"*: Quoted in *The Black Panthers: Portraits from an Unfinished Revolution*, ed. Bryan Shih and Yohuru Williams (Nation Books, 2016), 62.

298 *they did not conduct*: Seale, *Seize the Time*, 153–54.

298 *"The cadre doesn't relate"*: Quoted in Thomas Sugre, *Sweet Land of Liberty: The Forgotten Struggle for Civil Rights in the North* (Random House, 2008), 409.

298 *the problem for the Panthers*: See, for example, Yohuru Williams, "'Give Them a Cause to Die For': The Black Panther Party in Milwaukee, 1969–1977," in *Liberated Territory: Untold Local Perspectives on the Black Panther Party*, ed. Yohuru Williams and Jama Lazerow (Duke University Press, 2008), 251.

298 *"We had more members"*: Huey Newton, *Revolutionary Suicide* (Harcourt Brace Jovanovich, 1973), 150–51.

298 *"The party grew much too rapidly"*: Interview with Huey P. Newton, May 23, 1989, for *Eyes on*

the Prize II: America at the Racial Crossroads (1965–1985), digital.wustl.edu/cgi/t/text/text-idx ?c=eop;cc=eop;rgn=main;view=text;idno=new5427.0458.119.

298 *"The BPP [Black Panther Party] was not"*: Judson Jeffries and Ryan Nissim-Sabat, "Painting a More Complete Portrait of the Black Panther Party," in *Comrades: A Local History of the Black Panther Party*, ed. Judson Jeffries (Indiana University Press, 2007), 1.

299 *"the greatest threat to the internal security"*: "The FBI's Covert Action Program to Destroy the Black Panther Party," *Supplementary Detailed Staff Reports on Intelligence Activities and the Rights of Americans, Book III*, Select Committee to Study Governmental Operations, April 23, 1976, hsdl.org/?view&did=479831, 2.

299 *They were particularly lax*: Ahmad Rahman, "Marching Blind: The Rise and Fall of the Black Panther Party in Detroit," in Williams and Lazerow, *Liberated Territory*, 217.

299 *"the power of the gun"*: Quoted in Heath, *The Black Panther Leaders Speak*, x.

299 *"shootings, beatings, and a high degree of unrest"*: "The FBI's Covert Action Program to Destroy the Black Panther Party," 3.

300 *Of 295 actions launched by the FBI*: Bloom and Martin, *Black Against Empire*, 210.

300 *before dawn on December 4, 1969*: Bloom and Martin, *Black Against Empire*, 238.

300 *the police had fired eighty-two times*: Bloom and Martin, *Black Against Empire*, 246.

300 *In Chicago, as in Detroit and Los Angeles*: For Chicago and Detroit security chiefs being informants, see Rahman, "Marching Blind," 217; for Los Angeles, see Judson Jeffries and Malcolm Foley, "To Live and Die in L.A.," in Jeffries, *Comrades*, 279.

300 *In New York, three members*: Curtis Austin, *Up Against the Wall: Violence in the Making and the Unmaking of the Black Panther Party* (University of Arkansas Press, 2006), 278, 280.

300 *American law enforcement officials*: Judson Jeffries, "Revising Panther History in Baltimore," in Jeffries, *Comrades*, 41.

300 *likely that the true scope and reach*: See Harris Wofford, *Of Kennedys and Kings: Making Sense of the Sixties* (Farrar, Straus & Giroux, 1980), 204.

300 *"the ostentatious display of weaponry"*: Quoted in Peter Kraska and Victor Kappeler, "Militarizing American Police: The Rise and Normalization of Paramilitary Units," *Social Problems* 44, no. 1 (February 1997): 10.

301 *"May God help you to help yourself"*: Quoted in Garrow, *Bearing the Cross*, 565.

301 *"I don't feel like speaking to people"*: Quoted in Garrow, *Bearing the Cross*, 571.

301 *"I don't want to do this anymore"*: Quoted in Branch, *At Canaan's Edge*, 641. For more on the dissension at the Airlie House meeting, see David Varel, *The Scholar and the Struggle: Lawrence Reddick's Crusade for Black History and Black Power* (University of North Carolina Press, 2020), 177.

301 *"King was visibly angry at Bevel"*: Quoted in Branch, *At Canaan's Edge*, 653.

13. Memphis, 1968

303 *"If you miss me from the Movement"*: Mary King, *Freedom Song: A Personal Story of the 1960s Civil Rights Movement* (William Morrow, 1987), 328.

303 *"You know what?"*: Quoted in Michael K. Honey, *Going Down Jericho Road: The Memphis Strike, Martin Luther King's Last Campaign* (W. W. Norton, 2007), 303–304. This paragraph also reflects Michael K. Honey to author, email, July 13, 2021.

304 *the tactic was one that Gandhi had favored*: See, for example, Louis Fischer, *The Life of Mahatma Gandhi* (HarperCollins, 1997), 225.

304 *"One of the things he said to me"*: Interview with James Lawson by Joan Beifuss and David Yellin, July 8, 1970, "Sanitation Strike Tapes," Memphis and the Mid-South Files, Rhodes College Digital Archives, dlynx.rhodes.edu/jspui/bitstream/10267/33759/2/SS243_transcript.pdf.

305 *"Jim Lawson has been around for so long"*: Interview with Andrew Young, conducted by Blackside,

Inc., October 27, 1988, for *Eyes on the Prize II: America at the Racial Crossroads (1965–1985)*, Washington University Libraries, Film and Media Archive, Henry Hampton Collection, transcript, digital.wustl.edu/cgi/t/text/text-idx?c=eop;cc=eop;rgn=main;view=text;idno=you5427 .0112.179.

305 *about five thousand participants*: Richard Lentz, "Sixty-Five Days in Memphis: A Study of Culture, Symbols, and the Press," in *We Shall Overcome: The Civil Rights Movement in the United States in the 1950's and 1960's*, ed. David Garrow (Carlson Publishing, 1989), 2:575.

306 *two liquor stores had been looted*: Honey, *Going Down Jericho Road*, 341.

306 *"The people were trampling over my feet"*: Quoted in Honey, *Going Down Jericho Road*, 303.

306 *"It was just a mass of people"*: Quoted in Henry Hampton and Steve Fayer, *Voices of Freedom: An Oral History of the Civil Rights Movement from the 1950s Through the 1980s* (Bantam Books, 1990), 460.

306 *"Those assigned to marshal the participants"*: Andrew Young, *An Easy Burden: The Civil Rights Movement and the Transformation of America* (Harper, 1996), 453.

306 *"Jim, call off this march right now"*: Quoted in Flip Schulke and Penelope McPhee, *King Remembered* (W. W. Norton, 1986), 240.

306 *"I told Reverend Lawson"*: Quoted in Kate Ellis and Stephen Smith, "King's Last March," APM Reports, features.apmreports.org/arw/king/c1.html.

306 *"I consulted nobody"*: Interview with James Lawson, July 8, 1970, "Sanitation Strike Tapes."

307 *Behind them, the parade degenerated*: Hampton and Fayer, *Voices of Freedom*, 461.

307 *Looters ransacked stores*: List of looted stores is from Joan Beifuss, *At the River I Stand*, rev. ed. (St. Lukes Press, 1990), 300.

307 *with a full-scale law enforcement riot*: Honey, *Going Down Jericho Road*, 347.

307 *the first time that King had seen violence*: Young, *An Easy Burden*, 455.

308 *"Not having had that big of a march"*: Interview with James Lawson, July 8, 1970, "Sanitation Strike Tapes."

308 *"We should have had some intelligence work done"*: Quoted in Alan Westin and Barry Mahony, *The Trial of Martin Luther King* (Crowell, 1974), 264.

308 *"One of the things he said"*: Interview with James Lawson, July 8, 1970, "Sanitation Strike Tapes."

308 *Sitting in Suite 801*: Suite number is from Taylor Branch, *At Canaan's Edge: America in the King Years, 1965–68* (Simon & Schuster, 2006), 744.

308 *King stayed awake until dawn*: Garrow, *Bearing the Cross*, 614.

308 *"Martin Luther King is dead. He's finished"*: Quoted in David Garrow, "Martin Luther King, Jr., and the Spirit of Leadership," in *We Shall Overcome: Martin Luther King, Jr., and the Black Freedom Struggle*, ed. Peter J. Albert and Ronald Hoffman (Pantheon, 1990), 32.

308–309 *"Our demonstrations have been planned"*: Quoted in Ellis and Smith, "King's Last March."

309 *Lawson then held his own press conference*: Honey, *Going Down Jericho Road*, 378.

309 *"He was more depressed that night"*: Quoted in Hampton and Fayer, *Voices of Freedom*, 463.

309 *"The Reverend Martin Luther King"*: Quoted in Honey, *Going Down Jericho Road*, 377.

309 *"I'm just happy that God has allowed me"*: Martin Luther King Jr., "I've Been to the Mountaintop," address delivered at Bishop Charles Mason Temple, Memphis, Tennessee, April 3, 1968, Martin Luther King Jr. Research and Education Institute, Stanford University. Other quotations from this speech are from this same source.

310 *King was standing on a balcony*: Charles E. Cobb, Jr., *On the Road to Freedom: A Guided Tour of the Civil Rights Trail* (Algonquin Books, 2008), 338.

310 *requested that he include his favorite song*: "Timeline" in Marc Perrusquia, "Leading Up to 6:01: The Last 32 Hours of Martin Luther King, Jr.," *Memphis Commercial Appeal*, March 28, 2018.

310 *A moment later, at 6:01, a sniper's bullet*: Oates, *Let the Trumpet Sound*, 491.

310 *"I was the first person to get to him"*: Interview with Ralph Abernathy, November 6, 1985,

Eyes on the Prize: America's Civil Rights Years (1954–1965), repository.wustl.edu/downloads
/vx021g754.

310 *He instinctively prepared for great pain*: Interview with James Bevel by Katharine Shannon, Civil
Rights Documentation Project, Moorland-Spingarn Research Center, Howard University, 11.

310 *"I could see right down into his mouth and neck"*: James Bevel with Randy Kryn, "Declaring
Peace: James Bevel's 1960s Movements and Strategies; A Practical History and Guide to Nonviolence" (unpublished manuscript, 1988–2004), 142.

310 *forty-six people had been killed*: Harvard Sitkoff, *The Struggle for Black Equality* (1981; repr. Hill
and Wang, 2008), 144.

311 *"James Bevel and Jesse Jackson wasted time"*: Young, *An Easy Burden*, 484.

311 *"I was in a daze, functioning on autopilot"*: Young, *An Easy Burden*, 485.

311 *Young jumped over a conference table*: Young, *An Easy Burden*, 490.

311 *"I sank into a depression"*: Young, *An Easy Burden*, 486.

312 *"The Civil Rights Revolution"*: A. Philip Randolph, "The Crisis of the Civil Rights Revolution,"
address at the 25th Annual Institute of Race Relations, Fisk University, Nashville, Tennessee,
June 24, 1968, 4.

312 *"A year in the Movement"*: Interview with Bob Moses by John Biewen, "Oh Freedom Over
Me," February 2001, American Radio Works, americanradioworks.publicradio.org/features/oh
_freedom/.

312 *Lawrence Guyot, a Black Mississippian*: Howell Raines, *My Soul Is Rested: Movement Days in the
Deep South Remembered* (Penguin Books, 1983), 290.

312 *"I've always felt that many people"*: Quoted in Eric Etheridge, *Breach of Peace: Portraits of the
1961 Mississippi Freedom Riders* (Atlas, 2008), 126.

312 *some of the sexual adventurism*: See David Garrow, "The Troubling Legacy of Martin Luther
King," *Standpoint*, June 2019, 30–37.

313 *"for some vets, orgasm functions"*: Quoted in Jonathan Shay, *Odysseus in America: Combat Trauma
and the Trials of Homecoming* (Scribner, 2002), 118.

313 *Indeed, the clinical understanding of PTSD*: See David Morris, *The Evil Hours: A Biography of
Post-Traumatic Stress Disorder* (Houghton Mifflin Harcourt, 2015), 17, 143–44.

313 *"I think the people who believed"*: Quoted in Raines, *My Soul Is Rested*, 259.

313 *Donaldson pleaded guilty*: Martin Weil, "Ivanhoe Donaldson, Civil Rights Organizer, Confidant
of Marion Barry, Dies at 74," *Washington Post*, April 5, 2016.

314 *volunteer who had been tortured*: Raines, *My Soul Is Rested*, 273.

314 *"I just thank the Lord"*: Quoted in Etheridge, *Breach of Peace*, 232.

314 *"It comes as a great shock"*: "Transcript of the Baldwin versus Buckley Debate at the Cambridge
Union," in Nicholas Buccola, *The Fire Is Upon Us: James Baldwin, William F. Buckley Jr., and the
Debate over Race in America* (Princeton University Press, 2019), 381.

314 *"They just couldn't take the movement"*: Interview with Septima Poinsette Clark, Southern Oral
History Program Collection, University of North Carolina at Chapel Hill.

314 *"I don't think they were really aware"*: Quoted in Raines, *My Soul Is Rested*, 107–108.

315 *He fled to Canada*: "Robert Moses interview with Clayborne Carson at Harvard University,"
March 29, 1982, Civil Rights Movement Archive, crmvet.org/nars/820329_moses_carson.pdf,
51–56.

315 *"I've always felt that was a blessing"*: Quoted in John Blake, *Children of the Movement* (Lawrence
Hill Books, 2004), 44.

315 *He did not set foot in Mississippi*: Taylor Branch, *Pillar of Fire: America in the King Years, 1963–
1965* (Simon & Schuster, 1998), 613.

315 *Moses started the Algebra Project*: Robert P. Moses, "An Earned Insurgency: Quality Education as
a Constitutional Right," *Harvard Educational Review* 79, no. 2 (Summer 2009): 378.

316 *"He exudes tranquility"*: Blake, *Children of the Movement*, 41.

316 *Similarly, after splitting with James Bevel*: The first two sentences in this paragraph summarize David Halberstam, *The Children* (Random House, 1998), 631–35.

316 *"There is a satisfaction"*: Quoted in Fred Powledge, *Free at Last?: The Civil Rights Movement and the People Who Made It* (Little, Brown, 1991), 646.

316 *Some of the oddest*: Etheridge, *Breach of Peace*, 50.

317 *A study of a group of World War II veterans*: Margaret Lindorff, "After the War Is Over: PTSD Symptoms in World War II Veterans," *Australasian Journal of Disaster and Trauma Studies*, 2002, no. 2.

317 *"a worthwhile fellow"*: "Interview with Septima Poinsette Clark," Southern Oral History Program Collection.

317 *Jackson, having feuded with Ralph Abernathy*: David L. Chappell, *Waking from the Dream: The Struggle for Civil Rights in the Shadow of Martin Luther King, Jr.* (Random House, 2014), 33–34.

317 *"dishonest and vicious"*: Peniel Joseph, *Stokely: A Life* (Basic Civitas, 2014), 280.

318 *Dennis Sweeney, a former volunteer*: Affidavit of Dennis Sweeney on SNCC letterhead, Civil Rights Movement Archive, crmvet.org/docs/640708_sncc_mcc_sweeney_affidavit.pdf.

318 *Sweeney, who had been briefly married*: Information in this paragraph is from King, *Freedom Song*, 510, 517.

318 *"My wife loved people"*: Quoted in Kay Mills, *This Little Light of Mine: The Life of Fannie Lou Hamer* (University Press of Kentucky, 2007), 303.

318 *"Broadly speaking, religious belief"*: David Morris to author, email, July 7, 2021.

318 *"they came through in fine style"*: John Dittmer to author, email, July 2, 2021.

319 *Pauli Murray, who after helping*: Information in this paragraph is from Anthony Siracusa, *Nonviolence Before King: The Politics of Being and the Black Freedom Struggle* (University of North Carolina Press, 2021), 13, 103.

319 *"My mom says he was on the verge"*: Interview with Enoch Bevel by the author, December 27, 2020.

319 *may constitute a wound more painful*: Leo Bartemeier et al., "Combat Exhaustion," *Journal of Nervous and Mental Disease* 104 (July 1946): 378.

319 *"SCLC's Executive Board misdefined"*: James Bevel with Randy Kryn, "Declaring Peace: James Bevel's 1960s Movements and Strategies; A Practical History and Guide to Nonviolence" (unpublished manuscript, 1988–2004), 147.

319 *"where Judas was on trial"*: Bevel with Kryn, "Declaring Peace," 207.

319 *The following summer, at Paschal's Motor Hotel*: Andrew Young, *An Easy Burden: The Civil Rights Movement and the Transformation of America* (Harper, 1996), 504. See also John Lewis, *Walking with the Wind: A Memoir of the Movement* (Simon & Schuster, 2015), 428.

320 *"That weekend was like"*: Bevel with Kryn, "Declaring Peace," 237.

320 *frequently compared himself to Zeus and Jesus*: John Blake, "Survivors of a Revolution," *Chicago Tribune*, November 5, 2000.

320 *"I wanted to stand up"*: Quoted in Blake, *Children of the Movement*, 3.

320 *"a man who is totally concerned"*: Julius Lester, "Political Psychiatry: An Interview with James Bevel," *Evergreen Review* 15, no. 89 (May 1971): 48.

320 *In November 2005, ten of his children*: Enoch Bevel, "Faithful to My Father's Dream," *Dissent* 57, no. 2 (Spring 2010).

320 *Years earlier, his father had been*: Jakobi Williams, "Racial Coalition Politics in Chicago: A Case Study of Fred Hampton, the Illinois Black Panther Party, and the Origin of the Rainbow Coalition" (PhD diss., University of California, Los Angeles, 2008), 108.

321 *"He was my best friend"*: Information and quotations in this paragraph are from interview with Enoch Bevel by the author, December 27, 2020.

322 *They also took legal action*: Blake, *Children of the Movement*, 105. However, the *Washington Post*'s obituary of Hampton states that after being contacted by lawyers for the King children, Hampton

himself initiated a lawsuit charging that their threats and demands were having a chilling effect on his work. See "Documentary Film Maker Henry Hampton Dies," *Washington Post*, November 24, 1998.

322 *Ralph David Abernathy III*: Rosalind Bentley, "Cancer Claims Abernathy III, Ending His Fight to Revive Dad's Legacy," *Atlanta Journal-Constitution*, August 16, 2016.

322 *"I went out of my way"*: Quoted in Blake, *Children of the Movement*, 87.

322 *"Bo wants to be a millionaire"*: Quoted in Blake, *Children of the Movement*, 90.

322 *"I want to integrate the money"*: Quoted in Blake, *Children of the Movement*, 84.

322 *"One of the things that I have discovered"*: Interview with Jim Zwerg in *People's Century: Skin Deep*, PBS, aired October 20, 1996.

Epilogue

325 *"We live better because of it"*: Charles E. Cobb, Jr., *On the Road to Freedom: A Guided Tour of the Civil Rights Trail* (Algonquin Books, 2008), 232. For Cobb's role in conceiving the Freedom Schools, see, for example, George Chilcoat and Jerry Ligon, "Developing Democratic Citizens: The Mississippi Freedom Schools," in *Freedom Is a Constant Struggle: An Anthology of the Mississippi Civil Rights Movement*, edited by Susie Erenrich (Black Belt Press, 1999), 108. Also see Bob Zellner, *The Wrong Side of Murder Creek: A White Southerner in the Freedom Movement* (NewSouth Books, 2008), 138, where Zellner writes that "Cobb and some of the SNCC people developed the idea of the Freedom School."

325 *"I believe in states' rights"*: "Ronald Reagan's 1980 Neshoba County Fair Speech," *Neshoba (Mississippi) Democrat*, August 3, 1980.

325 *America's demographics and values*: For example, the people who assaulted the Capitol building on January 6, 2021, tended to be older, white males with jobs. "Those involved are, by and large, older and more professional than right-wing protesters we have surveyed in the past. They typically have no ties to existing right-wing groups. But like earlier protesters, they are 95 percent White and 85 percent male." Robert Pape, "What an Analysis of 377 Americans Arrested or Charged in the Capitol Insurrection Tells Us," *Washington Post*, April 6, 2021.

326 *"a North Star that would guide"*: "Barack Obama's DNC Speech," CNN, August 20, 2020.

327 *Stacey Abrams, a Black female lawyer*: The details in this paragraph are drawn from Stacey Abrams, *Our Time Is Now: Power, Purpose, and the Fight for a Fair America* (Henry Holt, 2020), 79, 59–60, 88, 64–69.

328 *"target[ed] African Americans with almost surgical precision"*: Carol Anderson, *One Person, No Vote: How Voter Suppression Is Destroying Our Democracy* (Bloomsbury, 2018), x.

328 *the son of a Black Army veteran*: Ben Jealous and Trabian Shorters, eds., *Reach: 40 Black Men Speak on Living, Leading, and Succeeding* (Atria, 2015), 227.

328 *American police culture*: This paragraph summarizes the findings listed in "Police Shootings Are Not Letting Up," *Washington Post*, August 20, 2021.

329 *"I can't breathe. NOT GUILTY?!?!?!?!"*: Alicia Garza, *The Purpose of Power: How We Come Together When We Fall Apart* (One World, 2020), 110–11.

329 *Then came more deaths*: Barbara Ransby, *Making All Black Lives Matter: Reimagining Freedom in the Twenty-First Century* (University of California Press, 2018), 101.

329 *two-thirds of white Americans*: Bob Harrison, "Policing in the Post-Floyd Era," *Rand Review*, July–August 2021, 7.

330 *"It's easy to be reactive"*: Quoted in Andrew Marantz, "How to Stop a Power Grab," *New Yorker*, November 23, 2020.

330 *there are some major differences*: The details here are from Ransby, *Making All Black Lives Matter*, 46, 106–107.

331 *"Movement people will sometimes say"*: Quoted in "That Movement Responsibility: An Interview with Judy Richardson on Movement Values and Movement History," in *Civil Rights History*

from the Ground Up: Local Struggles, a National Movement, ed. Emilye Crosby (University of Georgia Press, 2011), 372.

331 *"numbers, defections"*: Quoted in "Protests in Perspective: Civil Disobedience & Activism Today, with Erica Chenoweth & Deva Woodly," *Carnegie Council Transcripts and Articles*, November 16, 2020, 4.

332 *"civil rights app"*: This phrase was coined by my friend Cullen Murphy in his critique of an early draft of this epilogue.

333 *"start to think about themselves"*: Quoted in "Protests in Perspective," 3.

333 *"laid the foundation"*: "Freedom Summer," Movement for Black Lives, m4bl.org/freedom -summer.

333 *Woodly traces the roots*: Deva Woodly, *Reckoning: Black Lives Matter and the Democratic Necessity of Social Movements* (Oxford University Press, 2022), 136.

333 *"Black Lives Matter has struggled"*: Clayton, "Black Lives Matter and the Civil Rights Movement."

333 *"Activists picked places like Birmingham"*: Quoted in Sujata Gupta, "What the 1960s Civil Rights Protests Can Teach Us About Fighting Racism Today," *ScienceNews*, June 5, 2020. See also Omar Wasow, "Agenda Seeding: How 1960s Blacks Protests Moved Elites, Public Opinion and Voting," *American Political Science Review* 114, no. 3 (August 2020).

334 *Erica Chenoweth studied 627 resistance movements*: Erica Chenoweth, *Civil Resistance: What Everyone Needs to Know* (Oxford University Press, 2021), 255–85.

334 *Chenoweth counts James Lawson as a mentor*: Andrew Marantz, "How to Stop a Power Grab," *New Yorker*, November 23, 2020. See also Chenoweth, *Civil Resistance*, 10–11.

334 *regimes established in the wake*: Erica Chenoweth and Maria J. Stephan, *Why Civil Resistance Works: The Strategic Logic of Nonviolent Conflict* (Columbia University Press, 2011), 16.

334 *"High impact, low ego"*: Ransby, *Making All Black Lives Matter*, 152.

335 *"The Movement for Black Lives has a semi-federated"*: Quoted in "Protests in Perspective," 7.

335 *more effective in controlling its narrative*: Woodly, *Reckoning*, 179.

335 *BLM developed broader public support*: Woodly, *Reckoning*, 165.

335 *killings by police generally have declined*: Woodly, *Reckoning*, 181.

335 *electoral campaigns that target prosecutors*: Woodly, *Reckoning*, 185.

335 *a national discussion about policing*: Woodly, *Reckoning*, 190–91.

335 *"Hashtags don't build movements"*: Garza, *The Purpose of Power*, 137.

335 *"Protests are never enough"*: Garza, *The Purpose of Power*, 254.

337 *"There certainly will be no mass response"*: M. K. Gandhi, *Non-Violent Resistance (Satyagraha)* (1961; repr. Dover, 2001), 240.

ACKNOWLEDGMENTS

My decision to research and write this book was inspired first by reading Taylor Branch's marvelous three-volume history of the United States during the King years. Those books shaped my approach here. If you haven't read them, you have a great time awaiting you.

I am multiply in debt to David Garrow, author of numerous memorable books on Martin Luther King, Jr., and the civil rights movement. Garrow responded with alacrity when I inquired about reading some of the interviews he conducted for his books. And he gave an early draft of this book a vigorous reading, for which I am grateful. He also put me in touch with Jonathan Eig, who generously shared some of his research on Martin Luther King, Jr., with me. I wound up with the same editor as Eig—Alexander Star, whose enthusiasm for this project and whose probing questions have improved it again and again. He is an extraordinary editor.

Andrew Wylie played an essential role in steering this project past the shoals of the publishing industry and finding safe harbor for it. He could write a book on how to be a literary agent—and why authors need a deft one, like him. In moments of peril and doubt, I always came away better for having talked through the problem with him.

Andrew also introduced me to Farrar, Straus and Giroux and Alex Star. Working with him and with Julia Judge and her publicity team at the house has been a pure pleasure.

I also want to thank Randy Kryn for agreeing to share with me the unpublished manuscript he wrote with James Bevel. Likewise, I am indebted to Erica Muhammad, Bevel's wife, for locating that manuscript and sending it to me.

I am grateful to the Henry Hampton Collection at Washington University for posting the transcripts of the complete interviews done for *Eyes on the Prize*. Just by themselves, they provide a rich history of the civil rights movement. Another wonderful repository is the Civil Rights Movement Archive, which is a treasure chest of documents and interviews. I used it almost daily as I did research.

Several scholars generously provided aid and counsel along the way. Sir Hew Strachan of the University of St. Andrews, perhaps the preeminent writer on strategy today, gave the manuscript a reading with an eye to that subject. At the University of Texas at Austin, Paul Edgar and Catherine Evans helped me navigate the obstacles to research posed by the COVID-19 pandemic of 2020–2022. My old friend Thomas Remington of Harvard University posed a series of helpful questions, both when I was writing and then in reviewing an early draft of the manuscript. His wife, Nancy Roth Remington, provided a gimlet-eyed line edit that resulted in literally hundreds of changes. Also at Harvard, Erica Chenoweth, whose works have influenced this book in several places, was patient and helpful in responding to my repeated queries. Alan Draper of St. Lawrence University pointed me toward good studies of the Ole Miss confrontation. I look forward to his biography of Bob Moses, one of the most interesting but most elusive figures in the civil rights movement. Peter Onuf of the University of Virginia again gave me a smart and encouraging response to my writing. Michael Honey of the University of Washington Tacoma was a helpful critical reader, providing a thorough review of the entire manuscript and suggesting additional books to read. He also shared with me his collection of speeches by James Lawson; he and Kent Wong published these in 2022 as *Revolutionary Nonviolence: Organizing for Freedom* (University of California Press). John Dittmer, professor emeritus of DePauw University, and Adam Fairclough of Leiden University, the authors of two of my favorite books on the civil rights movement, saved me from several errors in fact or context. Both gave the first draft the kind of rigorous reading that every manuscript needs. Their perspectives were invaluable, and I am grateful to them.

I am indebted to several good friends who gave the manuscript a critical reading. Jonathan Kaufman of Northeastern University wrote a thoughtful critique that especially inspired me to revise the epilogue. Vernon Loeb helped me with recasting the prologue. He and Cullen Murphy both helped me sharpen the epilogue.

A number of leading military minds also stepped in. Adrian Lewis, a thoughtful military historian at the University of Kansas and a retired Army officer, brought to the manuscript a sure feel for Army doctrine and made some illuminating suggestions that are reflected especially in my discussions of command and control issues in the civil rights movement. The retired Army colonel Robert Killebrew helped me both in writing about strategy and in making sure I got the nuances of military terminology right. The retired Marine general James Mattis also brought his vast knowledge to bear on the first draft.

My family played an unusual and helpful role as I worked on this book. They didn't just root for the book; they improved it. My daughter, Molly Ricks, a terrific editor and a public historian, asked hundreds of penetrating questions, pushed for more examples, and helped me with considering a series of titles. My sister Sarah Ricks, a professor at Rutgers Law School in Camden, New Jersey, brought her knowledge of American legal history to bear in reviewing the manuscript, with a series of precise and thoughtful comments. Throughout, from start to finish, the development of this book was constantly informed by my wife, Mary Kay Ricks, a former coleader of the Washington, D.C.–area chapter of High School Friends of SNCC. She edited the rough draft of this book with skill and thoughtfulness, as one would expect from the author of a fine volume of history, *Escape on the Pearl: The Heroic Bid for Freedom on the Underground Railroad* (Morrow, 2007).

Most of all, my old friend Karin Chenoweth, whose own books on education in America today deserve a wider audience, did an extraordinary job in showing me how to frame the book. Some of the best words in the prologue are from a letter she wrote to me after reading an early draft. This is the third book of mine to which she has lent her intelligence and knowledge. I am grateful to her.

None of these people should be blamed for anything in this book. Try as I do, every book of mine has had mistakes. The ones herein are mine.

INDEX

civil rights movement (the Movement)
(*cont.*)
children in, *see* children, in civil rights
movement
children of activists in, 321–323
choice of times and places of
confrontations in, 67, 97
cohesion in, 91, 105
combat stress in, 312–315, 317
confrontations between leaders of, 163
consequences of, 185
corporations and, 167–168
daily life for activists in, 110
diminishing number of eyewitnesses
to, xiv–xv
discipline in, xviii, 105, 163, 196–197,
267, 331–332
division within, 185, 214, 237–238,
249, 273, 274, 278, 282, 309,
312
and educating the opposition, 143
endings and reconciliation in, 33, 129,
332
federal government branches and,
130–131, 293
and fighting specific targets versus
entire system, 115–116
goal of, 16, 20, 249
image of workers in, 245
innovation in, 67, 69
jail and, 88
"keep your eyes on the prize" in, 61,
62, 197
lessons of, for today, 331–332
life spans of activists in, 317–318
measurement of successes in, 35–36
military operations and warfare
compared to, xiii–xx, 3, 66, 201;
see also military and warfare
as national movement, 167–168, 184,
198
newcomers in, 105
noncommissioned officers of, 137
nonviolence in, *see* nonviolence, in civil
rights movement
opposition to, xiv, xvii

organization and planning in, xviii,
69–70, 116, 118, 267, 332
pioneers of, 8
political power and, 237, 293
in present day, 325–337
problems accompanying success in,
273–274
public opinion on, 128, 152, 165, 335
readiness and timing in, 49
reasons for success of, 331–332
records of, 151
recruiting in, 44, 65, 66
songs of, 61–63, 94, 210, 213, 214, 303
staff members of, 139–141
strategy and tactics in, xix, 16, 20, 21,
332
support structures in, 332
television coverage of, *see* television
training in, 40, 41, 65, 66, 105, 118,
139, 331
transformations brought about by, 325
victories consolidated in, 168
as viewed in today's political climate, 326
women in, 177–180, 238
women's movement and, 175,
185–186, 313
Civil War, xiv, 3, 166, 273, 277, 281
Bull Run in, 115
Gettysburg in, 79, 119, 133
Mosby in, 75
Sherman in, xvii–xviii, 153, 180
University of Mississippi and, 119
Clark, Jim, 151, 248, 251–256, 258–260,
268, 270, 272, 277, 278, 377n
Clark, Kenneth, 58, 361n
Clark, Ramsey, 257, 270
Clark, Septima Poinsette, 65, 116,
300–301, 314, 333, 356n, 386n
in Birmingham, 136, 137
cafeteria line and, 137
at Highlander Folk School, 12, 44, 333
on Jackson, 317
Clausewitz, Carl von, 81, 233, 351n,
373n
Clayton, Dewey, 333, 389n
Cloud, John, 268

A Note About the Author

Thomas E. Ricks is the author of multiple bestselling books, including *First Principles, Churchill and Orwell, The Generals,* and *Fiasco,* which was a #1 *New York Times* bestseller and a finalist for the Pulitzer Prize. A member of two Pulitzer Prize–winning teams in his years at *The Washington Post* and *The Wall Street Journal,* he lives in Maine and Texas.